Remembering Ruabon

Cofio Rhiwabon

T. W. Pritchard

Bill Pritchard

Ruabon & District Field Club

First published in Wales in 2000
by
Bridge Books
61 Park Avenue
Wrexham
LL12 7AW
on behalf of
The Ruabon & District Field Club
Millennium Book Committee, 2000

A CIP entry for this book is available from the British Library

ISBN 1-872424-90-2

Typeset and printed by
Bridge Books, Wrexham

Contents

Acknowledgements		*v*
Foreword		*vi*
Introduction		vii
1.	Beginnings and Settlements	9
2.	Wynnstay	41
3.	Churches and Chapels	63
4.	Schools	90
5.	Penylan	124
6.	Industry	135
7.	Health	158
8.	The Community in the 19th and 20th Centuries	172
	Notes	225
	Sources	232

Acknowledgements

The decision to publish a millennium history of Ruabon was made in February 2000 and without the co-operation of a number of people it would not have been produced in time for Christmas 2000.

Research material and illustrations were obtained from the National Library of Wales, Aberystwyth; Denbighshire Record Office, Ruthin; Flintshire Record Office, Hawarden; Wrexham Library and Museum. I am most grateful to the staff of these places for their kindness and assistance. Written material was provided by Audrey Bowen, A. C. C. Brown, Audrey Crosbie, John H. Davies, Helen Eardley, Roland Fenner, Christine Giller, Renée Giller, Rosemary Howard, Betty Humphries, Eddie Bowen Jones, the late Esther Pugh Jones, Derek Owens, Brenda, Graham and Jill Phillips, John Lawton Roberts and Marjory Williams. Many individuals generously searched for, and then lent photographs for inclusion as did the Society of Antiquaries, London; Clwyd Powys Archeological Trust, Welshpool; Mr Peter Smith (author of *Houses of the Welsh Countryside)* and Mr Thomas Lloyd (author of *The Lost Houses of Wales);* the Denbighshire Record Office, Ruthin; the Royal Commission on the Ancient & Historical Monuments of Wales. John Bradbury has been indispensable in providing a number of photographs specially taken for inclusion in the book.

The book was written in the congenial atmosphere of St. Deiniol's Library, Harwarden and I am grateful to the Warden, the Reverend Peter Francis, and his staff for their kindness. Without the cheerfulness and hard work of Wendy Hughes and Rowan O'Neill the text would not have been ready by the deadline. Geoffrey Veysey read the proof with his usual patience and expertise. John Smout produced an admirable design for the cover. The President of the Ruabon and District Field Club Ann Owens and members of the production committee — Malcolm Crosbie, Betty Evans, Roland Fenner, Wendy Hughes, Bronwen Jones and Dorothy Taylor gave me every encouragement. Alister Williams of Bridge Books has supported me with the benefit of his professionalism as a publisher and his kindness as a friend.

T. W. Pritchard

Foreword

I wish to commend this history to the people of Ruabon and those who have past or present connections with the village. The Ruabon Field Club wished to mark the Millenium in a memorable way and decided the Venerable T. W. Pritchard be invited to write a history of the village. A former vicar of the parish, he is also an expert on its history.

Ruabon is a very old settlement and this volume deals with various aspects of its development over the centuries. The text is illustrated with photographs, many of which have not before been published.

I hope that readers will find the book both interesting and enjoyable and put it down feeling they have deepened their understanding of this community and its evolution.

Thanks are due to the many people who have helped in so many ways towards the production of this volume, and especially to the Venerable Bill Pritchard.

Ann Owens
President
Ruabon Field Club

Introduction

This study of the community of Ruabon is confined to the area established in the local government reorganisation in 1994 and is limited to the electoral polling districts of Ruabon north and south which is virtually the same as the ecclesiastical parish of Ruabon . In the nineteenth century new parishes were created out of the old parish of Ruabon: Rhosymedre, Rhosllanerchrugog and Penycae. These are not included in the survey. However, the area covered includes Ruabon Village, Gardden, Gyfelia, Penylan, Plas Bennion, Rhos y Madoc and Wynnstay.

Ruabon Field Club are the sponsors of the book which reflects their long interest and dedication to the study and conservation of the local environment. It is their millennium project and provides as such an historical description of the community from its beginnings before the first millennium to the twenty-first century.

I was thrilled to be invited by the Field Club to write this book. I first took an interest in the history of Ruabon as assistant curate from 1960 to 1963 and vicar from 1977 to 1987. Previous to this study I have published articles on Wynnstay, the parish church, the endowed Grammar School and with the late Ifor Edwards a book of photographs. However, much new material is presented, although there are gaps in the story and I leave it to those who spot them to make up the deficiencies.

Each of the chapters is designed to give a record of the past as seen through the lives of the people, the shape of the landscape, the design of buildings and the establishment of settlements and communities. An assessment of the lives of forebears over the past two thousand years brings out the circumstances, struggles and achievements of successive generations and is illuminated by the exploration of the major themes. The importance of religion in shaping the lives, beliefs, customs and freedom to worship is seen in the discussion on nonconformist , Roman Catholic and Anglican places of worship. Community care, the provision made for the poor and sick, is discussed through the parish records to the establishment of the welfare state. One of the great achievements of the last millennium is chronicled: that is the availability of education and establishment of primary and secondary schools. Pastoral and arable farming dominated the economy of the community until the last two or three hundred years saw the landscape and workplace transformed by the exploitation of iron, coal and clay, the coming of the railway and the construction of roads and bridges. Over the centuries the community was influenced by the power of tribal leaders: the Lords of Bromfield and Yale, the squirearchy at Erddig, Penylan, Rhos y Madoc and above all by the vigour and wealth of the Williams Wynn family of Wynnstay. Their influence and legacy is described in some detail.

Sandstone and red brick are the chief building materials in this area and here are recorded the historic buildings of the community; mansions, the parish church, chapels, public buildings, industrial sites and dwelling houses.

Every effort is made to illustrate the narrative with maps and photographs to recall the richness of experience and the variety of activity enjoyed in the nineteenth and twentieth centuries when the community as we know it today was broadly shaped. Photographs in particular are an excellent medium for both the record and recall of buildings, work, housing shops, welfare, medicine, law and order, leisure, sport, public houses and the people involved, ranging from school groups, the baronets of Wynnstay, industrialists, doctors, ministers of religion, church and chapel associations and the variety of social activities which are indicators of the strength of community life.

Many people have shared their memories, knowledge and experience. The author and the members of the Ruabon Field Club are grateful to those who have generously contributed. Thank you.

T.W. Pritchard,
2000

The Parish Church of St Mary, Ruabon, 2000.
[John Bradbury]

1. Beginnings and Settlement

This first chapter of the history of Ruabon over the last two thousand years, beginnings and settlement, sets the scene for the story of the community area. The purpose here is to put the picture in the frame, and the type of description is reminiscent of a landscape painting. A wide canvas, distant horizons, a rural setting, and a few major topographical details.

Earth's formation over millions of years, the shaping of hills, rivers, valleys and broad plains clothed in woodland, beneath which are precious resources of iron, coal and clay, is part of that distant horizon. Brought nearer by the perspective of time are more familiar details. Through the mist there emerges our ancestors dressed in skins, hunters of animals, gatherers of food, and relying upon primitive weapons and tools made from stone. Palaeolithic (c.200,000BC), Mesolithic (c.10,000BC) and Neolithic (c.4,000BC) people, left hardly a footprint in the area before the Bronze Age (c.2,400BC).

Our pre-history in Ruabon begins with the discovery of archaeological evidence for the settlement of these bronze age people in the second millennium BC. Y Gardden hill fort is the first major topographical feature we recognise within the picture frame. This dates possibly from the Iron Age which began about 400BC and lasted until the Romans came at the very beginning of our history of the last two millennia.

Wat's Dyke and Offa's Dyke, the two great 5th and 8th century linear earthworks running along the borderland of England and Wales determine the community area of Ruabon. Set in the midst of these ancient boundaries is the parish church of St Mabon and St Mary. These dedications suggest religious influences over many centuries, as diverse as the semi-pagan origin of Mabon, the Celtic Christian influence of Collen and the Cistercian cult of the Blessed Virgin Mary. They are vague and uncertain until the permanency of the tradition, established by the building of the parish church on the present site.

More precise than the legends of the Celtic saints is the remembrance of the arable and pastoral farming practiced by the native Welsh tribes occupying this area for a thousand years before the Edwardian conquest of Wales in 1282. Field names mentioned in ancient deeds, church documents from the 17th. century onwards and the tithe apportionment of 1844, describe the nature of farming over nearly two millenia. Names more familiar to our forebears were those of the townships and their divisions within the community area — Ruabon township consisting of Hafod, Belan, Rhuddallt, Bodylltyn; Dinhinlle Isaf and Morton Anglicorum. These originated from the tref (township) of the tribal agrarian settlements going back to the Iron Age and influenced after the conquest in the 13th century by the creation of the marcher lordship of Bromfield and Yale. It is not until the 15th century that we can begin to see the emergence of landed estates and learn the ancient names of farms and their extent. These are the themes that make up the first fifteen hundred years of the history of the two thousand years we here relate.

Bronze Age Discoveries

Two archaeological finds were made in Ruabon in 1898 and 1917 which gave evidence of Bronze Age settlers in Ruabon in the middle Bronze Age, sometime between 1400–900 BC. The first discovery was made opposite the Baptist chapel in Cleveland Street in 1898 during excavations to put in a sewerage system. Digging four feet below ground the workmen discovered a cist, or what we would describe as a stone coffin. 'The sides, ends and cover of the cist were formed of fragments of a single rough slab between three and four inches thick. Inside the cist, in the centre, mouth upwards, was a cinerary urn containing a quantity of bones and some pebbles.'[1]

A notable archaeologist, Professor W. B. Dawkins, was later consulted about the find, and replied that 'the bones have been partially burnt. They are human fragments of shell and teeth, and belong to the Bronze Age, when cremation was first practiced in Britain'.[2]

The cinerary urn, made of pottery to contain the cremated remains, was taken out whole by the workmen.

Bronze Age urn containing cremated remains.
Found in Cleveland Street in 1898.

It was nearly fifteen inches in height and about a foot across the mouth, but tapered to a somewhat narrow base, $4^7/8$ inches in diameter. The inside was black, indicating that the bones had been placed therein straight from the funeral pyre. There was ornamentation consisting of triangular indentations on the upper part between the shoulder and on the inside of the lip, 10 rows on the former and 3 rows of the latter.[3]

The fragments of the urn came into the possession of the Rev. D. J. Bowen, later headmaster of Ruabon Grammar School. Bowen was a keen naturalist and amateur archaeologist, interests which led him to become a founder-member of the Ruabon Field Club. He was involved in the second Bronze Age discovery in 1917 made whilst he was supervising the digging of a potato patch in the school playing field. Here they found about three feet below the surface, human bones, a flint arrowhead and a bronze axe in a cairn of gravel. The boys and their headmaster had stumbled across a Bronze Age earthwork known as a round barrow.[4]

Other Bronze Age axes or palstaves were found in Ruabon, the places of discovery unfortunately not recorded. Two of these axes are in the British Museum.[5] Another, a 'looped midrib palstave with a slight droop to the blade', from an unidentified site was presented to Manchester University.[6]

Scarce as these discoveries are, they give important insights into the lives of the first people who settled in Ruabon somewhere in the region of three and a half thousand years ago. European in origin, they were the descendants of western Neolithic farmers and north European hunters. Their economy was based on the use of a metal-working technology which introduced a variety of copper alloys — bronze and lead

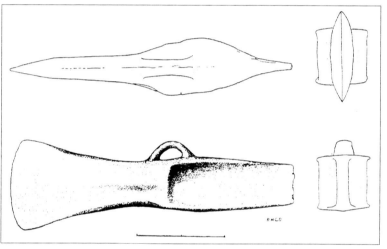

Looped midrib palstave, Bronze Age axe. This is now held in Manchester University Museum.

were a harder alternative to copper. Bronzesmiths produced palstaves, a type of flanged axe, which provided a much firmer seating for the haft, but needed a two-piece mould. These axes were used for export and exchange of goods, but more importantly, to clear patches of woodland for agriculture. It may be speculated that the closeness of the finds in Cleveland Street and the Grammar School suggest the clearance of common fields in the Maes-y-Llan area. The social organisation of those Bronze Age settlers is reflected in their burial rites with the cremated remains of the most important members of the tribe, chieftain, priest or king, being buried separately in a grave under a round barrow or cairn as shown in the Ruabon finds.

Y Gardden Hill-Fort

Y Gardden is an Iron Age hill-fort 585ft above sea level on an elevated plateau between the ravine formed by the Afon Eitha in the west and south of the valley of the Afon Goch to the north. In shape the hill-fort is an irregular oval with an interior area of four acres. Y Gardden has not been excavated, although a written description of the site has been published by Dr Willoughby Gardner. The hill-fort dates from *c.*400 BC and was probably occupied spasmodically for over a thousand years. Gardner summarises the defensive design of Y Gardden:

In brief, the scheme of fortification here consisted:— first, of a great stone-built rampart encircling the hill-fort with, secondly, a deep and wide military ditch immediately in front of it; there was apparently but little berm outside the rampart wall. Beyond this wall at an average difference of 50ft. there was a second or obstacle

Y Gardden hill-fort.
[Clwyd-Powys Archaeological
Trust 84-10-13]

rampart, while beyond this again there was in places a fourth — these earthen ramparts presenting further obstacles to attack upon the main rampart wall above.[7]

Gardner reaches these general conclusions about the hill-fort:

> There is no record of any early relics having been found upon this site. In the absence of excavation it is not possible to say definitely when the hill-fort was constructed, by whom it was occupied, or for how long. But it is visibly an early native stronghold, as opposed to anything Roman, and it was defended by remarkably well-engineered fortifications. It was sufficiently large to have afforded permanent occupation to a considerable tribal community. As suggested above, it is possible that it may have continued in occupation or have been re-occupied as late as the eighth century A.D.[8]

Thomas Pennant recorded what he found at Y Gardden in the 18th century:

> On the road (from Ruabon to Wrexham) I digressed a little to the left, to visit a great Caer in this parish (Rhiwabon), called the Garthen, *i.e.* Caer-ddin, seated on a summit of a hill commanding a most extensive view around … this caer contains about four acres of ground, protected in some parts by one, in others by two very strong dikes and deep ditches. The inner dike is made of loose stones, with a wall of vast thickness on the top. Within the area are many vestiges of buildings, the habitations of the old possessors. It lies 200 yards from Offa's dike. Part of the turn-pike road is formed for a considerable way along the top of the dike, which shows its prodigious thickness.[9]

Pennant's derivation of the name has been dismissed. Gardner, depending on Professor Ivor Williams, suggests that the most likely meaning of the name Y Gardden is an enclosure. The field inside the hill-fort is known as 'The Chesters', which in literary Anglo-Saxon, denotes any enclosed place.[10] Sir Cyril Fox noted that the Mercian builders of Offa's Dyke in the eighth century excluded the hill-fort because it lay within the territory of the princes of Powys.[11]

Wat's Dyke
Wat's Dyke runs through the community area of Ruabon. It is east of Offa's Dyke and may be seen along the ridge between Pentre Clawdd farm and the back of the vicarage where it crosses the road into Wynnstay Park. The former name Watstay alluded to the fact of a break in the dyke there. The total length of the dyke is forty miles and it runs parallel to Offa's Dyke following a more easterly alignment across mostly low-lying agricultural land from Basingwerk in Flintshire in the north to the river Morda at Maesbrook south of Oswestry. There has been a new dating of the dyke due to radiocarbon dating of sample excavations carried out at Maes y Clawdd, Mile Oak industrial estate at Oswestry, on a section of the dyke. A fire hearth was uncovered on the site and a sample of charcoal and burnt clay was sent by Hugh Hannaford, Shropshire County Council Archaeology Service, to Queen's University, Belfast. The exciting news was reported by Hugh Hannaford:

> The results of the test gave a calibrated date for the hearth of AD 446 (*i.e.* between AD 411 and AD 561). This suggests a 5th century date for the construction of Wat's Dyke, which should now, perhaps, be regarded as contemporary with other great fifth century linear earthworks, such as the Wiltshire Wansdyke and should be considered as an achievement of the post-Roman kingdom of northern Cornovii than a work of 8th century Mercia and a near precursor of Offa's Dyke.[12]

Wat's Dyke, looking south towards Wynnstay Hall. [John Bradbury]

The purpose of the dyke may have been to demarcate a political frontier between the Cornovii and other Welsh tribes, the Deceangli and Silures further west. The Cornovii were a powerful post-Roman kingdom and wanted to protect the western approaches along the Dee estuary to the Roman city of Deva (Chester) and their territory eastwards (modern Shropshire) which included Wroxeter. The earlier dating of Wat's Dyke may imply greater stability for agricultural settlements both above and below the dyke, pointing to the creation of a political boundary three hundred years in advance of previous knowledge.

Offa's Dyke[13]

Offa's Dyke is an 8th century earthwork running from north to south between Treuddyn near Wrexham and Sedbury cliffs on the Severn estuary. The dyke may be

Wat's Dyke, 'staying' at entrance to Wynnstay Park.
[Clwyd-Powys Archaeological Trust, 90-MB-338]

seen to advantage in Ruabon along the eastern side of Tatham road and continuing across the Penycae road along the footpath to the Llangollen road.[14] The basic structure of the dyke is a large earthen bank having a broad ditch on its western (Welsh) side.

King Offa of Mercia 757-796, of his day the most powerful of Saxon kings, recognised by his European contemporary Charlemagne as an equal, caused the dyke to be raised. Like all kings in England Offa was disturbed by the instability of his western boundary and the continual threat from the Welsh princes, particularly those of Powys, whose kingdom bordered Mercia. An inscription on the 'Pillar of Eliseg' at Valle Crucis states how Eliseg harassed the English settlements and turned the border 'into a sword-land by fire'. The major reason, therfore, for Offa to build the dyke was to defend and define his western frontier. It has been argued that the massive work of making the dyke was carried out by work parties levied from the local population, with each individual required to make a given contribution.[15]

Sir Cyril Fox saw the dyke as a frontier which represented a negotiated agreement between Mercia and the Welsh princes, to define an agreed limit to English settlement.[16] There is no doubt that the substantial structure of the dyke was intended as a warning by Offa to the Welsh raiders and cattle rustlers of his military might and resources. Once raised up, the dyke became a symbol

Offa's Dyke close to Ysgol Rhiwabon.
[John Bradbury]

of the difference between the Welsh and the English, a cultural frontier. The township names in the old parish of Ruabon reflect this dividing line; Morton Wallicorum, *of the Welsh*; Moreton Uwch y Clawdd, *above the dyke*; Morton isy Clawdd, *below the dyke;* and a township east of Wat's Dyke is called Morton Anglicorum, *of the English.*

Ruabon Place Name and the Foundation of the Church

Grave doubts have been raised about the whereabouts of the site of the first church in the parish of Ruabon. It is commonly claimed that when the parish of Ruabon was appropriated to the monks of Valle Crucis in 1274, they built a new church on the present site, and rededicated the church to St Mary in honour of the Blessed Virgin.

What are the grounds for believing that the present site is the original foundation? This site is in the township of Rhuddallt situated between Offa's and Wat's Dykes. The hill on which it is sited was more pronounced in those days before the road was raised up. One of the strongest arguments for this site is the nature of its churchyard being a typical early llan or enclosed cemetery. Near the church were the common fields Maes-y-Llan. It might be argued that the small Christian community in Ruabon from early times was gathered round the church in the area of the river in Tan Lan. The dedication of the church was to Mabon. The place name Ruabon/Rhiwabon, means Mabon's slope or hill. Who was Mabon and why was the church dedicated to him?

A Mabon fab Modron appears in the story of Culhwch and Owen and in her edition of *Troedd Ynys Prydein* Dr Rachel Bromwich makes Mabon a Celtic deity translating the name as, "the youth (God) son of the mother (Goddess)". A. N. Palmer described 'Mabon' quite simply as the 'Welsh Apollo.'[17]

Another source identifies him with the 6th century St Mabon the Confestor, son of Tegonwy ab Teon, and brother to St Llewelyn of Welshpool. There were two other churches dedicated to him: Llanfaban in Glamorganshire and Llanfaban in Anglesey.

What are the arguments for an alternative site for the parish church? In the taxation of 1254 the church in Ruabon is dedicated to St Collen. Twenty years later there was a dispute between the Abbot of Valle Crucis and Bishop Anian of St Asaph about the cure of souls in the area, when it was argued that Ruabon was only a capella or outlying chapelry to Llangollen. By the 1291 taxation there is no mention of Collen, and the parochial revenues are divided between a rector and vicar. But there is no doubt that there was a chapel in Ruabon dedicated to St Collen. The evidence for this is strong. Edward Lhwyd writing in about 1697, says, 'They call a field, where there is a cross in Ruabon parish, Kappel Kollen and a field Cae'r groes newydd (field of the new cross) and another Errw Armon and Erw Capel Kympas (Erw o gwmpas y capel) acre around the chapel. Nearby a little north-west of Crab Row, is a field called 'Cae Gosber', that is, the field of vespers or of evensong.[18] All these fields are in the township of Dinhinlle Isaf, recalling not only St Collen but also St Garmon, a saint connected with the Powys dynasty of kings as recorded on Eliseg's pillar. In the 16th century we read of a chantry chapel at Gyfelia which was dissolved at the Reformation but traces of which remained in 1620 when Norden in his Survey recorded, 'The same Owen Brereton holds the chapel and two gardens', against which, someone else added later, 'They suffer the chappel to decay'. Clearly there must have been chapels at Gyfelia and in the township of Dinhinlle Isaf somewhere near the present church of All Saints', Penylan. Perhaps the clue to the original site of the parish church Ruabon is the ancient *llan* enclosure, and this is where the investigation should begin.

The 13th century was a turning point in the affairs of Wales. The parochial system of parish, deanery and territorial diocese, was firmly established. The conquest in 1282 brought about major administrative changes with the banishment of the princes of Powys and the exercise of judicial power by the newly created lords of Bromfield and Yale.

The Relationship of Ruabon Church to Valle Crucis Abbey

By 1291 the abbots of Valle Crucis were receiving the rectorial tithes of the parish of Ruabon, and were responsible for the payment of a vicar to take care of the people and perform the divine office in church. This arrangement continued until the Reformation. The *Valor Ecclesiasticus* of Henry VIII made in May 1535, to determine the revenue of the church, estimated the yearly value of the rectory of Ruabon to be £29–7s–10d and the vicarage £13–6s–8d. Out of these two sums the main item of income was the tithe of corn amounting to £32.

There was bound to be a close relationship between the abbey and the parish. Advice on skilled architects would be available, the Cistercian knowledge of farming would be invaluable, and it may have been the influence of Valle Crucis which led to the making of the wall painting on the south wall of the parish church.

It appears to date from the first half of the 15th century. The inscription in Welsh (St Matthew 25 v 35–40) relates to the theme, the works of mercy, a recurrent medieval morality subject which has received various representation: sometimes as part of the 'Tree of Life', or as a 'Wheel', but here as a set of scenes. Five out of

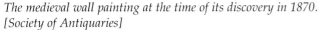

The medieval wall painting at the time of its discovery in 1870.
[Society of Antiquaries]

the seven Biblical scenes are shown, namely: feeding the hungry, giving drink to the thirsty, clothing the naked, receiving strangers, and half of another scene with a fragment of a sixth. The treatment is fairly normal, each person performing his good deed being inspired to it by an angel: as a rule the same man is shown performing all the acts, whereas in this case the principal character is different in each scene, and in one case is a woman. The priest at Ruabon in the middle of the 15th century, Maredudd ap Rhys, was a skilled poet who wrote a verse to teach his parishioners the meaning of the mural. The following is a translation from the Welsh:

> And the seven deeds (expected of) the believers
> Which should all be performed for the sake of the weak;
> Supply food and drink when they come seeking,
> Attend to the suffering of invalids,
> Carry the dead from the hill to the church,
> Befriend every jailed prisoner,
> Give board and lodgings to those in need of shelter,
> And clothing against the elements.

One of the Abbots of Valle Crucis, Adam, gave his name to the bridge at Pont Adam.

Welsh Townships
For centuries the people of Ruabon lived as members of a tribe communally and in kinship groups. Their descendants recognised the tribal obligations of the Welsh laws. In the years between the Norman invasion of England in 1066 and the conquest of Wales in 1282 important changes took place throughout Wales which in turn affected the people of Ruabon. The political situation was such that the Welsh had to defend themselves against attack from England. Ruabon was part of the kingdom of Powys in Bromfield. This threat united the princes of Powys and Gwynedd and in 1094 their leaders swept the Normans back across the Dee as far as Chester. The effect of this locally was to the advantage of the tribesmen living in the mountains of Ruabon and Esclusham. Under the leadership of Sandhe Hardd, Elidyr and Ithel ap Hunydd, they swept down from the hill and drove the English occupants across the Dee.

Another important change was the establishment of geographical boundaries for the ancient Welsh unit of the tref, the township, and the creation and demarcation of ecclesiastical parishes usually defined by a grouping of townships. The old parish of Ruabon for example contained the townships of Ruabon (with the four hamlets of Belan, Bodylltyn, Rhuddallt and Hafod), Dinhinlle Isaf, Dinhinlle Ucha, Coed Cristionydd, Cristionydd Kenrick, Morton Wallicorum, Morton is y Clawdd, Morton Anglicorum. The origin and character of the township was essentially communal. Basically it was a unit of human settlement, a collection of homesteads, either nucleated or, more commonly, dispersed … it exercised firm control over communal pastureland, waste and meadow; it appointed its own community shepherd; it determined the seasonal chronology of the communal agriculture of the village … Neighbourliness and necessity were close allies.[19]

The Lordship of Bromfield and Yale
The greatest change took place in 1282 with the conquest of Wales when Bromfield and Yale, part of the Welsh kingdom of Powys Fadog, was given by Edward I to John Warrene, earl of Surrey and became a Marcher Lordship. The earl had removed any possibility of reviving the claims of the prince of Powys by murdering the infant sons of Madog ap Gruffudd to remove any centre of revolt. Otherwise conditions in the new lordship were little altered. There was no deportation or removal of Welsh tenants. The only place where Englishmen were to be found in any number was in the borough of Holt. There were eight in Wrexham, but nowhere else throughout Bromfield and Yale were any to be found.

The first information about the people living in the lordship is found in the survey of 1315.[20] In this and later surveys we learn something about the effect of the English occupation on Welsh society. The primary objective of the English occupation was to exploit the resources of the lordship to the full to provide, men, money and power. 'There is a fair lordship there', remarked the Council of the Black Prince in its report on Bromfield and Yale in 1347, 'well worth 2,000 marks a year'.[21] English and Welsh law coexisted and the landed customs and civil procedures of native Welsh society emerged virtually untouched. The conditions in

Bromfield and Yale apply to Ruabon. There were three main classes of people: free tenants, unfree, and 'foreigners' or newcomers to the lordship. All of them had obligations to the lord. The survey shows a continuity of Welsh tenure and gives a detailed description of Welsh tribal communities as they existed before 1282 under the Welsh princes of Powys Fadog.

The greater part of the free and unfree tenants were organised into kin groups which depended on blood ties. They held their land communally. They were pastoral farmers who grazed their flocks and herds across a wide area on land situated in different and widely dispersed townships. These were the families who had migrated eastward after 1094. The names of the family of Elidyr, their dispersed holdings, and their obligations to the English earl are set out in the survey of 1315.

The Family of Elidyr

Extent of Ruabon, Marchwiel, Ruyton, Gwersyllt, Burras, Riffri, Erlas, Sutton, the lands in Eyton held in exchange for all the land in Eyton Fawr and Crew.

Madoc ap Llewelyn, Hywel and Griff his brothers, Eden Goch Madoc and Gronw, brothers of the same Eden, Ken ap Madoc, Eden and Llewelyn brothers of the same Ken, Madoc ap Hwyfa, Hywel and Ken, brothers of the same Madoc, Meuric ap Eden, Madoc, Ior, and Eigon, brothers of the same Meuric, Madoc ap Cadwgan Fychan hold jointly the ville of Burras (Riffri) and Acton Parva and one third of Ruabon, one quarter of Marchwiel and Ruyton, and two hundred and seventy five and a half acres of land in Eyton which they hold, in exchange for all the fields and lands which the Earl had from them in Eyton Fawr, by homage and fealty, and render annually jointly 22s. 3^1/$_4$d. at Michaelmas, and render annually at Michaelmas 10qr. 2bz. corn, Wrexham measure, worth 12d. per bushel by estimate. Also they pay 7s.–6d., each of them, by way of relief after the death of their ancestors. Also whenever a daughter of theirs shall marry or be led astray while unmarried by different men they pay 20s. Also they are bound to go to war with the Lord in England, Scotland and Wales with the body of the Earl at the cost of the said Earl, and they remain with the Earl at his will, and each of them gives for his share of £20–10s., which is paid in gross at Martinmas for the pannage of free men and their tenants of Bromfield. Also all their tenants who hold houses pay, that is each of them for himself, 1^1/$_2$d. at Michaelmas for gathering nuts. Also they come to the court of Wrexham or Marford whenever it is proclaimed. Also each of them gives for his own share towards the making of a hall, chamber and cookhouse and the new mill at Wrexham, and this with thatching with straw. And they turn the water at the lord's mill, namely those who remain within the bailiwick of Wrexham.[22]

Hwfa ab Iorwerth like many of his countrymen prospered in the service of the new regime. Earl Thomas appointed him his ewerer and in 1321 gave him lands in Ruabon. The tomb of Hwfa's father is in Ruabon church.[23]

When John Warenne, Earl of Surrey, was granted Bromfield and Yale, he gave in return for service 2,500 acres of land to ten English knights. John de Philibert held 207^1/$_2$ acres and John de Breous 59 acres in Dinhinlle.

By the end of the 14th century there was an increase in the use of money and individual proprietorship of land grew at the expense of communal tenure. The lords of Bromfield and Yale acquired portions of lands and became shareholders in corn mills. The Black Death in 1349 led to the availability of more land and to its purchase by individuals, members of other kin groups, and even strangers. From this time onward we see the beginnings of the growth of estates.

Another feature of the surveys was the description of the six seignural parks. The Lord's Park in Dinhinlle had a circumference of just over two and a half miles and an area of four hundred acres: the southern boundary

Effigy of John ap Elis Eyton and Elizabeth Calverley, Ruabon Church, c.1526.

was the river Dee and the northern limit was marked by a hedge and a ditch. Here the great stands of oak were grown for the repair and maintenance of Holt Castle and floated down the Dee on rafts. The surveys, as we would expect, notice the stone quarries within the wastes of Ruabon at Nant y Belan, for example, which provided the inhabitants with stone for their ovens and millstones for the mills of the lordship. Extensive deposits of marl were noticed. Already active was the mining of iron stone in Morton Anglicorum with forges set up in the adjacent township of Dinhinlle Isaf located near a supply of trees for the charcoal burners. The iron was sent to Wrexham market.

Emerging Estates and Farms

The purpose of this chapter is to review the beginnings and settlement in the community area of Ruabon. The first part of this task has been achieved with an account of the evidence for the first settlers in the Bronze Age, the hill fort in the Iron Age and the two dykes raised in the first millennium. The migration and settlement of Welsh tribesmen in the 11th and 12th centuries and their subjugation in the 13th has been described. By the 15th century a new class of land owners was beginning to emerge and this process was accelerated in the 16th century by the Act of Union in 1536 which absorbed Wales into British society giving Welshmen equality and greater opportunity of advancement in the professions and trade. These advantages were taken by the gentry to acquire landed estates, to be recognised as the *bonedd*, gentlemen with long pedigrees and heirs of the cultural traditions of the Welsh. In the second part of this introduction, their success will be seen from the survey and gazeteer of the estates and farms in the community area. This is arranged according to townships.[24]

The Township of Ruabon

This township contains the four hamlets of Hafod, Belan, Rhuddallt and Bodylltyn.[25]

The Hamlet of Hafod

Palmer states that the original name of the hamlet was *Hafod y Callor*, the summer dwelling of the cauldron, referring to the summer pastures of the tribesmen. Soon after 1536 the Eyton estate became known as Watstay. John ap Elis Eyton d.1524 was a freeholder of some substance. He fought at Bosworth field in 1485 and there is a fine monument to him and his wife Elizabeth Calverley in the parish church. The Eyton estate in Hafod ,in 1562, amounted to 846 statute acres. In the 17th century the estate descended to Eyton Evans whose daughter Jane married Sir John Wynn, baronet, who changed the name of Watstay to Wynnstay.

Pentre Clawdd, dyke, hamlet or dwelling, stands on Wat's Dyke. In 1620 David Lloyd sold Pentre Clawdd to Kenrick Edisbury. Included in the estate was Maesydd y Llan (village fields). In 1715 the farm contained over 282 acres. It passed from the Edisburys to John Mellor of Erddig and then to the Yorkes.

Cinders Farms; three farms of this name in 1620. The two Cinders farms near the Crimbal belong to the Wynnstay estate. There was another 'Cinder Tenement', part of the Erddig estate in 1715, but later leased under the name Caia Clapiog.

Cae Cyriog is noteworthy as being the home of the Griffith family who were antiquaries and genealogists. John Griffith (1654–98) was a notable genealogist and herald and possessed an extensive library. His son married the co-heiress of Pennant-y-Belan, afterwards called Pen-y-nant. In the 19th century Thomas Taylor Griffith (1795–1876) was a surgeon, antiquary and a founder of Wrexham Infirmary. The area of Cae Cyriog is now known as Parkside.[26]

The Hamlet of Belan

In the 19th century Belan Place belonged to Richard Jones (d.1862) then became part of the Wynnstay estate.

Pen-y-Nant

At one time the mansion and grounds of Pen-y-nant were quite a show place and in its earlier history was surrounded by an extensive estate. It was then that there was a rough and rocky common within called Nant-y-Belan, belonging to his highness's tenants, who pay for the same to the receiver bailiff of this manor a certain toll yearly and for the quantity thereof the jury knoweth not. There is a quarry of stone in Nant-y-Belan and no profit made of it, saving that some of the neighbours, thereabouts get thereof for the making of their ovens.

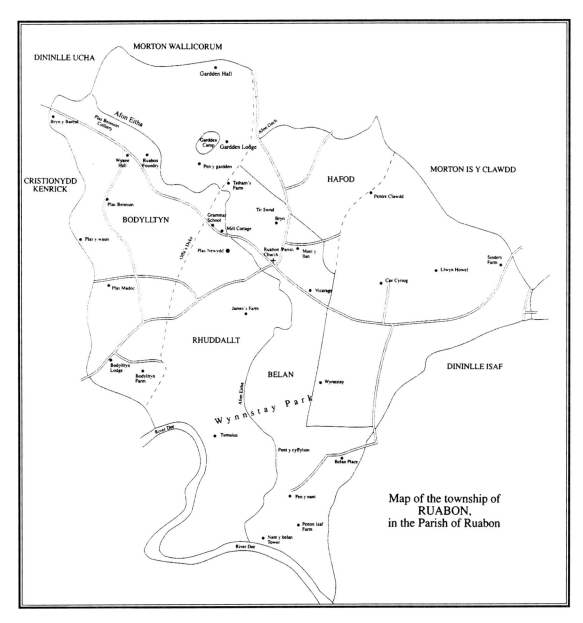

Map of the township of
RUABON,
in the Parish of Ruabon

There is another common called 'Nant y Glyn Ddu', being moorish and rough, overgrown with brambles and shrubs, which belongs to the free holders of the township of Ruabon as appertaineth to their local freeholds.

The Pen-y-nant estate at the beginning of the 18th century was in the possession of Thomas Hughes who in 1719 left £15 to the poor of Ruabon. His third daughter Rebecca married John Griffith of Cae Cyriog and the two estates joined. Pen-y-nant was extensively rebuilt by the Reverend Thomas Llewelyn Griffith (d.1904). His heir, Sub-Lieutenant Thomas Llewelyn George Griffith, 24th Regiment, was killed at Isandhlwana in the Zulu War. The estate was sold in 1906 to Wynnstay.[27]

The Hamlet of Rhuddallt

This means red cliff. There is now no house called Rhuddallt in the parish of Ruabon and the greater proportion of the hamlet is within Wynnstay Park. There were formerly two estates not annexed to Wynnstay, Rhuddallt Isaf and Rhuddallt Ucha.

Sub-Lieutenant Thomas Griffith.

Rhuddallt Isaf

An ancient estate with the ancestry going back to the eleventh century. In 1663 Catherine Edwards of Trevor, the mother of Richard Davies, was presented as a Quaker. Her son Richard Davies maintained a meeting place for Quakers in Rhuddallt, and two of his younger sons emigrated to Philadelphia.

Rhuddallt Ucha

The home of Dr David Powel, eminent for his learning, and assistant to Dr William Morgan in the translation of the Welsh Bible. His widow married Edward Eyton of Watstay. His second son Samuel was vicar of Ruabon, and his third son Gabriel was an eminent scholar and a prodigy of learning.

Plas Newydd

The earliest written reference which I have found to Plas Newydd is a Wynnstay document dated 10 February 1464/5, with the names of John, son of Elys Eyton and Elizabeth, daughter of Hugh Calverley, Kt.[28] The fine alabaster tomb of John ap Elis Eyton (d.1524) and his wife Elizabeth Calverley (d.1526) is in the north chapel of Ruabon church. It was the same John ap Elis Eyton who fought on the side of Henry Tudor at Bosworth Field and was awarded an annuity of ten marks for the space of his life 'in consideration of the true and faithful service performed for me … in the course of our triumphal victory'.

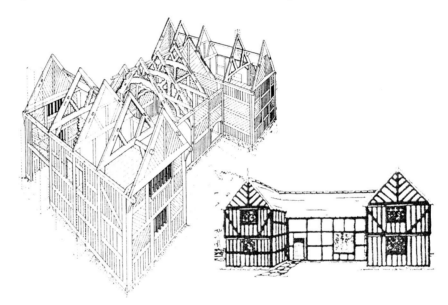

Conjectural drawings of Plasnewydd. Taken from Houses of the Welsh Countryside *by Peter Smith, HMSO, 1988. [Crown copyright: RCAHMW]*

The mansion houses of Watstay and Plas Newydd were built by the Eyton family. The date for the building of the latter has been revised because of the discovery in the course of restoration of the 'unsuspected use of herringbone and diamond pattern infilling, indicating that the house is probably later than first believed — early or possibly even mid-16th century, as perhaps also suggested by its height, as well as the Renaissance doorhead detail of the passage partition'.[29] One of the occupants in the 19th century was Sir Watkin's kinsman and agent, Owen Slaney Wynn. Rhuddallt, 'covered in the old days, a very extensive and important area, that portion in proximity to the Dee was occupied by woollen mills … Little or no trace is left of this once busy community. There were several mills running in connection with the woollen industry including one named 'The Sergeant Mill'.[30]

From early times there was a ferry across the Afon Eitha. In 1479 a bridge was built over the river probably quite near to the present Ruabon bridge erected in 1894.

The Hamlet of Bodylltyn

Means the dwelling place of Ylltyn. It gives the name of the hamlet and a house associated with the parish for over six hundred years. In the 18th century, together with adjoining land, Bodylltyn was enclosed in the park.

> Bodylltyn was a residence of some note, and the family connected with most of the leading personages in this area, from the Lords of Dinas Bran in the twelfth century to the Eytons of Watstay, the Lloyds of Plas Madoc and most of the Welsh nobility in the neighbouring manors and townships.[31]

Plas Madoc. Demolished c.1965. [Thomas Lloyd]

Plas Madoc
Watkin Ellis wrote the following:

I have no doubt that there was a demesne at Plas Madoc in the twelfth century, used by the Lords of Dinas Bran for their retainers, very possibly earlier than this.

Many readers have asked me to give the names of the past occupants of Plas Madoc for they realise, very rightly, that the hall and its people played a great part in local events covering six or seven centuries.

This is my reason for the following 'detailed' information.

Some, like myself, remember it in its former glory, with its well-kept park, surrounding a most attractive mansion. What the prospect was before the railway was laid, before the Wynnstay park was enclosed and before the existence of the present Ruabon to Rhosymedre road, when the Plas Madoc parklands extended as far as the old road near Bodylltyn and previous to the near-by colliery being sunk, can well be imagined — according to the records sixty acres in extent.

Howel Grach married Margaret, a wealthy heiress, and their only daughter Angharad married Madog yr Athro, the ancestor of the Lloyds of Plas Madoc. This was about the year 1250.

Iorwerth Fychan, who was living in 1332, and passing by some of the family, we come to David ap Llewelyn, one of the grand jury of the assizes held at Holt Castle in 1468. He married Margaret, daughter and heiress of David ap Hwfa.

Then followed John ab David, who married Angharad, the daughter of Sir Randle Brereton of Malpas.

Their son, Randle ap John, who married Angharad, daughter of John ab Ieuan ab Deicws ab Dio of Llanerchrugog.

Then John Lloyd, who was one of the grand jury for his county in 1547 and 1563. He married Janet, daughter of Geoffrey Bromfield of Bryn y Wiwer, Ruabon.

William Lloyd, who was one of the grand jury in 1596, married Catherine daughter of Owen Brereton of Borasham.

Edward Lloyd, (*c.*1620) married Anne, daughter of John Eyton of Leeswood, or Coed y Llai.

Edward Lloyd of Eglwysegl, M.A., their eldest son died in his father's lifetime, leaving two young children — Edward, who succeeded his grandfather at Plas Madoc, and Catherine who became the wife of John Powell of Rhuddallt, eldest son of Daniel Powell ab David Powell, D.D., vicar of Ruabon.

This Edward Lloyd bought the great tithes of Bodylltyn and Christionydd Cynwrig from the Lord Wooton, owner of Valle Crucis abbey. He died in 1636. Edward Lloyd the grandson of the previous owner, married his cousin Elizabeth. John their eldest son was a captain in the royalist army in the regiment commanded by Colonel Robert Ellis of Groes Newydd, Wrexham (the ancestral home of the late lord Howard de Walden). He died in his father's lifetime and the estate passed on to Samuel, the third son. The daughter, Anne, married William Lloyd of Plas Bennion and Trefynant.

Edward Lloyd died in 1691 and was succeeded by his third son, Samuel.

Another Edward Lloyd died in 1760 aged seventy-four, and was buried like all the other Plas Madoc family, at Ruabon. He left to the poor of Ruabon parish £150 to be distributed in coals and schooling for three boys and two girls from the townships of Cristionydd and Coed Cristionydd, secured by a rent charge on lands at Weston Rhyn. These lands were purchased from the Lloyd family by Mr Kenyon of Penylan.

The heiress to Clochfaen, Plas Madoc and Rhydonen mentioned previously, Sarah, married John Edwards of Crogen Iddon, Glyn, by whom she had no issue. She married secondly the Rev. Thomas Youde of Brasenose College, Oxford.

Mrs. Sarah Youde died in 1837, aged ninety-three. She had issue, Thos. Watkin, who succeeded to the Clochfaen and Plas Madog estates. He was deputy lieutenant of the county of Denbigh and High Sheriff of Montgomeryshire in 1816. He died unmarried in 1821. Edward, another son, succeeded to the estates on the death of his mother in 1837. There were also three daughters — Sarah, who died unmarried in her eighteenth year: Julia Elizabeth, succeeded to the estates on the death of her brother Edward, and died unmarried in 1857, and Harriet, who married Jacob William Hinde of the 15th Hussars. Harriet died in 1856 and Capt. Hinde in 1868.[32]

Plas Bennion

Rebuilt 1685, abandoned *c*.1800. In the 18th century Anne Lloyd, heiress of Plas Bennion, married John Rowland who had purchased lands in the parish of Ruabon and established the family of Rowland of Plas Bennion, Bryn, Acrefair, Delph, *etc*. The Plas Bennion estate was rich in iron and coal and the house became neglected and fell into a ruinous condition.

Wynn Hall

Built 1649 by Captain William Wynn. His descendants became Kenricks and lived here until the 1960s.

Map of the township of Dinhinlle Isaf. [W Alister Williams after A N Palmer]

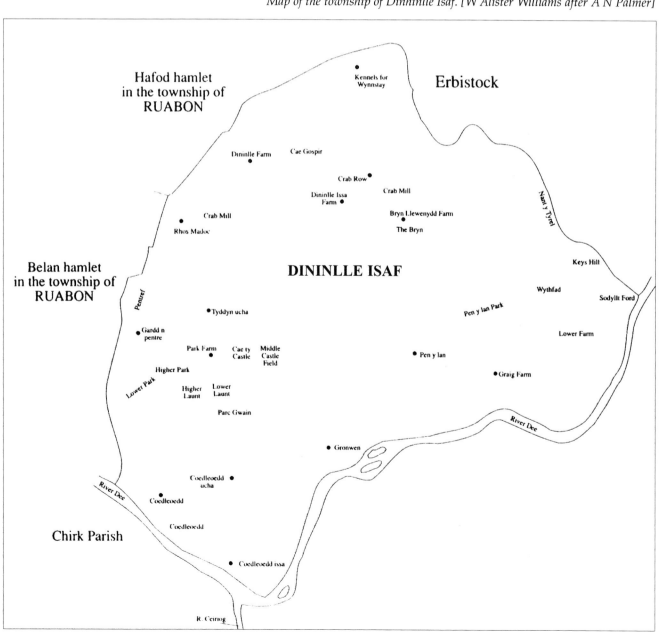

Ruabon Bridge, 1810. [National Library of Wales]

Gardden
At least four houses have taken their name form the camp Y Gardden.
Pen y Gardden, owned by the Parrys, later by Reuben Haigh.
Gardden Lodge in 1814 belonged to Edward Rowland and was owned by Richard Briscoe in 1844.
Gardden Hall sold to Ellis Lloyd of Pen-y-lan in the 17th century.
Tatham's Farm in 1840 belonged to the Hon. Frederick West from the Myddelton family.

The Township of Dinhinlle Isaf
The principal feature of the township was Dinhinlle Park, one of the princely reserves of the princes of Powys Fadog. It is mentioned in 1388-9 and in Tidderly's Survey of Bromfield in 1546. The park contained in 1620, 575 statute acres. Existing field names trace the boundaries of the old park, 'Launt', 'Lower Back Park', 'Upper Park', 'Park Farm' *etc.* The various holdings called Coed Leoedd (The Wood Houses) were not within the park, although adjacent to it.

The pentref, or village of Dinhinlle is old, Gardd y Pentre, a farm being mentioned in 1562. Bryn Llewenydd is the name of a farmhouse now called simply 'The Bryn'. There was in 1620 a moor or 'greene' in this township called 'Rhos John ap Madoc' — this name referred to the farmhouse and enclosed fields on this site. In 1767 Roger Meeson was the owner.[33]

Penylan
In the great surveys up to 1620 Penylan is not designated a large estate. In 1620 William Williams, Hafod House, Esclusham married Mary Lloyd, heiress of Penylan. In 1670 Ellis Lloyd, brother of Eubule Lloyd and of William Lloyd, Bishop of Norwich, resided here.

The Township of Morton is y Clawdd (Morton Below the Dyke)

New Hall
During the years 1664 and 1665 payments amounting to £1,154–13s–1d were made for building New Hall 'with the object of encouraging Mr Charles Myddelton and his second wife Jane Needham, the famous

New Hall, now demolished.

beauty, to settle in the country'. The hall was modernised in 1839 and chimney pieces, ceilings *etc.* were removed. Mr Henry Dennis bought the house from Colonel Cornwallis West *c.*1868 when it was faced with stone.

Farms along the western boundary of the township include the Clwt farm which belongs to the poor of Ruabon, the house called Crymbal with some land belongs to Ruabon Charities. The Wynnstay estate owns

Morton Cock Farm, Morton Below Farm and the Crymbals meadows. The *Cinders Farm* has forty-seven acres in Morton is y Clawdd and thirty-four acres in Dinhinlle Isaf. It was part of the endowment of Ruabon Grammar School, but in 1858 the farm was purchased by Sir Watkin as part of the arrangement for building the new grammar school.

The Township of Morton Anglicorum
The name means Morton of the English. Within the township is the village of Gyfelia, named after the smithies which flourished there.

Ruabon Village Settlement
We have seen that there was a church on the present site at the latest by the 13th century. The mansion house at Plas Newydd was built in the 16th century, and the river Afon Eitha used as a source of water power. It was probably the river more than the church which determined the settlement pattern. There is a record of a bridge being built across the river near the existing bridge in 1479, where there would be a small settlement.

The use of the river as a source of power is confirmed by evidence for the existence of mills in Ruabon by Robert d'Eggerley in his survey of 1391, and other surveys of 1562 and 1620, which record the existence of grain mills. The mill cottage in Pont Adam probably goes back before the building of Plas Newydd, with a bridge there built in the time of Abbot Adam of Valle Crucis. These mills became part of the Wynnstay/Watstay estate and accounts for their rent and repair are found in the 18th century:

> *1749, July 20th* Paid Roger Williams, Mill Wright, his years salary due at Lady Day last, for repairing Ruabon and Sergeant's Mills, Wynnstay Mault Mill, the engine and the Brew House pump £5.
> *1747.* Edward Jones for Ruabon Mills and two parcels of land being part of Plas Newydd tenement £17–0–0 (Rental).

There is evidence in the diocesan records of the existence of common fields in the Maes-y-Llan area which would presume early settlement. Maes-y-Llan farm and the vicarage are about the same distance from the church. The church terriers of the 17th century mention the dwellings around the church. The site around the church became a crossroads: to Plas Newydd across the bridge at Pont Adam; to Oswestry crossing the bridge and following a route different from now; to Wrexham part way along the road to Overton, the route of which was changed at the end of the 18th century. Near the church on all these roads was some habitation.

Church Street: the road to Plas Newydd. Along this street the Grammar School was built in 1618, the alms houses in 1711, and the mill at Plas Newydd much earlier. The will of Edward Pritchard, died 1679, curate of Ruabon, confirms the settlement around the church:

> Item whereas I bought one parcell of wast ground of John Powell of Rhuddallt in the parish of Ruabon in the County of Denbigh gent. lately deceased commonly called & known by the name y vron tan y dynwent extending itself in length & breadth, east, west, north & south from the churchyard road to two wayes, the first, the high road from Wrexham to a stone bridge of the brooke of Ruabon leading towards the new bridge, the other way leading from the west end of the school house in Ruabon to the said stone bridge (excepting a cottage wherein Joice Eyton widdowe lived (lately deceased) & a kilne, containing two bayes of buildings & another cottage with a garden at the stone bridge end, wherein one Phillip David Clogger now liveth) I give and bequeath the said parcell of wast ground together with a cottage called the bakehouse, that I built thereupon where one Ales verch Roger now dwelleth to the use of Humphery Powell, now curat & School Master of Ruabon, during the time he shall remaine curat and Schoole master here, & no longer, & after his departure to his respective successors.

Some of the existing houses in Church Street have timber framing behind 18th and 19th century facades.

Bridge Street: leading to Oswestry is below the church. The hill has been altered when bridges were built at the beginning and end of the 19th century. Settlement below the church was in the hamlet of Rhuddallt, the river divided the hamlet and the estates of Rhuddallt Isaf and Rhuddallt Ucha were across the river. These medieval estates were later absorbed into Wynnstay park in the 18th century.

Tan Lan: The area on the church side of the river, Tan Llan, Tan y Llan or Brookside is the site of ancient habitation. Several houses on the west side of Duke Street date from the 17th century and the building known as Brookside House, situated on the south side of the river below Bridge Street appears to be part-timber

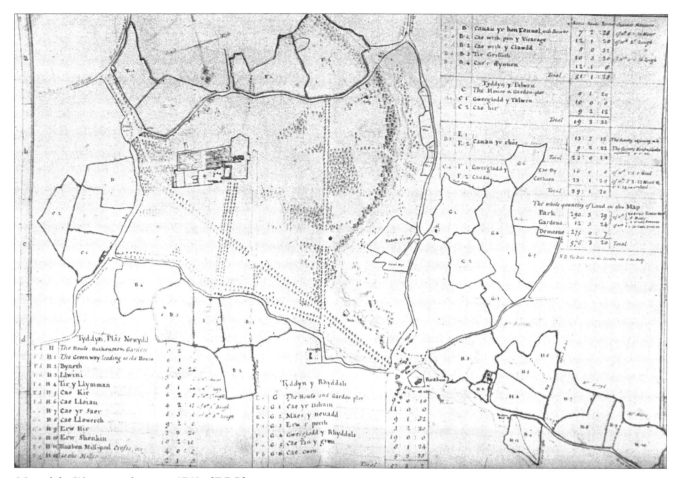

Map of the Wynnstay demesne, 1740. [DRO]

framed and its situation suggests that this may have formerly been a mill. A building called 'y Skabor tan y llan' is mentioned in a mortgage 13 February 1635/36.[34] Tan Llan is therefore an ancient settlement on the river bank, hence the name Brookside, which would have taken advantage of the water power and have been part of the Rhuddallt estates.

Park Street: The map of Wynnstay Demesne[35] 1740 shows what appears to be Park Street before the Park gates were put up in 1770 and a new turnpike road made to Overton later in the century. Another map, undated, but probably made between 1815 and 1824, again shows a number of dwellings here in the form of a square, formed by four blocks of buildings with the Market Place opposite the Wynnstay Arms, before the building of the Constitutional Club. On the south side of Park Street, at the back of the houses, dropping down towards the river is a group of houses, Tan Lan. The map does not show property belonging to other landowners. Clearly Park Street was built and laid out before 1841, the date when the Wynnstay Arms was renovated. I have found no evidence for the building of Park Street as late as the 1840s; on the contrary there is firm evidence that the Wynnstay Arms was built *c.*1749.

High Street: South High Street shows the same settlement pattern as Church Street, houses with small gardens at the back. In the 1740 demesne map it is not clear if the Wynnstay Arms (the Eagles Inn) is there. The north side development is not clearly shown but we know that it extended by 1823 to what became the residence of Dr Lawton Roberts. The 1740 map of the Wynnstay demesne lands is interesting because of the information it gives about the area surrounding the mansion.

Park	290a–3r–24p
Gardens	12a–3r–24p
Demesne	273a–0r–7p
	576a–3r–20p

Tyddyn Plas Newydd has 72a 1r 19p with 'Ruabon mill pool'. Some of the field names are prefixed cae, erw,[36] ... Tyddyn y Rhuddallt has 57a-3r-2p with field name prefixes — cae, maes, erw and gwerglodd. Wat's Dyke crosses into Wynnstay east of the vicarage, and Offa's Dyke is marked as dividing Plas Newydd lands.

The *c*.1820 'Map of Wynnstay Demesne and other lands in the parishes of Ruabon, Erbistock and Bangor'[37] gives an excellent description of the landscaping work undertaken for the fourth baronet, *c*.1775–85 by Capability Brown, J. Woods and J. Evans, with the upper and lower lakes clearly marked — and the Waterloo Tower at Newbridge. In the park to the west of the lower lake is James's Farm and James's Park in Rhuddallt township, (not mentioned by A.N. Palmer) to the south west of which is, first, a group of buildings identified as Thrashing Machine and second, Bodylltyn, with a number of large fields: Green Field, Lucerne Field, Barn Field *etc*. Outside the

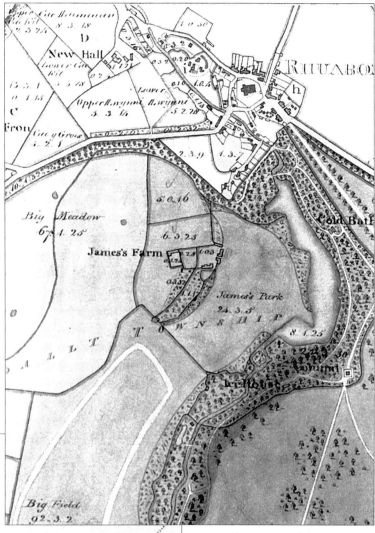

Above: Map of the Wynnstay demesne and Ruabon village, c.1820.

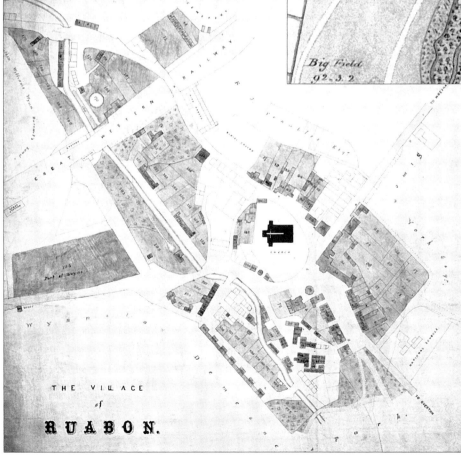

Left: Sir Watkin's property in Ruabon village, c.1865. [DRO]

Tan Lan, 1930.

park by the road turning for Rhos-y-madoc on the north side of the Overton road is Llwyn Howell, with its field names designating early settlement: *cae, erw, werglodd*. Common here but unusual is 'cinders' which occurs seven times and refers to early iron-making.

Another Wynnstay map,[38] no date but post-1863, records Sir Watkin's property in Ruabon village as 237 tenements, with tenants named. It shows that as late as 1863 the main settlement area was around the church, with the concentration of property in Tan Lan, Church Street, Park Street in which were the robing room, court house, Ruabon market hall and Goat Inn. The density of population and occupation in the Tan Lan area is seen from the 1891 census returns.

Park Street: butcher's shop, Robert Griffiths; Police Station, Frederick Jones, Sergeant of Police; John Roberts, butchers; Hannah Jones, living on own means; Joseph Ellis, stone mason (pensioner); Edward Richards, plate-layer; Sarah Howell, housekeeper; Ernest Reynolds, painter and decorator; Walter Jones, tram driver; Susan Hughes, laundress with three boarders; Isaac Smith, gate-keeper; William Hopley, saddler and harness maker; Henry Lloyd, brick wheeler; John Davies, joiner; William Jones, tailor; Edward Roberts, coachman; Ellen Drinkwater, widow; Joseph Jones, railway porter; George Eden, railway signalman; Thomas Jones, railway pointsman; John Edwards, foreman in brick terracotta works; Richard Williams, bricklayers, labourer; Samuel Rees, general labourer.

Tan Lan:

Duke Street: John Jones, railway wagon repairer; John Morris, blacksmith; William Bailiff, haircutter; John Jones, shoemaker; Thomas Jones, contractor; Charles Davies, labourer brick works; Mary Jones, labourer, in brick works.

Brookside: Edward Owens, labourer in brick works; Peter Crewe, railway porter.

W. M. Conservative Association Rooms: Thomas Pearson, messenger postman; Edward Samuels, general labourer.

Wesleyan Chapel.

Little Street: John Rowlands, railway plate layer; Wm. Richard, railway plate layer; Wm. Stanford, boiler maker;

Frederick Eaton, general labourer; Thomas Roberts, collier; Richard Barnfield, shunter on railway.

Paddock Row (from here onwards occupations only): general labourer, railway plate layer, modeller (terracotta), boiler maker, railway porter, road man, blacksmith, brick burner, plumber, coal miner, carter, railway signalman, patternmaker.

Tan Lan: Dress maker, char cleaner, coal miner, coal mine labourer, five general labourers, dressmaker.

The Court, Tan Lan: charwoman, coalminer,

Tan Lan hill, off Bridge Street: housekeeper, brickyard labourer, housekeeper.

Chapel House: grocer's shop, Mary Williams, grocer.

Working Men's Institute

Tan Lan Hill: general labourer, colliery labourer, Hannah Williams, shop keeper.

Tan Lan off Park Street: head brick-burner, coal miner, general labourer, charwoman, brick maker.

Chapel Square: labourer in brick works, fitter.

Tan Lan, rear of reading room: colliery labourer.

In the 1910 valuation[39] Sir Watkin owned 49 houses in Tan Lan, 13 in Paddock Row, 7 in Little Street and 5 in Duke Street.

Mr. Eddie Bowen Jones has fond memories of Tan Lan over 60 years ago:

In those pre-war days the early onset of the dusks of autumn was a very exciting time. We were allowed to play in the dark for a short while each evening. During this limited time, we managed to work the usual seasonal mischief of knocking on doors and running away, and tying black buttons to black thread to tap on living room windows. Another more antisocial prank was to spit on people from great heights, that is if you were tall enough! Two favourite spots for this exhilarating activity were the bridge above the railway platform at Ruabon Station in the summer when the station platform was crowded, and the Lady Steps in Park Street in the darkness of autumn. In the context of the popularity of twist chewing 'down pit' and industrial lung disease, spitting was rather like smoking now, frowned upon but not absolutely banned.

It was from the Lady Steps, I think, I had my first view of the roofs and smoking chimneys of the tumbledown dwellings of a part of Tan-y-Lan which has long since disappeared, being that area now occupied by the Royal British Legion buildings and its car parks. From our vantage point at the top of Lady Steps, under threat of eviction by Mrs. Wainwright and Mrs. Robinson, we could see by the light of the 'tancle' (a large gas street-light) a rough, un-made lane. This lane ran from the foot of the steps to the highway which still exists in front of the legion buildings. It then crosses the brook (Afoneitha) by way of a small bridge leading on to the Duke of Wellington Inn via Paddock Row.

On the right of the un-made lane, when walking down, was a ramp leading to the shop then occupied by Mr Dick (Tanylan) Jones and his family, including their youngest son, my friend Billy. On the left was a row of houses, and at the lower end of this row was the same tancle, close to the portable water standpipe. Immediately across the highway was another row of cottages backing on to the brook. If you turned sharp left at the end of the lane and walked in the direction of Wynnstay park wall towards the brick and slate built pumping station (which still stands today), there was another row of houses on the left, fronting the brook, and behind these houses was the 'square'. We never saw the square for the very good reason that it was outside the light of the tancle, and closer to 'Lady Harriet's Walk' than was good for one with a vivid imagination in the gathering dusk. On the other side of the brook from the pumping station was the well. Alas, I never knew the well save by name as it must have fallen into disuse with the advent of the street standpipe.

Downstream from the well were the cascades which was the point where the brook entered the park under the park wall, with its protective water-gate hanging under the bridge or archway in the wall. Long before our time, in fact before the First World War, the cascades fed the boating lake which was the centrepiece of the ornamental gardens within the park, of which the Bath House formed part.

It seemed a long time (we had probably been caught spitting) between one autumn and the next, and when we were able to sneak to Tan-y-Lan again, all was changed. The square was uninhabited and only a few houses above the tancle were occupied. Gone was Mr Dick (Tan-y-Lan) Jones and his 'treeping' whistle, together with his dog and his family. Gone were the roofs of many of the houses.

Only the tancle and the large rock or stone beneath it where people used to foregather remained, together with the leaking standing pipe. 'Sweet Auburn' could well describe the desolation. We enquired the whereabouts of the once teeming populace, remembering that there were some twenty or thirty dwellings in the area I have depicted, and each small dwelling invariably housed a good-sized family, only to find that they

Ruabon Vicarage, c.1900.

had in the year of our Lord 1937, under the auspices of the public health authority, departed to a place called Luxembourg, now better known as North Avenue, Wynnville, Ruabon.

As we grew up the remains of Tan-y-Lan disappeared. The area near the cascades became a salvage dump during the war, and after the war the area on the other side of the brook, which I have not dwelt upon, fell into ruin, leaving very little other than Paddock Row and Duke Street. How the face of nations change!

Our chapter on Beginnings and Settlement concludes with an examination of a small area of land that stretches from Maes y Llan to the vicarage. Records of land owned by the church and associated with the parsonage house was regularly made by the vicar and chief parishioners in the vestry meeting and sent to the diocesan bishop for his safekeeping. These records are called terriers and provide an inventory of landholding. Terriers exist for the parish of Ruabon for 1636, 1685, 1730, 1749 and 1856; from these is extracted a list of the pieces of land belonging to the vicarage as glebe land, that is land farmed by the incumbent. This list of items of land is invaluable for many reasons. It refers to the common fields in Maes y Llan which were originally held in strips, quillets or butts. Some of these strips were given to the vicarage as glebe, well before the 16th century. This list gives field names, occupiers and boundaries over a period of 220 years. These field names refer to the ancient Welsh agriculture practiced in Ruabon from the beginning of arable farming, over a thousand years ago. The terriers give a detailed description of the parsonage house showing the vicarage as a substantial building which took on the character of a farm with all the necessary outbuildings. For example in 1749 the vicarage had a large porch hall, kitchen, wainscotted parlour, boarded parlour, pantry, dairy, scullery and cellar. There were three staircases. The first led to four lodging rooms each with a fire-place: the second to two more, and the third rose from the dairy into a servants' room and thence to two garrets. There were three large outbuildings. The first included a threshing floor, three bays for corn, a stable, a servants' shop over which were two small lodging rooms for servants. The second outbuilding had two bays for hay or corn, a stable and a coach house. The third contained a brew house, a malt house and a gardeners' shop and above these, granaries. The kitchen garden was 40 yards square walled in on 3 sides. The pleasure garden 34 yards long and 25 yards broad. The small garden 37 yards long and 9 yards broad. Finally, there was the court before the kitchen 37 yards long and 11 yards broad. The terrier of 1856 described the house as it remained until it was sold in 1953:

> The house contains on the Ground Floor an entrance hall, dining, breakfast room and library, kitchen housekeeper's room, servants hall, larder, dairy, china closet and watercloset, bath room and dressing room — on the first floor a drawing room, seven bed rooms, three small dressing rooms and water closet, — on the second floor or attic, four bed rooms and a lumber room. Detached is a building containing a wash house and oven in it a shoe brushing room, poultry yard and three pig sties — In another detached building are two three stalled stables, cow house, calf kit, coach house, saddle room, cart house and shed. In another detached building is a laundry, a wash house, a kitchen and two bedrooms.

It is now known as the old vicarage. The residential part has been divided into three separate dwelling houses. The laundry and glebe was converted into a farm house sometime in the 1920s. The extensive garden of the parsonage house was sold and developed as a housing estate, Vicarage Fields, from 1953 onwards.

A description of the lands belonging to the vicarage and poor of Ruabon as given in the terriers of 1685, 1730 and *c*.1750. The extract below is taken from the terrier of 1685. The items follow the same sequence in the two later terriers with little variation in description:

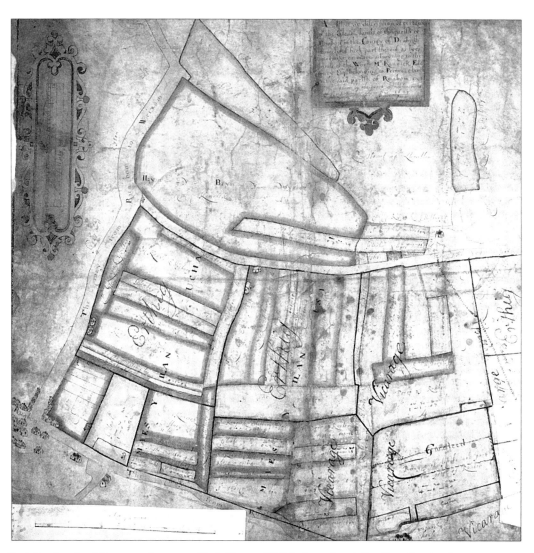

Glebe land in Maes y Llan, belonging to the vicarage of Ruabon, 1715. [Denbighshire Record Office, PD/89/1/3]

1. Item a Little Croft at the back of the cow house called Cae yr Kill being about the fourth pt. of an acre.

2. Item a Close by the Mansion called Cae'r Scrubon extending in length from a close called bryn fadyn felyn unto the way leading to the vicars house about four butts in a close called y gwastad ar cae yr pant lying next to the Court leading to the porch of the vicars house in length from the headlands in the east end of the said close unto Maes y Llan issa about one acre.

3. Item Two Butts near the hedge in the same close containing about the fourth part of an acre.

4. Item a Meadow called gwerglodd y pwllegweinion under known bound and limits about one acre and a half.

5. Item another meadow called gwerglodd y vicar lying in length from the meadow called gwerglodd y fron ddrys unto the lands called dryllie y mondri and in breadth fron ddrys unto the lands now in possession of Joshua Edisbury Esq., about one acre.

6. Item A parcel of lands lying in length from bryn yr uwch unto the fron goch and in breadth from the lands called Y Bronydd which John Eyton gent., deceased hath bequeathed unto the poore of Ruabon unto a close called y cae bychain containing about the fourth pt. of an acre.

7. Four Butts in Maes y Llan ucha lying in length from the headland of Joshua Edisbury Esq., unto a certain close late of Kenrick Edisbury Esq., called Erw yr fforddig and in breadth between the lands of the said Joshua Edisbury about one acre.

8. Item. One close hereby before expressed called erw yr fforddig which the said Kenrick Edisbury Esq., did heretofore give and bequeath to the church of Ruabon to be as pt. and p'cell of the glebe lands thereto also belonging and lying and adjoining to the street that leadeth from Ruabon to the town of Wrexham about one acre. (Note: added in 1750 the words: 'subject to a chiefty of one shilling yearly to Sir Watkin Williams Wynn Baronet')

9. Item. One Butt in Maes y llan ucha being the next saving one to Cae mab yr offeriaid about the fourth part of an acre.

10. Item. The one half of two butts in the same field lying next the highway leading from Ruabon to the Vicarage house whereon Joshua Edisbury Esq., aforesaid hath the other half about the sixth part of an acre.

11. Item. In the field called Maes y llan Issa four butts in length from the headland called talar y famog unto the highway leading from the Vicarage house to Ruabon having on the south side the lands of Joshua Edisbury Esq., and on the north side the lands of the Poor of Ruabon (half an acre).

12. Item. Seven butts in the same field divided in the midst four in the east end and three in the west extending in length from talar y famog unto Maes y llan ucha and in breadth from the east part between two parcels of land belonging to the poor of Ruabon and for the west part between the lands of Joshua Edisbury Esq., about one and a half acres.

13. Item. Two Butts in Maes y llan issa extending in length from the north end of talor y famog through the highway leading to Pentre Clawdd unto two other butts of the vicars land called cwisida'r dwr about the third part of an acre.

14. Item. Two other Butts in Maes y llan issa extending in length from a croft of the said Joshua Edisbury Esq., called y Erw hir unto the highway that leadeth from Ruabon to Pentre Clawdd and in breadth between the lands of the said (J. E.) (half an acre).

15. Item. Four Butts of land lying in Llwyni bryn wiwer set out by Edward Eyton Esq., under known bounds and limits — one acre.

16. Item. Two Butts and a pike called cwisiade yr dwr lying in the midst of a little close which is at the east end of the last mentioned four butts unto a p'cell of lands of the said Joshua Edisbury Esq., called dryllie y miondre upon which Elizabeth and the late wife of Anthony ab Edward deceased lately dwelt — accounted the fourth part of an acre.

17. Item. A house in Ruabon now in the occupation of John Owen shoemaker with a backside and garden belonging in the same. (Note, in *c.* 1750 Roger Jones the Parish Clerk lived there).

18. A house and tenement at the north west corner of Ruabon Church with a garden plot thereto belonging called y urdd lyn lying between the highway which leadeth from Ruabon to Cristionydd and a close of Sir John Wynn Knt & Bart. Which house and tenement is now in the occupation of John Wxall & Catherine (verch) Richard. (Note: the house was recorded as being re-built in 1730 and divided in 1750).

19. Item. A house and tenement in Ruabon now in the occupation of Edward Shone weaver and Elizabeth ych Edd and the ground whereon the same doth stand extending in length from ye crabtree at ye west end of ye same unto the highway yt leadeth from Ruabon to Rhuddallt adjoining to both sides to ye lands of John William ab William lately deceased.

20. Item. Ye vicars portion of the House by ye Cross in Ruabon now in ye occupation of Richard Williams Clarke of ye pish for which ye Vicar receiveth half a crown p. anno of Sr. John Wynn Knt. &c.

21. Item. A plott of ground where a house in times past did stand between ye barn called yr yscubor Ddegwin & a garden belonging to a house in Ruabon called y tydy where John Parry now dwelleth.

22. Item. A close called Cae mab yr offeriad under known bounds and limits and a house and garden on the same in the occupation of Catherine Wynn widow. (Note: about one acre and a half *c.* 1750).

23. Item. A close called erw eva under known bounds and limits. (Note: One acre 1730).

24. Item. A croft called gwerdd y llyn extending in length from the highway leading from Ruabon to Llangollen unto the lands of Sr. John Wynn Knt. & Bart and in breadth from ye late lands of John Williams ab William deceased unto the lands of the said Sir John Wynn Knt. & Bart.

25. Item. Three butts of land by ye house wch Jane ych Edward widow to Hugh ab Edward of Rhuddallt deceased now dwelleth butting fourth westward upon ye late lands of John Eyton Vauchan deceased and north eastward upon the late lands of John ab Edward Smyth and lying in breadth between the lane that leadeth from Ruabon to Rhuddallt and the land of Edward ab Rondle: one acre.

26. Item. A p'cell of lands in p'ish of Wrexham called Erw fair under knowne bounds and limits. (Note in 1730 — one acre and a half).

By 1856 the twenty-six items of land have been consolidated into eight fields.

Field names in 1856
1. The Vicarage area (which contained the house and garden). 4a-1r-11p.
2. The Meadow 6a-2r-30p which included 1a-2r-7p of Poors' land.

3. Gwastad 2a-2r-18p which included 2r of Poors' land.

4. The Gravel Hole Field 7a-3r-15p which included 2a-0r-1p of Poors' land and 1a-0r-18p belonging to Sir W. W. Wynn.

5. Brick-Kiln Field. 5a-1r-36p which included 3a-1r-25p. of Poors' land.

6. Cae Pen Plas Vicar. 3a-0r-18p 'on western portion of which stands the laundry cottage erected in 1843 and a portion of the same side forms part of the present back-yard.'

7. The Well Field 1a-2r-0p 'a portion of which now forms part of the lawn'.

8. The Fir Tree Field formerly called Bryn yr lwyd 3a-2r-25p.

What can we learn from these items of land described in the terriers? First that they preserve clues about the early settlement and agriculture in the community which would be difficult to find elsewhere. From the field names preserved here and mentioned earlier in the chapter (*erw, cae, gwerglodd etc.*), we are able to give an approximate date to the settlement or colonisation of Ruabon township.

   The first period of colonisation relates to arable cultivation and the ploughing of the land. Farming was a communal enterprise which demanded co-operation particularly where ploughing was undertaken. The ideal medieval homestead or *tyddyn* each theoretically contained four acres or *erw* of specified dimensions grouped together in a *rhandir*, or shareland in an open field. *Erw* oiginally indicated the amount of land ploughed in a day by a yoke of oxen. It later became generally used to describe a field. There are many words in the extracts from the terriers which relate to open field agriculture:

Butts, in an open field usage a strip, especially one abutting at right angles on another group of selions (strips).

Close, a small area of land enclosed for agricultural purposes.

Croft, a small field or paddock understood to adjoin the toft (homestead).

Headland, in an open arable field this was land at the head of the furlong on which the plough could turn.

Gweirglodd, the common hayfield.

Messuage, a dwelling and the land adjoining it.

Maes an open field, a plain.

Llan, originally an enclosure, but its association with the church finally stabalised its meaning as a church-place or church.

Pike, a gore or triangular piece of land as in a common field.

Quillet, an unfenced strip of land associated with communal aration

   The second period of settlement and colonisation occurs in the late 15th or early 16th centuries onwards. *Cae* is the most common field name and is generally applied to a field or an enclosure with a hedge. The third phase of settlement was the process of enclosure which took place between 1750–1850.

Farms in the community area of Ruabon

This list is based on information contained in the census returns up to 1891. The major source is the Inland Revenue Valuation Return for 1910, referred to by historians as the New Domesday. Another source of information is the Wrexham Rural District Council Rate Book for 1955. This source has its limitations, referring for example, to farm occupiers only, with no reference to acreage. The size of the land is the figure given, ignoring dwelling houses and out-buildings. It must be emphasized that this information is accurate as far as 1955 and must not be taken as correct at the time of writing in August 2000.

Astridge
1955 R. Barraclough.
1955 *Astridge Farm* Robt. W. Lloyd Jones

Bellan Farm, Belan Place
1891 Joseph Jones, farm foreman

1891 Roland E. Cheslyn Walker, Clerk in Holy Orders, chaplain to Sir Watkin

Bodylltyn
1861 Greville N. Wynne Esq. gentleman unmar. forty-five, with butler, housekeeper, cook and footman

Bryn Farm, Penylan
1861 James Stocker, farmer of 40a.
1881 William Cecil Roscoe
1891 George Mullock
1910 Own. Peter Ormrod occ.: Chas. A. Younger 152a-3r.
1955 E. Darlington. Sold 1945 by Penylan estate 151a.

Cae Clapiog
1861 Richard Wright, head gamekeeper
1871, 1881, 1891 William Leighton, gamekeeper and park keeper

Cae Cyriog
1861 Thomas Edwards, blacksmith
1871 Edward Green, labourer
1891 Thos. Jones, gardener

Castle Fields
1861 Frances Thomas wid 59, farmer of 83a.

Cinders (more than one property)
1861 Thomas Jones, farmer of 48a.
1871 l. Thomas Jones, farmer of 48a; 2. Owen Roberts, farmer of 88a.
1891 James Drake, farmer; Richard Davies, farmer; Thomas Jones, farmer
1910 Owner of all properties Sir Watkin. 1. James Drake 82a; 2. Samuel Wynne 18a-3r; 3. Mrs. Green & son 14.; 4. Griffith Williams; 5. Thos. Jones 46a.
1955 Occupiers W.J.A. Drake; J.N. Harris; K.P. Massey

Clwt Farm
1871, 1881, 1891. Thomas Roberts, farmer of 45 acres
1910 Owner Henry Dyke Dennis 41a-2r.
1955 Occupier Frederick E. Davies

Coedlleoedd more than one property
1861 1. Elias Rogers, late farmer; 2. Joseph Roberts, farmer of 50a; 3. Sarah Richards, farmer of 15a.
1871 1. Joseph Richards, farmer of 18a;
2. Thomas Roberts, farmer of 41a; James Phillips, farmer of 75a.
1881 1. Wm. Roberts, farmer of 20a;
2. Thos. Roberts, farmer of 41a;
3. Wm. Davies, farmer of 80a.
1910 Owner of both reps. G. Boscawen;
1. Wm. Davies 95a-3r;
2. Joseph Roberts 59a-2r.

1955 *Coedlleoedd Ucha*, S.T. Povey;
Coedlleoedd Issa, K.A. MacKenzie

Colomendy Farm
1871 J.A. Pruett, farmer of 18a.

Old Crymbal.

1881 J.A. Pruett, farmer of 80a.
1910 Henry Dyke Dennis, 14a.
1955 Mrs. Betty Beach

Crab Mill, Penylan
1910 Owner P. Ormrod; Occ. Joseph Dodd, 25a.
1955 Ogwen Williams

Crymbal
1861 Thos. Williams, farmer of 12a.
1910 Own. Trustees, Ruabon Poor; occ. Henry Stubbs 12a-2r.
1955 Francis A. Stubbs

Dynhynlle Isa
1861 John Lloyd, farmer
1871 John Lloyd, farmer of 119a.
1881 Rebecca Wilkinson, farmer 11a.
1891 Thos. Davies

Dynhynlle Farm
1881, 1891 Kenrick Kenrick, farmer 120a.
1910 Woodlands, Sir Watkin 18a; Peter Ormrod 144a-1r; reps of G. Boscawen, 56a.
Woodland — *Dynhynlle Isa* — 1910 Sir Watkin 18a, Peter Ormrod 144a-1r reps of G. Boscawen 56a.

Dynhynlle
1910 Sir Watkin own. occup. Walter Morgan 3a.
1955 *Dynhynlle*, Rhos Madoc, Edwin Kenrick
Mr and Mrs A.F. Phillips, *Dynhenlle Farm*, Penylan

Frongoch
1910 Own. Sir Watkin occup. Robt. Griffiths 34a-3r.

Gardden Hall
1910 Own/occ Reuben Haigh 81a.

Gardden Lodge
1910 Own. Ruabon Brick & Terracotta Co. occupier land, Reuben Haigh, 44a; house, Revd. D.J. Bowen

Gyfelia Farm
1861 Edward Massey, farmer of 96a.
1871 Edward Massey 98a; Edward Roberts, 60a; Robt. Williams 27a.
1881 Uriah Morgan, 70a; Robt. Williams 36a; Thomas Massey 96a.
1910 Own. R.W. Davenport, occ. Uriah Morgan 45a-1r; own. Uriah Morgan occ. Thos. Jones 10a; own/occ. H. Dyke Dennis 73a-1r.
1955 Wilfred Blake

Graig, Penylan
1861, 1871 Joseph Chapman, shepherd
1881, 1891 John Evans, farmer
1910 Own. P. Ormrod occup.
Edward Evans 139a-1r.
1955 C.K. Richards

Llwyn Howell
1861, 1871, Edward Griffiths, farm bailiff

Demolition of Mill Farm, Pont Adam.
[John Bradbury]

Mill Farm, Pont Adam
1861 John Jones, labourer
1871 Edward Wynn
1881 Elizabeth Wynn
1891 Ann Lloyd, laundress

James's Farm
1861 John Evans, groom
1871 Chas. Arthur, groom;
1881 Thos. Martin, ag. lab. Jn. Fletcher, farrier
1891 Thomas Milner; groom; Alfred Chapman, boarder; Tom Brotherton, blacksmith, Thos. Martin, farm lab.

Lower Farm, Penylan
1861 Wm. Rodenhurst, farmer of 80a.
1891 Hugh S. Sands
1910 Owner Peter Ormrod, occ. Edwd. Humphreys 96a-3r.
1955 C. L. Younger

(Lower) Moreton Farm
1871 John Griffiths, farmer 96a.
891 Sarah Griffiths
1910 Own. Sir Watkin occ. John Griffiths 98a-2r.

Lower Moreton farm
1871 Lewis Jones, farmer of 139a.
1910 Own. Sir Watkin occ. Thos. Lewis Jones 139a.
1955 Lewis Jones

[Census] Moreton Manor
1871 (under *Gyfelia*) Uriah Morgan, wheelwright, grocer;
1891 Uriah Morgan, farmer & shopkeeper
1955 John Cheetham

New Hall
1871 Hugh Rowe, farmer of 240a.
1910 Own. occ. Henry Dyke Dennis 210a-2r.

1881 Edward Jones, farm bailiff;
1891 Richard Jones, general farm servt.
1910 Own. Sir Watkin; occup. J.C. Murless 53a.
1955 T. Eric Davies

Machine Farm
1861 Thomas Walker, bailiff on farm of 60a.
1891 George Thomas, farm manager

Maes y Llan
1861 Sarah Roberts, farmer 94a.
1871 Wm. Williams, farmer 92a.
1881 Robert Roberts, farmer, 43a.
1891 Robt. Roberts, farmer
1910 Maes Llan Philip Yorke. Thomas Lee occ. 9a-2r; 2. Wm. Edwards 20a; 3. Robt. Lloyd — house buildings & land 43a.

Park Farm, Rhos y Madoc
1861 Richard Probert, farmer of 160a.
1871 William Jones, farmer 160a.
1881 Wm. Randles, farmer 160a; William Wall
1910 Own. reps G. Boscawen occ. Thomas Massey 161a-3r.
1955 W. D. Blanchard

Pentre Clawdd Farm
1861 Jane Rowland, farmer 150a.
1871 Charles Thomas
1881 William Williams, farmer 184a.
1891 Margt. Williams
1910 Own. Philip Yorke occ. Margt. Williams 164a.
1955 R. E. Blake

Pentre Issa, Rhos y Madoc
1861 Margt. Jones farmer 90a.
1871 John Jones, farmer 100a.
1881 John Jones, farmer 74a.
1910 Own. Sir Watkin; occ. R. Colby Evans 102a-1r.
1955 Stanley Davies

Pentre Ucha, Rhos y Madoc
1881 & 1891 Richard Price farmer of 84a.
1910 Own. Sir Watkin; occ. Richd Price, 70a-3r.
1955 (Pentre) J.T. Jones

Penylan Home Farm
1871 John Scott, land agent
1881 Saml. Jellicoe, bailiff & agent
1891 Saml. C. Moore, estate agent.
1910 Own/occ. Penylan Hall Peter Ormrod 177a-1r.
1955 *Home Farm*, Penylan. E. Darlington

Plas Madoc Farm
1871 George Pierce, groom
1881 Rowland Edwards, farmer 56a.
1891 Henry Jackson, farmer.
1910 own. Sir Watkin, occupier, Margt. Ann Jones, 101a, Richd. Gabriel 5a-2r; Wm. & Jonathan Roberts 10a-1r.

Rhos y Madoc Farm
1861 John Griffiths farmer 110a.
1871 Martha Griffiths 105a.
1881 Martha Griffiths 115a.
1891 John Taylor.
1910 Owner reps. G. Boscawen occupier Elias Thomas 12a. Edward Massey 100a-1r.
1955 Mr G. & Mrs. G.M. Monslow

Tathams Farm
1861 Kenrick Kenrick farmer 65a.
1871 Kenrick Kenrick
1881 Anne Jones farmer 12a.
1910 Own. Sir Watkin, occ. John Gibbons 14a and 13a-3r.
1955 Mr W. Allen

Tyddyn Ucha
1871 Edward Massey farmer 85a.
1881 Wm. Randles farmer 85a.
1891 Nathan Hutchinson farmer
1910 Own. Peter Ormrod occup. John Lloyd 86a-2r.
1955 W. Kearsley. Sold 1945 by Penylan Estate 87a.

Whitegate, Gyfelia
1881 William Roberts butcher & farmer of eleven and a half acres
1891 George Evans general labourer
1955 J. P. Brayne

Wynnstay Home Farm
1955 D. T. Evans & Co

Yellow Oak
1871 John Smith ag. lab.
1881 Edwin Vaughan game keeper.
1910 Own, Peter Ormrod occup. S.C. Caldecott 121a-3r.
1955 William Pugh sold 1945 by Penylan Estate 111a.

Yew Tree Farm
1891 Wm. Edwards
1910 Own. Reps. G. Boscawen occ. Wm. Roberts 16a-3r.
1955 Joshua Powell

A list of Wynnstay Lodges found in the census return

Baker's Lodge
1871 Thomas Baker, carter & servt. Resident in Drive Lodge;
1871 and 1891 Oven Lodge occupied by farm labourers.
These may well be the same building
The gates and gate piers at Baker's Lodge, situated on the road to Rhos y Madoc, are probably mid-19th century and perhaps designed by George Tattershall. It is listed as a gateway of some distinction on the Wynnstay estate and as part of an important series of 19th century improvements.

Bodylltyn Lodge
On the Rhosymedre Road
1871–81 Samuel Harper, shepherd
1891 Samuel Harper, shepherd. Richard Evans, wagonner

Broth Lodge
On the south side A539 Ruabon to Overton road.
1881 John Haynes, sawyer and Methodist local preacher
1891 Fdk. Smith, groom
and James Williams, wood sawyer
A two storey lodge faced in ashlar sandstone including an attached screen wall and gate piers

Green Lodge
1881 Edward Evans, ag. lab.
1891 George Evison, farm lab.

Dandy Lodge
1871 Richard Hall, farm lab.

1881 John Brooks, farm lab.
1891 uninhabited

Nant y Cae Coch Lodge
In Wynnstay Park south of the mansion house
1871 James Ellis, labourer.
1881 Llew. Ellis, gardener;
1891 John Colley, woodman

Park Eyton Lodge
1891 Robt. Jones, stationery engine driver. Old Kennel Lodge
1871 Jane Lewis wid. 39, schoolmistress.
1881 Dog Kennel Lodge Francis Caine, superintendent of works. Park Eyton Lodge situated 2.5 km east of Ruabon on turning for Penylan also known as Kennels Lodge. Perhaps designed by James Wyatt late 18th century, in the pedimented style of a Greek doric temple

School Lodge, Rhosymadoc.
[John Bradbury]

Park Lodge — Gate House — Park Street
Listed buildings — former lodge

School Lodge and School Room and attached house
1891 Miss Wms. Wynn's School Jane Lewis wid. school mistress, Jane Lewis dau. unmar. asst. mistress
1891 Jabez Wadey Clerk of Works building dept. 'The school room and house were designed as an architectural feature relating to the adjacent School Lodge with which they have group value.'

Lodge No. Eight
Formerly on the Oswestry road not far from the Bridge End. The marshalling point for processions to the church on special occasions

Other listed buildings

Ruabon Gates, Wynnstay Gates, Park Street
Gateway *c.*1770 by John Jones. Gates and railings erected to mark the coming of age of the future 8th Bart. Watkin Williams Wynn presented by Wrexham Rural District Council 1912.

Wynnstay Park, Ice House
Remains of a circular ice house 70 metres south west of Wynnstay Column. Receipt in Wynnstay accts.

Wynnstay Column
Designed by James Wyatt in memory of the 4th Baronet *c.*1790.

Boat House, Wynnstay Park
Part of scheme for landscaping the park by 4th Baronet. 'Rustic boat house thought to have been designed by Richard Woods'.

The Boat House, Wynnstay Park.

Wynnstay Kennels
Situated 2.5 km east of Ruabon running west of the by-road to Penylan off the A539. Built in 1843 to the designs of George Tattersall. 'Listed as a fine example of an extremely well planned and architecturally distinguished complex of the mid-19th century by one of the leading experts in kennel design.

*Left & below: Two views of the Wynnstay Arms.
[John Bradbury]*

Ruabon Railway Station

Tudor Gothic revival style. 'Designed by Henry Robertson in the 1860s replacing the original Shrewsbury and Chester Railway Station by T. M. Penson. Converted to offices in the late twentieth century and the platform canopy removed.'

Congregational Church

North side Pont Adam 'including attached Sunday School, gate piers, walls and railings, designed by W.I. Mason of Liverpool. Built at a cost of £1,400 and opened in 1858. Gothic Revival Style. Organ with painted and stencilled pipes by Wadsworth & Bro', Manchester. Chrome and glass electric lights of c1930. Listed as a little altered mid-Victorian chapel with contemporary fittings.'

Plas Newydd

South side Pont Adam Crescent.

Wynnstay Arms

Listed for special interest as a prominently sited, 18th and 19th century coaching inn.

Park Street estate cottages

Four blocks of estate cottages … listed as a fairly intact example of carefully planned estate cottages relating to the Wynnstay estate.

Henry Street, south side, Nos. 1 & 2 Oaklands
includes attached forecourt walls and gate

*An example of the local terracotta work on the front of Nos 1 & 2 Henry Street.
[John Bradbury]*

piers. Built 1895 of brick and terracotta produced by the Ruabon works.

Exterior: Pair of houses, the fronts of which are distinctive for their mixture of buff brick, red brick and red terracotta; slate roof with red terracotta Ruabon cresting tiles …. There is a large terracotta plaque centrally placed at first floor level in the form of a shell with bands of rosettes beneath; at second floor level is a central recess containing a terracotta figure of an owl.

Listed for the special interest of its eccentric design which is the most elaborate and best preserved example in the town, of a building incorporating locally produced Ruabon tiles, terracotta and brick.

Spring Lodge, Church Street.

Spring Lodge

Church Street north side. 'Listed as an imposing building of restrained early 19th century design, the house, gate piers and railings make an important contribution to the street scene'.

The Alms Houses, The Old Grammar School

'… the ground floor has been altered and rebuilt …'

St. Mary's Parish Church

Former Wynnstay Colliery

B5605 leaving roundabout S. of Ruabon. North side *Walker Fan House* — 'Built 1902 to ventilate Wynnstay Colliery which operated from 1856 to 1927… Listed as an example of a rare building type which survives relatively intact.' South side 'Vertical winding house, built 1855–6 as one of the original structures of the Wynnstay Colliery. It remained in use until the colliery closed in 1927. Listed as an exceptionally good example of the building type which is said to be the oldest surviving architectural monument of the north Wales coalfield.

Moreton Below Farmhouse (also known as Lower Moreton Farm)

2 km NE of Ruabon reached from a track which runs to the farm south of the B5426. The farmhouse originated as a 17th century timber framed building with cross-wing, cross-passage. In the 19th century the house was re-modelled and re-orientated. Listed as a house with 17th century origins which illustrates a sequence of development through the 18th and 19th centuries at the same time retaining elements of the original plan form and interior details.

Penylan Hall

Said to date from *c*.1690, the house was re-modelled in 1830 … Enlarged and altered in the late 19th century, much of these later additions were demolished in the 1950s. Exterior; Tudor Gothic Revival Style, stuccoed and castellated. Listed as an architecturally distinguished Tudor Gothic revival house of the 1830s which retains much of its original character both internally and externally.

Penylan Front Lodge

Built at the same time as the re-modelling of Penylan Hall *c*.1830.

A lodge at Penylan Hall.

Penylan Wyffydd
Near Lower Farm. Late-medieval half timbered and cruck framed hall-house, the west end of which has been rebuilt. 'Listed as a building of late medieval origin which retains a substantial amount of its original half-timbered, cruck-framed structure.'

All Saints' Church
'Listed as an architectural design of some distinction with an unusually good contemporary interior scheme'.

Bryn Llawenydd
The house is dated 1749 perhaps with earlier origins, re-modelled in the early part of the 19th century with extensions to the rear. After the opening of the church in Penylan in 1889, a private chapel of ease belonging to the Ormrod family, it became the residence of the private chaplain appointed by the Ormrod family. One of the chaplains, Reverend Thomas Buncome, was tutor to boys who resided at Bryn Llawenydd. In 1946 it became a dower house for the Ormrod family and was sold on the death of the widow of Major James Ormrod.

The view from the church tower looking along Church Street.

2. Wynnstay

The influence of Wynnstay as the family seat and the centre of activity and hospitality of the Williams Wynn family was enormous, from their arrival in Ruabon in 1719 until their departure in 1948. Although their ownership of land in north Wales has been considerably reduced from 150,000 acres to 26,000 acres at the beginning of the third millennium, the estate retains a considerable presence in Ruabon.

The purpose of this chapter is to describe the scope and development of the Wynnstay demesne, the architectural history of the mansion house and its grounds, and the development of the community on its doorstep as an estate village. This is reflected in the way the family remembered each successive generation in the parish church monuments and furnishings, and the involvement of parishioners in their rites of passage. The birth, coming of age, marriage and death, of at least six of the eight baronets was announced by the Ruabon church bells, and the ritual of these occasions shared with their tenants throughout north Wales in events which at times were both spectacular and lavish. Each baronet in turn made a contribution to both the Wynnstay demesne and the community of Ruabon.[1]

The previous name of the estate was Rhiwabon, and in 1620 was in the possession of Edward Eyton (d.1623) whose principal holding was in the manor of Isycoed. He was a descendant of John ap Elis Eyton (d.1524), who fought at Bosworth Field in 1485 on the side of the victor, Henry Tudor. Edward Eyton's sole surviving daughter Dorothy married Richard Evans of Treflach, Oswestry, and their son Thomas Evans (1591–1642) married Ann daughter of Dr David Powel, late vicar of Ruabon. Thomas Evans changed the name of the house to Watstay because of the dyke which runs through the grounds. Their son Eyton Evans (1609–55) married his kinswoman Elizabeth, daughter of Sir Gerard Eyton of Eyton. Their daughter Jane (1632–75), co-heiress, to whom Watstay was assigned, married Sir John Wynn knight and baronet.[2]

In order to understand the significance of Wynnstay as a political power base we begin our story in the 17th century with the advent of this Sir John Wynn (1628–1719). The great oak tree in Wynnstay Park illustrated by Moses Griffith reminds us of his pedigree and the succession of the estate. He was the grandson of his namesake Sir John Wynn (1553–1627) of Gwydir, described as 'unscrupulous, acquisitive, litigious and hot-tempered', who made his family supreme in Caernarfonshire. It was said that 'he combined the attributes of Welsh *ucheluriaeth* and the English Renaissance gentleman'.[3] He was proud of his descent from Owain Gwynedd (d.1169) prince of north Wales, and through him from Rhodri Mawr, the great king of Gwynedd, Powys and Deheubarth. His father Henry Wynn (d.1671) was Solicitor General to Queen Henrietta Maria, a lawyer and member of Parliament for Merioneth, and it was at his behest that Sir John married the heiress of Watstay, of which Henry said, when he went to spy out the land soon after the Restoration (1660), that for situation he had 'not seen its equal in Wales'.[4]

The new squire and baronet of Watstay inherited the Gwydir family qualities. He was loyal to the Stuart cause throughout his long life which witnessed the execution of Charles I, the restoration of Charles II, the flight of James II, the monarchy of William

Sir John Wynn's Oak, painting by Moses Griffith.
[National Library of Wales]

Wynnstay House (the 1612 house called Watstay can be seen on the left),water-colour by Moses Griffith.
[National Library of Wales]

and Mary, the reign of Queen Anne, and the uncertainty of the Hanoverian succession. Sir John succeeded his father as member of Parliament for Merioneth and later represented Caernarfonshire. Land-hungry and acquisitive, he purchased the manor of Much Wenlock and other lands in Shropshire. He acquired the former lands of Valle Crucis, including the township of Wrexham Abbot, and began to add to his estate in Ruabon. By the time of his death in 1719 he was possessed of a considerable estate in north Wales. Lady Jane, dying in 1675, left him Watstay to devise as he wished. He inherited Rhiw Goch, Trawsfynydd, from his mother, and Maenan, Eglwysfach, and Glasinfryn came to him as part of the Gwydir patrimony.

In 1616 William Eyton had built Watstay, of half-timber arranged around a courtyard, on the north side of which was a three-storey gatehouse. A modest self-contained dwelling house typical of that of the lesser gentry, it had none of the antiquity of Chirk Castle nor the grandeur of Plas Teg. Francis Jones has given a reconstruction of the old house based on his reading of the inventory which was made between 1683–86:

> This inventory seems to give a fair idea of the house of Watstay. On the ground floor were the hall immediately within the main entrance door; parlour and drawing room both furnished in much the same style; the old parlour, which from its contents appears to have served as a private closet was that of the late Lady Wynn and apparently was left undisturbed. A passage led to the old Parlour, and probably at the end of this was the little chamber described in the inventory. Another passage led to the kitchen next to which was the buttery. Strangely enough, there is no description of the dining room.
>
> On the first floor were four main bedrooms and a little chamber. This was reached either by a main staircase, or by 'ye staires downwards' from the little chamber which stood above the little chamber at the end of the passage on the ground floor ... On this floor perhaps was the picture gallery, which is suggested by the entry of the 'garrett over the Gallery'. There is one other garrett described which was above the bedroom over the kitchen ... [a] gatehouse ... the bedrooms over the milk house and brew house were obviously for the servants.[5]

Sir John Wynn,. Bt. (d.1719)

Sir John Wynn was more intent on buying land then spending his money on a house he would not live long to enjoy, but small improvements there were. In 1678 he walled in a deer park, an avenue was created, and many trees planted. He was highly regarded as an horticulturalist and was very fond of pears. A building traditionally known as the 'jewel tower', was his contribution to the architectural jigsaw of Wynnstay. In 1706 he erected in the courtyard the stout tower of stone which survives, although now completely surrounded by other buildings. Formerly it bore an inscription in Latin, intended to allude to the name 'Wynnstay', which translated reads: 'If a man has a decent house and livelihood, and a beloved fatherland, he has all that is needed for life: all else is mere care and trouble. John Wynn, soldier and baronet, built A.D. 1706'.

Sir William Williams, Bt.
(1634–1700)

The change of name of the estate from Watstay to Wynnstay was made after the childless Sir John had determined upon the heir to the estate in 1710. His choice was Watkin Williams (1692–1749), the eldest son of Sir William Williams of Llanforda second baronet, the son of Sir William Williams (1634–1700) of Glascoed, former Speaker of the House of Commons. It was through his mother, Jane Thelwall, that Watkin inherited Wynnstay because she was the heiress of Edward Thelwall of Plas y Ward and the great-granddaughter of Sir John Wynn, the first baronet of Gwydir. The young Watkin Williams shared the political views of the old man and had younger brothers who could succeed him if he too failed to produce an heir. What is more, after his succession had been determined, he married Ann, the daughter of an old political ally Edward Vaughan of Llwydiarth and Llangedwyn. The conditions of inheritance were that he add the surname of Wynn, quarter the arms of Sir John, and erect a monument in Ruabon church.

This monument represents the succession which made Watkin William Wynn the most powerful man in north Wales and in the eyes of his contemporaries the most important man in 18th century Wales. His father-in-law died on 5 December 1718 and Sir John Wynn in January 1719, and within the year an agreement was made with Robert Wynne, 'stone cutter' of Well Street, Ruthin, to erect a monument in Ruabon church according to the wishes of his benefactor. There are three statues, one standing of Henry Wynn (d.1671), and two kneeling, Sir John and his wife Jane (d.1675).[6]

Watkin Williams Wynn enjoyed his inheritance for thirty years. Politics was his stage and his relative success earned him the titles of 'the Great Sir Watkin' and 'the Prince

Monument to Sir John Wynn, Henry Wynn and Jane Wynn. Sculpted by Robert Wynne of Ruthin.

The Great Sir Watkin (1692–1749) by Michael Dahl.
[National Library of Wales]

in Wales'. Such was his power that at his approach to the capital Welsh gentlemen went out on horse back to greet him. Unfortunately, the Country and Tory party he supported were in the wilderness during the long years of Robert Walpole's administration, and the Stuart monarchy his fellow Jacobites schemed for, in exile. Great wealth gathered from the rent roll of six estates and over a hundred thousand acres supported the vast expense of electioneering. Defeat of the Myddeltons at the election in 1716 brought him the county of Denbigh representation in Parliament. Gradually he built up his own faction by the election of his own brothers to the House of Commons and he spent over a hundred thousand pounds at the poll. The Myddeltons were always a nuisance in opposition and in the election of 1741 Sir Watkin was illegally declared the loser by the corrupt sheriff William Myddelton, but was reinstated on appeal.

1742 Expences London. The cause of my master against Wm. Myddelton High Sheriff £397-19-0^{1}/$_{2}$d.

Power and patronage centred on Wynnstay was maintained on occasions by unscrupulous means and the fever brought about by national crisis and contested elections was stimulated by a liberal supply of drink to local henchmen. At the time of the Jacobite rebellion in 1715 and the elections of the 1720s John Mellor of Erddig reported the violent support of colliers for the Wynnstay cause in Wrexham who abused dissenters and other government supporters. In 1732 by a show of force in Chester, Sir Watkin influenced the Mayoral and a Parliamentary by-election in favour of the Grosvenor interest with the display of 800 tenants accompanied at their head by servants in Wynnstay livery, armed with pistols.[7]

By 1736, he was ready to begin his building works at Wynnstay. An interesting document which has survived from this period is *A Pocket Book of Maps of Demesne Land &c belonging to Sir Watkin Williams Wynn Baronet*, by Thomas Badeslade *c*.1740, recording the improvements recently made. There are illustrations of the new house and stables, the inside of the chapel, two lodges — one towards Ruabon and the other towards Oswestry, near Newbridge, where the existing lodges are. Interestingly, the bath house and the cold bath are shown. This cure was said to be extremely good against the headache and to strengthen and enliven the body and act against the vapours and impotence without giving too much pain.[8]

The map on page 26 shows the extent of Wynnstay in its three main areas: the Park 290a 3r 29p, the Gardens, 12a 3r 24p, and the Demesne, 275a 3r 7p. Providing a grand approach to the mansion house are the avenues already determined, and probably the work of Sir John Wynn (d.1719). Wat's Dyke is clearly seen running through the park and beyond the periphery wall is the estate village, other dwellings clustered around the church, with houses in Park Street, High Street and Church Street, and the extent of Tyddyn Plas Newydd which includes the Ruabon Mill Pool.

Francis Smith of Warwick (1672–1738) and his son William (1705–47), successful and distinguished master-builders, were chosen to carry out the work. What they achieved may be seen in the engraving of John Ingleby. His view of 1793 shows the house and stables designed by the Smiths. To the left of the house can be seen part of the Jacobean building. The new house 'appears to have been L shaped with the main front facing west. Of two storeys, over a rusticated basement, it had five bays, the centre three breaking forward and surmounted by a pediment. The north front had only three bays. The south front had eight bays, the centre four recessed'.[9]

John Ingleby's view of Wynnstay, 1793. L–R: Smith stables; 1612 house; Smith house.
[National Library of Wales]

Great use was made of local labour and resources in the building of the new house and stables. Information is available from the Wynnstay rentals which give details of frequent payments to 'John Rogers mason in payment for himself & workmen for takeing up stones' and 'for raiseing stones in Nant y Belan Rock for the new stables'. To Edward Davener and Richard Davies, brick makers 'for makeing brick at Wynnstay'. William Jones and John Edwards sawyers, and their partners were responsible for the timber, with oak being purchased from the Myddeltons and mahogany brought from Chester.

Wynnstay house was increasing in size and these selected entries convey some idea of the nature of the undertaking:

1737/8 Paid John Smith for sweeping 22 chimneys at Wynnstay 0-11-0
1738 Dec.23 Paid Thomas Pool Plaisterer … for plaistering the New Garretts at Wynnstay 10-3-0.
1739 Aug 22 Paid Mr Groome the Turner a bill for turning dresser feet for kitchen and scullery, pins for the Lodges gates and other work done for the use of my master. 4-6-6.
1739 Sept 6 Paid John Davies of Croes Voil a bill for nails and flooring dowells sold and delivered at Wynnstay from March 15 1737 to March 12 1738. 66-2-0.

It emerges from these accounts that work was proceeding at the same time in Ruabon village. The description 'work done at the New House and Brewhouse in Ruabon' refers to the building of the Eagles or Wynnstay Arms. Reference is also made to 'new houses in Ruabon'.

1749/50 Paid Peter Roberts and other Bricklayers a bill for building the new houses in Ruabon £19-4-7 1748/9
March 4 Paid Edward Davener for casting up clay to make two hundred thousand of Brick at Wynnstay 5-0-0.
1749 Sept. 9 Paid John Thomas for makeing 68 thousand of stock brick at 55s per thousand …

Ruabon village was beginning to expand to meet the service requirements of the Wynnstay estate, the surrounding gentry houses, and the growth of population which came with the industrial revolution.

Tragedy struck unexpectedly when Sir Watkin the third baronet, died from injuries sustained from a fall from his horse in returning from hunting on 26 September 1749.

Monument in the South Chapel of Ruabon Church to Sir Watkin (third baronet) who died in 1749. Sculptor Michael Rysbrack.

1749 Oct 26 Paid Mr Price of Wrexham Surgeon for attending Sir Watkin at Acton 10-10-0.

> Paid Dr Apperley of Wrexham for the like 5-5-0.
> Paid the Servants at Acton by my Lady's order 15-15-0.

It is said that the Methodists were holding a meeting on the same day and offered up the prayer 'O Arglwydd cwmpa Ddiawl mawr Wynnstay', 'O Lord, humble the great devil of Wynnstay',[10] a heartfelt petition brought about by his treatment of the local Methodists for holding an illegal assembly when the preacher Peter Williams and others were heavily fined and suffered the indignity of being detained in the dog kennels at Wynnstay. In spite of this the *Gentlemen's Magazine* appreciated his Anglican devotion:

> His piety towards his creator, was remarkable in his constant attendance on the service of the church. He revered religion, he respected the clergy, he feared God, the whole tenor of his conduct was one continued series of virtue. So prepared. He had little reason to be afraid of sudden death. Every day of his life was a preparation for heaven.[11]

The third baronet was buried in Ruabon church on 3 October. The *Gentleman's Magazine* gave this account:

> At the park gate of Wynnstay the corpse was solemnly received by multitudes of people, whose outward gestures of affliction pathetically represented the inward sentiments of their hearts. Few men have ever deserved so general a lamentation! In his public character, he was resolute and unmoveable, in his private character, he was generous, and of exceeding good nature. He loved his country with a sincerity which seemed to distinguish him from all mankind. His morals were untainted. He had an utter detestation of vice. His manners, like his countenance, was open and undisguised. He was affable by nature. He knew how to condescend, without meanness. He was munificent, without ostentation. His behaviour was so amiable, as never to create a personal enemy. He was even honoured, where he was not beloved. In domestic life, he was the kindest relation, and truest friend. His house was a noble scene of regular, yet almost unbounded hospitality … He feared God, the whole tenor of his conduct was one continued series of virtue.[12]

Fortunately there was an heir to the estate. Sir Watkin's first wife Ann Vaughan whom he married in 1715 died in May 1748 having failed to produce a surviving heir. It was her request that at her decease her husband should marry his god-daughter Frances, daughter of George Shakerley of Gwersyllt and Holmes Chapel, Cheshire. This he did on 19 July 1748, and the union produced two sons: Watkin born 8 April 1749, and William born six months after his father's death.

Accommodation for a suitable monument to the third baronet was made by the addition of a chapel on the south-east of the Parish Church in 1755. Michael Rysbrack was commissioned to erect a monument worthy of the baronet, and Sir Watkin in 18th century fashion is represented as a majestic reclining Roman senator.[13]

For the next twenty years, during the minority of the fourth baronet, the estate went through a period of consolidation with its resources sensibly husbanded by trustees. Debts were repayed, new lands purchased in moderation and a healthy surplus accumulated. Westminster School, Oriel College, Oxford and the Grand Tour gave Sir Watkin his education and by the time of his coming-of-age in April 1770 he had emerged as a young man of exceptional refinement, known for his exquisite taste and discerning patronage, gifts which were displayed to the full in the building of his great house at No. 20 St James's Square, London, by Robert Adam.[14]

Although treated in a more haphazard manner because of his inability to match his lavish expenditure with available cash, Wynnstay and Ruabon experienced the young Sir Watkin's exuberance for entertainment, appetite for building and landscape gardening, and his desire to uphold the family dignity and patrician obligations. What was the effect of all this on Ruabon?

The coming-of-age of the fourth baronet was celebrated at Wynnstay in April 1770. Preparations were made well before, particularly because the accommodation at Wynnstay was regarded as inadequate. Robert Adam and James Byres were both approached to make architectural drawings for a new Wynnstay in the grand manner. It was necessary to complete the work as soon as possible, and as an expedient Thomas Farnolls Pritchard (1723–75) of Shrewsbury, who at the time was engaged in restoring Ruabon Parish Church, was commissioned. Askew Roberts describes it as 'the Great Room', adding, that it 'was built for the festivities, and was only intended as a temporary creation, but so well proportioned and convenient was it found to be, that it was allowed to remain, and bedrooms were built over it.[15] In Sandby's view the Great Room is seen as the wing projecting southwards from the east end of the south front. Disbursements in the late 1760s and well into the 1770s show that work continued at Wynnstay on a modest scale. The kitchen, servants quarters and outbuildings were improved and considerable interior work completed. The coming-of-age of 1770 was the first of the legendary, spectacular and gigantic entertainments held at Wynnstay from time to time over the next hundred years. The *Gentleman's Magazine* estimated that there 'were at least

Sir Watkin, fourth baronet, 1749–1789 with Thomas Apperley (seated) and Lt-Colonel Edward Hamilton (right) by Pompeo Batoni, Rome, 1768. [National Museum of Wales]

Paul Sandby's view of Wynnstay. The Great Room can be seen on the extreme right of the building.

15,000 people at dinner in Sir Watkin's park all at the same time', and printed the gargantuan bill of fare:

30 Bullocks	60 Raised pies
1 do. Roasted whole	80 Tarts
50 Hogs	30 Pieces of Cut Pastry
50 Calves	84 Capons
80 Sheep	25 Pie Fowls
18 Lambs	300 Chickens
70 Pies	360 Fowls
51 Guinea fowls	96 Duckling
37 Turkeys	48 Rabbits
12 Turkey poults	15 Snipes
30 Brace of tench	1 Leveret
40 Brace of carp	5 Bucks
36 Pike	421 Pound of Salmon
60 Dozen of trout	24 Pound cakes
108 Flounders	60 Savoy cakes
109 Lobsters	30 Sweetmeat cakes
96 Crabs	12 Backs of Bacon
10 Quarts of shrimps	144 Ice Creams
200 Crawfish	18,000 Eggs
60 Barrels pickled oysters	150 Gallons of milk
1 Hogshead of rock oysters	60 Quarts of cream
	30 Bushels of potatoes
20 Quarts of oysters for sauce	6,000 Asparagus
	200 French beans
166 Hams	3 Dishes of green peas
100 Tongues	12 Cucumbers
125 Plumb Puddings	70 Hogheads of Ale
108 Apple pies	120 Dozen of wine
104 Pork pies	Brandy, Rum and Shrub
30 Beef pies	Rock work shapes,
34 Rice puddings	landscapes, in jellies, blancmange, &c.
7 Venison pies	
A great quantity of Small pastry	
One large cask of ale[16] which held twenty six hogsheads[16]	

The festivities were planned well in advance. For some time the mansion of Wynnstay was being prepared. The Great Room was built for this event, the house refurnished and decorated, the park wall built and Ruabon parish church restored. Nothing was spared to make the coming-of-age of Sir Watkin to his own memorable, and a fitting assumption of his position as head of the house.

The total cost of the birthday celebrations as recorded by Samuel Sidebotham in his account book for 1770 is £1,621-17s-11d of which nearly £1,200 was spent in London, the remainder being shared between disbursements at Wynnstay, travelling expenses, and the gratuities of waiters, constables, assistants, musicians, poets and bell-ringers for their laudatory announcement of the celebration.[17] The London purchases came by sea to Chester on the *King George* — wines, spirits, sugar, tea, mustard, fruit, fowls, asparagus, tickets (8,700) and favours, earthenware (Wedgwood was paid £98), cutlery — all that was necessary including the great cask and drinking horns. The estates of Llanforda, Llangedwyn, Llwydiarth and Glanllyn, added to the provisions. Cooks were brought in from London, Chester and Whitchurch, by the coach-load, and over a hundred waiters, constables and their assistants were employed to guard the feast and serve the multitude. Samuel Cook was in charge of '12 men beer-carriers and pumpers to the great cask 2 days'. Seventy-three hundredweight of bread was devoured. The church bells of Wrexham, Ruabon, Overton, and Bangor-is-y-coed, pealed out the welcome; drums, fifes fiddlers, harpists, morris dancers and the local poets joined in the jubilation. Mr Carter, the cook at Wynnstay, a talented performer, donned an old woman's

Betrothal portrait of Sir Watkin and Lady Henrietta Somerset, 1769, by Sir Joshua Reynolds.
[National Museum of Wales]

dress and sang ballads; David Mackender the groom dressed the horses in ribbons, and two post-chaises of London musicians added to the gaiety. At night the whole park was illuminated with Hardwick lamps and the fireworks of Dominico Jordan.

Later that year in September, Roger Kenyon of Gredington reported:

September 7 Overton
Our jubilee week at Wynnstay is at last over. We had a grand oratorio at the opening of the new organ at Ruabon Church, on the Tuesday, where several solos were performed by Mr Paxton, the first violincello, and Signior Giardagni, the first singer in the Kingdom. The company were all invited to Wynnstay to dinner, and a grand entertainment we had. About nine o'clock, we all went to the puppet show, where a handsome theatre and good music were exhibited... the whole must have cost Sir Watkin a couple of thousand at least ...[18]

No doubt John Parry, the blind harpist, played the organ on this occasion. This distinguished musician received £40 per annum as the organist at the church.

The restoration work at the parish church was extensive. In 1769 Faculties were issued in the diocesan court authorising the building of the north chapel, raising the roof and pillars, replacing the pulpit and reading desk, paving the aisles and renewing the pews. The church bells were added to and recast in 1768 to bear the strain of welcoming events and changing fortunes. The peals which greeted the arrival of the fourth baronet and his new bride in 1769 were muffled in mourning three months later on the death of Lady Henrietta in July. They had been married in April 1769 and Henrietta died on 24 July. She was the fifth daughter of the fourth Duke of Beaufort, a man of Jacobite sympathies who was reputed to have sheltered Sir Watkin after the collapse of the Jacobite rebellion in 1745. Charlotte, daughter of George Grenville and his wife Elizabeth Wyndham, became the second wife of the fourth baronet in December 1771. An heir, Watkin Williams Wynn (1772–1840) was born at Grosvenor Square on 26 October 1772. Robert Adam designed 'a new font for Ruabon Church to perpetuate the birth of Masr Williams Wynn'.

Wynnstay Park has always been popular with local people who have used it whenever they could as a playground, being the setting for annual shows, Sunday and Day School picnics, and military parades. The demesne as seen in 1740 was transformed by the fourth baronet between 1770 and his death in 1789. The work was carried out in stages, taking advantage of the scenery and topography and making much of its elevated position, the river Dee on its southern boundary, the Belan stream and the land sloping down hill to the village. Trees and water, designed walks, discreetly placed buildings contrasted with the walled gardens

John Parry (d.1782), the famous blind harpist of Wynnstay

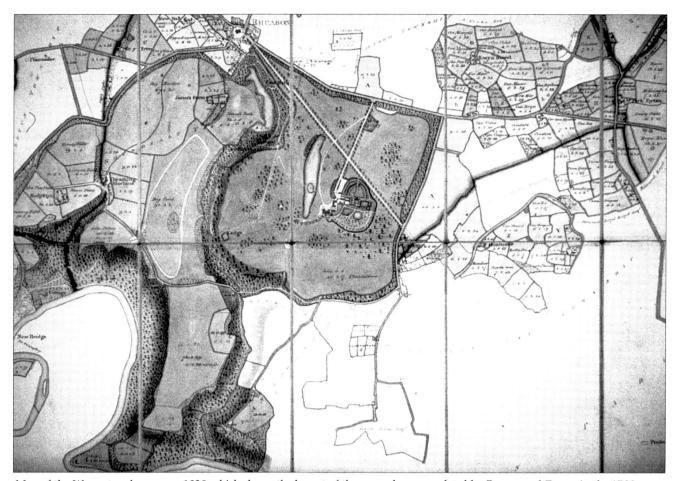

Map of the Wynnstay demesne, c.1820 which shows the layout of the grounds as completed by Brown and Evans in the 1780s.

and pleasure grounds in the shadow of the mansion house.

The first work was carried out in the early 1770s by Richard Woods, Edward Pugh, and Thomas Leggat. This was the upper lake or 'canal' lying to the right of the approach from Broth Lodge to the stables in line with Wat's Dyke as it entered the park. Sandby's view shows the Great Room and the 'canal'. Sir Watkin did not heed the counsel of his steward to 'Beware of your Architects & Modern Gardineur'[19] and engaged the services of Lancelot 'Capability' Brown who has left his mark. He planned the gardens in the immediate vicinity of the house, and extensive landscaping which included a lower lake. Brown died in 1783 and his design was completed by John Evans (1723–95) of Llanymynech, who dammed the Belan stream and constructed a cascade with artificial rock work. A description of it is to be found in the *Cambrian Directory* for 1808:

> Under the direction of John Evans, esq; of Llewenygroes … the waters of the small brook Belan, and some other pretty rills, were so concentrated as to form a considerable torrent, dashing over artificial rock-work, not distinguishable when covered with moss and lichens, from a natural cascade. Thence the waters spread into a majestic lake winding through the Bath or Belan grounds, in Wynnstay Park; its edges skirted with lofty woods, where only a few years since some stinted hawthorns, thinly scattered, were almost the sole possessors of the soil. To this park trees of a large size were removed, by appropriate machinery, from a considerable distance.[20]

The work at Belan water was officially opened in the autumn of 1784 in a grand manner and described similarly:

> Sir Watkin Williams Wynn having had in contemplation, for some time, the execution of a scheme proposed by the late Mr.Brown, of forming a beautiful piece of water, by constructing a dam below the bath in his park, determined to execute it in the course of this summer; accordingly he began it on the first of June, but finding all the teams and labourers he could hire unequal to the task, he had recourse to the assistance of the

neighbouring gentlemen and farmers, who cheerfully sent to his aid their teams, carts, and colliers by which means this immense work was completed on the 17th instant, when each individual concerned receiving a ticket of invitation, repaired to Wynnstay, and being properly marshalled by Mr Sidebotham, in pairs, formed the following procession to the Dam Head.

PROCESSION

Hugh Sands, the game-keeper, with a long staff.
A pair of bagpipes
Six tall men, with mattocks, by way of pioneers.
Six short men with, their clay maul.
80 colliers, armed with spades and pickaxes, with
A flag in their centre.
A waggon drawn by six oxen, in which was a large piece
Of roast beef, with the following motto:

THE SUPPORT OF LABOUR

100 carters, with their cart whips, and a flag in their centre.
A waggon drawn by four horses, wherein a hogshead of
Beer, with this motto;

TO MOISTEN THE CLAY

200 labourers, armed with their mattocks and spades, with
A flag in their centre
20 artificers, armed with their tools, ensigns of their arts.
Mr Midgley, with his levelling staff.
150 gentlemen and farmers, with red tickets, with a flag
In their centre
A band of musick.
The spirit level, carried by a tall man.
Mr Evans on horseback.
Sir Watkin and Lady Williams Wynn, with their eldest
Daughter in a phaeton, drawn by six ponies.
Master Williams Wynn and Master Charles, on horseback.
Several Carriages.
The servants and waiters brought up the rear.
S.Sidebotham, on horseback, who conducted the whole.

The company having formed a circle round the Penstock, the new lake received from Master Williams Wynn,
amidst the shouts and acclamations of a vast concourse of people, the name of
BELAN WATER

The procession then returned to the great avenue, where tables were laid, and most plentifully furnished. Dinner being over, many public and local toasts were drank, and not withstanding the number of guests amounted to 600, exclusive of double that number of spectators, the day concluded without one accident or act of irregularity to disturb its cheerfulness.[21]

Associated with Capability Brown and John Evans was the dairy finished in 1783. The role of dairymaid was a fashionable rural pursuit of the likes of Marie Antoinette and the Duchess of Argyll and was much the rage. The dairy at Wynnstay was supplied by the firm of Wedgwood and Bentley with prophyry and jasper tiles and vessels of 'the best Staffordshire earthenware'.

A spacious kitchen was concocted into a theatre for the coming-of-age celebrations. Capability Brown probably planned to remodel it. It bore the date 1782. From 1770 onwards there was an annual play season. Tradespeople and farmers were invited to the rehearsals, and tickets were sought after by the local gentry, some of whom acted. The gentlemen performers were often members of the Cycle Club[22] and probably belonged to the Freemasons Lodge at Wynnstay. Between 1773 and 1781 eleven of Shakespeare's works were performed as well as a great number of contemporary plays and farces. The major event in the theatre's

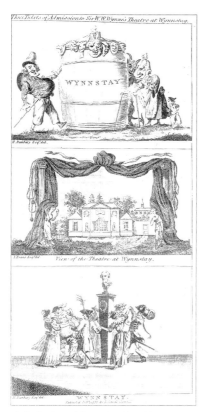

Admission tickets for the Wynnstay theatre, 1786.
[National Library of Wales]

thirty-year history was the visit of David Garrick who stayed for a fortnight in the autumn of 1777 although he did not act.

James Wyatt made the final architectural contributions in the life of the fourth baronet. Designs for a new mansion house were presented of which one small corner was built. Sir Watkin died in his forty-first year on 29 July 1789. His debts were enormous and reputed to be £160,000. Nimrod wrote a fitting tribute:

> The entire proceedings of the Sir Watkin of that day were most beneficial to society throughout, especially so to that of his immediate neighbourhood … there was a nobleness of character about this epitome of an English gentlemen, joined with the strictest observance of all moral as well as social duties, which has rendered his name nearly immortal wherever it is known, and his example had the best effect. His days were cut off prematurely; and strange to say of him, in so jovial a neighbourhood as his, the loss of his health was attributed to his not drinking a sufficient quantity of wine![23]

The fourth baronet's monument is the column erected by Frances Shakerley, the widow of the Great Sir Watkin (d.1749), and the mother of the deceased. It was designed by James Wyatt and is 116 feet high, surmounted by a bronze urn with goat's head handles. The inscription on the base reads:

FILIO OPTIMO MATER — EHEU — SUPERSTES
To the best of sons his mother who — alas — survives him dedicates this

It is seen quite clearly from the A483 road. Separated from the new mansion built *c*.1865, it seemingly broods over the neglect and destruction of the landscaping of the park.

Again there was a minority at Wynnstay when the fifth baronet (1772–1840) succeeded his father. His early manhood was marked by service in Ireland as colonel of the regiment of Ancient British Fencibles, a volunteer corps raised for defence against the alarm of French invasion in 1794 and eventually sent to Ireland in 1797, serving during the Irish Rebellion in May 1798.

Watkin's regiment bore the sobriquets 'The Bloody Britons' and 'Sir Watkin's Lambs'. The regiment was disbanded on 2 April 1800 when the whole corps of four hundred men sat down to a hot dinner provided for them in the Great Room at Wynnstay. Their comradeship in Ireland and the loss of so many companions in arms was not forgotten. A splendid memorial was erected to commemorate the fallen. Jeffrey Wyatt (later Sir Jeffrey Wyattville), the architect of Windsor Castle for George IV, was commissioned to raise a fitting tribute at Nant y Belan in the Wynnstay grounds on a steep majestic ravine, below which runs the river Dee. The tower was modelled on the tomb of Caecilia Metella on the Via Appia in Rome. The tower stood on a platform dominating the landscape. Beneath the platform a small cottage was contrived. Here, according to local legend lived Lucy, whom Sir Watkin had brought back from Ireland with him as a reward for having saved him from an attempt on his life by poisoning. The memorial tablet gives the names of the forty-five officers and men who were killed in Ireland and their epitaph:

Thus lives the soldiers' names who fought and fell
Thus Cambria to her latest sons shall tell
How her own Bands here ancient Britons bore
Her dragon Banner to Iernie's Shore
By courage zeal and discipline maintained
The ancient glory which their sires had gained
And true to Honour and their Country's cause
Sealed with their blood the triumph of her laws.[24]

Unfortunately, the ravages of vandalism, neglect and time, have contributed to the collapse of the memorial tower.

At home, when the nation was threatened with starvation, Sir Watkin assumed the role of an improving

The Column, Wynnstay, by James Wyatt, erected in 1790 as a memorial to the fourth baronet.

Sir Watkin, fifth baronet (1772–1840) in the uniform of Colonel of the Royal Denbighshire Rifle Corps of Militia. Painting by John Jackson,

Left: Nant y Belan Tower, the memorial to 'Sir Watkin's Lambs' by Sir Jeffrey Wyattsville.

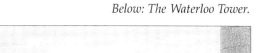

Below: The Waterloo Tower.

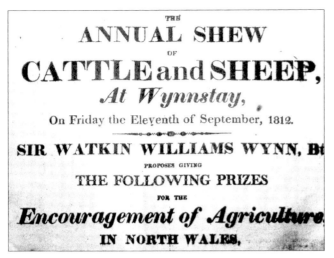

Wynnstay poster, 1812.

landowner. Agricultural displays replaced theatrical performances and Wynnstay became the centre of the North Wales Agricultural Society and the venue of the annual show:

> This agrestian fete is held in the month of September, on which occasion the shew of cattle is usually very great and a numerous and respectable assemblage of practical agriculturists, including nobility, gentry and yeomanry attend the meeting. Visitors to the amount from five to seven hundred have the honour to participate with Sir Watkin of the delicacies of his table; and others at the same time partake of the liberal hospitality of his house.[25]

Another building which commemorated warfare was the Waterloo Tower built in the Gothic style by Benjamin Gummow to act as a lodge on the Newbridge side of the park. Of three storeys high it provided a magnificent vista over to the Vale of Llangollen and flew the Wynnstay flag when Sir Watkin was in residence.

A violent storm on 23 April 1811 badly damaged a new range of hot-houses when 1,123 panes of glass were broken by meteoric hailstones which measured two and a half inches in circumference.[26] In 1820, hops were grown on the estates in Denbighshire, and in the same year, the enterprising baronet won a gold medal from the Society for the Encouragement of the Arts for planting over six hundred thousand trees on the mountainous land near Llangollen. No doubt part of his motive was to alleviate unemployment and soften the blow of the agricultural depression. He went further and took a compassionate attitude to arrears of rent, an act which brought forth notice in the *Gentleman's Magazine* when it was said that he 'has thus fairly claimed for himself the old title of the head of his family, "A Prince of Wales"'.[27]

The fifth baronet married on 4 February 1817, Lady Henrietta Antonia Clive, eldest daughter of Edward, Earl of Powis — a match which is said to have raised his income to £62,000 a year, and an heir, Watkin, the sixth baronet, was born on 22 May 1820. Family responsibilities gave the fifth baronet an urge to improve Wynnstay. The Wynnstay disbursements, 1819-30, record payments in the region of forty thousand pounds spent on improving the house and gardens. The mansion was given a new casing of stone in preparation for a visit by George IV in 1821. The Great Room was altered and redecorated to the scheme of C.R.Cockerell, employed to design a lodge, Sir Watkin used Benjamin Gummow as his 'superintendent' architect, and most of the payments of this period are made to him. Gummow lived in Ruabon. He was succeeded by his son Michael.

In her progress in Wales in the summer of 1832, the young Princess Victoria was entertained at Wynnstay in the first week in August. On entering Wales at Chirk they were met by Sir Watkin as Lord-Lieutenant. Edward Parry described the occasion:

> The roar of the cannon from the Castle announced the arrival at Chirk … At Newbridge, a royal salute was fired from four nine-pounders … The party turned to the right at the bridge and proceeded under the new entrance of the Dee into Wynnstay Park, the princely residence of Sir W.W. Wynn. The royal party attended Ruabon Church on Sunday, where the service was performed by the Rev. Rowland Wingfield, A.M. Their Royal Highnesses on the Monday following visited the acqueduct at Pontcysyllte, accompanied by Sir W.W. Wynn, Bart; and Mr Stanton, and inspected the great work for nearly an hour.[28]

The visit of the future queen anticipated a new reign. The remaining years of the fifth baronet were spent quietly. The world he knew was changing rapidly, his health was deteriorating and gradually death deprived him of his friends and loved ones. Of his own end, Askew Roberts recounts: 'He was buried in Rhuabon Church and the number of persons that attended his funeral was estimated by the newspapers of the time at ten thousand. An eye-witness informs us that the last carriage had not left Wynnstay when the first had arrived at Rhuabon; and hat-bands and scarfs were given to six thousand persons'.[29]

The sixth baronet succeeded in 1840 and remained at Wynnstay until his death forty-five years later. In some ways these were the most glorious and affluent years for the family and the estate and, as we will see in the chapter on 19th century Ruabon, for the community.

For splendour and as a widespread demonstration from the tenants in several north Wales counties, the coming-of-age celebrations surpassed those of 1770. 'The inhabitants of nearly every town and village assembled to greet the joyous day (22 May 1841) with enthusiastic devotion, and imitate the virtues of the family of Wynnstay, by promoting good neighbourhood and festivity amongst each, and plentifully regaling all who had not the means of providing for themselves.'

Ruabon people under the management of Mr Madeley, the schoolmaster, erected a magnificent triple triumphal arch before the gate in Park Street, leading to Wynnstay. Near the mansion a temporary pavilion 150 feet long by 50 feet wide was erected to provide both dining and ball rooms. The festive mood was encouraged by the band of the Royal Denbigh Militia and Mr Pugh the harpist who wore a splendid medal, presented to him by Princess Victoria when she visited Wynnstay in 1832. On the birthday there was dinner for five hundred, a firework display and entertainment for the children of the various schools. Throughout the celebrations there was an abundant supply of rare old ale, brewed to mark the birth of the young baronet in 1820. In Wrexham on 26 May dinner was provided for some 2,000 people in the High Street, fed on oxen, sheep, 2,000 loaves of bread, 10 cwt of plum pudding and 6 hogsheads of ale and it was announced that 'the children of the various day schools will be provided with tea and plum pudding and the poor in the workhouse will be regaled with roast beef and

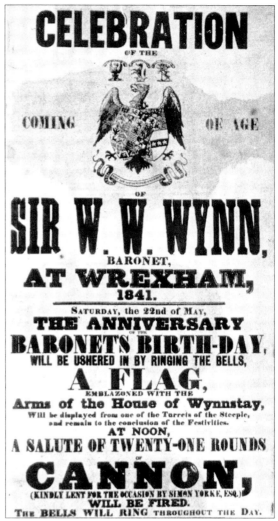

A poster advertising the celebrations in Wrexham for the coming-of-age of the sixth baronet, May 1841.

plum pudding'. At Wynnstay Saturday was set apart 'more especially for the entertainment of the tenants and trades people, and for the poorer classes resident in the vicinity'. The entertainment consisted of rural sports, a grand dinner to which between 600 and 700 friends and tenants were invited, and a display of fireworks. One of the highlights of the coming-of-age was the presentation of an address from the Dissenters of Ruabon by Edward Morris for the Independents; G. Roberts, Calvinistic Methodists; George Powell, Wesleyan Methodists; James Russell, Wesleyan Association; Richard Williams, Primitive Methodists and Jonathan Jones, Baptists; on behalf of 4,395 teachers and scholars of the 23 Dissenting Schools in the parish of Ruabon. (At this time the parish included Rhosllanerchrugog, Penycae, and Rhosymedre). The address solemnly concluded '… we shall retire to our schools and different places of worship to pray that you may as usefully and as honourably serve your generation as did your reverend parent …'

Askew Roberts' book *Wynnstay and the Wynns, a Volume of Varieties,* is devoted to the major public celebrations and public addresses to the sixth baronet: on his marriage in 1852, after the fire at Wynnstay in 1858, the birth of a daughter in 1864, his illness and recovery in 1875, his escape from an Irish terrorist bomb at St James's Square in 1884 and other events.

The impossible happened on the night of 5 March 1858 when a great fire destroyed the main block at Wynnstay. An account of this from the *Chester Chronicle* is given in the appendix to this chapter. As a result of the devastation, the major part of the mansion was rebuilt and is as we see it today. Benjamin Ferrey was chosen as architect.

The 16th century French classical style of the new house was a complete departure and the choice of Sir

SIR WATKIN WILLIAMS-WYNN,

"THE PRINCE IN WALES."

"I am monarch of all I survey,
My right there is none to dispute."

Punch cartoon of 1883 depicting Sir Watkin Williams Wynn, the sixth baronet, as the 'Prince in Wales'

Watkin, who was influenced by the new Louvre and other buildings erected in France in the 1850s. The great fire and Benjamin Ferrey re-shaped Wynnstay, and transformed it from a light elegant Georgian mansion into a gloomy chateau. 'Its huge size, bleak position, grey green stone, dominating French roofs and soberly elegant detail make it a house that remains in the memory' is the comment of Mark Girouard. It was indeed a change from the warmth and intimacy of the old house with its memories, to the Victorian hauteur of Ferrey's creation. One feels that both client and architect innocently begat a monster.

Holland and Hannen were entrusted with the building of the house over a period of at least six years (1859–65). Every item of expense in building is fully recorded in the disbursements:

1859 Dec 13 Thos. Dighton for a model of Wynnstay 42-0-0.
1860 Jan 17 Henry Smith ceiling for Lady Wynn's Room 2,311-0.
1860 Feb 1 Taylor & Son Llangollen Slate & Slab Co for Chimney pieces 17-0-0.
1860 Aug 28 W.B.Simpson for supplying and fixing the mosaic dado tiles in the new building 457-0-0.
1860 Oct 8 Henry Smith on account of a Chimney Piece 25-0-0.
1860 Dec 11 Edwards & Co. for two marble chimney pieces 20-5-0.
1861 Feb 18 T.Smith for carving Chimney pieces *etc*. 200-0-0.
1861 Mar 16 Maw & Co. (Brosley) for Tiles 106-7-6.
1861 Oct 11 Sahlgreen & Evrall for Freight and Charges on two packages of Figures from Copenhagen 7-10.-0.
1863 Mar 25 Coalbrookdale Co. for a Bronz'd Fountain 130-0-0.
1863 Nov 7 Bellman & Ivey on a/c of scaglio work executed at Wynnstay 100-0-0.
1863 Rich'd Dodson, for marble Chimney pieces and hearth Slabs 20-0-0.
1864 Feb 29 Charles Hudson the balance of his a/c for decorations to a suit of rooms at Wynnstay 427-0-0.
1864 Feb 29 Henry Smith the balance of his a/c for carving at Wynnstay 123-4-0.
1865 Feb 16 Gray and Davison for taking down Organ at 18 St.James's Square & entirely rebuilding the same complete at Wynnstay with an Hydraulic Blowing Engine 427-0-0.
1865 Jul 20 William Field for a Silican Marble Floor had in staircase Hall *etc*. 300-0-0.

An inscription in Welsh placed in the Great Hall of the new mansion expressed the determination of Sir Watkin to see Wynnstay arise from the ashes. This is a translation of the Welsh which was published in the Iolo Morgannwg manuscripts in 1848.

> Have you heard the story of Merfyn
> The man who was King of Powys?
> Without a beginning there is no end.

> Have you heard the story of the Chieftan of the Country
> Warning every sinner?
> It is easier to burn a house than to build it.

Wynnstay after the fire of 5 March, 1858.

The new Wynnstay, 1865. Architect Benjamin Ferrey.

Have you heard the story of Madog
Son of Idwal, loveable poet?
Success does not come to one without heart.[30]

The continuation of the line was assured by the birth of an heiress , Louise Alexandra, on 21 December 1864. Hunting[31] was the main activity of the sixth baronet. He was Master of Fox Hounds at the age of twenty-three and had the Wynnstay kennels built in the same year by George Tattersall near the Park Eyton entrance. At this time there were some fifty-five couples of hounds in the kennels.

1843 Nov 17 Geo. Tattersall architect balance of his account £207-17-6.

Tattersall's design provided a boiling house with an adjoining feeding room. Next to this was an ante-room in which was a bath through which the hounds were passed, having been fed after hunting and from there to a drying room where they were allowed 'to roll, revel, and lick themselves. before being shut up in their lodgings for the night'. The Wynnstay Stables were added to between 1845–7 by William Cubitt.

1845 Feb 5 Wm.Cubitt alteration of the stables £700.
1847 July 9 Wm Cubitt by a cheque from Sir Watkin on account of his balance for work done at Wynnstay Stables £700.

The census returns between 1861–91 show the employment of studgrooms and stablemen to be on average 25, indoor servants 30, and gardeners 10. In 1881 Charles Payne the huntsman and William Freer the dog feeder, lived at the kennels with the whipper-in William Render nearby at Park Eyton.

On 14 March 1885 shortly before Sir Watkin's death, the members of the Wynnstay Hunt presented Herkomer's portrait of her father as a wedding gift to his daughter, Louise Alexandra.

On his death on 9 May 1885 there was a break with tradition, for although plans had been prepared for the creation of a family mausoleum in Ruabon churchyard they were not implemented, and Llangedwyn became the family resting place.

Askew Roberts sensed the change that was to come about when writing of the consequences of the death of the sixth baronet:

> … Whatever the virtues of his successor may be, it is certain that there can never be another Sir Watkin like the one who has just passed away and those who preceded him. Sir Watkin, living through a time of social and political change, seemed to be in one sense, though not happily, in another, 'the last of the baronets', and it was for this reason, as well as for his geniality and kindness of heart, qualities made conspicuous by the greatness of his position, that his death created so much sensation in Wales.[32]

The seventh baronet, Sir Herbert Lloyd Watkin Williams Wynn, born 1860, a nephew of the sixth baronet, married in August 1884 his cousin Louise Alexandra, eldest daughter of the sixth baronet. An heir, Watkin was born in 1891, the marriage was dissolved in 1898, and Lady Louise Alexandra died in 1911.

An even greater sensation than the death of the sixth baronet was the defeat of his successor at the polls just seven months later in 1885. During the campaign in the week of the election Sir Watkin was nearly murdered.

RIOTING IN DENBIGHSHIRE
NARROW ESCAPE FOR SIR WATKIN

> A supposed attempt on the life of Sir Watkin Williams Wynn, Bart., Conservative candidate for East Denbighshire, was made on Tuesday at Brymbo, near Wrexham. Sir Watkin attended to address a meeting at the national schools, which were surrounded by a howling mob, who hurled stones and brick bats through the windows amid the shrieks of the ladies outside, who cowered beneath the seats and huddled together in corners of the room, while to protect them blackboards and seats were held up against the windows by the men. An effectual attempt was made to disperse the rioters, and Sir Watkin proceeded to address the meeting, amid the din of shattering glass, hooting and yelling of those outside, and shrieking of those within at the close of his speech. As cries had been raised to kill Sir Watkin, he was taken out through the back door, accompanied by two stalwart policemen and several of his supporters into the playground, with the intention of getting away along the railway, which runs near by. The manoeuvre was discovered by some of the mob, who raising cries of 'there goes Sir Watkin, kill him,' dashed after him…[33]

Sir Watkin escaped with his life. The mob proceeded to damage his coach and the school at Brymbo. The election took place on Friday 4 December, and a special edition of the *Wrexham Advertiser* appeared next day. The result was proclaimed as a great Liberal victory:

> Morgan, Liberal .... 3,831 votes
> Wynn, Conservative .... 3,438 votes

The extension of the franchise gave the miners on the coalfield the vote and led to the creation of a new parliamentary constituency in East Denbighshire which rejected the Conservative candidate in an area which was turning towards radical liberalism. There was an even closer majority of twenty-six in the election of 1886. After the 1885 defeat, the baronet of Wynnstay never regained his seat, but instead was prepared to play a leading role in county council politics after its creation in 1888. The community certainly appreciated his services.

The last coming-of-age to be celebrated at Wynnstay was that of his son, Watkin, the future eighth baronet, who attained his majority in 1912. This was marked by the erection of the entrance gates from Park Street, Ruabon, to Wynnstay Hall. The gates were purchased from a subscription fund and the occasion was marked by an address to him by the mayor, aldermen and burgesses of the borough of Wrexham. The address conveyed the good wishes of the borough:

> and that you may long be spared to worthily uphold the honoured traditions of your family ... your honoured father worthily maintains the traditions of his family in serving his country. We remember with pride and gratification his public-spirited work during the South African War and the example which he has shown as Lord-Lieutenant of the county of Montgomery in connection with the King Edward Memorial Fund. His work as a chairman of the Denbighshire Quarter Sessions, and as a member of the County Council and the Wrexham Rural District Council, is well known and much appreciated.

In reply to the addresses presented by Mr Dennis and the Mayor of Wrexham the young heir replied that the splendid gift they had just given him, would always be a remembrance of their friendship and kindness: and every time he came through these gates he would be reminded of the great kindness and good feeling displayed towards him that day. He hoped it would be one more lasting link in the friendship of those who lived at Wynnstay, and those who lived outside its gates.

Sir Herbert Lloyd Watkin Williams Wynn, seventh baronet (d.1944)

During the 1914–18 war, Sir Watkin established a munition factory at Wynnstay and took part in the actual manufacture of shells. In the Second World War Wynnstay was used by the army. The seventh baronet's services to the country were recognised when he was made a Companion of the Most Honourable Order of the Bath. He died on 24 May 1944 in his eighty-fourth year and the last of the family memorials in the parish church is a reading desk to his memory.

Tragedy struck the house of Wynnstay when the heir to the estate, Watkin, died in an accident in January 1946. The eighth baronet died on 9 May 1949 and was succeeded by his uncle. In the meantime the contents of Wynnstay were sold in 1947 and the mansion, five cottages and 150 acres of land were sold the following year for £17,100 to Lindisfarne College. Thus ended the association of the Williams Wynn family with the mansion of Wynnstay after a period of two hundred and thirty years.

Lady Williams Wynn, c.1890.

APPENDIX
The Great Fire at Wynnstay March 1858

The *Chester Chronicle*, 13 March 1858

We regret to state that, on Saturday morning, Wynnstay, near Wrexham, the principal residence of Sir Watkin Williams Wynn, Bart., M.P., was burnt to the ground, and the inmates barely escaped with their lives. The hall was situated on some rising ground in the midst of a magnificent park, facing the south, commanding some of the most beautiful scenery in Wales, including part of the Vale of Llangollen. The edifice had been enlarged from time to time, but its general style was Grecian, and it was built of brick with fine white stone facing. It had a semi-circular front with two wings the appearance of which was at once noble and graceful. It is said the celebrated architect Inigo Jones, in the time of Charles I designed the first portion, and within recent years, Professor Cockerell, R.A., had enlarged it with a saloon capable of accommodating from five to six hundred persons. Until late, alterations had been going on in the interior to construct a picture gallery, and effect other improvements. These had progressed so far that fires for some time past had been kept up for the purpose of drying the gallery, preparatory to the removal of a large collection of valuable paintings, chiefly those sent by Sir Watkin to the Manchester Exhibition, now at his town residence. At the north eastside of the hall were the servants' offices, and at the east side a small theatre. A distance off there is an extensive range of stables. On Friday last several guests arrived at the hall, with the intention of staying for a short time, including Earl and Countess Vane with two children; the Hon. Major Cotton and Mrs Cotton; Hugh Williams, Esq. of Leamington, brother-in-law to Sir Watkin, and Captain Bulkeley, of Windsor. On Friday night they all retired to rest at the usual hour, and a watchman was in attendance to walk round the hall, and to supply the gasometer fires. The night was exceedingly stormy, a strong wind blowing, with alternate showers of rain and sleet. At about three o'clock in the morning Lady Vane's nurse was awoke by a sense of suffocation, and getting up she felt convinced that she smelt something burning. She rushed to her ladyship's bedroom, and gave an alarm of fire. Lord Vane immediately alarmed the house. At first Sir Watkin and Captain Bulkeley proceeded to make an examination, when all doubts were removed by smoke issuing from under the door of the library, adjoining the new picture gallery. Sir Watkin exclaimed "My God, the house is on Fire." They opened the door, when out burst dense smoke, and the floor of the room seemed one red mass of fire. Ventilation having now been allowed, the flame spread with fearful rapidity. There was not a moment to lose, and the ladies had to rush out at the back entrance, with not an article of clothing but their nightdresses and thus they roamed about in the storm, almost unconscious with the intense excitement. The suddenness of the alarm, and the terrific sight which met their gaze, when the inmates began to recover their consciousness after being aroused from sleep, produced a scene at once heart-rending and indescribable. Lord Vane ran along a passage, exclaiming, "O God, where is my son" and he immediately hurried to the bedroom where his child was sleeping through fire and smoke, and brought him away in his arms. He next attempted to secure Lady Vane's jewels, but he was too late –– the flames extended too far. They were valued at from £4,000 to £5,000. The jewels of Mrs Cotton valued at £1,500, were also lost along with her clothing. A Bystander in condoling Lady Wynn, elicited the reply — "Yes, it is indeed, a great misfortune; but, thank God, no lives are lost." She expressed much regret at the loss of the portrait of her brother, the late Major Wynn, of the 23rd Welsh Fusiliers, who was shot at Alma, and whose servant their present watchman had been. On the alarm being given a small fire engine, on the premises, was brought into use,

The coming-of-age of the eighth baronet, 1912.
Scene in Park Street, Ruabon.

and 30 stable men, with numbers of the surrounding residents, promptly came to the scene, and rendered every assistance in their power. A man on horseback was also despatched to Wrexham, where he alarmed the town in the midst of its stillness. Two engines and a body of firemen were at once despatched for this place, as well as an engine from Chirk. The strength of the wind was such, coupled with the quantity of highly combustable material in the hall, and probably the gas, that the engines had not the slightest effect, though abundantly supplied with water from ornamental ponds close by. Even the rain and sleet seemed only to add fresh vigour to the flame. Sir Watkin, Captain Bulkeley, the Hon. Mr Cotton, and Mr Williams unremitting in their exertions to save everything possible, but to little effect. Sir Watkin had two or three narrow escapes. At one time he rushed into the drawing room and saved a portrait of his father; he returned to bring away that of his mother, but he could not succeed, and he stumbled out at the doorway from suffocation, and rolled a distance off. At another time a portion of the wall fell in just where he had been standing only a few second before. His left hand was so burned and cut that he has now to carry it in a sling. Fortunately the wind drove the flames from the quarter where the plate-chest was situated, and after forcing in the iron door the muniments and plate was saved, as well as Lady Wynn's jewels, and the valuable title deeds and documents belonging to the family. The plate is said to be worth £20,000, being the richest

The Park Gates, Park Street; the gift of the Borough of Wrexham, 1912.

probably in the country. The linen in store was also carried away. The flames reached their height about six o'clock when the scene was awfully grand. The flames streamed out through the roof and every window, and the effect was heightened by the country round about being covered with snow. From this time the fire began to sink from exhaustion of combustible matter, and the fears at once entertained of the extensive and magnificent range of stabling igniting now began to subside, though it was clear their safety was chiefly attributed to the direction of the wind. Dining-room, drawing-room, billiard-room, library with a rare and valuable collection of books and manuscripts, the entrance-hall, saloon, gallery, bedroom, alcove, pantries, and waiting rooms, were completely destroyed, with their varied treasures in furniture, decorations and apparel. The carpet on the drawing-room floor was quite a marvel in its way, having been manufactured expressly for the room, at a cost of from £500 to £1,000. The hearth-rug belonging to it was saved. Many very valuable paintings were lost, including one by Vandyke, another by Schneider, the portrait of Williams (Wilson) by Mengs, so much admired at the Manchester exhibition, and a number of family pictures — indeed only about four of the family pictures, by Sir Joshua Reynolds and Davie, have been saved. Fortunately the valuable collection by early masters, many of which were at the Manchester Exhibition, had not yet been brought down from London. The celebrated painting "Wynnstay Hunt" was amongst the saved. A quantity of china and glass, but comparatively a small portion, was saved, and so were two or three rich cabinets, a rich table, and a few articles of general furniture. The plate, linen and general furniture were stored in the stables; the painting and valuable pieces of furniture were taken to the residence of the gardener. When the confusion had a little abated, the gentlemen got an overcoat ot two for the ladies, so unexpectedly thrown almost shoeless into the night, and they were conducted to the house of one of Sir Watkin's employees, where they received every attention, and remained until late in the day. It is said that great difficulty was experienced in procuring articles of apparel to meet even temporary requirements, and that orders were sent to this town for the immediate despatch of considerable quantities.

By the exertions of the firemen the servants' premises at the north-east were kept from the general ruin; but much damage was caused even to these. It is said that considerable difficulty was experienced in rendering assistance from the absence of ladders — articles which it appears were not on the premises. On Saturday, Captain Burlinson, Sir Watkin's agent, and Mr Ferrey the architect were telegraphed for, and on arrival they

The eighth baronet (d.1949).

immediately commanded an investigation as to the cause of the fire, but with no satisfactory result. In the course of the day most of the gentry visited the site of the catastrophe and the feeling universally expressed towards Sir Watkin and Lady Wynn was such as could only be expected, when it was considered how highly they were respected.

This being probably the most destructive fire that has ever occurred in North Wales, on Saturday and Sunday crowds from all parts were congregating to see the ruins. On Sunday the engines were still playing, and the appearance of the edifice was most lamentable. That which, a day or two before was a stately mansion, surrounded by an exquisitely arranged garden, was now a mass of tottering walls and smoking embers. Portions of the walls were in a threatening condition, whilst other portions had fallen into the gardens, but more particularly the large ornamental stone work of the front. The garden had been completely trodden away in the scene and pieces of burnt beams, old iron, pieces of carpet, wood &c. lay like a wreck, strewn over it. Inside, where stood the dining room, is a mass of debris containing, it is supposed the jewels before named, as well as gold and other valuables. Marble chimney pieces lying fractured, door locks, Dresden china, iron bedsteads, glass miniatures, broken pedestals, fractured statues and statuettes &c. were mixed up with the embers. Here lay the bust of some illustrious character, headless; there lay the bust of the "iron Duke", without a nose; and round about were empty niches falling to pieces. Here and there, gold and ornamental work were still in small particles on some of the walls. The wine cellars were saved from fire, excepting one; but yesterday the rubbish that had fallen into that one seemed like red hot cinders, and hot water dripped through the brick arches which were three or four feet thick. Where the library had been masses of black substance lay of the shape of books but hard and wet, mixed with scraps of black letter books, music and engravings. In the gigantic kitchens, which escaped most of all, were wet, cold, and hungry firemen, and groups of 'helps' before an 'Old English' fireplace, in companionship with joints of beef and mutton, in quantity sufficient for a regiment, together with bread, ale &c. rendered palatable under the management of two or three French cooks.

It is estimated that the total loss consequent upon the fire will not be less than £100,000, taking into account the buildings, valuable paintings, furniture &c. not an article of which was insured, although Sir Watkin is the trustee for a Welsh insurance company (the Provincial). No doubt many valuables will be found in clearing away the debris. As to the cause of the fire, nothing is known as a matter of certainty. Speculation has been busy in naming three or four causes; one, that some joist or beam near the library was too near some fire or flue through the alterations recently made; another that in attending to the fires for drying the new rooms carelessness had been manifested; and a third that the gas may have ignited. The library is positively spoken of as the place where it first originated, yet it is said there had not been a fire there for several days previously .

A group of Victorian outdoor workmen, probably from the Wynnstay estate, c.1890.

3. Churches and Chapels

Introduction

The Protestant Reformation of the Church in England and Wales began in 1534 with the renunciation of Papal Supremacy. The new religious settlement was established by law in Parliament, which recognised the monarch as head of the Anglican Church, dissolved the monasteries and chantry chapels, suppressed the cults of the local saints and destroyed their images, introduced a new liturgy and translated the Bible into the Welsh and English languages. The religious wars of the 16th and 17th centuries, the conflict between Protestantism and Catholicism, brought persecution of those opposed to the church as established by law. Many of these were Roman Catholics who remained loyal to their faith (often known as Papists), others were called Protestant Dissenters because they refused to conform to the worship set out in the Book of Common Prayer.

These conflicting positions came to a head in the 17th century in the Civil War, culminating in the execution of Charles I in 1649 and the rule of Oliver Cromwell. Bishops and clergy were suppressed, churches vandalised, and religious groups given freedom of worship. This situation was reversed at the restoration of the monarchy in 1660, and in 1662 there was a mass exodus of clergy who refused to conform to the Book of Common Prayer. These groups called Nonconformists, Presbyterians, Independents (Congregationalists), Baptists and Quakers, were outlawed from holding office in public and local affairs, and sometimes imprisoned. Relief from these religious disabilities was eased in 1689 when the Toleration Act allowed Protestant Dissenters to licence their own buildings for worship. This licence was granted by the bishop of the diocese and allowed him to monitor the growth of nonconformity. Control over the local church was exercised by the bishop through his authority to inquire in the state of the church by means of questions to the local incumbent. These answers, known as visitation returns, provide much information about the church and other religious bodies in Ruabon in the 18th and 19th centuries.

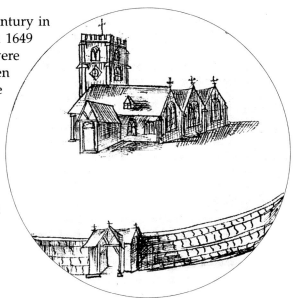

Ruabon Church, 1684. Sketch by Thomas Dineley.

By 1841 the number of nonconformists in the old parish of Ruabon were 4,395 teachers and scholars of 23 dissenting schools. Statistics are available in 1851 and 1905, which indicates the growth of nonconformity. A pattern emerges in religious life in the 19th century. Industrial developments in coal-mining, brick-making and the arrival of the railway brought in an influx of migrant labour from the Welsh-speaking countryside, many of whom found their spiritual home with nonconformity. Tan Lan, below the church, was the place in Ruabon village where Independents, Calvanistic Methodists, Wesleyans worshipped. Meeting houses were opened in Tan Lan with the assistance of the Williams Wynn family.

The old parish of Ruabon was divided and new parishes established in Rhosymedre, 1844; Rhosllanerchrugog, 1844; and Penycae, 1877. The 'new' ecclesiastical parish of Ruabon much reduced in size, took its mission to the agricultural village of Penylan and the industrial hamlet of Plas Bennion. The opening up of Bryn Fields in the 1890s saw the establishment of the Primitive Methodist congregation in Henry Street in 1892, the opening of the English Presbyterian Church, in Bryn Steet in 1895, and finally the presence of the Welsh Baptist Church in Cleveland Street 1894. The English Wesleyans built a new church in Park Road 1896.

Social and religious life in the community revolved around these buildings for the next fifty years until a decline in Sunday worship meant the closure of some.

Roman Catholicism grew slowly but steadily in the twentieth century and established a place for worship in Bryn Hall in the 1950s. An opportunity to share the parish church of St. Mary's was taken up with enthusiasm in 1980. Christians working together, ecumenism, is demonstrated in many ways: coming together for worship, a united mission, and witnessing together across denominational boundaries.

The evidence for the main themes of the history of religion in the Ruabon community, outlined above is now discussed more fully. A record of places of worship and their impact on the life of the people is given below, from whatever sources available.

The Reformation

In 1535, the notorious abbot of Valle Crucis, Robert Salusbury, was arrested for highway robbery and imprisoned in the Tower. The inmates of the abbey consisted of an abbot and three monks, and in 1536 the monastery was dissolved. Valle Crucis and therewith the rectory of Ruabon was leased by Henry VIII to Sir William Pickering. It was worth £29 16s 8d, the value calculated as:

> Tithes of corn and hay there in normal years   £24-0s-0d
> Tithes of lambs, wool and lactuals   £2-1s-4d
> Tithes of pigs, geese and other small tithes   10s-0d
> Offerings there in normal years   £3-8s-8d
> Glebe land there per annum   6s-8d

The tithes belonging to the vicar were valued at £12-17s-0d.[1] they included offerings to the Blessed Virgin Mary 3s, for holy water 6s 8d and for chrism, a mixture of olive oil and balsam used in Baptism, 20 pence.

There also disappeared after 1549, a small chapel in Gyfelia, possibly used as a chapel of ease for the use of ironworkers settled in the township of Morton Anglicorum. It was described as 'a chantry called our Ladyes service'. What this means is that rent from an acre of land, in this instance, was paid to a priest to celebrate regularly a private mass for the repose of the souls of the testator.[2]

Changes made before the return to Catholicism on the accession of Mary were recorded in the book of Ieuan, constable of Ruabon township, in 1554:

> a new font made by 'lewys mason' was set up on the 15 September 1538;
> on the 17 March 1548/9 the pulpit was made;
> on Whit Sunday 1549 mass was discontinued;
> or rather the service was altered, and on the 4th January 1550–1 the altar was pulled down;
> the first silver lost on the 12th August 1551.[3]

Queen Mary died in 1558 and the Reformation changes re-introduced and stabilised during the long reign of Queen Elizabeth (d.1603).

The most notable 16th century vicar was David Powel, vicar 1570–78. It is said that he was the first student to graduate at Jesus College, Oxford, in 1572/3. Powel was an outstanding scholar and was employed by Sir Henry Sidney not only as his chaplain at the Council of the Marches of Wales at Ludlow, but as an historian presenting the Tudor interpretation of history. In the introduction to his *Historie of Cambria, now called Wales*, 1584 he expressed the view: 'and if it, please God once to send them the Bible in their own language, according to the goodlie lawes alreadie established, the countrie of Wales, I doubt not will be comparable to any in England'.[4] This hope was to be realised in 1588 when William Morgan published his Welsh translation of the Bible. After naming the very special services rendered to him by the bishops of St. Asaph and Bangor and Dean Goodman of Westminster, Morgan adds 'Besides whom Dr David Powel, Archdeacon Prys and Mr Richard Vaughan contributed no inconsiderable amount of assistance.'[5] Dr Powel died in 1598. One of his sons, Daniel, speaks lovingly of his father, his care for the church of God and his 'costly travail' on his country's behalf and makes a half-promise to publish 'a Welsh Dictionary, my father's thesaurus.'

Wynn Hall, licensed as a Meeting House for the Independents in the 17th century.

The 17th Century

Nothing of note is known about the church in Ruabon in the 17th century, but it may be said that before and after the Civil War the parish was well served by the able vicars. Before the war, Dr Richard Lloyd established the Grammar School, the church fabric was maintained, its furnishings enhanced by new communion plate and a chest to house the parish documents, with a number of charitable bequests for the relief of the poor.

The troubles of the Civil War divided the loyalties of the leading families. The King found many supporters in the Wrexham area. In Ruabon, for example, Captain John Lloyd of Plas Madoc was a member of the Chester garrison. An entry in the burial register for 8 April 1644 is followed by the note: 'All the rest of the yeares were lost to the souldioures.' There is a tradition that Oliver Cromwell stayed at Plas Madoc. The vicar Dr Richard Lloyd was removed in 1646. His son Humphrey Lloyd was intruded into the vicarage in 1647 and deprived in 1650. In 1673 he became Bishop of Bangor. Both father and son were protected by Sir Thomas Myddelton of Chirk Castle, the Parliamentarian Major-General; Richard Lloyd was tutor to his children.

A prominent Parliamentarian and Dissenter was Captain William Wynn. During the first part of the Civil War he was imprisoned in Denbigh Castle. Palmer repeats a story that is told of him which is told of others, 'that a Bible, which he carried in his pocket, once received the impact of a nearly spent cannon ball and so saved his life'.[6]

Wynn achieved some prominence during the Commonwealth, 1649–60 and was made a Commissioner for the Propagation of the Gospel in Wales in 1650 whose powers extended to the appointment and expulsion of ministers of the gospel. As a member of the congregation of the charismatic puritan preacher and evangelist Morgan Llwyd, pastor of the gathered church of Independents, Presbyterians and Baptists, at Bryn y Ffynnon, Captain Wynn was at the centre of religious life in north Wales. He became an elder of the Independent church, Wrexham and remained so until his death in 1692. He was buried in the Dissenters' graveyard, Wrexham. He is said to have built Wynn Hall in Bodylltyn in 1649. The family remained prominent and steadfast dissenters through the marriage of William Wynn's granddaughter Sarah Taylor widow, to the Reverend John Kenrick in 1723. Kenrick's chapel was destroyed by the mob in the riots of 1715. The marriage was blessed by six sons and three daughters. The third son Samuel, was a noted classical scholar and founded with his brother the Old Bank at Bewdley in Worcestershire. The descendants of another son, Archibald, became directors of Lloyd's Bank, Midland industrialists and married into the Chamberlain dynasty. Wynn Hall was granted a licence to enable it to be used 'for the exercise of religious worship by Protestant Dissenters' during the periods of religious toleration, as for example in 1672 and 1689. Another licence was granted in September 1725.[7]

Another member of Morgan Llwyd's congregation in Wrexham was John ap John 1625–97, born at Pen y cefn in the township of Coed Cristionydd and living at Plas Eva (near the Sun Inn), Trevor. In July 1653 Llwyd sent him with a companion to meet George Fox, the founder of the Society of Friends, known popularly as the Quakers. George Fox and John ap John journeyed far into Wales to proclaim their faith, and established several Friends' meeting places. From the time of the Restoration in 1660, the Quakers met with heavy fines, persecution and imprisonment. One of those presented by the Grand Jury in October 1663, as Quakers together with John ap John, was Catherine ferch Edwards the daughter of Edward ap Randal of Rhuddallt Isaf; her son, Richard Davies, was 'one of the most influential of the early supporters of Quakerism in this district. A meeting began to be held at Rhuddallt which was continued in the lifetime of his son and successor, and was still in existence in 1724', after which it was removed to Cefn Bychan in the adjoining township of Coed Cristionydd.[8]

The Parish Church in the 18th Century

The old parish of Ruabon in 1738 contained 338 farms and about 500 cottages and its extent 'from east to west about five miles and from north to south about seven miles.' In 1809 it was reckoned that there were 621 houses and 4 to 5,000 inhabitants.

Churchwardens accounts and vestry minutes have been lost until 1796, although it is possible to get a good impression of the state of religion from the visitation returns dating from the beginning of the 18th century until 1753, and for the gap until 1790 there is some information in the Wynnstay manuscripts.

The account of the church life in Ruabon in the 18th century, generally speaking, shows a flourishing community ably led by its clergy and well supported by its influential lay men. In 1706 the Reverend Richard Davies, A. M. was appointed to the living on the death of John Robinson. He was the fifth and youngest son of Mutton Davies of Llanerch and Gwysaney in Flintshire. During his long incumbency at Ruabon preferment came to him regularly. He was Prebendary at St. David's in 1719, Canon of St. Asaph, 1710, and Precentor of Brecon College 1721, and this meant he was absent a month or two every summer but, he was no absentee, claiming 'I reside commonly at Ruabon in the Vicarage House & for some part of the year in the Parsonage House of Erbistock.' And in 1738 he gave this account:

> My curate Mr Robert Hughes, lives with me at my house & for these 26 years in one of the two parishes, the other being often supplied by Mr David Prytherch, when he can be spared from attending his school. I allow Mr Hughes £25 pa salary & his board.' He was still there in residence in 1745 with the amiable bachelor vicar. The Curate, 'who lives with me in my house & eats & drinks as I do.

Vicar Davies built the parsonage house at Erbistock and bequeathed to his successor there and in Ruabon 'the Boylers & Furnaces which shall be found in each house.' Whether or not he gave the same exacting attention to the parish church is open to question. In 1709 it was reported that the church was in 'very good repair', whereas twenty years later the south side needed repairing, two of the four bells, loose in the blocks, and the church wanted flagging near the belfry. The absence of essential church records makes it impossible to decide what repairs or additions were made to the church before the restoration of 1770.

The same pattern of worship was maintained throughout the 18th century. In 1738:

> The Publick Service is perform'd every Wednesday and Friday in the morning, & on Saturday in the afternoon, as also on every Lord's day in the forenoon & afternoon & all Holy dayes thro'out the year according to the Canons & Act of Uniformity.

and virtually the same reply was given in 1795 with a slight hint of criticism by the Rural Dean:

> The language used in Church is abt. Half Welsh, half English variable, according to the congregation the Vicar sees there. I believe, that if a greater proportion of Welsh was used in this church it would be more for the Edification of the generality of the Parishioners.

Exposition of the Prayer Book catechism was the main means of instruction in the elements of Christian doctrine and social ethics in order that the child 'learn and labour truly to get mine own living, and to do my duty in that state of life, unto which it shall please God to call me.' Vicar Davies had prepared his own scheme for catechising the children in the Welsh language.

The sacrament of Holy Communion was administered by vicar Davies on the first Sunday in the month and at the great festivals. The monthly attendance varied between 50-100 and Easter figures were 1744 — 300 communicants; 1753 — 340. In 1799 the number fell to 140, a decline blamed on the curate, and the situation had improved by 1809, 'the church is well attended & the parishioners in general are religious.'

Richard Davies died in 1746 when his will revealed a generosity equal to that of his predecessor Robinson. Both men endowed almshouses and gave liberally to the cause of education in the parish of Ruabon and remembered the poor of the places where they had ministered. Davies left £40 'to poor clergymen's Widows and Orphans' of the diocese of St. Asaph; £20 to the Dean & Chapter of St. David's towards erecting, or furnishing the library; £100 to his Cambridge college, Peterhouse, in grateful memory of his education there.

To one servant, Roger Philips, he left £20 'besides my wearing apparel, mourning and a year's wages and to his servant maid Elinor Hughes £10. Davies ordered his executors to examine his manuscripts '& do strictly require that he immediately commit it to the flames what he shall judge to be any ways trifling & jejune.' One that did survive is a notebook of sermons in Welsh 'Some of them became old friends one based on 2 Cor. 5 v 11, was given ten times, four of them being at Ruabon.'

Church patronage, the nomination of the vicar of Ruabon, was in the gift of the Williams Wynn family of Wynnstay. Of the vicars of Ruabon since the Restoration in 1660, Robinson, Davies and Puleston, were members of county families and others protéges of the patron.

Richard Davies, AM	1706–46
Richard Jones, MA	1746–56
Edward Davies, MA	1756–58
Lewis Jones, MA	1758–70
Thomas Trevor, MA	1770–84

He resided principally at Ruabon from 1770 but also at Worthenbury where he was rector. He was vicar of Oswestry 1736–1784. Trevor's memorial tablet in Oswestry parish church describes him: ' … of manners unaffected, he performed the services of the church with a peculiar grace; and by a propriety of elocution, attracted the attention and raised the devotion of his hearers.'

Philip Puleston, DD, 1784–1801

Rector of Worthenbury and vicar of Ruabon. In 1784 Sir Watkin when writing to his agent commented 'I am very glad to hear that Rector Puleston is so acceptable to the Parish. I do not think that he will distress anybody at Tythe or anything.'[9] The Rural Dean noticed in 1791 'The Vicar officiated himself occasionally but keeps a Curate.'[10]

Church enrichment was the prerogative of the aristocracy, particularly in the 18th and 19th centuries. Sir Watkin, fourth baronet, happened to be very rich, of an exceptionally refined disposition with the opportunity to 'do up' his parish church occurring after an intensive Grand Tour of France and Italy and a direct involvement with the leading sculptors, painters, and musicians. His major fault was attempting to do too much. There is no question that he took his responsibilities, both to God and mankind, seriously. He was the provider to his great army of tenants and his agents were instructed to care of the poor. Food and money was daily distributed at his gate.

The church was restored and enriched for the coming-of-age in 1770 of Sir Watkin Williams Wynn, fourth baronet (1749–89). His mother, the Dowager Lady Frances had prepared the way by raising a chapel on the south side to house a memorial to her husband the third baronet. In 1769 the family decided to remove their monuments from the crowded chancel and transfer them to another chapel to be erected on the north-east end, uniform with the newly erected one. A whole catalogue of church furnishings were introduced.The church bells were recast in 1768.

The monument to the first wife of the fourth baronet, Lady Henrietta Somerset, was raised by Joseph Nollekens, whom Sir Watkin may have met on his Grand Tour to Italy. He was the best and most expensive portrait sculptor of the period.

Ruabon Church as restored in the 18th century.

Thomas Farnolls Pritchard, architect of the 1770 restoration of Ruabon Church.

A choir or psalm singers were in existence before the organ was installed, and has continued ever since. Sir Watkin provided an annuity of £40 *pa* for the organist, the first of whom was John Parry, the blind harpist.

1750 pd for Ale to the Rhiwabon Salm Singers last summer 2s.
1810 8 June Ordered that new singers be stopped singing the better without them.
1771 12 Nov. Gave Mr Parry's maid for making fires & cleaning the Organ gallery a year in Ruabon Church £1-1-0.

The Wynnstay family pew was in the organ gallery at the west end of the church above the choir vestry and is now the vicar's vestry. It had its own stove and curtains, and must have been the equivalent of a box at the theatre.

The font, the design of Robert Adam and installed in 1772, is mentioned in Sir Watkin's accounts.

1773 17 Feb. — Pd Mr Hinchliffe for a Marble basin £13-13-0.

Mr Nelson, for a Carved Gothic Stand £31-2-9.
For a new Font for Ruabon Church to perpetuate the birth of Masr. Williams Wynn.
1774 2 Dec. — Pd Chrisining Fees at Ruabon Church.
Baptising Juba Vincent the Black Boy £0-3-6.
1776 9 Jan. — Pd Rev'd Evan Morris Curate of Ruabon.
Chrisining Fee on the Birth of Master Charles Williams Wynn £1-1-0. Pd him for Juba's Schooling £1-1-0.

The church plate, was remade in 1776, designed by Robert Adam. It included a flagon of ewer-form, originally a gift of 1679, two identical communion cups (one 'Originally The Gifte of Griffith Matthews Cyttizen and Vintener of London Sonne to Edward ap Madog of the Parish of Ruabon 1616 Remade Anno Dom 1776. Sr Watkin Williams Wynne Bart.), and two identical silver plates, one given in 1679.

The church memorials of the 18th century are representative of the estates in Ruabon in the 18th century:

Ellis Lloyd d.1712, Squire of Pen y Lan. Chief Inspector of the Public Revenues in the Duchy of Cornwall, Chief Notary in the North Wales Court of Sessions.

Randle Jones, gent d.1754. Agent to Sir John Wynn and to Sir Watkin. Recorder of the Lordships of Bromfield and Yale. He left £50 for the poor and educating two boys.

Edward Lloyd of Plas Madoc d.1760. Benefactor to the poor of Ruabon he left £150 the interest to be distributed in coals and schooling for three boys and two girls.

Ann Rowland d.1796 wife of John Rowland, esq coal owner and iron manufacturer of

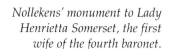

Nollekens' monument to Lady Henrietta Somerset, the first wife of the fourth baronet.

The 1772 Font, designed by Robert Adam.

Plas Bennion d.1796. At Nant y Gwalia in Pont Adam she left alms houses 'which she freely gave' to four poor families.

The population began to rise from the middle of the 18th century onwards: at the end there was a temporary decline in the number of Anglican worshippers and a growth in the number of meeting houses in the old parish of Ruabon for those who wanted an alternative to Anglicanism.

Evidence of the progress of dissent in the old parish of Ruabon is found in the visitation returns and the licences issued for meeting houses.[11] The answers given to the Bishop's question on the increase of dissent are:

1738 — 'there is one Quaker, two Presbyterians, & some few Antipaedo Baptists.[12]

1749 — I know but two Dissenters, one Presbyterian, the other Anabaptist. We have not any licensed Meeting house. Sometime ago an inconsiderable number of Anabaptists met at the house of one John Hughes near the New Bridge once in the month; but not for the twelve month last past as I am inform'd.[13]

1795 — No Papists. There are Presbyterians, Methodists and Anabaptists, the first meet at Wrexham, the second at Rhosllanerch in this Parish — their meeting house is unlicensed, their preacher Itinerant. The Baptists meet at Coed Cristionydd in this Parish — their meeting house is licensed, their teachers name is John Griffiths.[14]

1799 — By every account I could obtain the attendance upon the services of the church is dwindling and meeting houses crowded.[15]

1806 — It was stated that the number of Dissenters 'cannot easily be ascertained because there are many who attend both the church & the meeting houses'.[16]

1809 — there are no Papists in the parish. The dissenters of this parish are chiefly Anabaptists & Methodists. Their meeting houses are duly licensed & I understand their teachers are qualified according to law, their numbers increase.'[17]

There was an episode in the middle of the 18th century when Sir Watkin was harsh to the newly appearing Methodists. On a cold winter night in 1747, he arrested the Rev Peter Williams, who, together with some of the congregation, was imprisoned in the Wynnstay dog kennels, and heavily fined. Peter Williams had joined the Methodists that year, and was a fervent preacher as well as a distinguished Biblical scholar and commentator. The gentry had long memories of the humiliation and suffering of their families at the time of the Civil War in the 17th century. Sir Watkin regarded their gathering as illegal under the Seditions Conventicles Act of 1665 and was determined to set an example.

Calvinistic Methodism

Methodism began in Wales in 1735 with the conversion of Howel Harris. In 1742 George Whitfield and John Wesley quarrelled over theology, and from then on the majority of Welsh Methodists followed the Calvinistic Whitfield. Methodism grew from within the Anglican Church and a Great Awakening came as a result of the spiritual gifts of a number of ordained clergy. Griffith Jones possessed the fervent zeal to teach people to read the Bible in order to save their souls and set up Circulating Schools throughout Wales. George Whitfield and Daniel Rowland were able preachers and the hymns of William Williams Pant-y-Celyn gave fervour to the devotions and worship of the societies as the emerging groups of Methodists were called.

At the end of the 18th century north Wales benefited from the leadership and inspiration of Thomas Charles, an Anglican clergyman. He was ordained in 1778, came to Bala in 1783, and was made a member of the Methodist Society. Thomas Charles was a man of vision and organising ability. He established the Sunday school as a successor of the Griffith Jones Circulating Schools. In order to evangelise the newly literate, he issued a monthly quarterly magazine and published a Biblical dictionary and doctrinal catechism. As a founder member of the British and Foreign Bible Society he ensured that the scriptures were available in their own tongue for the masses. In 1811 when the decision was taken by the Calvinistic Methodists to ordain their own ministers it became a distinct denomination.

We now turn to the history of the buildings and congregations of the respective nonconformist chapels in the village of Ruabon.

Rhagluniaeth, Providence Chapel, Ruabon 1834-1981.[18]

Calvinistic Methodism took roots in the old parish of Ruabon, with the establishment of a congregation at Capel Mawr, Rhosllanerchrugog, in 1770. It took forty years for a chapel to be built in Ruabon village. Tan Lan was the popular centre for the colliers, craftsmen and immigrant workers: here about 1813, the cause began in a chapel which was used later by the Primitive Methodists. As with all groups which emerge out of persecution in their struggle for freedom of worship, there are folk memories and heroes. The first is Roger Lloyd who came as a young boy from Llangollen, joined a night school in the village, and began a preaching ministry at the age of twenty-three in 1817, which lasted for thirty-eight years. By 1819 the Cause in Ruabon numbered 49. The second hero is Rice Jones from Plas Newydd, Pont Adam. Rice Jones was a remarkable

Rhagluniaeth.

man, serving as a Captain and Adjutant of the Royal Denbigh Militia during the Napoleonic Wars, and afterwards was the agent to Sir Watkin, the fifth baronet, with whom he had served. A chance opportunity of hearing a Methodist preacher in Shrewsbury led to his conversion and support of the cause in Ruabon. It is said that once when the rabble were jeering at the new congregation, Rice Jones undid the buttons of his topcoat showing his military uniform and put fear into the mob. He died in 1825. Another assistant was John Jones, the weaver from Tainant, who helped with the Sunday school. Perhaps the greatest advantage gained was winning the support of Sir Watkin. Tan Lan was owned by him and it was through the persuasion of the wife of an estate worker that permission was obtained, and moreover the professional services of the competent architect, Benjamin Gummow, were generously given without charge. It was this set of circumstances which determined the name of the chapel Rhagluniaeth —Providence— with the words in Greek 'Glory to God', and the information that the land was 'generously given by the patriotic nobleman, Sir W. W. Wynn Bart.'

Thus the new chapel was opened in 1834. An idea of the social background of the chapel and its members is seen in the list of deacons. Evan Jones, the foundry; John Edwards, a carpenter at Wynnstay; Thomas Williams, who kept a bake house under the chapel, and Richard Brunt shopkeeper, Bridge Street.

The return for the Religious Census of 1851 gives the spaces available as: 'Free 300; others 20; standing 300; present morn. 75; afternoon 68 scholars; evening 77. Average (12 months) morn. 100; aft. 70.'

The church was reordered in 1865 — maybe this accounts for the reduction of seating from 300 to 170 in 1905. Membership figures as given by E. P. Jones are not always consistent with those found elsewhere; nevertheless it is possible to draw conclusions. The Religious Revival of 1859 brought an increase to the regular membership which increased from 100 in 1858 to 160 in 1859. Communicant figures showed a much smaller increase, from 27 in 1858 to 38 in 1859.

The years 1891 to 1905 are regarded as the most prosperous period in the life of Providence. The 1905 statistics confirm this:

Communicants 93; Sunday school 113; number of adherents 170; sittings in chapel 170. For the year 1901, E. P. Jones gives the strength of the Sunday school as being '14 teachers, 109 pupils,' and an indication of the strength of its instruction with the recitation of 5,569 Biblical verses, 184 hymn verses, 22 parts of the book of instructions.' The membership, that is communicant figures for 1884 is 47, which rises to 93 in 1905, and then falls to 47 by 1931 and 42 in 1933. Who were the members? E. P. Jones lists some of them for the second half of the 19th century. Thomas Edwards, smith; Evan Parry, shopkeeper, Duke Street; John Williams, blacksmith, Tan Lan; Morris Jones, 'The Tea'; John Samuel, stone mason; David Evans, High Street from Bala.

David Evans came from Bala through Ruabon in 1867, and decided to stay. He was not the only member, from Bala who was attracted to make his home in Ruabon, another was John Davies, 'the Gas'.

A preponderance of the members of Rhagluniaeth came from the farming community and the villagers referred to it as 'the Farmer's Chapel.' Prominent amongst these was the Williams family from Pentre Clawdd who were associated with the chapel for nearly seventy years (1867-1934), providing hospitality and lodging for Sunday preachers and deacons, and office holders for Rhagluniaeth. Other families were the Kenrick family Dinhinlle Isaf, the Taylors from Rhos y Madoc, and the Prices from Pentre.

An outstanding contribution to the life of Rhagluniaeth was made by the Reverend John Jones who was pastor from 1850 to 1901 apart from a brief stay in Birmingham in 1877-8. A native of Llangollen, a weaver by trade he read his Bible as he worked. In 1851, at the age of 22 he began to preach, and in 1855 entered the academy at Bala. He was called to care for Rhagluniaeth and Hyfrydle, Cefn Mawr.

John Jones lodged with Mrs Parry, the shop, in Tan Lan. Such was his knowledge of the scriptures that he was called by his brother ministers 'the Concordance' because he was able to say immediately the context of verses. His godliness impressed itself on Dr William Jones of Ty Newydd, who said there was only one person in Ruabon that was going to heaven, and that was the Reverend John Jones. He had a stroke which proved fatal, whilst in the middle of an address in the English Presbyterian Chapel, Brynfields. At his funeral in Ruabon cemetery at least a thousand people came to pay their respects.

One of the first things John Jones did at Rhagluniaeth was the formation of a literary society. In appreciation of this on Christmas Day 1861, he was presented with 'the whole of the works of the eminent Divine John Owen D.D. and the works of other divines of the Puritan period. The meeting which was a large one lasted three hours:

> The chair was occupied by Mr John Davies of Acrefair and short and appropriate addresses were delivered on the following subjects: 'The importance of forming the character aright when young,' by Mr Robert Roberts; 'Temperance' by Mr Robert Williams; 'Perseverance' by Mr Robert Cooper; 'Education' by Mr Brunt. There were also two 'dialogues', the first entitled 'Water and Alcohol' the other 'The Miser and the Spendthrift'. The reciting of these pieces created a good deal of merriment and the reciters were loudly cheered. Several anthems and sacred pieces were sung at intervals by the choir.[19]

Four years after his death, there was the 1905 Revival. Many meetings were held in union with the Baptists. A special mission took place, and Mr Watson, a Primitive Methodist, preached several times in Rhagluniaeth, and even though some had an unmistakable conversion no great things were felt in Ruabon.

In the period 1890–1900 many young men joined Rhagluniaeth having come to live in Ruabon; and many of them were a great help in holding literary meetings at the Sunday school. Two of them were William Bartley, a clerk at Wynnstay Office, and Frederick Jones, a grammar school teacher.

The period before the First World War was alive with community activity. At Rhagluniaeth a young people's prayer meeting was established, there was a Temperance group, the Blue Ribbon Army supported by the Ruabon Free Churches, the Literary Society was re-established by the Reverend H. H. Jones in 1914. The Great War brought the village together in support of the young men involved. The church membership suffered losses. Among the dead were Lieutenants D. Garfield Davies and Hubert C. Davies, the sons of Mr and Mrs E. T. Davies. After the war, a memorial was erected to Lieutenant Harry Harding (killed on 10 November 1917) and Private Thomas Hughes (killed on 21 August 1918).

With the possibility of transferring the Welsh Calvinistic Methodist cause to Bryn Fields, a plot of land was bought in April 1891 'comprising 738 yards with the intention of using it to build a new chapel.' This was sold in 1897 to pay for chapel repairs. Another plot was bought later for the same purpose and sold.

At the beginning of the twentieth century, E. P. Jones sees the appearance of signs of decline. Writing of 1904, he notes 'It was complained even in those days that it was the language that was the difficulty of the church. Familes were persuaded to practice the Welsh language at home to assure the maintenance of the cause in the future'. He observes of 1910, 'There is a suggestion in the annual report that whole families had started to leave Ruabon because the industrial advantages of the area had proved disappointing. In the period after the Great War decline continued:

> By now the industrial depression had an adverse effect on the life of Rhagluniaeth church, whilst the Welsh language lost its footing more and more on the hearths of our village. The number of new members began to

fall gradually, due to the number of men and young women moving out of our midst. Nevertheless, some came to Rhagluniaeth from other churches amongst them Miss A. Gower Jones, MA, the first headmistress of the Girl's Intermediate School, Ruabon.

It was reported that in the winter of 1926 over 100 of the village children came to the meetings of a Band of Hope, held at Rhagluniaeth 'and the English language had to be used because the children could not speak Welsh and it was felt that the Welsh church (Rhagluniaeth) was not benefiting from the endeavour'.

In 1925, the pastorate was united with Siloh (Johnstown) and Moriah (Rhos). An attempt was made in 1930, to form a pastorate with Rhagluniaeth church and the English Presbyterian church in Bryn Fields, 'to assure the presence of a minister of the Association in Ruabon and to promote the work of the Lord in the village.' It failed to reach an agreement.

Rhagluniaeth carried on for another fifty years and was closed in 1981 because of a lack of membership and the prospect of the prohibitive cost of repair. Members of Rhagluniaeth Church began worshipping in the Congregational Church, Mount Pleasant, on 21 June 1981.

The English Presbyterian Church, Bryn Street.
Opened in December 1895, closed in the 1960s, and used as a storehouse for plate glass before demolition in the 1990s. I have been unable to find any church records. The information given below, however, suggests that it followed the same pattern of religious life as other Free Church causes in the village of Ruabon. This pattern was primarily the provision of Sunday worship according to the denominations tradition. There would be morning and evening services and the Sacrament of the Lord's Supper, twice or four times a year. The Sunday school with its emphasis on the catechism and learning of verses of scripture was central to the life of the church. Prayer, Bible study and worship would take place in 'midweek', and if there was a choir it would meet for practice and rehearsal for concerts and performances. The pastor would be assisted by the deacons.

The opening of the chapel December 1895:

> The New Presbyterian Chapel — with a view of providing for the regular needs of the fastly developing Bryn, the Monthly meeting of the Calvinistic Methodists (Llangollen District) decided to erect a Chapel which was opened on Sunday. The building is built of pressed bricks with terra cotta facings with cathedral glass windows. The seats which are pitchpine are stained and varnished. There is a large classroom and boiler room and the building which is heated by gas, will seat about 250 persons. Messrs Jenkins and Jones were the architects and builders. The services on Sunday were conducted by the Rev'd D. C. Davies, MA, who preached powerful sermons, and there were encouragingly large congregations. Mr Hywel Jones, Johnstown, presided at the harmonium. Services being held during the week, when the ministers were the Rev'ds D. Williams, Wrexham; R. T. Williams, BA, Wrexham; David Williams, Summerhill; R. E. Morris, MA, Wrexham; and W. Foulkes, Llangollen'[20]

The statistics for 1905 show that the church is slowly establishing itself: 22 communicants, 100 Sunday school members, including teachers, estimated number of adherents 120, estimated value £520, sittings in chapel 180. The newspaper reports indicate the nature of activity:

Sept 26 1896 — The members and friends of the New English Presbyterian cause had tea when Mr Clough the newly-appointed evangelist was welcomed. In the evening a public meeting was held … [21]

Presbyterian Church Members, c.1934.
Adults: Llew Williams; Emlyn Davies; Herbert Hughes; Albert Harrison; Mark Thomas; Teddy Jones; Maldwyn Jones; Daniel Hughes.
Boys: Kenneth Owen; Eric Williams; John Jones; Laurie Davies; Glyn Edwards; Ronnie Pemberton.

Presbyterian Church Members, c.1934, 'Buds and Blossoms'.
Included in the photograph are:
Margaret Humphreys; John Edwards;
Edward Williams; Eva Thomas; Eddie
Griffiths; Mark Thomas; Eric Williams;
Ron Pemberton; Lizzie Davies; John Hough;
Florrie Phillips; Nan Jones; Nancy Jones;
Ethel Hughes; Herbert Williams;
Ken Owen; Myra Hughes; Laurie Davies;
John Jones; Marjorie & Arthur Davies; Iola
Griffiths; Mary Wright; Nancy Evans;
Phyllis Nicholas; Gladys Hughes; Glyn
Edwards; Raymond Nicholas; Leslie Jones;
Joe Hughes; Peggy Venables; Brenda
Hughes; Marion Jones; Ena Evans; Betty
Williams; Mary Jones; Pat Morgan; Tommy
Jones; Tom Jones; Betty Williams.

April 12 1913 — Another performance of the sacred cantata 'The Passion of the Cross' by Challinor was given before a crowded attendance at the English Presbyterian Church on Sunday night by the choir. The Reverend James Roberts presided. The choir conducted by Mr Dan Davies, consists of fifty voices.[22]

August 2 1913 — Well over a hundred members of the English Presbyterian Church Sunday School drove to Eccleston Ferry on Sunday.[23]

1930 — English Presbyterian Schoolroom. Address on Prohibition.[24]

Mount Pleasant English Congregational Church.[25]

The history of the Congregational Church in Ruabon has its origin in the foundation of an Independent Chapel in Tan Lan in 1813. William Williams of Wern, a member of the Independent cause at Penstryd, became a student of the Wrexham Academy and was called in 1808 to the churches of Wern and Harwd near Wrexham from where he founded new churches at Rhosllanerchrugog, Ruabon, and Llangollen. He remained as pastor until the summer of 1822. He is regarded as one of the greatest of the Welsh 19th century preachers. A new chapel was built which later became the British Legion Club.[26] The Religious Census 1851 gives the date of erection as 1823 and supplies more information:

Independent Chapel, Tan Lan.

Space free 208; other 100. Present: morn. 96, aft. 93 scholars, even. 91. Remarks: It being a wet showery day several in the distance did not attend. William Jones, Deacon and Superintendent, Butcher & Grocer'. From the information given above, the church in Tan Lan was flourishing. However, in 1858 it was decided to erect a new chapel. Once again Sir Watkin provided a new site, this time purchasing for £151-3s-6d the vacant chapel.[27]

Mount Pleasant as the name implies is situated on a hill above Church Street and over the railway bridge. The area above the church was opened the same year, 1858, as the new cemetery. The church was designed in the Gothic style by W. I. Mason of Liverpool at a cost of £1,400 and described 'as well built, neat and commodious and as having a very fine barrel-vault roof.' It was a bigger and more imposing building than the chapel at Tan Lan, and in 1905 provided 350 sittings. There was an adjoining

Mount Pleasant Congregational Chapel, built in 1858.

schoolroom which became much used later on by the Girl's Secondary School.

Somehow, the pulpit installed came from Wrexham parish church and may have been the one from which Bishop Heber read, for the first time, his famous missionary hymn 'From Greenland's Icy Mountains', composed the evening before in the vicarage. It was removed in 1957 because of dry rot.

The original harmonium was replaced by a fine pipe organ suitably installed in its chamber in 1897. A lightning strike on the church in 1880 resulted in great expense.

When the church moved from Tan Lan in 1858, a decision was made to conduct the services in the English language. At the end of the19th century the church was flourishing.

1890 — Membership 110: Sunday school scholars, 150.
1905 — Communicants 120: Sunday school 113, Adherents 154.

The Church accounts for 1914 give the receipts as £142-18s-11d of which the major expenditure was 'Pulpit Supplies' £71-15s. Chapel keeper's salary £7. The Sunday school receipts were £53-13s-10d, with the major item of expenditure being the trip to Southport £17-10s-1d.

In 1958 amongst the church officers are 16 persons responsible for the Sunday school, Women's Guild, Junior Guild, Young People's Guild and Efforts Committee.

Church life: newspaper extracts from the *Wrexham Advertizer*.

1884 Jan 25 — The Congregational Sunday school — teachers and scholars tea meeting — speeches — solos — recitations. Pastor Rev D. J. Benyon.

1884 Feb 15 — Lecture on Martin Luther 'The attendance however was not very large.'

1884 Feb 15 — The Blue Ribbon Army.

Prior to the meeting, a procession at which there was a strong muster, paraded the village, headed by the Cefn Drum and Fife Band, speeches also being made in the streets' … 'an experience meeting was held during the evening, when a band of abstainers related their experience.

1884 Oct 4. — New instruments received by the Blue Ribbon Army Committee for the drum and fife band to be formed. Instruments, thirty fifes and piccolos, a large drum and two side drums. A class of young men and boys are receiving instruction from Mr Peter Darlington at the Congregational School Room.

Interior Mount Pleasant Congregational Chapel; pulpit and organ.

1913 January with her customary generosity, Mrs R. A. Jones, on Tuesday entertained at her residence the members of her Sunday school class.

Mrs R. A. Jones (1874–1946), the widow of Alderman R. A. Jones lived at Bryn View, Ruabon. She was an able woman, capable of making public speeches in both fluent English and Welsh. A member of Denbighshire Education Committee, School Manager of the Council School, member of the Board of Governors, Ruabon Boys and Girls Grammar School, member of Wrexham Rural District Council and an active Liberal in politics, she played a leading role in county and village affairs.

Another outstanding member was Mr Edward Morris who died in 1876. He took 'the initiative in rearing the edifice … Having secured the promises of Mrs Kenrick, Wynn Hall, Mr Barnes, Quinta, and a few other friends, he then generously gave £50 towards the building of the same'. He was senior deacon and shopkeeper in High Street.

Centenary Congregational Church, 1958.

The *Centenary Booklet* gives a list of ministers to 1958:

1861	H. C. Welsford
1864	Edward Edmunds
1867	John Lewis
1872	W. Tiller
1882	D. J. Benyon
1886	E. M. Edmunds
1905	Pandy Thomas
1910	Ambrose Evans
1915	J. M. James
	Wynne Evans
1927	H. S. Cresswell
1935	David Harries
1940-3	I. James Rees
1940-6	J. W. Emrys Shepherd
1955	C. Withers

Wesleyan Methodism
Wesleyan Methodism came to Ruabon before 1807, we know this because it is included in the weekly 'Plan of Appointment of the Preachers' in the Llangollen Circuit during 1806-07, when John Morris preached.[28] A building was registered on 8 June 1812,[29] for worship described as 'A room in the dwelling house of Mr Edward Roberts … set apart for divine worship.' The witnesses included Edward Jones, minister. There were four Edward Jones' who were Wesleyan ministers at the time. The best known of these was Edward Jones of Bathafarn, Ruthin, who was involved in the Welsh mission at this time. We know from the Religious Census of 1851 that the cause was stable and had a healthy membership.

Wesleyan Chapel
Erected 1838
Day School
Present: morn. 70 + 55 scholars; even. 100.
Joseph Jones, carpenter. George Powell.

This new chapel of 1838 is referred to in the Wynnstay records as 'A messuage at Tanyllan, Ruabon, formerly used a a public house called The Swan, and now converted into a chapel called Wesley Chapel.'[30] Associated with this chapel were George Jones, plumber and glazier; George Powell, grocer; Joseph Jones, joiner and Edward Hughes, tailor all of Ruabon. When the Park Road Chapel was built in 1895 'the old Ruabon Wesleyan Chapel was conveyed to the Trustees of the Wynnstay settled estates' after the building of a schoolroom at Park Road in 1901.[31] No records survive for this building or an account of 19th century Welsh Wesleyanism before plans to build a new chapel at Park Road in the last decade.

The names of the first trustees appointed in June 1891 were Thomas Ames, foreman at the brick works; John Davies, builder; Thomas Jackson, manager of the brick & tile works. The second trustees appointed in December 1894 give some idea of the social background of the members. The list includes: Robert Griffiths, butcher; William Peters, book-keeper; William Jones, brick maker; Joseph Morris, carriage examiner; Thomas Ellis, grocer; John Hall, brick maker; Samuel Newns, sawyer; Anne Hatton, pensioner; Thomas Evans, brick maker and Alfred Whittingham, clerk.

These were the artisans and craftsmen who formed the core of the membership of the old chapel, who now wished to build a new one and change the language of worship from Welsh to English. It was decided in 1890, to approach Sir Watkin for land on which to build a new chapel and schoolroom and he gave them a 'portion of the Paddock at Ruabon next to Griffiths' shop, where the old double door used to be in the wall.[32] Specifications were prepared by Thomas Jones, architect, Wrexham, for the 'completion of church and schoolroom for the trustees'. The stone-laying ceremony was arranged for 17 July 1895. Many fund-raising activities were held in the autumn. The highlight was a bazaar in Wrexham, six lantern entertainments, a series of 'coffee suppers' with a minimum charge of 6d and 'It was resolved to make the suppers as equal in quality as possible and without hams.' To give some extra income pew rents were charged: ninepence per quarter for a single sitting, and three shillings and sixpence per quarter for a whole sitting.

The new Wesleyan Church was opened on the first Friday in March 1896:

> … the ceremony was performed by Mr Nuttall of Llangollen in the absence of Miss Nuttall his sister, through indisposition. After a few remarks by the Rev W. Mellor, Wrexham, Mr Wm. Thomas, JP, Wrexham, presented Mr Nuttall with a silver key. Shortly afterwards Mr Ralph Darlington FRCS, Llangollen, unveiled a coloured window, which was presented by him in memory of his two brothers. A service was also held at which Professor Waddy Moss, of Didsbury College, preached. A service was held at 7.30 at which the Rev C. Garrett preached. At the services which were very largely attended, large collections were made … the cost of the building was approximately £1,100.' The sum of £654.19s.4d. had been collected in Ruabon alone.[33]

Methodist Chapel, Park Road.

Between 1896 and 1902, the old chapel in Tan Lan was used a schoolroom until the debt on the new chapel was paid. In March 1901, Mr Darlington was deputed to approach Sir Watkin for more land on which to build a schoolroom. Sir Watkin agreed to give the trustees 20 feet more land, on condition that the old chapel was handed over to him and that the plans of the new schoolroom be submitted for his approval. The tender for the schoolroom submitted by Mr John Davies, Ruabon, was for £732.[34]

The strength of the new church membership in 1905 was: 38 communicants; 91 Sunday school members including teachers; 130 adherents; estimated cost of property £2,320, chapel sittings 150, schoolroom 100.

The chapel and the schoolroom were built at a time of fierce competition between the religious denominations in Ruabon. The Primitive Methodists and the English Presbyterians set up new churches in the Bryn Fields area which became the 'new' housing development area from 1891 to 1914. The Wesleyans

Wesleyan Chapel Sunday School, tea and games in Vicarage Fields, July 1914.

decided to remain in Tan Lan, and as part of their strategy to entice new members changed the language of worship from Welsh to English. This succeeded until after the Second World War and the migration of families from the Tan Lan. In the meantime however, an active membership was maintained with a strong Sunday school, attractive worship with instrumentalists providing the music, and a tradition of preaching. At an anniversary service in 1913, 'Special music was rendered by the choir and band under the leadership of Mr Harold Wright. The band consisted of six violinists and a clarionette, flute and cello.' The schoolroom was used for instruction and weekday evening activities and lectures. In 1930 Dr E. K. Jones of Acrefair, gave an address on the League of Nations.

By 1957 plans were being made for 'the disposal of the Church buildings in view of its impending closure through lack of attendance'. In 1959 the chapel trustees approached the Freemasons to increase their payment for use of the schoolroom from £50 to £100 per year. They refused to do so, and a year later offered the sum of £2,000 for the purchase of the building. In October 1960, the trustees put a reserve of £2,500 on the building and advertised its sale in the *Wrexham Leader*. The trustees offered to make a gift of the chapel to the parish church, this was turned down because of anxiety over the cost of repair, and in the end agreed to accept the offer of £2,300 from the Freemasons.[35]

Ruabon Methodist Church, Henry Street, 1892

In 1932 the Primitive Methodist Church united with the Wesleyan and United Methodists to form the present Methodist Church. The origins of the Henry Street Methodist Church lie in Tan Lan.

> On the afternoon of Monday, 5th September 1892, the members of the chapel and Sunday school assembled for the last time at Tan Lan before making their way in a procession from the old to the new schoolroom. The dedication service at the Primitive Methodist Sunday school, Henry Street, Ruabon, was conducted by the Rev Thomas Guttery of Southport ... [36]

The Primitive Methodist Church developed from the work of Hugh Bourne and William Clowes both of whom were expelled in the early 19th century from the Wesleyan Methodist Church. In 1811, their two organisations united under the name of the Primitive Methodists. It was a church of evangelical fervour and later of close relations with trades unions, especially among miners and agricultural workers.

The first notice of the Primitive Methodists Church in Ruabon is given in the *Returns for the Religious Census* in March 1851. From the description it appears to have been a small building. 'Space; free (seats) 20; other 70; standing, 8 yards. Present: afternoon 31. Average: 12 months; afternoon 25; evening 70, John Haghivery, Steward'. The building, now demolished, was situated at the foot of Chapel Hill, Tan Lan.

A list of trustees of the chapel in 1891 gives some idea of the social background of the members and the variety of occupations in the expanding village community.

> Joseph Langford, postman; William Richards, plumber; Richard Barfield, miner; Edward Hall, signalman; James Richard Postle, labourer; Joseph Davies, bricklayer; Edward Evans, labourer; William Edwin Richards, draper's assistant; Alfred Henry Hall, labourer; Joseph Charles Langford, grocer's assistant; Pryce Davies, brickmaker; George Daniels, stonemason; William Price, miner; John Williams, blacksmith; Edward Jones, miner — all of Ruabon.

The church was built on land purchased from the sale of the Bryn Hall estate in April 1891. 654 square yards of land were purchased on behalf of the trustees at 4s.-3d. per square yard. The site purchased was

Methodist Church, Henry Street, built 1892.

conveniently situated on the thoroughfare to Wrexham at the end of the old village of Ruabon next to the hospital, built in 1886, and at the beginning of the new phase of development in Bryn Fields:

Building work at Henry Street was completed in August of 1892, the schoolroom being constructed of Ruabon brick, relieved with stone copings, jambs and sills, in the Gothic style. It was described as having a neat and prepossessing exterior, with a comfortable and bright interior, which was to be fitted up and used for services until the funds were forthcoming for the contemplated new chapel. It also had a two-storey building attached at the west end; this comprised of an upstairs classroom which could be opened to provide a choir-balcony to the schoolroom, a vestry with facilities for making tea, and a cellar held the coke-fired boiler for the heating system in the schoolroom, lighting being supplied by town gas. The cost of land, building, and other items was about £700; fittings were additional.[37]

When the church was restored in 1976, the building attached to the west end was demolished.

Figures for the year 1905 endorse the justification for the move from Tan Lan with a solid core of 70 communicants, a flourishing Sunday school of 252 scholars and teachers, and 270 adherents.

The life and energy of church life was seen in the way in which they approached raising the funds for the Henry Street schoolroom. Fund-raising activities in 1891 were centred on the Assembly Rooms at the Wynnstay Arms Hotel. A choir of 40 voices gave a concert there. A grand Oriental Bazaar was organised by a committee consisting of 32 men and 37 ladies!

Advantage was taken in 1892 of raising money at the Ruabon Fête in June and the Flower Show in August, both in Wynnstay Park, at which the church members were temperance caterers. The solidarity of the Nonconformist churches was shown by support from Congregationalists and Calvinistic Methodists.

It was said that because of the use of the chapel, caretakers found it difficult to obtain free periods for cleaning. Being so conveniently situated it was ideal for the Sunday school, Band of Hope, temperance meetings, mid-week prayer meetings, mission services, choir practices, concerts, and other activities.

A feature of these early activities was the support received from the Presidents of the Primitive Methodist Conference. Circuit links are now established with Rhosymedre in the south and Regent Street Church, Wrexham, in the north. Membership declined in the 1970s, and building problems and general maintenance threatened the church with closure.

Mrs Sheila Brookfield described the situation on the eve of the new millennium and the new hope which has arisen:

The members became exhausted by the effort to maintain the building: A 'spiritual lift-off' was quite sorely needed. By 1985 prayers were being answered — a trickle of young people, some with families, came along, and soon more were added, reviving the spirit of the older members. The number of children increased and a fresh challenge was being made: there was a need for a Sunday School, and for premises to hold it on Sunday mornings. In 1987, two young committed Christian people of the church leased adjacent shop premises and there, with help offered by the church members — and that of friends from other churches in the Circuit and from other denominations in the area — they were able to fulfil a vision of outreach work in the community in the opening of 'The Lamp' Christian Coffee Shop: coffee and refreshments, together with Christian books and craftwork are available at the shop, offered in a ministry of friendship and communal support. The Sunday School has been held in these premises since it recommenced in November 1987. Once a month the children come into church to worship together in a family service. Mid-week fellowships have revived too; and these have reverted to the earlier Methodist form of house-fellowships.

With the spirit of the church revived, mission has featured prominently in recent times. In 1986, the church

Methodist Church Sunday School trip, c.1937.
Back row: Wilf Richards; Linda Clarke; Harry Green; driver; driver; Lizzie Owens; Maggie Jones; -?-;
Annie Owens; -?-; driver; Sallie Owens; Ruth Colley; -?-; Johnnie Hughes; Jane Hughes.
Middle row: Ernest Reynolds; -?- Reynolds; Iris Richards; Gertie Green; Martha Evison; Baba Williams; -?-;
Renée Clarke; -?-; Minnie Hall;Mabel Evison; Olwen Evans.
Front row: driver; -?-; Marjorie Formstone; Jean Evison; Glenys Green; Mary Evison; Doreen Owens; Kathleen
Pumford; Margaret Pumford; Sheila Owens; -?-; Dorothy Evison; driver; Phyllis Williams; Megan Evans.

Methodist Church Junior Guild
(Football), 1956.
Back row: David Jones; Michael Parry;
John Cryer; Towyn Ffoulkes; Ken
Roberts; Tudor Jones.
Middle row: Merlin Hughes; Charles
Riley,; Bryn Roberts; Harold Pumford;
John Page; John Edwards.
Front row: Tudor Owens; Keith
Hughes; Phil Jones; Gwilym Austin;
Gwyn Watkins; Ronnie Jones.

took part in ecumenical door-to-door visitations, inviting people of Ruabon to one of the Wrexham Circuit's performances of *The Witness*, a modern Christian musical, which told of the ministry of Jesus Christ and of his gift of the Holy Spirit to all who follow and believe in him — as witnessed by his disciple, Peter. This was held at St. Mary's Church, Ruabon, kindly loaned for the occasion, enabling a large number of people to be present at the challenging performance. Then, in 1989, the church hosted a team of students from the Capernwray International Bible School; the students encouraged the members by the freshness of their evangelical witness; the students also took their witness into the schools and other establishments of the community. Later, in the same year, the church was involved in the 'Tell Wales' mission when the members made door-to-door visitations in Ruabon as preparation for the visit of Dr Luis Palau, the Argentinian evangelist, who held meetings at various places in the Principality, at which many people came to know of the love of Jesus Christ. And in 1990, the church shared in the Ruabon Mission with the Anglican and Catholic churches of Ruabon; this successful mission was led by a team of Catholic missioners; and through working and sharing together the mission helped to bond the spirit of ecumenicism which has been important in all the years of witness of the Methodists at Ruabon.

In 1992, the church had 35 members, the Sunday School had 24 scholars and there are several babies in the crèche. The signs of growth are encouraging, and there is a new sense of joy in worship. The development of the Sunday School — inspired by a band of dedicated teachers — is already outgrowing "The Lamp" premises; a fresh challenge faces the church, that of accommodation for the growing Sunday School. It is perhaps not dissimilar to the challenge faced by the Methodists of the Tan Lan chapel so long ago, and met in the building of the church which is now celebrating its centenary.

The Methodists at Ruabon thank God for the faithfulness of their forefathers and, together with friends, they rejoice at the 100 years of worship and fellowship at Henry Street. They go forward with confident faith and a real sense of hope and expectation as the pilgrimage continues into the next century.'

Bethania Baptist Church, Cleveland Street. Closed 1999.

Bethania Welsh Baptist Church, Cleveland Street.

The Baptist presence in the old parish of Ruabon was strong in the 19th century. In 1851 at Capel Mawr, Cefn Mawr, the general average congregation was 700, with an addition of 398 scholars and with another 300 at Cefn Bychan, 200 at Penycae, and 800 in the evening at Rhos.[38] The only reference however to the village of Ruabon is that the house of John Edwards, stone mason, was licensed by the Baptists as a meeting house in August 1805.

A hundred years later, the statistics of 1905 show that in the Bethania Welsh Baptist Chapel schoolroom, newly built in Cleveland Street, the membership was made up of 48 communicants, 58 Sunday school scholars and teachers, 90 adherents, with the number of sittings in chapel counted as 180.

We have seen that Ruabon began to develop rapidly at the end of the 19th century and the Bryn Hall estate sale gave the opportunity for land to be purchased in small lots suitable for chapel building and working-class housing development. In June 1891, Sarah Wright purchased 1,369 square yards of land at 38 pence a yard, lots 30 to 35, of the Bryn Hall estate, from Henry Dennis for a place of religious worship and instruction. Mrs Sarah Wright sold the land for the price she paid for it £220, to the trustees of Bethania Chapel. At a meeting on 10 March 1893, the trustees decided to build a chapel and paid Mr Owen of Liverpool £5 for his services as architect and the builders J. T. Jones, £315. The trustees proceeded cautiously and built the schoolroom. This proved in the long run to be sufficient. It was opened on 29 April 1894. As a means of maintaining the building and perhaps supporting the membership numbers, 11 to 16 Cleveland Street were built as chapel houses. These were modernised in 1973 with the help of a gift towards the cost of £3,175.20p.

A minister was shared with Johnstown, successive pastors being: R.L. Thomas, D. Cynnon Evans, R.J. Thomas and J. Morgan Thomas.

The pattern of services was Sunday Worship, a Sunday School, Bible Reading and a Prayer Meeting on weekdays. There was an annual Preaching Festival on the last weekend in April, with a Thanksgiving Service coinciding with the Harvest Festival at the end of October. The Quarterly Meetings of the local Baptist Associations were held on occasions at Bethania.

The small chapel schoolroom provided a centre not only for worship but also some kind of social diversion for its members.

In December 1896, on a Monday evening, the third of a series of literary and competitive meetings was held at Bethania with singing and recitation and the Penycae choir in attendance.

On New Year's Eve 1912, a pleasant service was held in the chapel when various games 'were indulged in' and refreshments were provided.

In 1913, the Preaching Anniversary began on Saturday evening, and was continued on Sunday with preachers from Carrog and Bangor College. Large congregations were reported.

To lighten the dark days of war, a social was held on Christmas night 1917. 'Mr Aubrey gave some delightful selections on the concertina. Private D. Jones who is home on furlough gave a solo, Mr J. Thomas and party sang some carols'.

The jubilee of the opening of the chapel was celebrated on 29 and 30 April 1944, when the Annual Festival preachers were Humphrey Ellis, Caernarfon, and W. Arthur Edwards, Ebenezer, Cefn Mawr. The latter preached in English.

An effort was made to encourage children when in 1949, the minister, J. Morgan Jones, set up a branch of Urdd when eight children made vows of membership and received badges.

The deacons in 1915 were William Davies, R. L. Edwards, John Thomas, John Wright and Griffith Griffiths, who stood down as secretary on 26 May 1946 and was a Sunday School teacher for fifty years. He died on 29 May and his years of devoted service were an example to others who came after him. Arthur Boast was secretary for thirty years, Alexander Evans for twenty-two years and Iola Evans for twenty years.

Year by year the membership was reduced by death until in 1997, with only four members remaining the chapel was closed after 103 years of witness in Cleveland Street.

Bethania Baptist Church, Ladies Sunday School Class, 1920.

Bethania Baptist Church. Presentation to Ada and Arthur Boast after 30 years service to the church.
Left (front – back): Iola Evans; Phyllis Jones; Irene Jones; Ruth Roberts; Edith Davies; Ada Boast; Arthur Boast; Harry Manning (Senior); Olwen Edwards; Towyn Jones; Dilys Davies.
Right (front – back): Josie Davies; Annie Griffiths; Olwen Davies; Mabel Hughes; Emrys Davies; Harry Manning; -?- Manning; Rose Griffiths; Emlyn Griffiths; Norman Edwards; Isfryn Evans.

The Parish Church in the Nineteenth Century

The church has always been well served by its officers, particularly Parish Clerks — Roger Jones for 65 years, died 1780 aged 92 years, and Edward Jones, for 73 years clerk, died March 20 1810 aged 89 years. The old adage he would be late for his own funeral was true in Ruabon, when the vestry ordered 'that any funeral being fifteen minutes after the time fixed by the Minister shall pay to the sexton one shilling for the irregularity.' So important was time that, when Mr Thomas Rogers, the parish clerk in 1851, was appointed to wind the church clock, it was resolved 'that he be directed to set the clock by the proper railway time, on Friday evening, in each week, under penalty of half-a-crown fine, to be deducted from his salary.'

It was perhaps through being over-zealous that the first great disaster occurred in the church in January

Benjamin Ferrey, architect of the 1870 restoration of the Parish Church.

1819, when there was a fire caused by the overheating of the flues. Six weeks before Edward Jones, the sexton, had been given an increase in salary 'for making fire in the church flue, finding wood, and carrying the coal. The fire did considerable damage, and Sir Watkin came to the rescue with the gift of a pulpit and payment for repairing the organ.

Extensive alterations were made to the church in 1846. Open seats were substituted for box pews, the north chancel arch opened up and the fine altar rails and a Gothic reredos added to the furnishings.

Drastic work of restoration was undertaken. J. Hardcastle, Esq. of Penylan had the memorandum entered in the Church Book 'That it may be desirable to obtain the erection of a new church … upon the foundations of the present existing church leaving the tower undisturbed.'[39] Fortunately this was not done and Benjamin Ferrey was asked to make plans which were radical enough. These were described by Sir Stephen R. Glynne, Mr W. E. Gladstone's brother-in-law, in 1872.

The restoration has been completed. The arcades have been replaced; five pointed arches on pillars alternately octagonal and circular; also a new clerestory of which the windows are alternately square-headed, and of spherical triangular form. The roofs are all new. A chancel-arch is added on marble shafts, and a new east window. The aisle-windows are, decorated, of three lights; the organ removed to the south aisle, and the Wynnstay seat into the tower. A curious mural painting has been discovered in the south aisle, appearing to represent the corporal acts of mercy.'[40]

The handbook prepared for the re-opening in March 1872 contemplated further alterations:

These, however, are not all the improvements Sir Watkin intends making. He has very generously promised to present a new stone pulpit and reading desk, and to remove the communion rails under the chancel, in order to afford more space. The interior will be framed with encaustic tiles, and new chairs will be placed within.

Fortunately this work was not carried out. No structural alterations have been made since 1872. North and south porches were added in the next decade.

The average Sunday attendance at the parish church in 1888 was Sunday morning 300, evening 450, service in Welsh 3.30pm 20, children's service 3.30pm first Sunday 178. Services were held on Wednesday at 7pm; Saint's Days 11am with additional services in the seasons of Advent and Lent. The service of Holy Communion was held in the parish church on the first Sunday at 11am and on the second, third and fifth Sundays in the Wynnstay chapel. There was no organised District visitors but 'several lady visitors.'

The district of Penycae was made a separate parish in 1877 and mission work was then centred on the Bryn, an agricultural district centred on the Penylan Hall estate, and Plas Bennion, a mining hamlet bordering on Penycae and Rhosymedre parishes.

Plas Bennion Mission Church

Plas Bennion was a mining community between Wynn Hall and Plas Madoc on the newly established boundary of the parishes of Penycae and Ruabon.[41] To make a religious provision for the fifty odd dwellings there in the 1880s, cottage lectures were held during the winter on Thursdays. This was the strategy that the vicar, Canon E. Wood Edwards, had used in Penycae twenty years earlier.

It was described in H.C. Ridley's 1829 handbook *Parochial Duties*:

The clergyman rings the bell … and on entering the room a short prayer is offered up. The portion of scripture is then begun in continuance with the last reading. From ten to thirty verses are gone through, almost word for word, with the distinct meaning of every passage and its reference to others, and explained as simply as possible. The whole passage is then repeated in a sort of paraphrase, and lastly the practical duties arising from its consideration are summed up under three particular heads. This, with the Lord's Prayer and another … occupied one hour.[42]

Right: St Mary's Church bellringers, 1894.

Below, left: St Mary's Church bellringers, 2000
L–R: Sam Erlandson; Janet Erlandson; Anna Lena
Bradbury; John Griffiths; Mary Jones; Ian Cole; Gareth
Erlandson; Matthew Cunningham.
Absent: Richard Perry.

Mr Derek Owens, 1998 . The six bells of
St Mary's Church awaiting restoration.

St Mary's Church choir, 1966.
Standing: Adrian Maurice; Herbert Kilfoyle (Churchwarden); John Mathias; Trevor Wilkinson; Mervyn Rogers; Alan
Crewe; Frances Fowles; Janet Matthias; Raymond Williams; Lynn Jones; Anne Morris; Rowland Jones; Leslie Hill; John
Page (Verger); Eric Bowen (Churchwarden); Ian Roberts; Paul Williams.
Seated: Mary Crewe; Phillipa Rees; Audrey Higgins; H.L.T. Smith (Organist); Rev. Geoffrey Davies (vicar); Rev. Glyn
Iball (Curate); Joshua Evans; Heather Pearson; Susan Kilfoyle; Mary Davies; Kevin Williams; Angela Rees.

A mission room, probably in the same building was held on Friday, at *7pm* and a children's meeting at *6pm*.[43]

There was no lack of support for this missionary enterprise and a permanent site for a church was found in 1893. A new Iron Mission Room supplied by R.C. Harris, iron church builder of Coleman Street, London, was purchased at a cost of £117. The site of this 'Tin Tabernacle' was just south of the railway line on land owned by Mr Ll. Jones, Penycae.[44] The building was 45 feet by 20 feet with four windows on each side, two in the front end and one window in each gable with a porch fronting the road. In the 1950s, this building was encased with Ruabon red brick and was used until the church, then in a dangerous condition, was closed at a service of thanksgiving on 13 November 1982 in the presence of the Bishop of St Asaph, Alwyn Rice Jones. Some of the money realised from the sale of the site funded the building of the church hall at the parish church of St Mary's, Ruabon. By this time the row of houses built for the mining community had been demolished and their residents dispersed.

Members of the community were proud of their little church and recruited a surpliced choir with music from a harmonium. The services were generally in charge of the assistant curate of Ruabon, a lay reader and sometimes the vicar. Mr William Parker was faithful in the first part of the 20th century as lay reader, and in the second half, Mr H.L. Brown, Mr R. Breeze and, on occasions, the last squire of Erddig, Philip Yorke, officiated. Organists I remember from 1960 onwards were Betty Miller (née Davenport) and Mrs Kenrick. The Brellisford family, Mrs Annie Roberts, Betty Ellis (née Humphries) and Brenda Ellis (née Tunnah) and many others were faithful and active members of the church and community.

Near the church was a building known as 'the Room' used for the social events. In February 1913, Miss Agnes Bowen and her concert party from Ruabon consisting of Misses Sallie and Nan Bowen, Gwen Crewe and Lily Sharpe, performed. In September 1919, the church choir, through the kindness of Mrs Pugh, Tai Clawdd, and Mr Watkin Rogers the lay reader were invited to a picnic tea at Belan and went on to Belan Tower and 'indulged in games'. By 1922 the choir was re-organised when it was reported that it 'now consists of about forty members, including a number of well-known singers. The practices are held weekly, under the conductorship of the curate in charge, Mr A. Hervey, assisted by the Rev H. J. Croasdale.'[45]

Across the railway tracks in the parish of Penycae was a Wesleyan Methodist chapel and both congregations used to support each other's services on special occasions.

The 20th Century

It has been sad to chronicle the decline and closure of places of worship but on the other hand, there have been signs of growth. Christians openly came together in the last twenty years of the twentieth century. Circumstances on more than one occasion gave the opportunity. One area of religious life in Ruabon which has not been recorded is that of the Roman Catholics.

The Roman Catholic Church of St. Michael and the Shared Church of St. Mary

The Roman Catholic parish in the year 2000 covers the area which the old parish of Ruabon embraced, until Rhosymedre, Rhosllanerchrugog, and Penycae were separated from Ruabon in the 19th century. It has two churches, Mair Wen in Acrefair, and St. Mary's Shared Church in Ruabon.

By 1960 the Catholic population of the area described above had grown to almost 350.[46] This growth was largely the result of the influences of the Second World War. Roman Catholic schools were evacuated to Ruabon and children attended the local school and received their instruction from local Catholic priests centred at Wrexham. Wynnstay Park was a camp throughout the

Plas Bennion Mission Church.

war for the Royal Engineers, and a mass centre was available for them. After the war, the huts in Wynnstay Park housed refugees from Lithunania and Poland. Some Italian and German prisoners of war remained and married and introduced new Catholic families into the area. Mass was said in the Duke of Wellington Inn in Tan Lan in 1939. The upper room of the Village Room was used as a mass centre as was the Parish Hall for evacuees during the war. The mass centre post-1945 was the Village Room.

The faith and devotion of the small Roman Catholic community is recaptured in the petition they made to Bishop Petit:

> Petition for the building of a new Church in Ruabon from Duke of Wellington Inn, Ruabon. 22nd January 1953.
>
> Your Lordship,
> Since we have heard that a Church has been acquired at Acrefair, may we respectfully beg your Lordship to consider the position of your people in Ruabon …
>   Your Lordship will be mindful of the fact that in Ruabon about 14 years ago was said the first mass since the Reformation in the very shadow of the lovely Parish Church, that was once the treasure of Welsh Catholics of this area. You will know that we have struggled hard to keep together since that time always with fond and cherished hope that one day God will bless us with a Church of our own. From a tiny family — perhaps the least in God's household — of five or six, we have lovingly watched Our Lady's family grow in the service of Her Divine Son. Now our gathering in the bare loft we hire for Holy Mass seldom numbers less than 90, and on a good day, when the older, the infirm and the younger members of the congregation are not prevented by the inclemency of the weather, we number over 100, and always 50% will join in Holy Communion.
>   In between buses we have little time to enjoy one another's company, but we have all grown to know and love one another. Now, as many of us who can, come together every Thursday evening when we endeavour to practice the hymns we sing during Mass, and enjoy one another's company in a Catholic Social evening. Our children too, meet together, and Sunday afternoon sees many of them walking, and we may say, running, not a short distance to join their friends where at least 20, sometimes, 30 will be gathered together to pray, play, learn their catechism, and sing their hymns.

The Bishop acknowledged the petition by sending his young secretary, Father Owen Hardwicke, to prepare the way for building a new church. This was not without its difficulties. Ruabon Free Church Council protested to the Wrexham Rural District Council and to the Welsh Office of the Ministry of Housing and Local Government:

> Viewing with alarm the encroachment of Roman Catholicism on a Protestant Community, the Ruabon Free Church Council, representing all the Nonconformist churches in the district, protest strongly against the

St Mary's Church Parochial Church Council
Back row: Ronald Breeze; Anna Lena Bradbury; Mary Jones; Jill Bottomley; Linda Tracey; Jennie Bailiff; Richard Elmore; Barbara Ormrod; Pauline Davies; Irene Giller; Barbara Cunningham; Helen Eardley; Ian Cole; Barbara Ellis; Gareth Erlandson; Jane Davies; John Griffiths; Rowena Jenkins.
Front row: Roland Fenner (Treasurer); Brian Robinson (Churchwarden); Terry Jones (Chairman); Rev. Godfrey Caine Jones (Vicar); Berwyn Thomas (Churchwarden); Audrey Powell (Secretary).

allocation of a plot of land in Ruabon for the creation of a Roman Catholic … .The site … is situated at a new estate and has not yet been purchased.[47]

Not to be thwarted Fr. Hardwicke bought Bryn Hall and set about turning the property into a church and presbytery. The first mass was said in a room of the house on the feast of Saint Richard Gwyn, the Welsh martyr, on 17 October 1957.

Major demolition work had to be done and over 500 tons of rubble were moved by voluntary labour. This effort made its impression on the local community who admired the enthusiasm and dedication of the workforce. Not surprisingly news reached Dublin and 800 employees of the Irish Glass Bottle Company who had just finished paying for the erection of a factory oratory decided to give similar financial assistance from their weekly wage packets to help finance the transformation of Bryn Hall into St. Michael's Church at a cost of £7,000.

The building was ready by the end of May 1959 when Bishop Petit of Menevia opened the church, inducted Fr. Hardwicke and three days later raised to the priesthood Brian Jones in his native Ruabon.[48]

The background to the sharing of the parish church is recorded in the church guide book.

However, during the next twenty years serious structural faults were discovered and the building unhappily had to be abandoned as being unsafe. We are ecumenically-minded in Ruabon and the most exciting thing that has happened is the inauguration of a sharing agreement between the Anglican and Roman Catholic congregations. The Roman Catholic Bishop of Menevia and the Anglican Bishop of St. Asaph were present when the Sharing Agreement was inaugurated by a joint service of evensong on Sunday 20 January 1980 during Christian Unity Week. Both bishops warmly welcomed and endorsed the sharing and gave it their blessing. As we have seen, the possibility of sharing arose because of the dilapidated state of St. Michael's Roman Catholic Church. It seemed hypocritical, foolish, and uncharitable, for £100,000 to be spent on the building of a new church. We have put into practice the famous dictum of Cardinal Mercier, 'We cannot love each other if we do not meet each other'. The Roman Catholics use the north chapel as the Blessed Sacrament Chapel. We share all things, cleaning, grass-cutting, the cost of insurance and church maintenance. On occasions we worship together and run joint social events. The administration of the church is the responsibility of a joint council composed of Roman Catholic and Anglican members.

The Church Hall.

Church and Community Hall

The first fruits of our fellowship is the building of an extension on the north-west

Opening of St. Mary's Church Hall, 1984. L–R: Stephen Scott; Canon Bill Pritchard (vicar); Father Anthony Jones; Father Bernard Morgan (parish priest); Ronald Breeze (lay reader); Rev. John Tarbrook (deacon).

Ruabon News *production team. c.1988..*
Farewell to the editor at the home of Miss Bronwen
Jones. L–R: Ann Owens; Daphne Thorne (editor);
Michael Williams (vicar); Anna Lena Bradbury; Sheila
Brookfield; John Bradbury; Derek Owens.

side of the church for church and community use. We are grateful to the Community Task Force for sponsoring the scheme, for providing free labour and the excellence of the craftsmanship. The architectural partnership TACP of Wrexham under the guidance of Mr R. B. Heaton, B.Arch., FRIBA, has supervised the work. The cost of materials has been met by the shared congregation and was in the region of £33,000.

New Pipe Organ

In 1987 the opportunity arose to install a pipe organ to replace the old organ taken out in 1970 and replaced by an electronic instrument. The organ was built in 1909 for the Church of St John, Hightown, Wrexham, by James Jepson Binns, organ builder, Bramley, Leeds, and was the gift of John Jones of Grove Lodge, Wrexham, who erected the church to the memory of his wife in 1909. When St John's was made redundant the rector of Wrexham was approached and he generously offered the organ to the shared church of St Mary's. Mr John S. Evans of Ruabon was responsible for designing and making additional casing in oak from the choir pews of St John's Church. The cost of the installation and improvement to the Binns organ was over eleven thousand pounds shared between the Anglican and Catholic congregations. The organ was completely overhauled and rebuilt with new electropneumatic actions throughout by Leonard Reeves, organ builder, Stoke-on-Trent. It was dedicated on 5 May 1987 by the Right Reverend Alwyn Rice Jones, MA, Bishop of St Asaph, and the Right Reverend James Hannigan, Bishop of Wrexham.'

Ecumenism

It is the spirit of sharing, ecumenism, meeting together which has brought the various Christian traditions together. This was described by Sheila Brookfield in her centenary account of Methodism. It has been

Below: Father Owen Hardwicke climbing the stairs to
the village room. Also present are Jeffrey Evans,
Maureen Cookson and Vicky Law.

Abovet: Bishop Petit, Secretary James Hannigan and Deacon Brian
Jones bless the outside of the new church of St, Michael and All
Angels. Servers include: John Jones; Doug Williams; Terry Bishop;
David Bellingham. The musicians include: Roger Newsom. Architect
Fred Roberts.

demonstrated by the members of Rhagluniaeth and Bethania being offered accommodation, and welcomed by the members of the Congregational Church. The Ladies Guild meeting regularly together in the Church Hall is another example of Christians meeting together. The right spirit in which to celebrate the millennium.

Vicars of the Parish

1404	Reginald, son of John Cedewain, Vicar of Halkyn.
1414	David ap Madoc.
1430	Meredydd ap Rhys — a Welsh poet and tutor of Davydd ap Edmwnd.
*c.*1500	John Elys.
1537	John Burras — younger brother of William, valet to Henry VIII.
1539	David Edwards.
1570	David Powel, DD, Prebendary of Llanfair. Distinguished historian.
1578	Robert Salusbury, DCL.
1598	Samuel Powel, AM.
1600	Peter Williams, AM., Prebendary of Meifod.
1617	Richard Lloyd, DD, Canon of St. Asaph.
1647	Humphrey Lloyd, DD — ejected 1650, restored 1660. Dean of St. Asaph 1663 and Bishop of Bangor 1675.
1654	R. Hill. Intruder during the Commonwealth.
1675	John Robinson. AM. He endowed the Grammar School and Almshouses.
1706	Richard Davies, AM, Precentor of Brecon. Canon of St. Asaph and St. David's — he founded and endowed four almshouses.
1746	Richard Jones, AM.
1756	Edward Davies, AM.
1758	Lewis Jones, AM.
1770	Thomas Trevor, AM.
1784	Philip Puleston, DD.
1801	Rowland Wingfield, MA, Canon of St. Asaph.
1842	Richard Bonnor, MA, later Dean and Chancellor of St. Asaph.
1859	Thomas Thomas, MA, Canon of Bangor.
1862	Ebenezer Wood Edwards, MA, Canon of St. Asaph.
1897	Evan Morgan Roderick, MA.
1901	James Sculthorpe Lewis, Canon of St. Asaph.
1921	Clement Reynolds Thomson, MA, Canon of St. Asaph.
1926	Joseph Herbert Davies, BA.
1939	Benjamin Peredur Jones-Perrott, BA, Canon of St Asaph, Archdeacon of Wrexham.
1963	David Geoffrey George Davies, BA, BD, Canon of St. Asaph.
1970	Maurice Coburne Donaldson, BA, BD.
1977	Thomas William Pritchard, BA, LLM, FSA, Rural Dean of Llangollen, Canon of St. Asaph and Archdeacon of Montgomery.
1987	David Michael Rochfort Williams.
1993	Godfrey Caine Jones, BA, MEd, Rural Dean of Llangollen.

Roman Catholic Priests

1977	Anthony Jones.
1982	Bernard Morgan.
1989	Terence Carr.
1998	Joseph Stewart.

Ruabon United Choir, c.1922 (photographed at Corwen).

Practices held at the Primitive Methodist and Presbyterian Chapels, Ruabon.

Back row: Albert Pumford; Willie Price; David Charles; Ed. O. Davies (Pearl Ins.); -?-; Emlyn Griffiths (Garddan View); E. O. Phillips (Gwilym's uncle); -?-.

Second row: Edward Edwards; Ben Edwards; Tom Price; David Jones; -?-; Edward Griffith; J. P. Dodd; Harold Wright; Mark Thomas; Bill Jones (Potts) Forresters Terrace; -?-; Ernest Jones (railway guard); Manny Williams (Cllr); Bill Williams (Bryn View).

Third row: George Hughes (joiner); Charlie Price (Willie's brother); Sam Edwards; Joe Edwards (Sam's brother); Marjorie Griffiths (butcher's neice); Plas Newydd maid; -?-; Mrs Bill Roberts (Mrs Steele's mother); Enid Samuels; Dilys Griffiths (Mrs R. E. Davies); Annie Mathews; Olwen Williams; Gwen Williams; John W. Mathews; Bill Greasley; Cyril Wright (Curly's father).

Fourth row: Susie Edwards (later matron, Lindisfarne); -?-; -?-; Sarah Williams (Plas Bennion); Ada Boast (née Griffiths); Sallie Samuels (Gaynor's mother); Carrie Rogers (Offa Terrace); May Owens (Mount Pleasant); Celia Roberts (Mrs Steele's sister); Jinnie Hughes (schoolteacher); Celia Hughes (George Hughes' daughter); -?-; Maggie Humphries (Forresters Terrace); Fred Davies (schoolmaster); Robert Samuels (Enid's father).

Fifth row: Ben Davies (Pearl Ins.); E. T. Jones (Denzil's father, Church Street); Mrs E. T. Jones; Edith Hough (Herbert's mother); Mrs Hannah Price (Willie's mother); Sallie Rogers (Cefn); Annie Hough (S. Hughes' sister); Sarah Owens; John Charles Powell (accompanist); Sam Hough (conductor, Rhos); Dai Owens (Sylvia Johnson's uncle); Polly Edwards; -?-; Cis Griffiths (Bobby's mother, Forresters Terrace); Eva Parry (Mrs Mark Thomas); Hannah Thomas.

Front row: Sam Hughes Jnr (Herbert's father); Charlie Nicholas (Railway Terrace); Lewis Owens (Forresters Terrace); Mary Price (Mrs W. Price); Winnie Roberts (Mrs Steele); Lizzie Owens; Gertie Hughes (Stanley Hughes 'Co-op's sister); Sarah Davies; Percy Price (W. Price's brother); Olwen Powell; -?-; -?-. The children are from Rhos.

4. Schools

Records giving an account of education and schools in Ruabon go back 400 years to the beginning of the 17th century. What today is called primary and secondary education was provided in the first school, the Endowed Grammar School, founded about 1618. From this time the post-Reformation Anglican Church controlled education in the Ruabon community for nearly 300 years. It was not until the beginning of the twentieth century that non-sectarian schools were provided.

This chapter relates the story of the Anglican foundations: the Endowed Grammar School, 1618–1896, and the provision of primary education under the auspices of the local church and the National Society of the Church of England from 1824 to the present day. Welsh Intermediate Schools were provided in 1889 in the control of county councils, and under this legislation a County Secondary School for Boys was reconstituted from the Endowed Grammar School in 1896, and a Girl's Secondary School opened in 1922. These two schools became one in 1967–8 when comprehensive secondary education was introduced in Ysgol Rhiwabon. In the meantime, non-sectarian primary education became available in Ruabon in 1912 with the opening of the council school now known as Ysgol Maes y Llan. From the middle of the 19th century there was a primary school in Penylan until it closed in 1968. Both primary and secondary education have been available in the private or independent sector, the most notable of which was Lindisfarne College, 1948–94. These schools are described under three headings:

> I.   The Endowed Grammar School, 1618–1896
> II.   Secondary Education 1896 onwards
> III.   Primary Schools 1824 onwards.

I. The Endowed Grammar School, 1618–1896[1]

There is no evidence that the endowed grammar school was founded earlier than 1618. This date is probable because of a document dated 1637 which refers to:

The old Grammar School seen from the churchyard.

'a decent schoolhouse erected upon the north side of the church yard about these nineteen years by the general consent of Mr Doctor Lloyd, vicar of Ruabon and gentlemen, free-holders and inhabitants of the said parish … for the educating and instructing of the youths of the said parish and others, with learning in the fear of God'.

This petition addressed to the chancellor of the diocese of St Asaph is signed by Richard Lloyd, vicar; two churchwardens, Roger Kynaston and John Peck, and other gentlemen, Edward ap Randle, John Lloyd, Thomas Evans and Eyton Evans.[2] The licence and letters of orders of the schoolmaster Jeremiah Davies, dated 1626, who signs the petition are to be found in the Wynnstay papers.[3]

The earliest known benefaction, or endowment, was that given by Thomas Nevitt, citizen and draper of London, and a member of the Girdler's Company, who in 1632 left a legacy of £2 a year to the schoolmaster at Ruabon which was paid out of the income from a tenement and twenty-four acres of land in Romney

Marsh, Kent. Jeremiah Davies was succeeded as schoolmaster in 1637 by the Reverend Edward Pritchard who kept the school until he left in 1668. His period of office was disturbed by the Civil Wars but he had a great loyalty and affection for the school and in his will left a parcel of waste land 'y vron tan y dynwent' and a cottage called the bakehouse to the use of Humphrey Powell curate and schoolmaster of Ruabon and to his successors as such.[4]

John Robinson became vicar of Ruabon in 1675 where he remained until his death in 1706. He had first-hand knowledge and experience of most of the 'classical' or grammar schools of North Wales — Llanwrst, Hawarden and Ruthin — and was a graduate of St John's College, Cambridge. It is probable that the thirteen curates who officiated during Robinson's thirty-one years at Ruabon were schoolmasters. Between 1706 and 1757 Ruabon Grammar School received its major endowments.

The Reverend John Robinson 1706, was the chief benefactor to the endowed school. His will left a number of directions. First that the rent from a farm called the Cinders, in Crimbal Lane, of 74a 0r 31p should be the major source of income for the better support and maintenance of a grammar school in Ruabon. Second, Robinson directed his trustees to ensure 'that the master of the said school be orthodox and well qualified in learning, and industrious and free from public scandal'. Third he left other land in Wrexham, Bersham, and Esclusham, to support the education of the poor and directed that the nature of the curriculum was to be that of a typical 18th century charity school. Robinson stipulated:

> That six poor children of Ruabon parish, from 6 to 12 years, should be chosen by the vicar and wardens of Ruabon parish, for the time being out of Ruabon School, or out of the parish of Ruabon, to have blue coats and caps, shoes and stockings … given them at Christmas … such children should be taught gratis in Ruabon school, to read, write and cast accounts till they were 12 years old, and then to be dismissed and other elected in their room; and the said children should be obliged to wear their caps and coats abroad and at school … And they shall be obliged to learn the Church Catechism … and write the same in the Church upon Sundays in the afternoon when called upon to do so.

A Review of Other Educational Endowments

Griffith Hughes' Bequest 1706

The benefaction was secured on lands adjoining Pentre Issa Farm in the parish of Ruabon. The will directed that poor children of the parishes of Oswestry, Whittington, and Ruabon, should be taught 'to reade the Bible and the Church Catechisme'. The vicar of Ruabon and his successors and John Griffith of 'Kae Cariog' were appointed 'to order and admit whom & how many poore children they shall think fitt to be taught within the Parish of Ruabon.'

John Probert of Church Lawton, labourer, 1708

In his will, he directed that £8 be given to the 'School of Ruabon the interest to goe to the schoolmaster of Ruabon School for teaching some one poor child of [Rhosllanerchrugog] yearly for ever it being my Will that such child may be chosen out of some of my own relations if such there be and for want of such at the direction of the schoolmaster ….'

Richard Davies, Vicar of Ruabon, 1706-46

In his will left £200 that 'should for ever be vested in the Vicars & Churchwardens of Ruabon in Trust, for the use of the Master of the Free School there, one moyety for his trouble & pains in teaching six poor children to be plac'd in the School by the Vicar of the aforesaid Parish for the time being. Which children I desire may be taught to repeat the Church Catechisme, to write & read English, & if capable, to learn to cast Accounts, in order the better to prepare them for being made Apprentices, to which purpose I do assign the other moyety, to be expended in placing out Apprentices one or more of the Children of the said School according to the discretion of the Vicars of Ruabon...'

Ellis Lloyd of Pen y Lan, 1712

Bequeathed £200 for certain charitable causes. £100 for the 'binding out' of poor children apprentices and £100 towards the support of a grammar school to be kept in the usual parish school in Ruabon. This sum,

The Rev. D. J. Bowen's choice of the year of foundation.

together with £200 more, vicar Davies' legacy, were vested 1753, in the purchase of the Nantir Farm, in the parish of Llancadwaladr.

Randle Jones of Pen y Bryn, Ruabon, 1753

Amongst other charitable bequests to the poor he left 'the interest of the remaining twenty pounds to pay for the schooling of two poor boys of the said parish yearly in Ruabon School upon the nomination or appointment of my said sons and their heirs.

Edward Lloyd of Plas Madoc, 1757

Instructed the vicar and churchwardens of Ruabon

… to lay out the sum of £2-18s yearly for the teaching at Ruabon free school of three poor boys of the townships of Christionydd Kenrick, Coed Christionydd Trevechan and Ruabon, to read, write a plain legible hand, and spell well, and also for instructing them in arithmetic, in the knowledge of the four first rules, at least. And upon further trust to lay out the sum of 12s yearly … for the schooling and teaching of two girls to read and sew plain work in a sufficient manner. And in case any savings should at any time or times be made for want of proper objects of the said charity such savings were to be applied for the apprenticing one or more of the said boys. And it was thereby declared that such boys and girls who shall be objects of the before mentioned charities, were to be chosen from amongst the children of the workmen belonging to Plas Madoc collieries and iron furnace preferably to all other...

In all about five hundred pounds was bequeathed to be applied for educational purposes in the parish. Of this sum £400 was invested in 1753 in the purchase of the Nantyr Sheepwalk. Randle Jones' £50 and John Probert's £8 were lost in the 18th century, as was Edward Lloyd's rent charge in 1841. Griffith Hughes's bequest, a rent charge, was transferred to the National School in the 19th century. In 1837 the Charity Commissioners gave the following summary of the emoluments of the school:

Rent of lands, devised by Mr Robinson	£74 - 0 - 0
Nevitt's rent charge	£2 - 0 - 0
Edward Lloyd's ditto	£2 - 18 - 0
Rent of Lloyd and Davies lands	£15 - 0 - 0
Interest on Jones's money	£1 - 0 - 0
Ditto of timber money	£5 - 0 - 0
	£99 -18 - 0

Schoolmasters

Thomas Evans

The first definite mention of a schoolmaster in the 18th century is when Thomas Evans in the customary manner displayed his licence at the Wrexham Visitation in 1710. 'Thomas Evans, Ludimagister.' He appears not to have been in Orders. His burial is recorded in the Ruabon register '1711 Oct. 8th Mr Thomas Evans Schoolmaster buried.'

Reverend David Prydderch

He was Evans' successor. He is first mentioned in the registers in 1711 and regularly exhibited his licences as a clerk and schoolmaster until his last entry in the parish book in 1759. Although officiating regularly in the parish he was licensed primarily as a schoolmaster and did not act in the capacity of a curate. Prydderch's character is revealed by Richard Jones (vicar of Ruabon 1746-56), who found it difficult to get on with the old man in the matter of a dispute relating to the execution of the will of his predecessor, Richard Davies. In his correspondence with the Bishop of St Asaph, Jones describes the truculent schoolmaster, 'Mr Pryddech is strongly obstinate...I had before heard a good deal of his temper...! He is 'a clergyman above seventy years old and who has been schoolmaster of this village above forty-one. His perversness may be in some measure owing to his age and therefore I compassioned him — at the same time that he gives me the utmost trouble.' His son Stephen, baptized in Ruabon, 18 November 1719, is the only recorded pupil of Ruabon Grammar School until the 19th century.

Stephen Prydderch received from his father in Ruabon school 'the first rudiments of learning', but it is significant that he was sent to Wrexham school before entering Jesus College, Oxford, where he graduated. After ordination he became first a master at Wrexham School, and then returned to be curate of Ruabon. Coming to the notice of Sir Watkin he was promised the next vacancy of the vicarage of Great Wenlock, unfortunately his patron died in 1749 before this materialized. Nevertheless, Lady Frances fulfilled her husband's intentions when in 1752 he was inducted to that living.

A contemporary gave this description: 'he is an agreeable, and well accomplished man, reads distinctly, sings admirably and so is an agreeable companion, as well as a good scholar.'[5]

The inability of Ruabon Endowed School to compete with Wrexham School for the provision of a grammar school education is borne out by the report of the rural dean in 1749. 'The number of boys is eighteen and all (taught) in the English language. Six of them are cloath'd but none maintained or lodg'd. All must be taught to read and six to write and account if they be found capable. They are not employ'd in working but some of them apprenticed to trade. They are duly brought to church and instructed in the principles of the Christian religion according to the Church of England.'[6]

By the time of the last endowment in 1757 the number of boys entitled to free education varied between twenty-five and thirty, depending on those supported by Griffith Hughes's bequest. Any additional pupils had to pay entrance money. The Visitation Return for 1799 illustrates this fact: 'The income amounts to about £60 a year for the education of 30 children — there are about 60 in the school.'[7]

Schoolmasters and Curates

1759–72 Edward Jones, AB, Jesus College, Oxford
1772–86 Evan Morris, AB, St John's College, Cambridge
1786–1824 Robert Saunders, AB, Christ Church, Oxford

Our knowledge of the school is virtually non-existent during the sixty-five years of these schoolmasters. What we do know is that towards the end of this period the vestry meeting was dissatisfied and resolved that 'A Committee be appointed to meet ... to examine the state of the Parish School, the Funds thereof, the number of Boys educated and the Progress they have made in Learning. In order that should it be deemed necessary that a proper representation may be made to the Bishop and other Trustees of the School' and by August 1816 they were prepared to present to the Bishop 'the Petitions relative to the Will of Mr Robinson respecting a Grammar School in Ruabon.'[8] Unfortunately no copy or record of its contents has survived.

However the document had its desired effect and the parishioners and trustees were determined to raise the intellectual level of the school. Two significant steps were taken. The first was the building of a school room by the market place in Park Street, later the Court House, which housed Thomas Madeley's School. He was the parish clerk and was appointed to the office of schoolmaster, charged by the vestry, with providing elementary education. The second significant act was the appointment of another lay person who was capable of providing a grammar school education. The choice fell on George Bagley, aged forty-two years, experienced as a junior under-master of Shrewsbury school under the eminent Dr Butler and for the past six years headmaster of the reputable Hawarden Grammar School which offered 'Instruction in the Classics and every branch of mathematics.'

To the trustees, Bagley appeared to be the right man to restore the status of the school to that of a grammar school with the reputation of being proficient in the classics and mathematics, and the experience of responsibility and teaching in at least two good schools.

The new schoolmaster entered into his office with enthusiasm and began at once to effect improvements to the living accommodation:

George Bagley.

In 1825 Mr Bagley built, at his own expense, a kitchen and brewhouse, with two roomes over them, adjoining the school: the cost was about £200. After his appointment and before he resided he paid an under-master a salary less than was allowed to him by which he saved £50. This went towards building the above rooms, and the remainder he paid by other means...[9]

The numbers in the school 'which would accommodate 81 scholars' appeared to be satisfactory as 'in 1824, he employed two assistants'. The school was still active at the end of 1832 when the vestry 'Ordered — that Mr Bagley be allowed one pound to purchase books for the school boys out of the Nanthir fund.'

The earliest account of Bagley's headmastership is that of the Commissioners for Charitable Endowments in 1837. The report hints at decline and lack of enthusiasm. The emoluments of the school then amounted to £99-18s.:

For this the master considers himself liable to teach 24 boys reading, writing and accounts gratis including six boys clothed, appointed by the vicar, and 12 are placed in the school by the churchwardens, and apprenticed as reported. He is also bound if required, to instruct the boys of the parish gratuitously in the Latin tongue. This, however, did not seem, for some cause or other, to be in high request, there being at the time of the Inquiry only three so taught. For these boys a charge of half a guinea a quarter was made for reading, writing and accompts, with 2s. 6d. or 5s. as entrance money when it can be obtained. The foundation boys are allowed a months holiday at Christmas, and the same at Midsummer.[10]

From the year 1837 onwards, the story of Bagley's tenure of office and its disastrous effect on the school until his eventual resignation in 1853 is a sad one. It may be traced through the evidence provided by the Commissioners Inquiring into the State of Education in Wales conducted in 1847, and from the vestry minutes.

In 1837 the vicar of Ruabon transferred part of the endowments for the education of the poor to the Ruabon Free School. Bagley himself testified to the visiting Commissioner and admitted the utter decline of the school. His evidence shows a complete incompetence and lowering of the standard of the school so that in his time it reached its lowest ebb.

The Commissioner reported in 1847:

I visited the school January 21. I found the school-room, which would accommodate 81 scholars, partly filled with coals, and the remainder used as a lumber-room, being covered with broken chairs and furniture. The glass of the windows was broken, and the room neglected and filthy in the extreme. The lumber and dirt appear to have been accumulating for several months, and except some tattered books without covers in the window seats, there was no vestige of the school which is said to have been once held there.

The master stated that he had been in ill health for several months; that when he commenced school in 1824, he employed two assistants, but that when the school discontinued he was teaching, and had been for some time teaching alone; that within his recollection no one had visited the school; that he had no register to produce, and that no record of the attendance of the scholars had been kept for years. He could give no exact account of the period when his school expired, or of the attendance at that time, but stated that the opening of the schools at Rhosymedre and Rhos Llanerchrugog had drawn off all his scholars. He stated, that when the school was in operation he did not consider himself bound to give anything besides classical instruction gratis, and that for writing and arithmetic a quarterage was paid by all, except a few boys, for whom, to the number of 18 provision is made upon a distinct foundation.

On the other hand, he stated that there are no persons in the neighbourhood at all disposed to give their children a classical education, and that practically the subjects taught in his school have been the same as in the average of Church and British schools in north Wales, the classical instruction having been late confined to such rudiments as are necessary to understand the meaning of English words …

The testimony of the vicar, the Rev R. M. Bonnor, and of the principal Dissenters at Ruabon, concur in proving that for the last six months nothing has been done in the grammar school above mentioned, and that for a long time previously it was utterly useless as a means of instruction; that although it professes to be a grammar school for giving instruction in the classics, it has for years been in the practice upon the same footing as the free school for the poor, the same class of persons sending their children to both; that all the respectable inhabitants are obliged to send their children to Chester or elsewhere in order to be educated; and that the school would not have been kept alive so long but for a collateral fund for clothing, and apprenticing scholars belonging to the school …[11]

The Education Commissioner's report was published in 1847 at the time of the completion of the new National School at the end of Park Street. It took the trustees of the Endowed Grammar School and the vestry over five years to make proposals to the Charity Commission for a scheme of reform. In October 1852 the vestry requested the trustees to grant the headmaster a small retirement pension and

that in consequence of there being three National Schools for educational requirements of the labouring classes this Vestry would deem it greatly for the benefits of the Parish if the Trustees would adopt a scheme for the future Government of the Grammar School which would afford a superior education for a higher class of Boys than those educated in the National School.[12]

Bagley was removed, a suitable replacement was found, and the Charity Commission were approached on the lines suggested by the vestry:

That the school should be restored to its original character of a Grammar School for the education of the Middle Classes and that in future a Schoolmaster in Holy Orders, or a graduate of one of the Universities be preferred … at the same time they would propose (in accordance with the provisions of the Revd. Robinson's Will) that six blue coat boys (supplied as directed out of the Alms House Fund with Coats, Caps, Shoes and Stockings) should be selected from the National Schools of the Parish if such can be found likely to benefit by the Charity & that the Education of these boys in the Grammar School, or in the national schools, (if the Trustees shall see fit to retain them there) should be gratuitous.[13]

The vicar, R. M. Bonnor, made the same point to the Charity Commissioners.

The Poor Children of the Parish have no need of a Grammar School…What parent would send his child to a school where every dirty boy in the Parish might claim an admittance'. He argued that the 'value of the school' will depend upon fees paid 'and will virtually exclude the poorer class and raise this Grammar School above the National Schools of the Parish thereby supplying an Education for the sons of the respectable farmers and Tradesmen'[14]

A. L. Taylor, headmaster 1855–1901.

New trustees were appointed including the diocesan bishop, the rural dean of Wrexham, the vicar of Ruabon, the Honourable Lloyd Kenyon and Sir Watkin. A new headmaster was appointed: Alfred Lee Taylor (b.1827), the son of a Rochdale solicitor educated at Corpus Christi College, Cambridge. When appointed in 1855 he was a layman, but was ordained by the bishop of St Asaph deacon in 1856, and priest in 1857. He was headmaster until 1901. The Charity Commission insisted on Robinson's will being observed which directed that six poor boys chosen from the National School should, as foundation scholars, receive a free education at the Grammar School.

A new school building was urgently required as the Headmaster made clear to the trustees in the summer of 1855:

The number of Day Boys who have attended during the past Half year is five, and I fear that there is little prospect of this number being materially increased in consequence of the unhealthy position of the present School Room…inasmuch as the graves are carried close up to the Premises, and the position of this portion of the church yard renders drainage impracticable, there is a constant saturation through the walls, and moreover in warm weather the effluvia arising therefrom is most obnoxious. I am informed that several persons would most gladly avail themselves of the Educational advantages offered to their sons in the present school, but that they are deterred from so doing by reason of the unhealthiness of the building — and, as regards Boarders, it is quite impossible to think that any Parent would allow his child to remain in a house, the position of which most necessarily be so prejudicial to health — I have already had complaints from the Parents of some of the Boarders I brought with me from Carnarvon, and I can hardly expect that they remain with me much longer … no Master however capable and experienced can ever hope to succeed, when his exertions are constantly thwarted by such insuperable obstacles, as an unhealthy House and School Room.[15]

A solution to the problem was proposed by vicar Bonnor who suggested an exchange with Sir Watkin of the Grammar School farm at the Cinders with a rent of £88 per annum for the new school house, when built, with two or three acres of land around it, and an equivalent in tithe rent charge. This arrangement was accepted by Sir Watkin who provided the required building and a piece of land called weirglodd croes containing 3a-0r-24p.

The school moved to new premises in 1858 and in 1864 was in a thriving condition as shown from the report made by Mr Bompas to the Schools Inquiry Commission.

The new school buildings, 1858.

Day Scholars — 24: three-fourths between 10 and 14 years old; sons of professional men, tradesmen, and artisans; from distances up to two or three miles; pay for drawing, music, and French £6-6s each.

Dancing £4-4s. These subjects optional. General work, parishioners £8, six on foundation are free.

Boarders — 26: of whom three-fourths under 14 years of age; sons of professional men, all in the headmaster's house. Four meals a day; meat once.

Terms for board: under 15, £44-10s, above 15, 50 guineas. Washing, £31-3s.

School bills: highest. £101, average £74, lowest £50. Cubical contents of bedrooms 612 feet per boy. Hours 6.30 to 7.30*am*, 9*pm*.

Instruction, Discipline, &c — Boys on admission must be able to read English fairly.

School classified uniformly by one leading subject. School course modified to suit particular cases. Religious instruction in Bible and Church Catechism. School work begins and ends with prayers taken from Prayer Book.

Promotions by examination.

Examination half-yearly by an examiner selected by head master. A half-holiday given each month to the boy who has gained the greatest number of marks in his class. Prizes of books given once a year.

Corporal punishment not used; impositions inflicted.

New playground 40ft x 70ft recently added, open to all scholars. Field for cricket and football open to all boys on payment of 10s. a year. Boys except elder ones, walk out accompanied by a master.

The following distinctions gained within the last ten years were:

R. B. Kirby, elected to an open Mathematical Scholarship at Caius Coll., Cambridge, 1864.

R. P. Forsham, lst class Local Examinations (Oxford) 1863.

Many of the boys have passed the Cambridge and Oxford Local Examinations.

The comments of Mr Bompas reflect the middle class attitude to education expressed by the Endowed Schools Commission, enforced by the trustees and headmaster in Ruabon, and modified to a certain extent by local circumstances as the following extracts reveal:

The instruction given is an ordinary grammar school education, modified, however, by the wishes of the boys and their parents … there are some boys, who come only for a short time, who do not learn Latin at all, and less than a quarter of the boys learn Greek. Drawing, especially mechanical drawing, is learnt by many of the boys

... the grammar school as at present conducted seems to supply the wants both of those who seek only a commercial education, and of those who wish to prepare for one of the Universities. The boarders are mainly from England, and come to the school mainly from some personal knowledge of and connexion with the head master .... The day scholars are on the average from rather a lower class than the boarders; no distinction however, is made between them, though a small fee is charged for the use of the cricket field, which practically excludes from it some of the boys .... The six free boys, though all of them are poor, are not socially the lowest in the school. It was originally intended to let the free admission to this Grammar School be prizes for the boys in the National or British Schools. This, however, was not found to work well, owing partly to the unwillingness of the masters of the National schools to lose their best pupils, and partly to an unwillingness of the boys in many cases to extend the time of their education — to move to a different school; they are now therefore chosen by the vicar from the boys who he thinks need a grammar school education, but are unable to afford it'.

At the end of his report Mr Bompas paid tribute to the work of the headmaster. The moderate endowment 'has been sufficient to draw to the town the present master, and so to obtain for the neighbourhood a very much better school than would probably in any other case have been found in so small a place.'[16]

A thorough government inspection was conducted in November 1870 by J. L. Hammond, one of the assistants of the Endowed Schools Commission, whose findings were presented to the Trustees in 1872.[17] Under their new scheme for the management of the school, the old trustees were replaced by non-sectarian governors six nominated by the Ruabon School Board and six co-optative governors nominated by the Endowment Commission, who were replaceable only by the authority of the Charity Commissioners. Scholarships were made available by competitive examination. The curricula was reading and spelling, history, writing, geography (political and physical), arithmetic, drawing, the elements of algebra and geometry, vocal music, mensuration and land surveying, natural science, English grammar, composition, and literature, Latin and Greek to be taught as an extra during the present master's tenure of office. Parents had the right of exempting their children 'from attending prayer or religious worship...or from any lesson or series of lessons on a religious subject. The governors were to pay the vicar of Ruabon the annual sum of £12 for a catechetical lecture, as provided by the will of vicar Robinson.

In 1880 Gladstone appointed Lord Aberdare to inquire into higher education in Wales and Monmouthshire. Ruabon School was again under scrutiny and the head, A. L. Taylor, gave evidence to the commission at Bala in November. He stated that there were on average sixty to seventy day boys some of whom came by train from Llangollen and Chirk. They belonged to various religious denominations although 75% were nonconformists. The average number of boarders was twenty, all churchmen. He judged that the school was doing thoroughly good work for the neighbourhood and was becoming more integrated in the local community. He concluded:

> Schools like Ruabon Grammar School are sadly in need of certain things. We have very little funds; the nett endowment is only about £100 a year. The building erected 25 years ago served the times very well then, but now we are behind the times. Fresh buildings are wanted, scholarships are wanted, and so forth ... I think it is doing its best now, but sadly wants those aids'.[18]

The Aberdare Commission's recommendations were implemented in the Welsh Intermediate Education Act of 1889, and Ruabon Grammar School was part of the scheme for Denbighshire Intermediate and Technical Education introduced in 1894, and in June 1896 a new building was opened:

> The first school erected in Wales under the Intermediate Education Act was opened at Ruabon, on Friday ... Although the school is now a County School, the inscription over the entrance hall is the Ruabon Grammar School. The school buildings consist of a schoolroom, 40 feet by 20, a class-room 25 feet by 20, a science demonstration room, 24 feet by 20, and a chemistry and physics laboratory and workshop, 30 feet by 20. The rooms are airy and well ventilated, and are built on the very latest type ...[19]

Ruabon County Boys School, *Absque Labore Nihil*, 1894–1967

Although no longer an endowed school and classified as a County Secondary School, it was still known locally as Ruabon Boys' Grammar School guided by the same headmaster, A. L. Taylor, cherishing the traditions and safeguarding the reputation he had built up over forty-eight years. Taylor's place as

The new Intermediate School, 1896.

headmaster was taken by J. R. Roberts, another inspiring teacher. The school report received in June 1908 noted:

There has been a further increase in the number of pupils — from 72 to 97 and the Headmaster and his Assistants have again had a heavy session.

Previous reports have pointed out the need for extension of buildings, and the further increase in numbers has emphasised the urgency of this need. Two classes are always held in the main Schoolroom, out of which three doors lead towards other classrooms: this arrangement results in noise and great inconvenience. More cupboard accommodation is sadly needed, especially in connection with the Science teaching. There is no system of heating by hot water pipes: the classrooms are warmed by open fireplaces. This, combined with the lack of storage accommodation, makes for dust and dirt. The Science Lecture Room and Laboratory are not as smart and clean as might be wished. But the Laboratory is overcrowded in every sense: it is not easy to warm it, and the practice of keeping a number of gas jets lighted is unhealthy. Woodwork is taken only in Form III, and not even by the whole of this Form. The workshop cannot accommodate the whole of this Form, and it is also used as a cycle shed. There is no Art Room, and Model Drawing is done from flat copies instead of from actual models.

Private and Confidential, and for the Members of the Education Committee only.

Extension of the buildings has been delayed, in the hope of carrying out a project for converting the School into a dual School; but sketch plans have now been prepared for a new Science block, and it is understood that the extension will be carried out in such a way as not to interfere with the later erection of a Girls' Department.[20]

The school report for the session 1915–16 gives the number of pupils on average about 80. It gives the occupations of school leavers:

J. R. Roberts, headmaster 1901–17.   *J. T. Jones, headmaster 1938–53.*

Thirty-two boys left the school during the year. Of these three became elementary school teachers, one a clerk in a county asylum, one a clerk under the Wrexham Union, one a clerk in the office of the Surveyor of Taxes, one a clerk in a merchant's office, three clerks in colliery offices, three bank clerks, one railway clerk, two clerks (general), two medical students, one an ironmonger, one a chemist's apprentice, one a draughtsman, one an engineer, one a draper, one an apprentice to a colliery manager, one a farmer, two became munition workers, two entered a chemical works, and one left the district.

The progress of the war was taking its toll. About 130 old boys joined the army in the first twenty months of the war, and nine of these were killed in action, viz:

> Engineer Captain C. G. Taylor, MVO, HMS *Tiger*,
> Arthur Leslie Pritchard, King's Shropshire Light Infantry
> Dyke Davies, Corporal, Royal Engineers
> Captain De Bel Adams, MC, King's Liverpool Regiment
> Clifford Parry, Corporal, Seaforth Highlanders.
> W. Stanley Jones, Royal Field Artillery
> R. Lund
> Leonard Shirley, Canadian Expeditionary Force
> W. Sparling

A tablet was erected in the schoolroom to the memory of Captain Taylor. The design of the tablet was the work of the celebrated architect, W. C. Caroe — himself an old boy of the school, — and the cost was borne by those who were Captain Taylor's contemporaries in the school. Mr R. A. Jones was the originator of the movement, and deserves the thanks of the school, for securing for it a precious memorial of one of its most notable old boys.

It is to be hoped that when the war ends, the question of adequate buildings will be immediately taken up by the Governors, and carried through as speedily as possible.[21]

J. R. Roberts left in 1917, on his appointment as headmaster at Cardiff High School, and was succeeded by the Reverend D. J. Bowen, who retired as head in 1938. In the meantime in 1926–27 laboratories and classrooms were added at a cost of £8,850, and major extensions and a remodelling of the school took place between 1938 and 1941.

J. T. Jones was headmaster 1938–53, and was succeeded by R. R. Pearce from 1953–64. The last headmaster from 1965 until the the establishment of Ysgol Rhiwabon in 1967 was Eifion Ellis who later became the principal of Yale VI Form College in Wrexham.[22]

Eifion Ellis, headmaster 1965–72

II Ruabon County Secondary School For Girls 1922–67 (From 1945 Ruabon Grammar School for Girls) — *Goreu Trysor Enw Da*

Secondary education for girls was not available in Ruabon until 1922, twenty-eight years after control had passed to the Denbighshire Education Committee. Girls had to travel either to Llangollen or Wrexham to enjoy this advantage. But it was regarded as implicit in the building of the Boys School in 1896 that a dual school for boys and girls would be centred on the Ruabon site. This was proposed in 1905, when it was alleged that 'many girls from this district are at present debarred from secondary education as the travelling expenses are formidable to people of small means', and it was resolved that a special committee attend at Ruabon to hold a public inquiry. Their proposals were defeated in committee, and nothing was done for another ten years when once again a decision for providing additional accommodation at the Boys School was deferred until a scheme had been approved for boys and girls.

Pressure for the extension of secondary education in other parts of Denbighshire in 1919 highlighted the fact that Ruabon was a neglected area, and protests were made. In March Cefn Mawr Parish Council proposed to the Education Committee 'that a separate County School for Girls, and not a dual school should be established at Ruabon as soon as possible.' Rhosllanerchrugog Parish Council forwarded a resolution of 15 July passed at a mass meeting of Hafod, Bersham and Vauxhall coal miners, opposing the proposal to build the school at Ruabon'... such a school should be erected at Rhos, which is the most populous part of the Ruabon area'. A letter was received by the Education Committee from the governors of the Llangollen County School deploring the possibility of losing Ruabon Girls because they had erected 'a new Science and Arts Department at a considerable cost which has placed these School Governors in a very serious position'.In June 1919 the matter was brought by a deputation to the Board of Education in Whitehall. Here 'it was stated that local feeling at Ruabon ran very high in the matter, and that in the recent local elections the votes were given on this very issue. The population of the Ruabon District is now 25,000, of which number 7/8 are within two miles of the school. There are 200 boys and girls to be provided for. Wrexham County School had to close its doors. Fares were too heavy, and miners on that account actually had to withdraw their girls from that school.' By November 1919 a meeting of the Education Sub-Committee held at the Boys County School Ruabon, came to a firm decision to build a new girls County Secondary School: stating, that Ruabon was the most convenient site for the district as a whole: that a suitable site can be found on land belonging to the County School: that the proposed new school should be a separate Girl's School with a separate head teacher and that temporary buildings should be erected, and that accommodation should be provided in the first instance for 180 pupils.[23]

It was the temporary nature of the buildings which was to influence the character of Ruabon County Girls Secondary School for most of its lifetime. The crude limitations of the site demanded rugged endurance, indomitable leadership, and a spirit of determination and adventure from staff and girls alike. The school was established on a shoe-string, at a cost of £7,000 for the buildings. A modest rent was charged for the site on land belonging to the Boys County School which was part of the endowment of the former Ruabon Grammar School Foundation.

Three huts formed the basis for the new school opened in 1922. W. D. Wiles, the County Architect, reported in July 1920 that it was impossible 'to obtain any second hand army huts' and 'the type of building recommended for erection is that similar to the American Red Cross hutments constituted entirely of wood lined with 'beaver board' all built with standardised sections.

Two of the huts provided two blocks of building '111 ft long by 21 ft wide each divided to form three class rooms and a folding partition is arranged in each block between two of the classrooms, that may be opened, converting two of the classrooms into use as an assembly room giving accommodation for 30 students in each, making the total classroom accommodation 180. There is also provided in each block ... cloakroom accommodation, a store and a teacher's room'. These plans were forwarded to the Board of Education in Whitehall for approval. The Board suggested that a third building should be erected to give instruction in domestic subjects for girls which would be available for the elementary schools in the district, This became the third hut on the site. The Board of Education suggested covered awnings to the latrines:

> I am directed to point out that in Secondary Schools for Girls it is the practice for the pupils to change into indoor shoes and it is very desirable that in wet weather they should not be obliged to go out of doors to reach the offices.

To which the County Architect retorted:

> With regard to the question of pupils changing into indoor shoes, this School is in Ruabon, and not in a high class suburban district. I know the class of students that will attend this school, and I don't see there is any hardship in passing a few yards to the conveniences without cover. From observation, the only time shoes are likely to be changed is for physical culture and not always then.

Work went on steadily in 1921 in the preparation of the site, the architect observing that 'the quantity of soil that has had to be removed because of the cutting through of the Offa's Dyke, has been rather more formidable than I had anticipated.' In May 1922 the architect was 'empowered to tar asphalt the ground space between the two huts, also in front of the cookery and laundry room, and that wire net guards be erected to

The Girls' County Secondary School buildings.

the side windows of each as a protection necessary on account of the ground space between the huts being utilised for tennis.'

The school buildings were opened on the last Wednesday in September 1922 by Mrs Margaret Lloyd George, the wife of the great First World War Prime Minister.[24] The new headmistress, Miss A. G. Gower Jones, was there to greet her, together with Alderman R. A. Jones, Chairman of the School Governors, and other dignitaries. Mrs Lloyd George was presented with bouquets of carnations and roses, and to mark the occasion a rhododendron was planted. It was an occasion the people of Ruabon rejoiced in and the children from the council and church schools were lined up to greet her en route. The newspaper account reported rather uncertainly that 'there are between 50 and 60 pupils.'

The first headmistress went on to Grove Park in 1925, and her successor, Miss Mary Jones, was chosen out of twelve applicants. By 1929 there were 159 pupils on the register with 7 teachers. By 1940 the figure was 226, to climb to 271 in 1946, and 368 in 1959.

Weeks after the school was opened, the question of shared facilities between the Boys and Girls Schools was raised. Should the Boys School science laboratory be used for the instruction of both boys and girls? No, was the answer given by the headmaster and headmistress, and that the Girls School be immediately provided with the necessary equipment. From the very beginning the building was inadequate, and a fourth hut was added in 1928: a room size 40' x 30' for the purpose of a dining room, assembly hall, gymnasium, etc. and an annexe kitchen fitted up for the preparation of mid-day meals; a staff retiring room and two form rooms.' The work was carried out by W. F. Humphreys & Co. of Acrefair, at a cost of £2,537.

Further representations were made to the County Education Committee in 1934.

Ann Crewe, Audrey Higgins and Pam Wilkinson.

The opening of the Girls' County School, September 1922. Dame Margaret Lloyd George holds bouquets. Seated either side of her are Alderman and Mrs R. A. Jones. The headmistress, Miss A. G. Gower Jones, is seated wearing a 'mortar-board' hat.The Rev D. J. Bowen, headmaster of the Boys School, is standing in the centre of the back row.

   The headmistress made a statement with regard to the need for new permanent buildings. The accommodation of the present buildings was inadequate for the number of pupils attending the school; they were too hot in summer and very cold in winter, and owing to the lack of room, particularly in the laboratories, the staff and pupils were severely handicapped. The domestic subjects room was inadequate for the needs of the school, especially in view of the fact that it was also used as a centre for children from elementary schools. The cloakroom accommodation was unsatisfactory and altogether inadequate. The Governors present also expressed their opinion, and stress was laid on the fact that the girls were handicapped owing to the lack of laboratory accommodation; for instance, it was now impossible for a girl from the school to have the requisite preliminary instruction to enable her to become a qualified domestic subjects mistress.

   During the discussion it was pointed out by the members of the sub-committee, that the time was not opportune for pressing the matter for permanent buildings, and the Governors decided to ask the Education Committee to provide, with as little delay as possible, two form rooms and two laboratories on a new site to form the nucleus of a new permanent building.[25]

Two things happened as a result of these representations. Anticipating delay from the county council, the school governors found extra accommodation at the beginning of 1935 in the school-room of the English Congregational Church, half a mile down the hill, at a rental of 15s-6d per week including cleaning. The 1858 school buildings were also used.

The second achievement was the county authorities acceptance in principle of a scheme for new buildings for the Girls School, although during the financial year 1937/8 it was placed number twelve out of thirteen in order of priority. In January 1938 the Education Committee appointed members to consider plans for the new school and a decision with regard to phase one and as a preliminary, visited new secondary schools in Lancashire and Cheshire. These plans were rejected as being excessive, and once again the school governors were driven to temporary expedients suggesting that the sports pavillion required for the playing field should be erected at once and adapted for use as a temporary classroom. They obtained permission to purchase the geography room for not more than £150 from the Boys School which ironically was being taken down at the beginning of their building programme of £20,000. The outbreak of the Second World War in September 1939 meant an inevitable postponement.

Mrs Renée Giller, both pupil and teacher, has contributed the following memories.

Speech Day, 13 July 1938.
L–R: W. H. Evans (HMI); Evan Jenkins; Sir Watkin Williams Wynn; Miss Mary Jones (Headmistress); Dr. Geoffrey Fisher (Bishop of Chester – later Archbishop of Canterbury); Mrs T. W. Jones (Chairman of the Governors).

The School Buildings

There were six wooden huts in 1939. The largest was painted green, and housed the assembly hall, two small classrooms, and two small additional rooms. The hall had a raised platform in one corner, used as a stage for assemblies, eisteddfods, examination invigilation, and dinnertime supervision. The hall, as well as being used for assemblies, was the Central Welsh Board and Higher examinations hall, the dining hall, the music room and the gym, with climbing rails along the two long walls. Time-tabling needed juggling. The two small classrooms at the back had a dividing screen and a small cloakroom. The two rooms at the other end were small and used variously as a staff room, storeroom, and for cooking school dinners.

Parallel to the hall was a smaller white hut which housed the cookery/needlework room and larder, with two smaller rooms used as a pan storeroom and a physical education store. This was the hut where in addition to domestic science teaching, cold lunches were eaten. In this room there were three long tables, a shorter demonstration table, two gas cookers, three electric cookers, a gas boiler, and an open fire.

The remaining three huts were around the tennis court with Offa's Dyke making the fourth boundary. The smallest hut was the toilet block. The two largest huts faced each other across the length of the tennis court. One had two classrooms, the headmistress' study, and the staff room. The fifth hut housed the chemistry laboratory, a classroom, and another classroom, which was converted into a biology laboratory. A small room provided the sixth-form science work room, and a corridor cupboard contained the school library which opened at lunchtime. Joint arrangements were made for girls taking chemistry and physics at Higher School Certificate level to go to the Boys School laboratories, and for boys taking Latin at this level to be taught in Miss Ethel Wood's classroom. A later addition in 1938 was the 'hut on the field', lit by gas, and used at various times for art, science, and commercial subjects.

A survival from the 1858 endowed Grammar School was the School House. This was separate from the Girls School and was approached by means of a path alongside the gym and by crossing the boys yard. It was a stone building used mainly by the sixth form. On the ground floor was a large boardroom with an open fire and desks for about thirty pupils. There were three other smaller rooms used by the sixth-form for commercial subjects. A storeroom led to the cellar. This was out of bounds but nevertheless used by some of the adventurous girls who enjoyed a quiet cigarette. A flight of stairs led directly to the bathroom, which had a hole in the ceiling with buckets on the floor to collect the rainwater. There were three other smallish rooms on this floor used by sixth-form arts pupils. One of these was designated the 'Silence Room' for the use of scholars to pursue their studies. The other two rooms were form rooms and general study areas. For some time after 1935, English lessons were given in the Congregational Chapel on the hill which we shared with the mice. And all this time, despite the war the talk was of 'the new school'.

The layout of the school meant that we were never short of fresh air and exercise! In all weathers we tramped from building to building for each time table change. Eight lessons per day in a five-day week.

School Life

Welsh was a compulsory subject for year one only, after which it was a choice with French. For competitive activities there were four houses — Glyndwr, Madoc, Offa and Wynnstay — later reduced to three when Glyndwr pupils were divided between the other three. The annual Sports Day and Eisteddfod, inter-house hockey and rounder's matches, were opportunities for keen but friendly rivalry, and there was never difficulty in getting teams and supporters for Saturday matches.

School uniform was a green-pleated gym slip, long-sleeved white blouse, red and green striped blazer, navy gaberdine coat, velour hat with band and badge, and black shoes and black woollen stockings. The uniform could be obtained locally or from a Lancashire supplier. In 1939–40 first years were allowed to wear ankle socks in summer. Despite clothes rationing and difficulty in obtaining some garments, the uniform was never abused and was worn with the pride we felt for our school.

Ruabon Girls Grammar School (as it was called after 1945) was a very happy school, small enough for staff to recognise the needs of the pupils, and for pupils to respect their peers and their elders. Discipline was firm but friendly. We had an all-female staff for most of the time, though we finally shared an art master with the Boys.

From 1939–45 this was a school in a country at war, but although we accommodated a small number of private evacuees, we were not greatly affected. We had to carry our gas masks, and for air raid practice we had to proceed initially to lie under the hedges on Offa's Dyke and by the brook at Tyn-yr-agi, and later to crowd under one of the staircases in the boys school. There was one genuine air raid, which was scary. One of the highlights of the war years was the distribution of bars of chocolate from time to time. We also had concerts twice a year given by the Bangor Trio. The Head Girl was nominated by the teaching staff and headmistress and second year sixth form girls were prefects.

The headmistress from 1925–52 was Miss Mary Jones, MA, a graduate in history. She was of severe appearance, but with a smile which lit up her face and betrayed a very warm heart. In her black gown and on special occasions wearing her 'mortarboard', she cut an impressive figure. But in later years, as her health declined, the 'mortarboard' was replaced with a balaclava helmet and, retaining her dignity, she was followed by a pupil 'page' who ceremoniously carried her footstool and cushion. Quite naturally she was a true eccentric, although this was more obvious to her staff than her pupils. The permutations of time-tabling was at times problematical, with Tuesday afternoon's lessons being replaced by those of Monday morning. In this *Alice in Wonderland* atmosphere it was not unusual for question one on the English examination paper, delivered to the class room on a small piece of paper, to be — multiply 1234 x 1234 — with the direction to await for question two.

When she resigned in 1952, it was minuted 'the Governors are convinced that generations of pupils had benefited by her personal integrity and fine moral example, and her unstinted and almost selfless service to the school and the parish had been a vital factor in the development of the school.'

She was very well loved and even now when groups of her former staff meet, the conversation drifts to 'do you remember when she said this, or when she said that.' She lived near the school at Maes y coed with her younger sister Anna, who was the school meals organiser for the county.

Major changes took place in secondary education brought about by the Butler Education Act in 1944. School fees were abolished in April 1945. In 1946 there was a recommendation made by the Local Education Authority Reconstruction Committee to amalgamate the Boys and Girls schools. This was turned down, and the Governors continued the petition for the erection of the

Prefects, 1945–6.
Back row: Anne Jones; Brenda Clayton; Mair D. Jones; Dorothy M. Tomlinson; O. Jean Crewe; Pearl M. Evans.
Front row: Sheila E. Davies; Margaret Howard; Marjorie E. Harrison; Renée Topping; Barbara Trevor Jones. Prefects not photographed: Margaret E. Williams and Mair E. Humphreys.

Speech Day, 1954.
Front row: Glyn Simon, Bishop of
Llandaff with his wife, Sheila (née
Roberts) a former pupil of the school;
Miss Ethel Woods, headmistress, is
second from the right.
Back row: R. R. Pearce, headmaster of
the Boys School, on the left;
Archdeacon and Mrs Jones-Perrott,
third and fourth from the right.

long-promised new school building.

In these years the Old Pupils Association continued to flourish with an active drama group and a choir. Miss Mary Jones retired in August, 1952, and was succeeded by Miss Ethel Wood, classics teacher at the school from the late 1920s. Born at Cefn Mawr in 1904 and educated at Grove Park and the University of College of North Wales, Bangor she was highly respected as a first-class teacher and administrator.

Out of school she was an active member of Ebenezer Baptist Church, Cefn Mawr, and Secretary to the Baptist Union in North Wales, the League of Friends of the Wrexham Maelor Hospital, and a member and representative of other organisations. Both in ability and temperament she was the ideal person to steer the school through its many changes during her headship from 1952–1968.

Early in 1953 building work was actually started! The first phase consisted of canteen, library, science laboratories, the cookery room, and medical room. By 1954 there were lunch time crocodiles of pupils being escorted along Tatham Road and Penycae Road to the new canteen. At other times less structured groups proceeded to the new block for lessons, and 'library periods' were introduced. The building of the rest of the school followed fairly quickly, made easier by the use of pre-cast structures with the Assembly Hall — Gym — Examination Hall — Music Room still shared, class rooms and sports areas.

In 1961, the long hutments introduced as a temporary measure in 1922 were disposed of. One was transferred to the Boys School playing field, and the second was allocated to the Girls School to provide playing accommodation during dinner hours on wet days. On 9 January 1962, the school moved into the new buildings, and Miss Mary Jones and Miss Gwladys Jones former deputy head, attended the first morning service. The 'Miss Mary Jones Organ' was installed in May 1964. At this time of the redevelopment of the site, the 1858 School House was demolished and the space used as a collection area for pupils travelling by bus.

The school built up a reputation for extra-mural activities. There was an outstanding production of one of the York Nativity Plays by Mrs Dan Jones and Mrs Lottie Williams Parry during the 1950s. The first production was in Ruabon parish church, and subsequently in the churches at Chirk and Johnstown, Cefn Baptist church and finally and gloriously in St Asaph Cathedral. The very successful second Ruabon Guide Company and Sea Rangers continued until Miss Melvin's retirement in 1958. A number of guides and rangers represented Wales at international celebrations.

Once again in 1964 the recommendation that the two schools be amalgamated was put forward and at a special meeting of the governors on 19 January 1965 the resolution was accepted 'that the Governors of the Ruabon Grammar School are agreed on the principle of establishing bilateral schools and abolishing the eleven-plus examination, but believe that it is impracticable to establish at Ruabon a bilateral school of the size envisaged by the Education Committee.' Nevertheless it was decided in 1966 that a comprehensive school of about 1,600 pupils be established at Ruabon with no change in the present catchment area, and that it be constituted as soon as possible. It was agreed that there be a joint headship between Mr Eifion Ellis and Miss Ethel Wood 1967/8, and the headship to revert to Mr Eifion Ellis on Miss Wood's retirement in 1968.

*Girls Grammar School Staff, 1957.
Back row: Alan Williams; Margaret Barlow; Megan Leyshon; Rosa Williams; Frances Mercer; Joyce Margison; Olwen Thomas; Dorothy Barnes; Irene Topping.
Front row: Betty Hughes Jones; Ethel Wood; Malayan student; Malayan student; Alice Moorhouse; Mary Saunders; Kath Ambrose; Linda Norton.*

Miss Ethel Wood left her mark on the school. Although it was in existence for a comparatively short period from 1922–67, she had been a member of staff for most of that time. She inspired both awe and devotion in her staff and pupils. The high standards she set others were demonstrated in herself. She was a very fair head, quick to give praise where it was due, but very firm. Miss Wood did not tolerate lapses in effort or appearance, especially as far as uniform was concerned. In her own person she was small, elegant, dignified, but with an intelligent awareness, sense of humour, and unfailing presence in any company.

Ysgol Rhiwabon 2000

Ysgol Rhiwabon is an 11–18 co-educational comprehensive school with 570 students currently on roll. There are four forms of entry, with 90 students in the sixth form.

The School Environment

At the beginning of the third millennium the school environment is better than ever. Though the school is split-site, 85% of teaching takes place on the upper-school site. The school has already benefited from a major LEA remodelling programme. Planning permission has been obtained and drawings are complete for sports hall, drama and music facilities, and a new library, which will bring it onto one site. All classrooms have been refurnished within the last five years, and have been carpeted. The school regards the teaching environment as important, and pupil's work is on regular display.

Internal Organisation

During the last three years there has been a review of many of the beliefs and practices, and a range of new or revised policy documents has resulted.

All departments produce an annual development plan, which is structured around target-setting, governors, parents and pupils are included in the process. Staff meet regularly to discuss whole-school issues, as well as in subject and pastoral teams.

The school has a senior management team consisting of the head, one deputy and three senior teachers. The curriculum management structure is departmental; the pastoral structure is horizontal.

Head Teachers

1967–68	Eifion Ellis and Ethel Wood
1968–72	Eifion Ellis
1972–88	Elwyn Roberts
1988–92	Brenda Boydell
1992–	John Mackay

III Elementary Education

It was not until the 1840s that the main foundations for lasting elementary education were made for the community of Ruabon. Previous to this attempts were made to establish elementary schools. Two of these were precursors of the National School established in 1848.

Lady Harriet's School

Lady Harriet Williams Wynn was the daughter of the fourth baronet. Her school is first mentioned in 1809 when it is described as a charity school for girls in Ruabon, at which 20 girls are taught to read, sew etc.[26] In 1836 it was described as being kept at a cottage near the lodge, and supported entirely by Sir Watkin who gave the mistress £35 a year.[27] In 1839 there were 43 girls in the school divided into 3 classes, no ages are given. There is an itemized account of 'articles made: sheets, napkins, knife clothes, dusters, plate clothes, pillow cases, petticoats and hemming and darning.'[28] The Education Commissioners reported in 1847 that there were 53 scholars, fees 1d per week, subjects taught: the scriptures and church catechism, reading, writing and arithmetic. When the school was examined in January there were 13 scholars present who were mostly ignorant of the scriptures, 'four could repeat the Church Catechism correctly, but this was their only attainment. The mistress has never been trained to teach. She gives instruction in knitting and sewing .... The vicar informed me that the progress of the children is very unsatisfactory; that the mistress is continually bringing complaints of their misconduct; and that she appears to want both method of teaching and natural disposition for the management of children. There is no other school for girls in the town of Ruabon.'[29]

Thomas Madeley's School

This was the name given to the elementary school built by the parish in 1824 on land belonging to Sir Watkin in Park Street. This building became the Court House when the school was closed in 1848 at the opening of the National School. It was built by public subscription, of which £137 was raised.[30] The subscribers were the main estate owners: the Williams Wynn family, Lord Kenyon, Frederick West, Edward Lloyd Williams, Simon Yorke and Thomas Griffiths. The carriage of materials was done without charge by the parishioners. The parish had requested on 17 Feb. 1824 Simon Yorke's permission 'to build a National School on the vacant ground between the blacksmith's shop and Connah's cow house.' He agreed but the parishioners changed their minds.[31]

Thomas Madeley (1787–1861) was a son of Sir Watkin's chief huntsman and, as a young man, was apprenticed to a chemist in London but, because of his delicate health, obtained employment as a gardener. About 1820, he was stated to be a schoolmaster at the Pentre near Rhos y Madoc and removed to Ruabon and kept school in a room near Dr R. C. Roberts and sons surgery in the High Street, Ruabon. It was this school which moved to Park Street in 1824. Madeley held many parish offices, sexton, vestry clerk, secretary to the Association for the Prosecution of Felons, secretary to the Reading Room and Library, and surveyor of the Highways. In the old coaching days, Madeley was a booking clerk.

The school was described in 1837 as 'a very good lofty room built of stone, and well situated by the Market Place.'[32] The evidence he gave in 1842 on the Report of the Employment of Young People is informative:

> [Madeley] Has kept school at Ruabon for 18 years; has every year about 100 boys at school from 6 to 14 years of age, they are the sons of farmers, handicraftsmen, and farming labourers; has none of the sons of colliers or forgemen. He charges 1d a week for teaching reading, 2d for reading and writing, and 3d for reading, writing and arithmetic... There is a penny a month subscription library here, the books have been bought by subscription, in the first place of the gentry and others, and is kept up by the penny subscription; the books are lent out; there are about 200 volumes of useful religious, and entertaining books, and about 60 monthly subscribers of 1d each; they are much read, especially in winter. None of the colliers or miners subscribe. There are several schools in and about Ruabon, but the colliers and miners take no advantage of them. [Madeley] is sure that education has a good tendency among the lower orders; from experience of long standing 'can say that it gives them a greater feeling of independence and propriety of conduct; and that marching children to places of worship from the school, all walking in order, gives them ideas of reverence and decorum which are apt to remain with them hereafter'[33]

Madeley's School, Park Street (1824). Now the Constitutional Club.

Five years later, in January 1847, the Education Commissioners reported that there were 35 scholars and in addition to the 3 Rs the church catechism was taught. The Commissioner, Mr John James, did not think highly of Madeley's abilities.

The master has never received any kind of training ... the school continues as it was originally, a second-rate private adventure school. There are no traces of improved method in his mode of teaching; his classes are ill arranged, and there is not a child competent to be employed as a monitor ... Although the school is called a free school, the master does not profess to teach any pupils gratuitously. The usual payments are required from the pupils, and the master alone is benefited by the endowment.[34]

Madeley was not as dumb as the Commissioners made out. Wynnstay accounts record — '1843 Feb 8 T. Madeley. Contribution towards instruments for the school band £9'. This was either contrary to or ignored the Report of the Charity Commissioners of 1837 who reported that 'twenty boys are selected from the parish at large, who are taught reading, writing and accompts free.'

Ruabon National School (Now St Mary's Church in Wales School).

The first plinth stone of the National School was laid 13 September 1846 and the school opened on 1 February 1848. The cost of the building was £1,600. The Wynnstay accounts reveal that Benjamin Gummow built the 1824 school (later the Court House), and his son Michael the 1848 National School. Sir Watkin paid £200 for the Court House, and subscribed £250 to the National Schools. In 1854 an infant school was added at a further cost of £245. The school was subsequently enlarged on two occasions. A new school on the same site was opened in June 1976.

The school was built on land bordering on the Overton-Ruabon road. Simon Yorke of Erddig voluntarily conveyed the land of 3r-20p to the Reverend R. M. Bonnor and his successors. The first report we have for the school is for 1851:

... two Pupil Teachers and two new candidates passed creditable examinations ... The schools were found to have made fair progress since the last examination, and although there is much room for improvement, especially with respect to the girls, no pains have been spared by the master to render the school as efficient as possible, both in discipline and the mental and moral improvement of his pupils. A ladies committee has been appointed to superintend the sewing school. Boys on the books 89. Girls on the books 92. Average attendance 144.

The Lending Library was in the charge of Mr Humphries, the schoolmaster, 'who attends at the school after service on Sunday afternoon to exchange the books'. The Reading Room, established in 1850, was described as 'an important institution as connected with education, and the mental and moral improvement of the neighbourhood.' It was held in one of the school classrooms every evening from 6 till 10 and on Saturday from 4 to 9. There was a library and a daily paper. The subscription was 6s per annum.

The school was financed by means of annual subscriptions, donations, rents from schoolhouses, *etc.* The income for the year 1851 was £129-18s-1d of which £20 10s. came from local charitable endowments, the chief of which was the Griffith Hughes, Tai Nant, bequest of £18. The expenditure with a balance in hand of 6s-11d was spent mainly on salaries.

Mr Humphreys schoolmaster £50*pa*, and three quarters salary 'To Mrs Hughes late Miss Gittins £13-2s-6d'.[35]

Ruabon National School log books[36]

In the log books of the National School which begin in 1863 we have a continuous record of its varying fortunes which illuminate the local community it struggled to educate. An examination of the twenty years, 1863–84, will serve to illustrate this.

It was the period of 'payment by results'. If the government inspectors thought the school had done badly, the government grant was decreased accordingly. A sad business, for upon this grant depended the salaries of the staff. The log books are full of information — curricula, behaviour, staff relationships, the fabric, visitors, the weather, social conditions, epidemics, local events, *etc.* — all are meticulously entered in their season. In these pages we see the great change in method and outlook which has taken place in the past hundred years.

The visit of Her Majesty's Inspectors was the judgement day and a bad report often meant that the headmaster would lose heart and resign, for upon their report, depended the government grant. Mr James Allot, the first headmaster to keep the log book, greatly improved the standard of education. He was succeeded by Mr W. Garratt-Jones, whose first report in February 1870 was most encouraging.

> The boys are in excellent order and have passed a very creditable examination. Some of the geography papers were very well done. Religious knowledge is imparted with care and judgement. Mr Jones deserved praise for the improvement he has effected in this school. If as much progress is made next year, I shall be able to pronounce the School in all respects excellent.

No: presented	93	Passed in Reading	92
		do. Writing	90
		do. Arithmetic	91
		Examined in Geography	23

In the 1870s there were frequent staff changes. Mr Garratt-Jones left, and the new headmaster Evan Williams resigned in 1875, to be succeeded by Mr Mascall. The inspectors reported in 1876 that if the school was to thrive, 'a better staff must be provided for it'. 'This school can hardly be said to be doing satisfactorily.' The logbook noted in April 1877, 'Master completed his time and left for the scene of his future employment and labours.' John Parr was the unfortunate successor. The Inspectors report for 1877 was sharp in its criticism:

> Results of examination deplorable. But I fully expect better things from Mr Parr. Order needs attention. Singing commendable. The rooms have a musty smell and untidy appearance. The floor should be washed every fortnight — and the windows cleaned once a month. Some of the old maps might be renewed with advantage. A few bright pictures would help to make the rooms look cheerful. A few more desks are needed.

Mr Parr did his work well and 'affected a praiseworthy change in the attainments of the scholars of this school.' The situation once again lapsed under Parr's successor: '1884, Aug. 13. No School, Owen drunk.'

The attendance at school during this period averaged about one hundred, and the schoolmaster was helped by pupil teachers and monitors. This was before a pupil-teacher centre was opened and the headmaster was entirely responsible for their training. Sometimes they were censored in the log book: 'Jones' class very noisy and disorderly —spoke to him about it.' (1862)

The National School (1848).
Now demolished.

Mr Garratt-Jones on his appointment in 1869 allowed his pupil teachers the privilege of marking the class registers, and gave them instruction before morning school between 7–8*am*. The inspectors warned in 1872, 'the pupil-teachers must materially improve.'

The unsuccessful Mr Mascall when he commenced school, in 1875, 'appointed two monitors at one shilling per week each & gave them private lessons.'

Curricula

In the early days the curricula was determined by the government policy of payment by results. A successful examination in the three Rs earned a considerable bonus payment to the school. For example in 1871.

No: presented 95	Passed in reading	90
	do writing	86
	do arithmetic	87
Govt. grant	do	£20-4s-0d
Examination		£35-1s-4d
Standard VII		£ 2-0s-0d
Geography		£ 8-0s-0d
		£65-5s-4d

If candidates were to give a creditable performance it was necessary to eradicate copying.

> Examined the 2nd Class in arithmetic thus: Gave each boy a different sum from that of his neighbour, to do, instead of giving out the same sum to all. I found a very small proportion correct. Copying is carried on to a much greater extent than I supposed. (1863)

In an effort to stimulate the intelligent child the reading of newspapers was introduced in 1863 but with little result — 'the 1st Class make but little progress.'

With the imperialist sentiments of the age, geography was a favourite subject of the examiners and map drawing and physical geography were taught from 1868/9.

If the school was not judged proficient in the three Rs, additional subjects were sternly discouraged.

> With the present staff grammar, geography & history had better be left alone until the children acquire a fair proficiency in reading, writing & arithmetic. (1876 Report).

Sometimes a subject was introduced with a view to educating the parents: 'sanitation prepared as a home lesson.' (1870). Religious instruction and the teaching of the catechism had primacy of place in the curricula of the National Schools and there was a close link, which is still maintained, between the parish church and the school. There were frequent visits of the parish clergy who gave regular instruction, and in 1875 the Bishop of St Asaph, Dr Joshua Hughes, questioned the 1st and 2nd classes in 'historical portions of the Old Testament.' On saints' days, and when there was a confirmation service, the children attended. The diocesan inspector made his annual examination. The school was a natural recruiting ground for the church choir, and the school was used for divine worship when the church was extensively restored 1870–2. But, no matter how much religious instruction they receive, 'boys will be boys'. The log book was a 'black book' recording every prank. 'Complaints made today about the school children robbing fruit gardens.' 'Many boys absented themselves from school to witness a fire. Cautioned them.' 'A boy ran out of school to escape punishment for fighting.'

Frequent entries complain of the boy's personal habits. 'Many boys came late and dirty.' 'Had to keep many boys in school for uncleanliness.' It is not surprising that disease was prevalent and school attendance diminished by epidemics. 'William Jones, a fourth class boy, died of scarlet fever.' ... 'Small pox and measles prevalent in the district, especially Rhos.' 1864. 'Dismissed the school on Thursday morning, drains cleared, closets emptied, *etc.*'

Attendance and distraction

The log books give a picture of the social life of the period. Every month was marked by an event which provided either a school treat or lead to poor attendance. A holiday was provided for the Ruabon fairs in

February, May and November, and the Ruabon Wakes in August. Cefn fair in June, Rhos fair in November, and the Wrexham fairs in March and October, could hardly be resisted. In August 1886 it was recorded: 'Aug. 5. Registers not marked this afternoon. Only one boy present at 2.15 the time for marking registers, owing to a circus in Ruabon.'

Many of the school children supplemented the family budget by helping in the harvest. 'April. The attendance of the children at this time of the year is rather irregular in consequence of their being employed in planting potatoes.' 'July. Thin school. Many children working in the hay field.' 'November. Attendance very poor today owing to a large number of boys being beaters for Gentlemen pheasant shooting.'

Poverty and industrial disputes also affected attendances. '1882. Dec 22. The attendance has suffered very much this year. Owing in the first place to 'strikes' and the bad state of trade and secondly from the weather, which has been very inclement during the last three months.'

The Williams Wynn family took a great interest in the school and there are many entries which speak of their generosity to the school:

> School treat. Children visit to Wynnstay.
> Half holiday to prepare for Lady Wynn's treat.
> Dinner given to the children by Lady Williams Wynn.

There was always the unexpected to surprise and delight the children especially if it meant release from school.

> 1878 Aug. 20 — School closed this afternoon owing to the review of Rifle Corps in park.
> 1863 — The school children were admitted free to the exhibition of the panorama of South Africa.
> 1863 Mar. 9 — Holiday — the joiners in school putting up tables for a tea to the children on the Prince of Wales' Wedding Day.

From the time of its foundation in 1847, the Ruabon National School had been influenced by the government's educational policy. One of the landmarks was the School Board Act of 1870, another the Welsh Intermediate Act of 1889, and the introduction of free education in 1891. Elementary schools were provided in other districts of the old parish of Ruabon. '1865 June 9th. Many Rhos boys have left school during the week, a new British School being opened at Rhos to which they have gone. Better facilities were provided for the training of teachers and a centre opened for the instruction of pupil teachers. By the end of the 19th century there had been a great step forward.

The 20h Century

Two log books cover this period. The first from 1895–1940: unfortunately the second does not cover the war, and only contains entries from 1946–85. These give some indication of the nature of the school building before it was demolished in the 1970s.

A new classroom was added in 1895. 1895 4 Feb. A rummage sale and an American bazaar in aid of the building funds for the new classroom. 1895 6 Aug. The recess in the Boy's School has been boarded off during the holidays on account of the building operations. 1896 4 Mar. Small classroom abandoned in consequence of new room being available.

In 1899 a letter from the Education Department stated that the accommodation of the school is not recognised as sufficient for:

Boys	185	185 present
Girls	149	204
Infants	75	135
Total	409	524

The school was remodelled in 1903 and described in 1948:

> It consists of seven rooms, three of them large ones, together with cloakrooms for boys, girls and infants. There is ample accommodation for the number of pupils now attending, but improvements to heating, lighting, cloakroom and sanitary arrangements, as well as to the playground will be necessary in order to meet modern

requirements. There are 142 pupils on the register, of these more than half are in the nursery and infant classes... They are organised into six classes.

The 20th century log book entries are in chronological order to evoke the period referred to and 'the march of progress.'

Chapel trips always denuded the school attendance and it was wise to play safe:

1895 8 July — The vicar allowed a holiday because the majority of the children had gone with the combined chapels trip to Llandudno.

The Boer War played on people's emotions.

1900 21 May — Holiday given today to commemorate the Relief of Mafeking.
8 June — This has been a very broken week, the village very upset with the war news, & on Wednesday a review of the Yeomanry was held in the Park, and a half-holiday had to be given.

Many local men were serving with Sir Watkin in South Africa. The school was directing its efforts to prepare the young school-leavers for work. The annual report of 29 October 1901 observed: 'I am glad that visits of observation under special guidance are being arranged to Terracotta Works, clay pits and coal mines in the neighbourhood, as well as to Wynnstay Park, gardens and home farm.

For those already at work:

1906 12 Feb.— ... Agricultural lectures given under the auspices of the Parish Council.

The school was a recruiting ground for the church choir.

1905 4 April — Very poor attendance this morning, the Bishop holding Confirmation: hence all the choir boys to the number of 16 being absent.

Proposed additions to the National School, 1895.

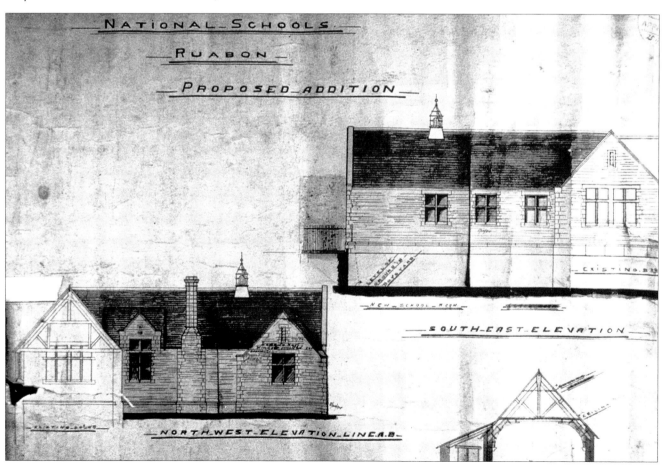

*Girls class group. c.1900.
This photograph includes Mrs Marjorie Williams (centre back) and Miss M. Parker (right) who later taught at the school.*

Football skills were encouraged.

1908 16 March — ... dismissed at 3.15 taking the football boys to see the International, England versus Wales at Wrexham.

1909 19 Nov. — There are several cases of tonsilitis among the children and the strike at Wynnstay Colliery affects the attendance also. The attendance officer reports great poverty in the neighbourhood tho' I have not seen any children at school suffering as yet from want of food. Boots and clothing seem to be the greater want.

The coal strike of 1912 was disastrous for the families:

1912 8 March — Low attendance is due to the coal strike, so many of the children picking coal on the colliery bank.

4 April — Have been taking 150 children to New Hall for dinner each day this last fortnight. Also, soup is provided in the Village Room by Sir Watkin to over a 100 children at 4.30*pm* & bread and cheese for lunch at 12 o'clock by him also for 150 children. Free breakfasts are also provided for close on 200 children each morning at the Presbyterian Chapel.

In spite of the deprivation there were examples of amazing attendance records:

1911 3 March — An interesting ceremony took place this morning. George Raymond Nicholas was presented with an inscribed silver watch for an unbroken School Attendance of 7 years.

The opening of the council school in August 1912 reduced the school number drastically:

1912 26 Aug. — Reopened after midsummer holidays. A very wet morning, 115 present. This low number accounted for owing to a new council school being opened today in the village. As far as I can make out now 51 boys have left for the council school: and 10 boys left for work.

On the eve of the First World War the children were being prepared by a good dose of nationalism, patriotism and imperialism:

1913 3 March — Mustered in the morning when an address on St David was given by self. Children of three departments then marshalled to playground, where the Union Jack was saluted. The vicar spoke to the children on patriotism and love of country. The Welsh National Anthem was sung. A few words given on the Empire followed by *God Save the King*. A half-holiday granted.

16 June — A flag staff has been erected in the school yard.

The realities of war soon came.

1916 3 Nov. — This morning the boys were taken to Cefn to see [a film of] the Battle of the Somme.
1917 7 March — Dr Williams (the Director of Education) called this afternoon and spoke about food production at the present time, and requested the managers to provide a plot of ground for raising food.

A year later in March 1918, food rationing was introduced and when the Armistice came in November the school was closed because of epidemics of influenza and fever. At the beginning of 1919 the school was closed because of a shortage of food. Peace Celebrations were celebrated in July 1919 when all the school children were given a treat in Wynnstay Park.

For every generation of school children the Christmas season has always been a special time:

1938 21 Dec. — Santa Claus visited the school and presented each child with a 6d. toy. The children took home the calendars, lanterns etc which they had made. The excitement cannot be described.

22 Dec. — At 3.15, the children are to have their annual party, a new penny and orange.

After the Second World War, on 3 December 1949, a party of thirty scholars were invited to the Polish Re-Settlement Camp at Wynnstay Park to the Festival of St Nicholas. There is information available in the log books which cannot easily be found elsewhere. For example there is a comprehensive account of the celebrations which took place on the Investiture of Charles as Prince of Wales in 1969. The enthusiastic and patriotic headmaster Mr H. L. Brown gave this account:

The Investiture Celebrations in Ruabon have been outstanding and worth recording. On Saturday 21 June the Youth Club staged a carnival and fête which was well attended. On Monday the British Legion organised a very good successful comical football match on the Recreation Ground. On Tuesday night 24 June, the senior citizens had a mystery trip by bus. On Wednesday the Rhos Girls' Choir gave a concert at the Parish Hall. On Thursday the Guides held a tramp's supper which was very enjoyable. On Friday night the dance was a big success. On Saturday there were sports and in the evening at 10.30*pm*. The enormous bonfire was lit and a display of fireworks took place on the Conker Field. Sunday night the Rhos Orpheus Choir gave a concert at Lindisfarne College. July 1st was a holiday and a great day for the crowning of HRH Prince of Wales a really unforgettable sight. The old people had colour television in the Parish Hall and a running buffet. 3 July was the school party day when the children were presented with a mug to mark the Investiture. The rooms were beflagged and a model of Caernarvon Castle made by Standard Two was on show. 215 pupils sat down to tea and were joined by the pupils from Penylan who attended Eyton School.

This was the last big effort of many for Mr H. L. Brown, headmaster for twenty-nine years, who retired the following month. A native of Cefn he came to teach in Ruabon when he was appointed headmaster in 1940, and until the time of his death in the 1980s, immersed himself in village life. He was a parish councillor, district councillor, member of the Burial Board, church warden, lay reader, army cadet officer and an extremely conscientious and forceful headmaster whose whole life was dedicated to his pupils, staff, and the community.

By the beginning of the 1970s, discussions began for the provision of a new school and community centre which could be used as a school assembly hall and gymnasium. It was an enterprise backed by the Church in Wales, Education Committee and the local authority with the negotiations and oversight being conducted by the parish councillors, the school governors under the chairmanship of the vicar the Reverend Maurice Donaldson, and the headmaster, Mr T. R. Evans.

1973 18 June — Work commenced this morning on the building of the new church school and community centre at a cost of over £170,000. It is scheduled that the building will take 105 weeks to complete.

It was built on the area which was the Girls' playground.

1975 18 July — School closed for the summer vacation ... As from today the work of demolishing the Old Church School will begin.

The new school was opened on the 15 September. It was officially handed over to the governors by the contractors, Messrs Gittins of Johnstown, on 12 September. The architect was Mr John Davies. The total cost of the school building was £129,529 and the community centre cost £61,945. The parochial church council's contribution towards the project amounted to £7,031. A plaque in the school entrance commemorated the event.

1976 7 June — The Dedication and the Official Opening of the New St Mary's Church in Wales School by the Bishop of St Asaph, The Right Reverend H. J. Charles, MA. The Community Centre opened by the Mayor of Wrexham, Maelor Borough Council. Councillor N. J. Wright.

Headmaster	Mr T. R. Evans.
Vicar	Reverend M. C. Donaldson, BA, BD.
Foundation Managers	Vicar, Mr J. R. Fenner, Mr H. L. Brown, Mr R. Breeze.
Representative Managers	Mr D. T. Hughes, Mr Stuart Jones.

Church School, 1930s.
Included are: Gwen Hayward; Hilda Jones; Eileen Jarvis; Ethel Edwards; Dot Rogers; Betty Hughes; Peggy Roberts; Patty Davies; Phoebe Williams; Laura Edwards; Winnie Jones; Olive Edwards; Emmeline Harris.
Jennie Davies; Mabel Jones; George Jones; Arthur Wayne; Jim Jones; Tom Bailiff; -?- Griffiths; Eddie Roderick; Evelyn Robinson. Bobbie Cartwright; Bert Lightwood; Eddie Griffiths; Frank Wainwright; Trevor Taylor; Frank Yarwood; Dilwyn Edwards; Teddie Jones; Stanley Halton.

Correspondent — Mrs Audrey Powell.
Director of Education — Mr John Howard Davies, BA.
Chairman of Diocesan Schools Committee — The Venerable J. E. Davies, BA.
Diocesan Director of Education — The Reverend T. P. Davies.

Mr T. R. Evans retired as headmaster on 31 Aug. 1983. He had served the school faithfully over many years, first as an assistant master in the 1950s and 60s, and then as headmaster from 1969 onwards. He was for a number of years a churchwarden at the parish church. He was succeeded by Mr T. M. Powell, BA, MEd.

St Mary's School

Extensive refurbishment has taken place and facilities improved since the new school was opened in 1976.

The school is able to accommodate 210 pupils along with nursery provision. At present there are 184 full time pupils.

The headteacher in July 2000 was Mr W. S. Wallace, BEd.

The Council School — Ysgol Maes y Llan

In the 19th century, primary education in the community of Ruabon was available only in the National School, which was a Church of England foundation. There were many parents who were not members of the Anglican church and preferred their children to receive a non-sectarian education. These were mainly nonconformists who experienced an active religious life in the thriving Baptist, Independent and Methodist

Church School, Standard IV, 1946.
Back row: Mr H. L. Brown (Head Teacher); Raymond Page; Jean Jones; Mary Prydderch; Margaret Edwards; Colin Whittal; Edmund Phillips; John Wright.
Middle row: Ronnie Roberts; Richard Everitt; Harold Davies; Heather Jones; Meryl Edwards; Pat Davies; June Dodd; Philip Williams; Brian Heath.
Front row: Barbara Ward; George Adams; Rachel Brown; Audrey Higgins; Thelma Samuels; Elizabeth Davies.

H. L. Brown, with his dog 'Boots' who invariably slept under his desk.

churches in Ruabon. By the beginning of the 20th century they were active in their demands for the provision of a non-sectarian school built under the auspices of the Denbighshire Education Committee.[37] They began their campaign in 1909 with a petition signed by 62 parents residing in the village of Ruabon.

It is believed that the present unsanitary and dilapidated condition of the Ruabon non-provided schools, out-offices, and playgrounds.... considerably endangers the health and welfare of the children ... a large number of parents have been compelled to withdraw their children ... and to send them considerable distances to other schools, namely, Acrefair and Johnstown Schools, which entails a hardship both upon the parents and children.

A joint committee was formed to represent the district managers of the Education Committee with Mr R. A. Jones being the leading Ruabon representative.[38] The petition was submitted with a list of 56 children from Ruabon attending Johnstown and Rhos Schools, and it was reported that about 35 children from Plas Bennion in the parish of Ruabon attended the new Penycae council school. This led to a proposal that a new council school should be erected at Ruabon, to accommodate not less than 250 children, and Mr R. A. Jones was to approach Mr Dyke Dennis, New Hall, Ruabon, for the sale of land 'a part of the Maes Llan Field, a very suitable and convenient site'.[39] The vendor of the land for the school was eventually Mr William Edwards.

These resolutions were met with strong opposition from the ratepayers objecting to the proposals 'based upon the belief:

1. That there is no necessity for further school accommodation.
2. That the cost of building the proposed school, as well as of its annual maintenance, would entail a serious charge upon the ratepayers.
3. That there is no religious difficulty, and no demand on the part of any considerable number of the parents for an additional school on religious grounds.

The petition was signed by W. Williams Wynn, Ruabon, Peter Ormrod, Penylan, Ruabon, and eight other ratepayers. The Local Authority responded by submitting the following information to the Board of Education:

Without commenting on the fact, the Committee beg to point out that of the ten signatures to the petition eight are tenants of the remaining two, who are known to be very strongly opposed to the provision of council schools for reasons other than those mentioned in the petition. Two only out of the ten are parents of children attending the school, and two only reside in the village...

With reference to the question of accommodation, the committee submit that the present provision is inadequate to meet the needs of the parish, as the following figures abundantly prove, viz;-

Accommodation of existing schools, 464

No. of children on registers, 501

No. of children attending schools outside the parish, 100

No. of children between the ages of 3 and 5, 153

It is calculated that the additional charge upon the parish would not exceed a penny rate.

... The 62 parents who signed the original petition in favour of the school were actuated by a strong desire for a school free from all sectarian influences. We also find that there are close upon 300 children of school age attending Sunday Schools connected with the various nonconformist places of worship in the village.[40]

The opposition failed, and plans were drawn up by the County Architect, Mr Wiles, for the new council school and submitted to the Education Committee in May 1910. The plans were for mixed and infants

St. Mary's (CinW) School Staff,
July 2000
Back row: Mrs A. Griffiths;
Mrs D. Erlandson; Mrs G. Pugh;
Mrs N. Roberts; Mrs V. Thomas;
Miss R. Williams.
Front row: Mrs L. Williams;
Mrs H. Jones; Mr R. B. Thomas; Mrs C.
Lloyd Jones; Mrs A Mates-Jones.

Pupil representatives from St. Mary's
(CinW) School, July 2000.
Back row: James Alec Hughes; Lucy
Mackreth; Kirsty Thompson (Head Girl);
Amy Platt; Anna Davies.
Front row: James Antony Hughes;
Andrew Roberts (Head Boy); Charlotte
Armstrong; Oliver Meredith.

departments, for two classrooms for infants' use, and for the mixed department. The scheme was to provide accommodation for 276 scholars, the six classrooms, all being placed in such a position that the maximum amount of sunlight is obtained to each room during school hours. The corridor principle was preferred to that of the central hall. The corridor was 13 feet wide by 130 feet long, with a portion of the same, 50 feet long, divided off for infants' use.

Such a corridor is found to be of the most convenient width for drilling and marching purposes. Separate cloakrooms are provided for boys, girls and infants, together with a master's room, teacher's room, two school store rooms, caretaker's store, staff lavatories and W.C.s.[41]

The new building was erected on a site which covered two acres at a cost of nearly £5,000. The school was designed according to the latest principles and in accordance with the open-air school movement. Two open-air classrooms were a feature of Ruabon council school, the first built in Denbighshire. Doctors were increasingly concerned at conditions in school: the seating of children, the arrangement of light, the supply of fresh air and the importance of a hygienic environment.

Ruabon council school was opened on 25 July 1912 by Mrs R. A. Jones as a fitting and just compliment to her husband for his untiring energy. She was presented with a silver key with which to open the door on behalf of the contractors, Messrs Dallow and Sons, Blackheath, Birmingham, and responded that:

> … she could hardly tell them with what pleasure and interest she had watched the building of that school until its completion and she trusted that she might also have the privilege of witnessing the growth and development from an educational standpoint of the children who would be taught in the school. As that building was looked upon as a model school, so she trusted would the lives and characters of the scholars be models, and thereby be a credit to their teachers and parents, as well as to the village to which they belonged.

Mr R. A. Jones was magnanimous and said that 'whatever difficulties they had to encounter, that is now ancient history.' County Councillor Edward Roberts, Brymbo, was equally tolerant when he 'said that Ruabon really wanted a council school: but at the same time they wished to speak with the greatest respect of the non-provided school (the church school). It had done splendid work for generations and had been the only school in the village for time immemorial.'[42]

The school log books are a commentary on life in the school and the community of Ruabon as seen from the perspective of head teachers.[43] How did the school use its model premises? One gets the feeling that they didn't know how to use the open-air classrooms. But from the early days it was a show school.

> 1912 4 Sept. — School visited by Mr Wiles, County Architect, who is anxious for open-air classrooms to be utilised.
> 5 Sept. — Visited during the week by several visitors who expressed delight at buildings and equipment.
> 1913 12 Feb. — Heard Mr Ellis student teacher give a history lesson. Beautiful day. Used open-air classroom on infant's side.
> 1913 16 April — Owing to increase in numbers I have decided to place the top class in the open-air classroom.
> 1914 24 June — Visited by Miss Roberts of Wrexham Girl's NP School and Miss Jones, Alexandra Girl's School, Wrexham. These teachers came particularly to see open-air rooms and the method of furnishing.

The HMI Report on the Infant's Department commented:

> 1920 1 June — At the time of inspection, two divisions had to be taught in one undivided room owing to the impossibility of using the open-air room which is occupied during warm weather only.
> 1943 8 Feb. — Open-air class room converted into a cook house. Dinners were served for the first time today.
> 1981 3 Sept. — Local Play Group moved to open-air room.

The School Report of 1947 makes no mention of the open-air classrooms:

> The fairly wide corridor is used for dining, but for school assemblies, a partition is drawn between two classrooms. There is a large garden and there are good playgrounds'. It was suggested that a portion of the garden might be allocated to each class for nature study. 'No Welsh is taught here and as yet no attempt has been made to provide the children with a Welsh background through the study of History and Geography'.

In 1963 the inspector reported 'that not a single child in school is Welsh speaking,' and added that 'Welsh is taught conscientiously as a second language.

The first headteacher was Mr Fred Davies who served from 25 July 1912 to 14 November 1929 and died in post. He had recorded on 22 Sept 1925 — 'Alderman R. R. A. Jones our esteemed chairman died this afternoon. We have lost our best friend. He was keenly interested in this school for it was entirely due to his zeal and energy that it was erected. He was always eager to help us in every way he could to make the school a success. His place in our school life will be hard to fill.'

The second headteacher was Mr A. W. Bassett: 1 March 1930. He too died in office on 20 June 1949, to be succeeded by Mr Iorwerth Griffiths 10 January 1950 to 13 July 1973 and in turn came Mr Delwyn Vaughan Jones, 3 September 1973 to July 1977 with Mrs Christina Heather Giller, 1 September 1977 to July 1985.

Head Teachers of the Infant Department

1915–18	Miss A. B. Jones
1918–27	Miss Margaret Hughes
1927–60	Miss Doris M. Hirst
1961–62	Miss D. E. Davies (Acting)
1962–82	Miss Marian Jones

Reports of school treats, trips and closures express delight at being out of school and enjoying these events, whether educational or not. In 1912, the school was closed to enable the children to attend the National Eisteddfod at Wrexham, and a month later a good attendance half-holiday 'coincided' with a carnival in Ruabon and a flying exhibition at Wrexham. Another such holiday was given in October 1914 'as one of the Royal Welsh Fusilier Battalions of Lord Kitchener's army marched to Wynnstay Park'.

This was not the age of the family holiday and all the more valuable was the Sunday School treat to take you to the seaside. On 13 July 1920 thirty children were taken to New Brighton, without leave of absence, and

Ysgol Maes y Llan — exterior.

Ysgol Maes y Llan — interior.

on successive days the following week two other Chapel Sunday School trips took place. In 1923, sixty-five children were taken to Wrexham to see the Prince of Wales 'space being reserved for them in Parciau on sloping ground where every child has an excellent view.' On 18 May, 1925, the last of the Wynnstay family events was celebrated:

> Closed school this afternoon by order of the managers to enable the scholars to go to Wynnstay to a tea party. This was given by Sir Watkin to celebrate the birth of a son[44] to Mr Watkin Williams Wynn. A beautiful day, a splendid tea, enjoyable games with money prizes and various other forms of amusements including a Punch and Judy Show.

An 'out of this world' experience was the eclipse of 1927:

> 29 July. Whole day holiday given today to enable 64 scholars accompanied by the whole staff and a few parents to travel to Criccieth to view the unique spectacle of a total eclipse of the sun, Criccieth being on the centre line of totality. We left Ruabon at midnight. The morning broke with heavy rain. So severe that we saw nothing except extreme peculiar coloured darkness. We remained in the train until noon when the weather cleared and the rest of the day was spent in warm sunshine on the beach and promenade. We left at 5' o clock and reached Ruabon at 8pm.

The next year the scholars were taken to Port Sunlight 'where scholars were presented by the management with tea and buns,' and then on to the Overhead Railway and Gladstone Docks, Liverpool, to view the Canadian Pacific Steamship *Montrose*, with four hours on the New Brighton sands.

From time to time, there were misdemeanours:

> 1920 14 June — Have spoken seriously to scholars upon the dangerous practice of running after charabancs. Some legal steps will be taken to stop this 'ere we have fatal results.

> 1922 25 June — Received a complaint from the Station Master at Ruabon about boys from this school throwing dust and small gravel at engines on the railway whilst in motion. I find that they are country boys who stay to dinner. I have spoken very seriously to them about it in the presence of the whole school and written to their parents.

The history of 20th century education, as we have seen, is available in the pages of log books and more can be read about the changing curricula, courses for teachers, the introduction of new technology, the greater

Left & below right: Two classes from Ysgol Maes y Llan, 1920.

Ysgol Maes y Llan Infants, 1969.
Back row: Marion Jones (head teacher); Steven Williams; -?-; David -?-; Peter Brookfield; -?-; Malcolm Jones; Arfon Hughes.
2nd row from back: David Morris; Joseph Mark Williams; -?- ; Ann Millington; Lynn Jarvis; Ann Jarvis; Mark Hughes; -?-.
3rd row from back: Patsy Ann Williams; Joanne Jones; Debbie Waters; Wendy Edwards; Marcia Samuels; -?-; Janice Davies.
Front row: Martin Roscoe; -?-; John R. Dodd; Jeffrey Paite; Keith Wright; -?-.

involvement of parents, and many other topics. It is impossible to hide the joy and wonder which is at the heart of primary education and the delight which chance entries in the log books reveal.

1978 22 March — The girls paraded through the village in their Easter bonnets. The police stopped the traffic for a few minutes. Later we took them to visit the Old Age Pensioners at their meeting.

Ysgol Maes y Llan 2000
The school has a population of 137 children which includes 20 nursery.

Ysgol Maes y Llan, July 2000. Rehearsal for 'The Feast of Life'.
Back row: Heather Roberts; Stephanie Davies; Abbie Jones; Beth Burke; Jessica Davies; Gareth Lloyd; Anna Chung; Marcus Dodd; James Griffiths.
Front row: Faune Ellis; Lucy Price; Matthew Jones; Ashley Bostock; Lyndsey Saffy; Andrew Swarbrick; William Ellis; Emma Barker; Ian Hall.

Ysgol Maes y Llan Staff, September 2000.
Back row: Anne Swarbrick; Siân Wright.
Front row: Christine Jones; Sue Glover; Siân Matthews (acting head teacher); Joanne Davies.

The Bryn

The Bryn was a boarding school conducted from 1883 to 1890 at Bryn, Ruabon, and then moved to Plas Madoc Hall for fifteen years. It was advertised as a Lady's School conducted by the Misses. Booth. E. K. Jones left this account:

> The proprietress was a cultured lady of good family, who was assisted by her four sisters. One took charge of the domestic side of the house, and occasionally assisted with French. The youngest acted as teacher. The other two would also help, with Music and French, at pleasure. Special teachers were engaged for special subjects. When the eldest sister died, an experienced and qualified headmistress was engaged to conduct the work. But, inasmuch as these ladies were not dependant upon the school, it was closed in the year 1905.

> At one time, there were as many as twenty-seven boarders at Plas Madoc. Children would come from a distance, as well as from Rhos, Ruabon, Cefn, and Penycae. Fees ranged from ten to twelve pounds per term. Often, parents would send their girls to be 'finished up'.

> The whole school, for purposes of health and nature study, would take daily walks into the country, and long walks on Wednesday and Saturday. On these occasions pupils would walk two and two, in an orderly column, with a teacher walking in front and another bringing up the rear. On Sundays, the school would march in order, for divine service at the chapel at Wynnstay. The Plas Madoc Boarding School did not compete with any other in the neighbourhood, as it stood in a class apart. The proprietress was also firm in keeping down the number of boarders taken in, so as to avoid overcrowding.[45]

Lindisfarne College, Independent Boarding and Day School at Wynnstay 1950–94

A school founded in 1891 by Robert William Grace in Southend-on-Sea in Essex and called 'Lindisfarne' in honour of St Cedd who brought Christianity to East Anglia from Holy Island off the coast of Northumberland. Grace hoped his 'Lindisfarne' 'would produce young men of principle and vision who would go out into the world carrying with them knowledge and sound spiritual values'.[46] The school moved to larger premises in nearby Westcliff in 1904. Robert Grace's great love was of literature, music, and art and Sunday evening services were the centre of the college life. He retired in 1920 to be succeeded as Headmaster by A. E. C. Saunders; when he died in 1928 Mrs Saunders remained as proprietress. Mervyn Gotch was Head from 1929–32. Edward Daws succeeded him, and with his wife Jean became the backbone of the school for 31 years. He was an old boy of Lindisfarne and knew the high ideals of the founder. The school prospered and won a reputation for cricket, football, and drama. On the outbreak of the war the school was evacuated and arrived in June 1940 at Newburgh Priory, Coxwold, in Yorkshire. It was here that Lindisfarne developed into a mainly boarding school. The two world wars took their toll of old boys, and 105 names, 55 from the First World War, and 50 from the Second World War, are engraved on the white marble memorial to be seen near the lych gate in St Mary's Churchyard, Ruabon.

At the end of the war there were about 120 boarders at Newburgh; the buildings at Westcliff had been sold, and the future of Newburgh was uncertain. In 1949, Wynnstay came on the market. 'Negotiations finally fixed the price at £17,000. The electricity fittings cost £3,500 and the drainage £1,000. The interior of the building painted at a cost of £700. The move from Newburgh cost over £500. The total cost to the school was £22,700, probably £450,000 in today's money.'[47] The school finally opened at Wynnstay in January 1950.

The first thirteen years at Wynnstay, were under the headship of Edward Daws. 'Dorrie' as he was affectionately known, established the traditions of the school at Wynnstay. He attracted and encouraged an increased number of boarders, recruited and won the respect of a well-qualified and efficient staff of teachers. Furthermore, he restored and renovated the grounds, the chapel, the stable block; created a dining hall, kitchen, dormitories, staff accommodation, a gymnasium, swimming pool, tennis courts, cricket and rugby pitches. A dedicated and loyal staff created the ethos of the school by their diligence both inside and outside the classroom. Harold Simpson and Joe Sellars were in charge of the school Army Cadet Force. Roy Jones, John Williams, and Donald Anderton were the Scout leaders. The Rugby XV under Gerry Cochrane and the Cricket XI guided by Donald Bowie, Len Lay and J. A. Lightowler did well. John Williams produced some memorable drama, and the school orchestra performed well. The school grew in size and by 1963 there were 300 pupils, most of whom were boarders. 'Lindisfarne attracted a large number of pupils from overseas so that it often resembled a mini United Nations. Boys came from Scandinavia, the Far and Middle East, and Africa.'[48] Boys and girls came from the United States and Canada in receipt of English Speaking Union scholarships. The college catered for a wide span of academic attainment and university entrance. From the beginning it received the benefit of advice from Ministry of Education Inspectors, and academic standards were achieved which reflected the abilities of pupils. Dorrie inspired with his addresses on Sunday evenings in the chapel and the school walk, the name for the outings 'invariably unplanned and usually decided up the night before' journeyed by train and bus to as far afield as Snowdonia, Cader Idris or Caernarfon. The Lindisfarne Old Boys' Association, Old Lindisfarnians, continued their custom of annual cricket and rugby weekends, and in general supported the College.

Strong links were established with the community of Ruabon. School governors, teaching staff, secretarial and financial assistance, domestic staff, maintenance workers and day pupils, were attracted from the neighbourhood. There was constant mini bus traffic and taxis to and from Ruabon.

The school for a number of the early years attended the Sunday morning service in the parish church and the annual Commemoration Day was observed there. The relationship between town and gown was friendly and affectionate. Those who were invited to the Christmas carol service in the hall, many times with snow on the ground, never forgot the experience, nor the hospitality of the Commemoration Day luncheon.

Edward and Jean Daws retired in August 1963, their wisdom and character had served the school well in observing old ideals and in introducing new patterns of life.

R. W. S. Carrington was head from 1963 to 1966. He resigned when school numbers halved in spite of a favourable HMI report after a full inspection. He was succeeded by L. Roy Jones (1966–86). The twenty years he was head were to match those of Robert Grace and Edward Daws for their influence on the school. A native of Wrexham, and a graduate in geography of the University College, Aberystwyth, with a war-time army commission, Roy Jones arrived in 1951. His ability, sincerity and Christian commitment, drew him close to Dorrie with whom he shared the ability to tackle daunting problems and work through a crisis, whether it was related to school numbers or financial matters. They were never allowed to effect the smooth running of the school. Throughout, he maintained a sense of dignity and equilibrium. Roy, together with his wife Lyn, inspired the whole school family by their example, compassion, and sense of fun. When he retired in 1986 there was a quiet conviction that the ongoing plans for the development of a preparatory school and £150,000 appeal for a new sports hall would be realised.

He was succeeded by Trevor Wilson (1986–90), head of the Sir James Henderson British School in Milan. The high point of his short stay was the opening by Roy Jones of the £250,000 sports complex, and the expansion of the primary school department. Trevor Wilson resigned in June 1990, and the school was in the care of deputy headteacher Ian Mullins, with Stephen Moore as his assistant.

In January 1991 John Dobinson, senior housemaster at Stowe School, was appointed head at the beginning of the Lindisfarne centenary year. He did not stay long as headteacher, and was succeeded by Keith Morgan who faced the same problems as his predecessors. The falling number of school pupils, with a drastic reduction in income, made it impossible for the school to remain economically viable. These pressures forced the school to close in 1994.

L. Roy Jones, hadmaster of Lindisfarne College, 1966–86.

High Street, c.1935.

5. Penylan

Penylan has almost the distinction of being a small village, but whatever status we arbitrarily confer, nothing can take away from it the beauty and serenity of its surroundings. As such, it has since the 17th century been the centre of the Penylan estate, although the village has been known as the Bryn, a hill which is more appreciated if approached from across the river Dee on its Shropshire side. The Bryn most probably refers to Bryn Lawenydd.

The Estate

Ellis Lloyd,[1] who died in 1712, was a lawyer who held the offices of Chief Inspector of the Public Revenues in the Duchy of Cornwall, Chief Notary in the North Wales Court of Sessions and Chancellor to his brother William, Bishop of Norwich. A native of Leighton Knowle in Shropshire, he came into the estate through marriage to Elizabeth, daughter of Edward ap William ap John ap David. Ellis's purse was as long as his father-in-law's pedigree, and he increased the size of the Penylan estate by judicious purchases. Dying without issue in 1712, his will directed that his heirs should assume the surname of Lloyd. This wish was honoured throughout the 18th century. The survey of the estates of Edward Lloyd Lloyd Esqr, made in 1797 by F. Bennion, reveal that he owned 2,217 acres scattered about in the parishes of Ruabon and Erbistock and over the border into Shropshire, of which there was a consolidated block of 1,234a-1r-4p which constitutes the Penylan demesne. In the 19th century, the Kenyons, through marriage, became squires of Penylan, the last of whom, Edward Lloyd Kenyon, died in 1843 aged twenty-eight years, leaving an only child, Louisa Mary

Penylan Hall from the River Dee.

Beaumont Kenyon. In 1854, the greater part of her estates were sold by the trustees to James Hardcastle of Bolton, Lancaster. He was succeeded by his brother-in-law, James Ormrod, who bought the estate in 1870. The sale particulars give an exact and interesting description of Penylan.

Particulars *etc.*

The Freehold estate called 'Penylan', in the parishes of Ruabon, Erbistock, Ellesmere, and St Martins, in the counties of Denbigh and Salop, comprising:

The mansion of Penylan and various farms, woodlands, and other hereditaments. The particulars whereof are as follows:

Tyddin Ucha and Castle Farms	85a-2r-4p
Part of Yellow Oak and Part of Crab Mill Farm	35a-3r-32p
Bryn Farm	125a-1r-8p
Plas Golborn Farm Erbistock	115a-0r-20p
Penylan Farm with	146a-1r-3p
Outer Park and	76a-2r-38p
Woods	24a-2r-3p
Lower Farm and Wyffydd with	73a-0r-1p
Wood	2a-1r-20p
Mansion and Domain with	311a-0r-29p
Woods	109a-2r-6p
Gamekeeper's Cottage, Garden & Orchard	0a-2r-23p
Gardener's do	0a-0r-27p
Prince's do	0a-0r-23p
Flannog and Caebedw Farms with Ellesmere	117a-0r-15p
Woods and	50a-0r-9p
Cottage and Garden St Martins	0a-0r-8p
Total	1,276a-3r-32p

NB. Five furlongs of the River Dee in its full breadth, and ten other furlongs in its half breadth, are within the limits of the estate, and not included in these measurements. Total about 1,300 acres.

The estate is in a ring fence, and nearly the whole of it has been thoroughly drained, and is in high cultivation. There are farm buildings, labourers' cottages, school-house, tilery, and other buildings, luxuriantly growing timber, extensive covers for game, and good trout and salmon fishing in the river which flows rapidly over and along about two miles in length of the property, and in which there are five good salmon pools. The grounds are disposed in knolls and sweeping lawns; with woods, shaded walks and rides, flower garden, kitchen garden and orchard, conservatory, hot-house, ice-house, etc.

The climate is delightful, and very salubrious. The parks are extensive and well-wooded, the surface being much varied with undulations, slopes, and holme lands to the river. The position of the mansion, near the centre of the demesne, commands extensive panoramic views, the scenery over every portion of the estate being beautifully varied and picturesque. The house is approached by a lodge entrance and carriage-drive, winding through the park; and contains entrance hall, lofty drawing room, 27ft by 19ft, dining room, 26ft by 18ft, library, 16ft by 16ft, seven best bedrooms, two dressing rooms, ten other bedrooms, housekeeper's room, servants' hall, two kitchens, laundry, dairy, bread-house, scullery, larders, and other offices and good cellaring. There are two three-stalled stables, five loose boxes, coach-houses, saddle and harness rooms, cow-houses, barn and other convenient outhouses, and yards attached.

The estate is bounded in Denbighshire by the Wynnstay property of Sir W.W. Wynn, Bart, and by that of the heirs of Boscawen; and in Shropshire by the lands of the Rev Cyrus Morrell, and others, all of which are strictly preserved; and the land is well adapted for game. There are fox hounds in the immediate vicinity, the Wynnstay kennels being close to the estate.

There is a commodious family pew, besides several pews for servants and tenants, in the parish church of Ruabon; and sittings or pews in the churches of Erbistock and Dudleston.

The mines in the Shropshire portion of the property do not belong to the estate. In the Denbighshire part, (in which there are several valuable beds of coal), the mines and minerals go with the property. The estates are

Penylan Hall — castellated and enlarged c.1830.

subject to tithe rent charge which average about 3s-8d per acre on the agricultural land.

The mansion is three miles from the Ruabon station, on the Shrewsbury and Chester portion of the Great Western Railway, where the railway of the Vale of Llangollen commences. This first-class station is about one hour from Liverpool, two hours from Manchester, and five hours from London.[2]

The mansion house was remodelled in 1830 in the Tudor-Gothic revival style, stuccoed and castellated. It was enlarged and altered in the late 19th century, much of these later additions were demolished in the 1950s.

James Ormrod was a deeply religious man and he built churches on the Lancashire estates with which he was connected. He believed that his wealth should be used to the glory of God, and this benevolence and liberality endowed Penylan with a school and a church, to provide religion and education for his tenants housed in the new cottages he erected in the hamlet.

The School

Notice of a school at Penylan is given under the name of Bryn in 1847:

Bryn School: A school for Boys' and Girls'. Taught together by a mistress in a room built for the purpose. Number of girls 28; of boys 12. Subjects taught: the scriptures and church catechism, reading and writing. Fees 1d per week. This school was examined January 21, when only three children were present. These scholars had made no progress in any subject. The mistress was formerly a dressmaker. She has never been trained to teach, but has kept a Dame-School for 30 years. She teaches the girls to knit and sew.

The schoolroom and outbuildings were out of repair. The former contained no kind of furniture except a table brought from the mistresses' cottage in the morning and returned at night.

The mistress is provided with a house rent free, and receives £6 salary which is said to be derived from endowment. In other respects the school resembles a Dame School.

There are records of unmarried schoolmistress living in the area — Mary Elizabeth Edwards born in Liverpool is a lodger in 1861 at one of the Bryn Cottages, and Mary Leich lived at Penylan Lodge in 1881.

The school is dated 1885 and has the initials J. O. and at that time must have been in the ownership of the Ormrod estate.

In 1920, Penylan School was formerly handed over to Denbighshire Education Authority for educational purposes subject to certain conditions. To put the school fabric in order, Captain Ormrod spent £700 on getting the school up to standard, and received in return a lease of £25*pa* for 21 years. For this he was to keep the main fabric of the building in repair and the Education Authority were responsible for all interior fittings, furniture, books, *etc.*, and all expenses in connection with the heating, lighting and maintenance of the school.

The Penylan community were allowed to make use of the school as a Sunday School and for evening meetings. The records relating to the school are to be found in the Denbighshire Education Committee minutes and the Penylan School log book which exists from 1938–68.

In 1945, the school was purchased by the Education Authority from the executors of the late Major Ormrod. The newly appointed headteacher noted:

Sept. 4. I attended a meeting of Manager and members of the Education Committee on Aug. 14 1945. It was to purchase the school building (at present on lease).

The first school report entered in the log book is good:

School Report. Penylan Council School inspected 2 February 1938.
The children read and write well but more attention might be given to speech-training and dramatic works to overcome shyness and diffidence of the children.
A daily period of dancing and games would also be very effective, but the condition of the playground is a serious handicap to this branch of the work, part of the space sufficient for physical exercises, should be asphalted … The Head Mistress has high educational ideals. Her outlook is modern … Despite their shyness, the children are all pleasant to talk to, and their behaviour is exemplary.
There are two teachers, the Head Mistress and her assistant, Miss Parker.

The number of children on the school roll is given:

1938 20 Jan. — Miss D. Smith, assistant school dental surgeon, treated dental cases during the morning and afternoon sessions.
21 Jan. — Dental treatments continued in the morning … No on roll 35.
1938 19 May — The Education Authority made a grant for £1-11s-6d with this amount. 19s was spent on library books and 12s.-6d. for four gramophone records, one march and three Scandinavian dances.

In the following year the first indication of war is soon apparent:

1939 11 Sept. — Received instruction stating that the Denbighshire children should be excluded from school until the evacuated children had been medically examined.

This led to a disproportionate rise in school numbers.

15 Sept. — Number of Denbighshire children in school 39: evacuated 39, privately evacuated 3. Total 66. One extra teacher accompanied by evacuees. They continued to arrive in 1940. 'Admitted 9 scholars of Chatsworth Street School, Liverpool'; and the school experienced an air raid warning during the period of the Battle of Britain.
5 Sept. — Air raid warning at 2.15*pm* children sent home: and took precautions.
20 Sept. — Received 34 yards of anti shatter muslin for the windows.
14 Nov. — Received one stirrup pump from Education Officer.
5 Dec. — Air raid shelter being built in cloakroom.

The war began to destroy the parochialism of the village life.

1943 3 Sept. 11–11.15am — Teachers and Scholars listened in to service of prayers and dedication on the fourth anniversary of war. Portable wireless set loaned to school by Reverend H. J. Croasdale.
20 Sept. — School meals commenced. These were conveyed by Messrs C. T. Clarke Ltd, from Whitegate Central Kitchen at Wrexham, and 18 were supplied. No: on roll 20.

Penylan School, built 1885, now a private residence.

In 1945 the end of the war was celebrated in the company of the children from the Church School at Ruabon:

29 Sept. — Miss Parker and I took the children to Ruabon to attend a Victory Tea Party provided by the Ruabon Parish Council. All thoroughly enjoyed a cinema show. Tea at the National School, sports in Wynnstay Park and bonfire and fireworks display at the Recreation Field. The number on the roll was reduced to eleven.

Normal schooling was resumed, children enjoyed their nature rambles and picnics, and annual church trips organised. In June 1947, they went to Rhyl. The Reverend H. J. Croasdale who had lived at the Parsonage with his family from 1916 left in 1946 to take up a living at Hornby.

Some of the fabric of the school its curricula, staff, and pupils, is contained in the report of June 1948.

21 June 1948 — Report by HM Inspector on Penylan Council School. The premises of this school include two pleasant class rooms separated by a glazed partition, a small store room, and a cloakroom, which is provided with running water, but has no fixed wash basin. Enamel bowls are used with buckets for waste.

The school is centrally heated, the playground is large but unsurfaced, and a portion is used as a school garden. The office accommodation which is of the bucket type is adequate: one each for staff, girls and infants and two for the boys. There is also a small cycle shed at the back of the school.

The twelve pupils on the register are taught in two classes, pupils over seven years of age by the Head Mistress, and the infants by a supplementary teacher of long experience.

Pupils are well grounded from the start in reading, writing and arithmetic, and good work in these subjects is done throughout, plenty of practice being given in writing free composition. Much attention is paid to nature study both out of doors and in the classroom. All the children have collections of pressed flowers, and illustrated nature diaries and records are kept by the joint effort of the top class.

Both girls and boys over seven years of age work under the supervision of the Head Mistress in the school garden, two to each plot … The school has a percussion band and attention is paid to modulator work as well as to choral singing … The infants join the upper class in the opening act of worship … All the pupils take the milk provided, and the school meal which is prepared in the Wrexham Central Kitchen … This is a very pleasant little school and everything is done to maintain in it the atmosphere of a happy family.

As if to celebrate this excellent report the Headmistress was married, and at a school party was presented with an engraved silver tray and a silver condiment set by the staff. Mrs Jarvis, as she became, remained at the school until her retirement in 1961. In the meantime, Miss Parker retired in December 1954 having taught at the school for thirty-nine years. The children continued to excel in music and needlework and bookbinding was introduced in the 1950s.

In 1961, the number on the roll was twenty-four. The log book noted:

18 May — Visit by County Librarian with fresh consignment of books. He congratulated the children on their various 'Book projects' on Wild Flowers, Geology, Fishes, Costume and promised to find suitable books so that they can read further about their chosen subjects.

In 1965 there was an outstanding report on the musical ability of the children:

19 May — Visit by Mr Humphrey William, BBC Education Officer, accompanied by Mr Murphy, writer and producer of the Music Workshop series. He was very impressed by our 'Follow up' work in connection with Music Workshop. He was particularly pleased with the children's own compositions. Jill Fletcher demonstrated how she composed,

Music and Movement, 1960s.
L–R: Victoria Goddard; Susan Whatmore;
Anthony Flynn; Carl Goodwin; -?-;
Helen Fletcher; Ronald Goodwin;
Roger Jones; Philip Jones.

Paintings and Collages.

then got the children to sing it and worked out the percussion accompaniment. His quiet remark about Jill was: 'this girl is brilliant'. Jill and Linda Richards played their tunes on the two organs. Jill, Linda, Carole, Clive and Rosemary, played their recorders.

31 Mar. — Mr H. Williams sent a tape of the children's interview and recording of their joint songs, words and music.

The whole area and community was distraught by the outbreak of foot and mouth disease in the winter of 1967. On one farm, the children were hysterical, and their father lost his voice after seeing cattle destroyed by the Ministry men. Other children had to stay at home to avoid spreading the disease, and 'Mrs. Jones had to go to hospital for the birth of her sixth, a baby boy'.

The next year, 18 December 1968, saw the closure of the school on the amalgamation of Penylan and Erbistock School with Eyton Controlled School in January 1969. Pupils, staff, parents, friends and families, gathered at an evening function 'for the formal ceremony of closing the school. Chaired by Major Ormrod who gave some of the history in the 127 years the school had been in existence.' The teachers, Mrs Edwards and Mrs Green, together with the pupils were photographed.

All Saint's Church

The site of the church of All Saints', Penylan, has been hallowed by the association with the Celtic saints. Edward Lhuyd, writing about 1697, says 'They call a field where there is a cross in Ruabon parish 'Kappel Kollen' and a field at Home Farm is 'Cae'r groes newydd'. Another field name is 'Errow armon'. Near Crab Row is the field 'cae gosper', meaning evensong or vespers. There must have been a place of worship in the township of Dinhinlle Isaf of which the above field names bear the holy testimony.

The Reverend Thomas Thomas, vicar of Ruabon in 1858, opened a mission room for divine service and this building was enlarged by his successor, Canon E. Wood Edwards, who recognised the necessity for a permanent place of worship. Communion was held at midday at Bryn on the last Sunday in the month. In 1883 there were 70–120, attending public worship in Bryn School room and the average number of communicants was twenty. The pastoral area of the township of Dinhinlle Isaf was the respon-

Staff and pupils on closure, December 1968.
Back row: Helen Griffith; Mrs M. T. Edwards; Trudi Holland; Helen Fletcher; Phillip Jones; Mrs Green; Jane Griffith; Brian Boothby; Ronald Goodwin.
Middle row: Susanna Goddard; Carol Goodwin; Sarah Griffith; Robert Griffith; Susan Whatmore; Janette Jones; Victoria Goddard.
Front row: Alice Ormrod; Tina Jones; Vivienne Jones.

sibility of the vicar of Ruabon with its centre at Bryn.

It is against this background that the generous act of building the church of All Saints', Penylan, took place. Now that over 100 years have passed since the laying of the foundation stone on 13 September 1887, we may record with gratitude those responsible and notice their good works.

In 1854 the Penylan estate was bought by James Hardcastle of Bolton, a rich and successful cotton spinner of the firm of Ormrod and Hardcastle. James Hardcastle died in 1869 and is commemorated by a memorial tablet in the lych gate. He was succeeded as owner of the estate by his brother-in-law, James Ormrod, who was later described in his obituary as 'a man of unbounded liberality and good friend to the church'. This is almost an understatement for James Ormrod built the church at Scorton, Lancashire, 1878–9, in memory of his brother Peter, who had himself largely paid for the re-building of Bolton Parish Church, by E.G. Paley, 1867-71, and contributed to the church of St Peters, Halliwell, which he was in the habit of attending.

It was on Tuesday 13 of September 1887 that James Ormrod laid the foundation stone of All Saints', Penylan, in the presence of the vicar of Ruabon, Canon E. Wood Edwards, and other clergymen. The formal ceremony was completed by Mr Ormrod's little grandson, who was lifted up in order that he might tap the stone three times with the mallet. A brass plate at the west end of the church records 'This Church, dedicated to All Saints' is built and endowed by James Ormrod, of Penylan, in the Jubilee year of Queen Victoria, to the glory of God and in memory of his wife Cordelia, September 13th, AD 1887.'

In the same decade James Ormrod built a school and houses, in the small hamlet. This small community was spectator to the building of the beautiful church of dressed sandstone, of a dark red colour quarried from the estate and strawberry-coloured tiles manufactured in the parish. The altar, choir stalls, pulpit and litany desk, were made from oak felled on the estate.

In under two years from the laying of the foundation stone, the church was opened on midsummer day, 1889. After the service there were sports and dancing in the park near the Hall. At the end of the proceedings, the aged benefactor, Mr James Ormrod, spoke to the guests, words which are equally relevant today to the people of Penylan: 'My dear friends I wish to thank you all for your presence here today and to remind you that the Church I have been privileged to see opened is a memorial to my dear wife. I trust you will make good use of it, and that it will be a great spiritual benefit to you and your families. We all owe thanks and praise to God for many mercies, and I am grateful that he has given me the power to devote some of my wealth in this way to his honour … whether we have good seasons or bad, we must never forget One who rules over everything. Again thanking you all for coming, and begging you to be regular and frequent in your attendance at the services in the Church'. The speaker died a few months later on 12 November 1889.

The architect of the church was R. Knill Freeman of Bolton. The windows in the chancel and the apse illustrate the dedication of the church to All Saints, and represent our Lord in glory, throned and surrounded by the Blessed Virgin Mary, the apostles, prophets and martyrs, all in adoration (St Augustine, David King and Prophet, the Blessed Virgin Mary, St Mary Magdalene, St Paul, St Stephen and St Alban). The tracery in the heads of the windows is filled with angels. The inscription running round the three windows is taken from the communion service: 'Therefore with angels and archangels, and with all the Company of Heaven.' The chancel ceiling is finished in light blue, powdered with stars and with ornamental designs on dark blue, in the lower part with sacred emblems in the centre panels and texts 'O praise God in His holiness, praise Him in the firmament of His power.' 'Let everything that hath breath praise the Lord.'

The chancel floor is of antique encaustic tiles supplied by J. C. Edwards. James Ormrod left his property in Lancashire to his eldest son, Cross Ormrod. The Penylan estate passed to his second son Peter, whose wife Sarah Emma, was laid to rest on 22 December 1905. The reredos of carved oak with its arcaded panels painted with the emblems of our Lord and the Evangelists and scenes of the Annunciation and Resurrection, and the two manual pipe organs, were installed as a memorial to her. Her husband died in 1919, and is commemorated by the nave window (depicting St Barnabas), and by the pulpit.

The pastoral care of Penylan from 1889–1946 was undertaken by a chaplain appointed by the Ormrod family. One was a devoted chess player, another eventually found his vocation in the West Country, and was a friend of the Rev Jack Russell, the hunting parson. In contrast, another chaplain left Penylan because he was chased by a cow.

In 1959 the church was conveyed, by way of gift, to the Church in Wales, by Colonel Peter Ormrod, MC, JP, the great-grandson of James Ormrod. It was consecrated on 21 February 1960 by the Right Reverend Dr D.

All Saints Church, Penylan.

D. Bartlett, Bishop of St Asaph.

Before the Second World War, work on the land was hard with long hours, low wages, no electricity and very little mechanisation. But diversions were found in the weekly market at Oswestry, and the local whist drives and dances across the fields at Rhos y Madoc and Ruabon. There are no records to tell us what people did, apart from the occasional newspaper report:

1913 22 Feb. — Church History. One of a series of lantern lectures dealing with the history of the church was given by the Revd. D. R. Davies at the school room.

1913 26 July — Sweet Pea Growers, Success. Mr Thomas Jones, Bryn, exhibited sweet peas with great success at the Crystal Palace Show last week, winning no less than four cups.

1922 24 June — Penylan Fête in aid of All Saints' Church

At Penylan Hall … to raise £300 towards the improvement of the organ … there was a large attendance. The programme included an American tennis tournament, concerts, and attractive stalls. The Ruabon Band played selections, and for the dancing in the evening … The tennis tournament was won by the Rev. and Miss Rossendale Lloyd.

1930 23 August — Cottage Gardens — Captain Ormrod, Mrs Mainwaring (Ottley) and her gardener have made their awards as follows. For the best kept and best cropped cottage gardens — 1. Mr George Humphreys; 2. Mr Harry Dodd. Special prize Mr William Tibbott.

On the outbreak of the Second World War, the Penylan detachment of the Home Guard, commanded by Major James Ormrod, made their headquarters in the school, prepared to defend the land of their fathers against the Hun. For this task they were not without experience and if drill would win the war they had their sergeants, Archie Drake and Ted Massey, old sweats of the First World War, to show them how. In the darkness of the night, they patrolled the roads of Penylan and Erbistock always prepared to repel the invader. Not so on Sundays, when the traffic was one-way across the Penylan bridge to go to the pubs in St Martins, unchallenged of course!

All Saints Church Choir, 1920s. Rev H. Croasdale (Chaplain); R. Parker (Lay reader).

Young people from Rhos y Madoc and Penylan prepared for courtship and other rites of passage outside the Bryn shop, admirably administered by Mrs Pike (not from *Dad's Army*) as a post office and supplier of sweets, pop, and cigarettes, *etc.*[3]

Major James Ormrod, died in the last year of the war and his young heir, Captain Peter Ormrod, was faced with heavy death duties. The inevitable step was taken to sell off part of the estate. Five farms were sold before the auction, together with Bryn cottages, totalling 509 acres. Another twelve lots which included Keys Hill Cottage, Wyffryd Cottage, Laundry Cottage, the Shop, New Cottages (4), Field Cottages (3), Bryn Smithy, Crab Row Cottages (4), Lower Farm, Crab Mill Farm and Flannog Farm, St Martins, with 209 acres of land were put up for sale. The estate bought in 1870 was reduced by half, and the church, with a generous endowment, conveyed to the Representative Body of the Church in Wales in 1959.

In spite of this turnover of property, the community in Penylan remained stable, former tenants became landowners, Penylan Hall was slimmed down and Captain Peter Ormrod, MC, and his family came into residence after the Korean War. Loyalty to the community and the church has continued. Colonel Ormrod always cheerful and supported by his wife Barbara, has now retired, and lives in one of the lodges on the estate. At the beginning of the third millennium, a new generation are taking up the challenges of life in the 21st century. One of these, Helen Eardley (née Fletcher), gives her personal view:

> My first glimpse of the village I have grown to love took place on the 22nd August 1959. I was born in my parents bedroom on a hot, sultry morning. My father who had grown tired of waiting for my arrival had left for Wrexham with a despatch of wilting lettuce grown on our small market garden.
>
> I grew up here amongst the beauties and dangers a small holding provides in a fairly close-knit community. During my so far short life in the village, I have many memories and impressions I would like to share with you.
>
> I couldn't wait to attend the village school and did so as soon as I was three. The school consisted of two class rooms — the Big Class and the Little Class. There was a large folding partition between the rooms which would be folded back to open the rooms up for social gatherings and concerts. There was also a large store room — which I remember being locked in on a number of occasions, a cloak room where dinner was served, and where the same floor tiles remain to this day. The toilets were of course outside, situated next to a large coal shed. The teachers at this time were Mrs Lloyd (infants) and Mrs Tudor Edwards (juniors). These well-loved ladies were Welsh speakers, so the children were encouraged to use the Welsh language as often as possible. Simple commands such as 'shut the door' 'open the window' 'play time' and 'all in' had to be proclaimed in Welsh. The arts were the main structure for our education, so music (including making our own musical instruments) art, drama, and creative writing, were high on the agenda. Nature walks were a real treat for all the children, and I feel that my own interest in wild flowers stems from that time.
>
> It was a sad day in the winter of '69 for the whole village. Despite great efforts to avoid it the school was closed down for ever. Erbistock school received the same treatment, and the seven children from there along with the seventeen from Penylan were bussed to Eyton school, which was developed for this purpose. This was a blow from which I feel the village has not yet recovered. The school formed a focal point for the village. Here parents would gather, meetings were held, social events experienced, and the church annual vestry held.

Choir

We didn't have a Sunday School in those days but the choir, with practice on a Wednesday evening, and the Sunday morning service, kept us on the straight and narrow. The choir played an important role in village life. More-or-less all children from Penylan and Rhos y Madoc joined at some stage, with the choir stalls practically bursting at the seams. During my childhood the choir's summer outing was a big incentive. It was a real village event. A bus would be hired for whole families to enjoy a day in Rhyl or Southport, along with the choir from St Mary's, Ruabon. The part enjoyed by most was the raucous singing in the back of the bus on the way home. Not hymns or anthems, anything but!

Festival-wise, harvest was the highlight. We would have help from St Mary's choir and Elwyn Powell, our choir master, would organise friends from Fron Male Voice Choir to give us a boost. People from all around would squash into church for Friday and Sunday night services. It was an emotional experience.

Penylan Village, c.1910.

Sunday School

Many years later, a questionnaire was sent out to families in the villages of Penylan and Rhos y Madoc to calculate the interest in a Sunday school being formed. Nearly every family responded positively, so in January 1992 All Saints' Church had its first Sunday School with twenty plus children in attendance. After eight years, the children who attend are still eager to join in family services and attend termly events. They also have a small collection each week which they split equally between the church and a charity of their choice.

Social Events

Before the church took a leading role in holding social events for the village, a social committee was set up in the 1970s . This committee organised quite a few enjoyable occasions, one of which was for the Queen's Silver Jubilee in 1977. A grand barbecue and dance was held in the outbuildings of Bryn Farm

Other major celebrations from the latter part of the 20th century included the churches' centenary, and New Year 2000, when a function was held at Dinhinlle Farm for the villagers to bring in the new century together.

Other Information

Tom Jones, famous sweet-pea grower, lived at 'Sweet-Pea Villa'! He introduced a new system for growing sweet-peas that even Percy Thrower was jealous of. Legend has it that Percy attempted to spy on Mr Jones to discover his growing techniques.

Hailstones — 6 June 1983

Freak hailstones as big as golf balls fell in a two-mile band across Cheshire and north-east Wales, leaving destruction in their path. Greenhouses were destroyed, cars were dented, plants were shredded and some houses were flooded. Blackcurrants from one garden were washed down the lane over quarter of a mile to another house

Foot and Mouth Outbreak — 1967–8

A black time for the village as with the rest of the country. People were so cut off from each other trying to avoid cross-contamination. Most farms in the village were affected, with children seeing their favourite cows slaughtered. I remember our own two cows being locked up in their shippon receiving constant attention, and eventually escaping the dreadful disease.

Tragedies

Dennis Pugh who played the church organ was tragically drowned around 1960. Wendy Jones can remember having been to Wrexham on her bike for the first time to buy a record 'Tell Laura I love her'. She returned to

Penylan Sunday School Outing, Llangollen Canal, 1999.
Back row: Amanda Madsen; -?-; Sally Bottomley; Vicky Kearsley; Kayleigh Jones; Laura Kearsley; Timmy Madsen;
Alice Eardley; Sam Eardley; Matthew Jones; Michael O'Brien; Tom Lees; Edward Bottomley; Andrew Clutton.
Front row: Mini Hedley; Emma Clutton; Lily Hedley; Barbara Hedley; Joe Jones.

the village to find Lindisfarne College boys out searching the woods for him. He was found eventually in the river at Bangor, opposite the house where he was born.

There used to be a deep pit down Crab Lane and here a little girl was drowned. Her mother who was with child at the time tried to save her, and lost the child she was carrying too. This happened around 1910.

George Humphreys had two sons. One was lost to the First World War, the other drowned himself in the river.

Houses

There were other houses in the village which no longer exist At Dinhinlle Farm there was a small cottage in the grounds where Lillian and Edwin Jones lived when they were first married around 1915–20. Lillian worked on the Wynnstay estate, and Edwin at the kennels. There was a cottage attached to the kennels where the whipper-in lived.

Tom Jones 'Sweet Pea'.

6. Industry

This chapter, attempts to explain how, in the second half of the second millennium, the inhabitants of Ruabon earned their living from the exploitation of iron, coal, clay, and working on the railways.

The great industrial enterprises of the 19th and 20th centuries lie outside the scope of the community area of Ruabon. The Dennis brick works at Pant and Hafod are in Rhosllanerchrugog. When George Borrow saw the sky illumined on his way from Wrexham to Llangollen, it was the glow from the furnaces of the New British Iron Company in Acrefair that caught his eye, and when the chemical industry established itself it was nearby at Cefn Mawr. The majority of the coal measures in our part of Ruabon were either worked out or flooded by the middle of the 19th century, and deeper mines had to be sunk at Hafod and Bersham. There is however, a great deal of material from the 17th century onwards associated with the Ruabon community area. Gyfelia was the centre of an iron industry from the Middle Ages until the 18th century. Plas Madoc had a flourishing furnace in the 18th century, and came under the control of the great ironmaster, Edward Rowland, who controlled a vast industrial empire from his home at Gardden. The Kenricks of Wynn Hall exploited their lands and owned a brass foundry and spelter works. Wynnstay Colliery boasted the latest technology when opened in 1856. The Green, Plas Madoc, Plas Bennion, Afon Eitha, Gardden, and the Brandie, were all coal-producing areas. Brick making at Tatham and Gardden lasted for a hundred years until eclipsed by Henry Dennis and his successors who, for a long time, conducted operations from their red brick offices in Ruabon High Street. Without first the canal, and then the railway, these various industries would have failed. Canals, tramways and railways, sustained the viability of industry and made Ruabon a by-word for the brick and terracotta industry. The railway was something which belonged to Ruabon village, and gave the inhabitants a sense of pride.

The census returns indicate various patterns of work. Mine workers were scattered amongst the community — with the exception of Green Pit Cottages, where a miner lived next door to James Darlington, a collier manager, and in Bodylltyn Row which was home for a cross-section of colliery employees: over-man, time-keeper, lamp-man and deputy manager. At Plas Bennion in 1881 colliers lived in at least half of the twenty-six houses. Railway workers — stationmaster, inspector, engine-driver, ticket-collector, porter, plate-layer, points-man and wagon tapper — either lived or lodged within walking distance of the station, and for neighbours had a mixture of workers — colliers, bricklayers, plumbers, carpenters, glazier, plasterer, shop assistants, clerks, blacksmiths, and numerous other occupations. On the western boundary of the community in 1861, there were connections with the iron industry. At Rock House on the Penycae Road lived Thomas Shone, manager of the iron foundry, and nearby at Wynn Hall, 'William Kenrick, spelter, master of 50 men and coal-master of 82 men, ' whose mother-in-law, Rachel Edminson, aged 75 years, was described as an 'ironfounder'. At Gardden Hall in 1861, lived William Wright, a zinc-smelter and colliery proprietor. Scattered about the village lived brick and tile makers and the labourers who won the clay.

It is clear that Ruabon was a crowded community: children, lodgers, paupers, servants, tradesmen, craftsmen, charwomen, professional men, medical men, etc. The workplace, colliery, brick works, clay pit, iron foundry, railway passenger traffic or cartage of freight, was within the community. Everyone walked to work and back. The various industries were subject to fluctuations, trade cycles, good times and bad times. In the coal industry in particular, the conditions were dangerous with the outcome sometimes fatal. If there was a sudden death, disease, industrial injury or a prolonged strike, the family suffered.

The Iron Industry[1]

Some of the place-names in the community indicate the existence of the early iron industry: 'Cinders', the 'Manor of Faborum', 'Gyfelia' (the smithies or forges). We saw in a previous chapter that there was a medieval chapel in Gyfelia, possibly erected there for the welfare and ease of a settlement of English iron workers. An early record of 1472 refers to a lease of a mine for ironstone from the Lords of Bromfield to two Welshmen, Robert ap Griffith and Ieuan ap Deicus, to mine iron over an area which stretched from Wat's Dyke to Ruabon mountain. In this first period iron was produced in small quantities by a process known as direct reduction, in primitive hearths and bloomeries, and produced a form of wrought-iron.

An agreement of 1634 between Sir Thomas Myddelton (of Chirk Castle), Edward Eyton (of Eyton), and William Wilson (of Eyton), is evidence for the existence of the Ruabon furnace near the present village of Gyfelia which was 'already made and now used by Roger Hill within the township of Ruabon.[2]

Relying on waterpower, the local coal-measure ironstone came from Myddelton and Eyton lands. The furnace was conveniently situated for a good supply of cordwood from the woodland of Edward Eyton. The second phase of technology in iron making used charcoal as a fuel and reducing agent.

The Ruabon furnace was part of the East Denbighshire/North West Shropshire complex of furnaces operated by the Myddelton family and their partners. Its prime function was to produce pig iron which went to the Pont-y-blew forge at Chirk. The Ruabon speciality was forge-hammers, and iron was sent down the Severn to Bewdley and Wilden for slitting. The furnace appears to have survived destruction during the Civil War, probably because the Eytons were Royalists and the Myddeltons Parliamentarians, and the iron was essential to the Parliamentarian forces, providing them with ammunition and ordnance.

The most successful period in the affairs of the furnace came at the Restoration when, in about 1662, an ironmaster named William Cotton entered into partnership with the Myddelton family. Succeeded by his son William Cotton II, the two families worked together until 1690. From 1660–74 the supplies of charcoal from Eyton Park began to dwindle, and coal from the land of Charles Myddelton in Moreton Above were used either for domestic purposes or in the chafery for drawing out iron.

Ifor Edwards lists a succession of iron-masters to prove the existence of the Ruabon furnace to 1763:

c.1693–1710	Thomas Lowbridge and Richard Knight
c.1722–31	William Wood and Thomas Harvey
c.1731–35	Under Daniel Ivie and a member of the Wood family
c.1763	William Higgins

From the end of the 17th century there was competition from the Plas Madoc Furnace, and iron production was established on the west side of the parish for the next two hundred years.

A local product of the iron dustry, dated 1709 — iron chest, St, Mary's Church.

Plas Madoc Furnace

Of all Welsh furnaces the records of none have remained more obscure than those of Plas Madoc. Fuller's list of 1717 shows a furnace producing 300 tins per week, as compared with Bersham's 250, *ie* 6 tons per week as compared with Bersham's five. Despite its importance in the charcoal era there are now no known records of this iron-works, of which there still remains the base of one of the early blast-furnaces with a grown tree in its centre, in the field by the present Plas Madoc Hall.[3]

Edward Lloyd (d.1691), owned an extensive estate rich in coal and iron stone and in his life time the Plas Madoc furnace was active from the 1670s producing cold short pig-iron and castings, and hammers and anvils. The family inter-married with the Lloyd family of Plas Bennion, an adjoining estate sharing the same minerals. The Lloyd family, at the beginning of the 18th century, exploited ironstone and coal in Plas Bennion, Penycae, Acrefair, and Trefynant. The family also leased the iron mills at Pont y Blew. The Wynnstay accounts show disbursements made to the Lloyds:

1749 19 May — Paid Mr Lloyd of Plas Maddocks (by John Rowland) a bill for iron to Wynnstay £31-15s-0d.

Gardden Lodge, now demolished, the home of Edward Rowland, ironmaster (1752–1815). [Crown copyright:RCHMW]

1750 10 Nov. Paid Mr Lloyd of Plas Maddock a bill for iron had from Pont y Bleau forge for master's use £19-1s-0d.

A succession of ironmasters centred on the Plas Madoc and Plas Bennion estates was ensured by the marriage of Ann Lloyd (1725–96) to John Rowland (d.1805). But it was the arrival of Isaac Wilkinson and his celebrated son John, at Bersham, in the neighbouring parish of Wrexham in the middle of the 18th century, which was to have a revolutionary effect on the iron and coal industries in east Denbighshire. Others were not slow to learn from the Wilkinson's technological innovation, particularly the smelting of ironstone exclusively by the means of coal, and the development of engineering skills to obtain the accuracy needed in the making of modern machinery. Coal ownership and iron production went hand in hand. These techniques provided the engineering skills for the building of the Pontcysyllte aqueduct, and the laying down of tramways and railways to provide communications for the supply of raw materials and new markets. When John Wilkinson died in 1808, Edward Rowland (1752–1815) of Gardden Lodge, became the foremost iron-master in north Wales. He was the inventor of double blast in the furnace. The production figures for 1805 show that only one furnace was active in north Wales, producing 1,925 tons, and for 1806 there were two furnaces producing 2,075 tons. In each case, one furnace can be assumed as being active in Ruabon. The ironworks were described by the Rev J. Evans:

> Mr. Rowland's furnaces are well conducted, but principally confined to the manufacturing of crude iron, merchantable in the state of pigs. The foundry is, however well worth the attention of the inquisitive traveller for the peculiar ease, convenience and economy, with which the various parts of the process are conducted.
> Almost everything is done by the aid of a most powerful steam engine, and Mr R[owland] appears to have been the first who invented, appropriated to fusion, the double blast, to give greater facility and expedition, the result is iron of a superior quality to that obtained by the old method … [The coal pits are] as deep as those at Bilston, Staffs …[4]

The Ruabon furnace of Edward Rowland was probably situated at Acrefair. This is indicated by the route of the Ellesmere Canal railway to link up with the Trevor basin and the Pontcysyllte aqueduct (completed in 1805), 'a railway three and a half miles in length already extends from the aqueduct through an extensive coalfield to Ruabon brook.'[5] This was the Ruabon brook or Pontcysyllte tramroad which was of great advantage to Edward Rowland, running from the Trevor basin through the Acrefair, Plas Madoc and Plas Bennion collieries to the Afon Eitha and Wynn Hall.[6]

Edward Rowland died in 1815 and was succeeded by his son, Edward Lloyd Rowland, who, with his partner George Homfray, set up the British Iron Company's iron works in *c.*1817 at Acrefair. Ifor Edwards states:

> Prior to that, the old Ruabon Ironworks, situated near the base of the Pant Hill, Rhosllanerchrugog, about half a mile from the Brandy Colliery, was in existence from at least 1790 onwards. Nothing remains but a protrusion from the bank covered with turf.[7]

Edward Lloyd Rowland lacked any business acumen, was bankrupt by 1822, and dead by 1829. The trustees offered the estate for sale in 1825 in thirty-four lots. It makes very interesting reading and throws light on the scale of the enterprise.[8]

First it shows the extent of the development and the potential of the Lloyd lands in 'Acrefair', Cristionydd Kenrick and Trefynant in the same township.

Acrefair estate 49a-1r-38p. The Acrefair iron works comprised two blast furnaces, 43 feet high; a large double casting house; a blast steam engine on Boulton and Watt's principle, rolling mill steam engine; 16 puddling furnaces; sundry dwellings for workmen, coal, ironstone and fire clay.

Trefynant estate 103a-3r-22p. Farmhouse with outbuildings; lime kilns; workmen's dwellings, coal, ironstone and fire clay. A colliery, open on this lot, had been partially worked for supplying the iron works and nearly thirty pits sunk.

Secondly, it provides a description of 'the freehold estate of Plas Bennion in Bodylltyn, Ruabon, containing 71a-3r-24p, with coal, ironstone, clay, etc, the old mansion being in ruins, but there were stables, outhouses, and some small houses, yielding in rent £15-2s-0d yearly, and the farm was held by three yearly tenants who paid £136 yearly. Many pit shafts had been sunk, but the coal had been only partially worked, and it was estimated there was sufficient coal and ironstone to supply two furnaces making 3,750 tons of bar-iron for 30 years, and yet leave vast supplies of coal for sale, as well as ironstone. This lot included engine and pump, railroads, and machinery. '

Thirdly, it gives some details of the unexpired mineral rights in the old parish of Ruabon. 'On the Delph estate — 52a-2r-1p of ironstone, coal, cannel and slack. At Plas Kynaston — 7a-2r-16p. Also under a tenement in Morton House — 23 acres (probably Pant) of ironstone. There were four coal pits open. '

Fourthly, there was some property in the Ruabon community area — 'a handsome modern stone mansion called 'Garthen' (Gardden Lodge) with 70a-0r-9p, and a pew in Ruabon church, purchased with the timber at the sale for £8,121-3s-10d. Lot XVI — two fields of 12a-2r-1p and two small houses and gardens in Bodylltyn being "a detached of Garthen estate" and "a fine quarry of excellent stone" thereon, sold at the auction, with the timber, for £1,311-18s-5d. Lot XVII — 'Morton farm in Morton below' 93a-2r-9p sold to Sir Watkin Williams Wynn for £4,309-5s-8d. Lot XXXII — a freehold estate of 7a-2r-22p called 'The Green' within a quarter of a mile of Ruabon village and close to Wynnstay Park containing three fields of pasture and nine dwelling houses. Lot XXXIII — a family mansion called Bryn on the right of the turnpike road from Wrexham to Llangollen and Oswestry containing four acres, with two pews annexed in Ruabon church (this was Bryn Hall in Bryn Fields) and Afon Goch field containing 12a-1r-8p, part of the Gardden Lodge estate, on which there were two dwelling houses and underneath a vast quantity of red marl.

The Acrefair estate and ironworks was sold to the British Iron Company for £72,000, out of which, a new company, the New British Iron Company, was formed in 1843, and operated until 1888. It was followed on the same site by Hughes and Lancaster, and later by Air Products. Other industries, mostly metallic, and all of them outside the Ruabon community area, occupied the Plas Kynaston Estate. J. C. Edwards established a brick works at Trefynant. In the 1870s Robert Graesser founded his chemical works at Cefn Mawr, which became known as Monsanto Chemical Works in 1934. All these industries employed men from the Ruabon community area, particularly in the 20th century.

Thomas Jones, an ironmaster, lived at Gardden Hall until he was declared bankrupt in 1829. He had iron works at Ponciau and Gutter Hill, Rhos. The two Greenhow brothers, Richard and Thomas, were owners of the Pant Iron Works, with Richard living at Gardden Hall. The land at Gardden was later developed as brick-making factories and clay holes.

Another area developed for metallic industry was along the Afoneitha stream below and beyond Wynn Hall. The Ruabon Tithe Apportionment for the township of Bodylltyn 1844 gives as landowner and occupier of Wynn Hall, William Kenrick, an estate of 79 acres, some of the field names are — coal pit field, brick meadow, railway, field by the foundry, field by the furnaces, field by the copperas. In the 1861 census, William Kenrick aged 60 is described as spelter master employing 50 men and coal master employing 82 men and his mother-in-law, resident at Wynn Hall, Rachel Edminson aged 75 iron-founder.

A trade directory for 1883 has Ruabon Foundry Company — John Holliday, managing partner, and spelter manufacturers, Kenrick & Son, Wynn Hall, spelter. The 1873 Ordnance Survey map shows along the Afoneitha stream below Wynn Hall and above the Gardden Lodge, quarries — Ruabon Foundry — and above Wynn Hall, in the parish of Penycae, near Plas Bennion, collieries, Wynn Hall, spelter works.

The Coal Industry[9]

Two of the four separate tracts into which the Denbighshire coalfield is divided in the Geological Survey of 1928, are to be found in the old parish of Ruabon. The early history of the Ruabon coalfield was concerned with the exploitation of the tract described as being:

> On the west, with Rhosllanerchrugog and Acrefair as its chief economic centres, is a tract in which all the coals below the Cefn Rock crop out and have been worked at comparatively little depth, as well as much ironstone in former times. Coal mining has, however, long been discontinued except for the exploitation of certain lower seams in conjunction with their fireclays. The later history of the coalfield until the last colliery in the old parish of Ruabon, Hafod, was closed in 1969, was concerned with the exploitation of the area described as 'a crescent formed by the Minera, Cefn and Wrexham fault and has long been the principal mining area of Denbigshire, with Brymbo in its northern part, Ruabon in the south, and Wrexham upon the eastern margin.[10]

Early 16th century records give an account of coal being mined at Pant, 'on a highway leading from Cristionydd Kenrick to Wrexham a gutter was made to avoid the water from the coal pit.'[11]

A document of March 1631 mentioned the sinking of a coal pit in the land of Owen Baddy at Morton Wallicorum.[12] Morris Jones is recorded as being the reeve of Ruabon coalpits in 1655.[13]

In an 'account book of the coal pits at Ruabon 1661–65' there are references to wages and outputs.[14]

In the 17th century the Myddeltons exploited the coal on their estate in the parishes of Chirk and Ruabon. In the 18th century they were joined by the Lloyds of Plas Madoc, the Wynns of Wynnstay, and the Wilkinson and Rowland families. The diminishing supplies of wood for household purposes proved an incentive to coal mining. The ironmasters saw the potential of coal. Coal obtained from the Ponkey banks burned in the furnaces of Charles Lloyd and John Hawkins, the Quaker relatives of the first Abraham Darby of Coalbrookdale. Coal pits dotted the hills between Wrexham and Acrefair, as *Brittania Depicta* 1724, with its references 'to ye Cole pits', bears testimony. '[15] Edward Lloyd of Plas Madoc became a negotiator for mining land leases in the middle of the century. The Court Leet Books of Bromfield and Yale, 1719–33, and 1762–80, contain entries relating to coal pits, for example:

> 1719 … We present Richard Griffith collyer for not filling two coal pitts in the roade leading from Ruabon to Llangollen amerced 40s.
>
> 1733 … We present Gabriel Jones for not filling up two coal pitts made in the highway near Rhos Llanerchrugog in the township of Morton Wallicorum, which are dangerous to neighbours and passengers, unless filled before midsomer next £2.

Estate owners are regularly presented at the Court Leet in the 1760s for enclosing waste land possibly to dig for coal:

> 1765 … — Mr John Rowland for inclosing abt. 15 roods in length and abt. five yards in breadth on the side of the Offa's ditch in the township of Morton Wallicorum adjoining to his own lands.

The disbursements contained in the Wynnstay rentals for the 18th century show that they had mining interests throughout the old parish of Ruabon.

> 1737, 18 July — Paid Edward ap Owen and Daniel Griffiths, labourers their bill for taking up coal at Acrefair £25-10s-11d.
>
> 1755, 4 Oct. — Paid John Rowlands a bill for coals carryed from Plas Maddock to Wynnstay £12-18s-5d.[16]

At the time of the fourth baronet (1749–89), the Wynnstay estate exploited coal in the Ruabon area. The traveller John Byng observed in July 1784: 'the country beyond Ruabon is full of coal pitts, some close to the road side; and I wondered at the immense coals I saw craned up, which are sold at 2s-4d the cart load. Winstay Park is a bed of coal, untouch'd.'[17]

In February 1777, Sir Watkin wrote to his agent Francis Chambre:

> Have you thought anything abt. the coals in the neighbourhood of Wynnstay, whether it will be advantageous to work them myself or let them, they will certainly be of great value to me either way.[18]

Jonah Barff reported to Francis Chambre in 1779:

You may tell Sir Watkin that the workmen have got top coal in Bodylltyn, eighteen yards deep. I brought some home in my pocket and it lights with a candle, so I hope it will be cannol.[19]

We have seen how Wilkinson and Rowlands opened collieries to provide the fuel to smelt their ironstone. They were followed by Thomas Jones of Llanerchrugog Hall and Edward Lloyd Rowlands. A rapid development noted by Samuel Lewis in 1833 when writing of Ruabon: 'it's mineral wealth in coal and iron-ore, particularly in the southern and western parts of it, which till the year 1830 were in full operation, and extensive mines have been formed; so that a great part of the parish is now occupied by pits, charcoal hearths, and mineral works of various kinds, and is intersected in different directions by rail-roads. ' [20]

1830 was a year of crisis on the north Wales coalfield with a coal strike centred on Ruabon in December 1830 and January 1831. In the late 1820s there was economic depression which led to the decline in the coal and iron works in the Ruabon parish as elsewhere in north Wales. Many coal owners and ironmasters were bankrupt, and industries requiring coal moved to other parts of the country, and south Wales soon outstripped the north.

The *Shrewsbury Chronicle*, 5 June 1829, reported that:

Much distress prevails among the working classes in the neighbourhood of Wrexham. Ruabon and other parts of Denbighshire, in consequence of the decline of the iron and coal business… The privations endured by the families of these poor men are very great, and they are a grievous burden upon the tradesmen and shop keepers of the district.

The Troubles of 1830–31.[21]

By the end of 1830, the north Wales coalfield was organised by the Friendly Association Coal Mines Union Society (originating in Lancashire), for co-ordinated strike action to remedy the evils of bad housing, fluctuating wages, tommy shops, and bad working conditions. The parish of Ruabon was deeply involved in the strike, which erupted into violence between the colliers and coal owners, and placed the Lord-Lieutenant, Sir Watkin Williams Wynn, in a delicate position.

The strike in north Wales began in Hawarden on Monday 27 December 1830. By the following day it had spread to Ruabon. Three of the leaders were arrested at Gutter Hill, Rhos, but were released by the strikers who went off to Cinders Hill where they sat down contentedly with their wives and children. In vain Sir Watkin tried to persuade them to disperse, and the Riot Act was read. The strikers wives pelted the troops with stones and clinkers, who in turn fired shots over their heads and charged the Cinder Hill. No one was hurt, one man was arrested, and later released. On Wednesday 29 December, despite a heavy fall of snow, the srikers met at Acrefair. The day's business brought forward Mr Wood, principal agent for the British Iron Works. Sir Watkin and Captain Morris implored him to abolish the tommy shop, but they were met with a blank refusal. It was agreed that Sir Watkin should act as mediator between the owners and workers the following day. On the Thursday, as arranged, the coal owners met six of the men's deputies, but refused to accede to their wishes, and the mob of colliers attacked the owners in the Wynnstay Arms, Ruabon.

'Mr Wood agent to the British Iron Company, had endeavoured to conceal himself behind a hayrick in the garden where he was discovered and dragged out with great violence'. He was rescued and escaped to Wynnstay dressed as an old woman.

That same afternoon, Sir Watkin summoned the miners' six representatives to meet several of the owners. The miners put forward their complaints about the royalties exacted by the ironmasters when coal prices declined, the high rents of cottages, the failure of air in the mines, dangerous machinery and other working conditions, the seasonable decline and loss of wages. Mr Pickering, representing the owners, promised to accede to the miners' wishes if all other masters would do the same.

On Friday it was reported that Mr Wood and his family had left the district and the other coal owners, with the exception of Mr Parry of Gardden, agreed to the miners' demands. Saturday was a day of violence. Colliers from Acrefair joined the Chirk colliers and met the North Shropshire Yeomanry at Chirk Bank in what was known as the 'Battle of Chirk Bridge'. One report stated that the Hon. Thomas Kenyon was injured by a blow on the head, and that Samson Jones, one of the strike leaders, escaped arrest by swimming across the river Ceiriog.

The troubles continued into 1831. The coal owners were not in sympathy with Sir Watkin's role as Lord-

Lieutenant and mediator. The British Iron Company sent a report to the Home Office about Sir Watkin's inability to arrest the leaders of the trade union movement. Under the order of the Home Secretary, troops were dispatched to north Wales and the notorious Mr Wood received the assistance of three officers from Bow Street, supported by forty constables, armed with warrants, to arrest six of the ringleaders. Two were caught and charged at Ruthin Assizes on the charge of assault with intent to murder. Sir Watkin did not escape without censure from the Home Office, and criticism from the coal owners and ironmasters. Throughout this year, under the influence of the union's chief organiser, William Twiss, accompanied by William Hughes from Rhos, the mines consolidated.

By June 1831 the 'Friendly Society of Coal Miners' had a large membership in the Ruabon Lodges. The trade union movement was denounced by the Calvinistic Methodists, but found its leaders from among the Baptists and Wesleyans.

The coal trade improved between 1835–40, but again declined in the 1840s, with the consequent ills for the miner of reduced wages, unemployment, and the bankruptcy of Mr Greenhow, the owner of the Pant Iron Works. Emlyn Rogers observed:

> In Rhosllanerchrugog, meetings were convened to discuss this abnormal poverty. A petition signed by eight hundred and fifteen persons was sent in March 1840 to the House of Commons, to be followed in June 1843 by another with one thousand five hundred and fifty seven signatures … A petition of 4 Oct. 1841 … stated that two thirds of the iron and coal works in the district were at a standstill. [22]

Another combination of the colliers was formed at Newcastle in November 1842, the Union of Miners of Great Britain and Ireland, and it is said that a union conference met at the Plough Inn, Rhosymedre, in April 1845, but before the end of 1848 this second miners' organisation had faded away. [23] Despite the miners' efforts, economic stagnation continued to delay any improvement.

Children in Coal Mines

The demand for coal, the opening up of the pits, the numerous tasks to be performed on the surface and underground, put a strain on the available labour force. By the 1840s the Government was concerned, and appointed a Children's Employment Commission to inquire 'on the State, Condition, and Treatment of such Children and Young Persons in Mines and Mineral in North Wales'. [24] It is from this report that we learn what life was like for the young in the colliery districts of Ruabon.

At each pit, two females assisted in banking the coal and turning the winding-barrel, by which the coal and ironstone were brought to the surface. They worked from six in the morning till six in the evening, earning 6d to 1s a day. Other girls under eighteen were employed at the pit mouth. No females worked underground. If the coal seams were thin, boys from the age of seven upwards were employed underground from six in the morning until late afternoon, or from six at night till four or five in the morning. Their jobs were varied, 'keeping the air doors, filling the wagons, riddling coals, pumping, drawing, hooking on, and driving the horses and asses underground. '

The report presented by H. H. Jones Esq made reference to the heavy and uncomfortable work required:

> Drawing or pushing the coal-waggons, which in North Wales are called pyches, forms the principal employment of children and young persons in the pits. Drawing is performed by means of a chain passing from the pyche between the boy's legs, and fastened to a girdle around his waist; being thus attached to the load he draws it by stooping down, proceeding along on 'all fours'. Some push the pyches from behind, which is done by the hands and forehead. The children describe it as immaterial to them which method they pursue. [25]

Jones was sympathetic:

> The work of these children is a grievous subject for reflection and a sad spectacle to behold: they pass the day in working many fathoms underground, where daylight never enters, and in excavations that will not in many instances admit them to stand in an erect position. The air they breathe is full of dust and noxious gases, and dangers surround them on all sides.
>
> Pitiable indeed is their sad condition . . . but it does not appear that there is any inclination to oppression; on the contrary they are treated with humanity and propriety by the charter-masters and colliers, many of whom are religious and good moral characters, and often pray aloud in the pits, and give good advice to both children

and adults.[26] Children at work in the pits and mines breakfast before they leave home; their dinner is brought to them by their friends, and consists of bread, butter, potatoes, a little bacon occasionally, with milk or broth. They have supper at home on their return from work; most of them have a piece of bread and butter to eat between breakfast and dinner, and between dinner and supper, which is eaten at work.

Their physical condition is proof that they have a sufficiency of nutritive food to maintain health and strength … Their clothing is in most instances well calculated to their work and station. The collier boys thick coarse woollen jackets, is common wear, and the boys at the mines are sufficiently clad; none whom I examined in either class had less than two suits and three shirts.[27]

Giving evidence about the children's health, Mr Roberts, surgeon at Ruabon, stated:

that fever, when once in a colliers's house, generally runs through the family; and in crowded villages through all the families. He attributes this to no peculiarity brought on by the nature of their work, but to the smallness of their cottages, the want of due ventilation, the total neglect of external cleanliness and drainage, the cottage floors being on a level with the ground, and the pig-sty and dunghill close to the door. The medical men allege that the colliers and miners bear the usual means of cure, such as bleeding and depletion in inflammatory diseases, and amputation when necessary, as well as others differently employed. [28]

Jones compared the educational attainments of the collier boys and those in the lead mines:

Amongst the collier boys not one in ten can read with anything approaching correctness, or so as to comprehend the sense of what he reads; those in the mines are almost, though not quite, as illiterate, probably because they do not go to work so early. Both classes are, however, utterly ignorant. It is an uncommon circumstance to meet with one who can read, write and cast accounts.[29]

The evidence of a pit lad who worked at Gardden Colliery, corroborated what Jones reported:

Gardden Colliery, Ruabon, Denbighshire. (April 30th, 1841)
N° 17 — John Tinna, aged 11.
Has been working two years. Drove the pony in the pits for six months. Now draws the pyches by girdle at 1s a day. Had 1s 4d a day at first; but wages have been lowered. Works from 6 to 6. Half an hour for breakfast, and hour for dinner. Has not always so much. Has sometimes come up to eat, though but very seldom. Men never beat him. Goes three times every Sunday to worship at Methodists' chapel, and to the Sunday school. Is learning to spell words, Can't read yet. Is questioned in the Testament. Never has been at a day school. Has sometimes worked all night when the pits had to be cleared. Is very healthy. Never hears the bad language in the pits. Some of the men often pray aloud.[30]

1846. Flooding in the old coal field.
Natural disaster was more severe than trade depression in its effect on employment, when in 1846, the flooding of the collieries on a large scale in the tract west of the Minera and Cefn fault bed extinguished coal mining in many pits. The flooding extended from Plas Madoc Colliery to Wynn Hall Foundry Pit, N° 2 of Gardden Lodge Top Colliery, and N° 6 Brandie Pit at Ruabon Colliery.[31]

New Collieries
    1856 — Wynnstay, originally known as Green Pit, situated between the railway line and the old road from Ruabon to Rhosymedre near Wynnstay Park
    1857 — Kenyon, Vauxhall, near the railway line between Johnstown and Ruabon. Closed in 1928.[32]
    1867 — Hafod, near Johnstown station between Wrexham and Ruabon.[33]

Henry Dennis came to north-east Wales in the 1850s as a young mining agent and became an outstanding entrepreneur in the coal-mining and brick-making industries. New Hall in Ruabon became his residence in 1878. George Lerry has summarised his career:

Leaving Cornwall, Henry Dennis was entrusted by a firm of eminent mining engineers with the construction of a tramway connecting the Llangollen Slate Quarries with the Shropshire Union Canal. He subsequently became manager of Bryn-yr-Owen Colliery, a position he relinquished in 1857, in order to join his brother-in-law, Mr Walter Glennie, as surveyors and mining engineers, but from 1870 Mr Dennis continued the business alone.

Wynnstay Colliery.

Later he became Chairman and Managing Director of the Westminster Colliery, and Managing Director of the Wrexham and Acton Colliery. In 1880 Mr Dennis was prominent in the purchase of Hafod Colliery and Brandie Coke Works by the Ruabon Coal & Coke Company, Limited, from the old Ruabon Coal Company and the subsidiary firm of the North Wales Coke Company. Later he acquired the Pant Brickworks, and established the Hafod Brickworks. Shortly before his death, plans for the sinking of shafts at Gresford Colliery were settled, and soon sinking was begun by the United Westminster and Wrexham Collieries, Limited, of which Mr Dennis had been Chairman and Managing Director. He was also Chairman and Managing Director of other important commercial undertakings in Denbighshire and other parts of Wales, comprising Rhos Gas Company, Ruabon Water C° ; Barmouth, Dolgelley and Dsynni Gas Companies, Cefn Stone Quarries, the Glyn Valley Tramway C°; and in Shropshire and Snailbeach Lead Mines. The various concerns under his control gave employment to upwards of 10,000 workpeople. He was a prominent member of the Institute of Civil Engineers, and in 1894 was elected President of the Mining Association of Great Britain. On the formation of the Denbighshire County Council he was elected one of the first aldermen in recognition of his wonderful business aptitude, and as a pioneer and captain of industry.

After his death in 1906, he was succeeded by his son, Henry Dyke Dennis, New Hall, Ruabon (Chairman and Managing Director of the United Westminster and Wrexham Collieries, and Managing Director of Hafod Colliery until its sale to the Carlton Main Company in 1933).[34]

Ruabon Collieries
The criteria for this choice, is the association of the collieries with the old Ruabon coalfield and their nearness to the historic mining sites in the community area of Ruabon.

Afoneitha
This was a small colliery by the side of the road leading from Rhos to Wynn Hall … the owner was John Wright … Coal was being raised in 1856, but soon afterwards the mine was abandoned.[35]

Gardden Hall
The pits at Gardden Hall Colliery were known as the Moreton Pits, and are half a mile from Johnstown to the west of the Wrexham–Ruabon road near the Moreton Inn. There are two disused shafts, 40 yards apart. Main coal was reached at 330 feet.[36]

Gardden Lodge
The main shafts of the disused Gardden Lodge Colliery (between Johnstown and Ruabon) are about 700 yards south of the Moreton Pits of Gardden Hall Colliery. Gardden Lodge Colliery was 'drowned out' in 1846 when the water spread from the Plas Madoc Colliery.[37]

Plas Madoc
The disused Plas Madoc Colliery was 'drowned out' in 1846.[38]

Wynn Hall Colliery
This had two pits, the Foundry Pit and the Rock Pit … In 1846 water spread from the Bee Pit (Plas Madoc)

Wynnstay Colliery Offices and staff.

and 'drowned' the Foundry Pit. Apparently some portion of Wynn Hall Colliery was working in 1854 and in 1868. The Foundry Pit was re-opened in 1876 to work the higher seams which alone remained above water.[39]

Wynnstay Colliery, 1856–1927[40]
Wynnstay Colliery was originally known as Green Pit and was sunk in 1856 to a depth of 1,244 ft with two shafts, sixty yards apart. The owners in 1856 were the New British Iron Company, and when they ceased to operate in 1886 a new company was formed as Wynnstay Collieries Ltd. This colliery worked Sir Watkin Williams Wynn's coal. House, steam, gas and shipping coals, were raised. Further changes took place in 1895 with the appointment of J & P Higion of Manchester as consulting engineers. Mr G. R. Mayers, resident engineer; Mr T. Doxey, agent, and in this and succeeding years the Colliery was equipped with the most modern machinery both above and below ground. In 1901 the work force was 1,033 (866 underground), increasing by 1914 to 1,361 (1,127) underground. Coal production ceased in July 1927, and the pit was abandoned by September. Some of the oldest industrial archaeological remains on the North Wales coalfield are to be found on the site, a holding which housed a vertical steam powered winding engine house of *c*.1856, and a Walker fan house of 1902.[41]

Various newspaper reports provide some history of the colliery. Two serious accidents occurred at the Green Pit. In 1860, ten men were killed and fourteen injured and on 12 December 1862, in which nineteen were killed and injured. The bodies of those killed and injured in the explosion were conveyed to their respective dwellings in carts, most of them passing through Rhosymedre. It was reported 'as soon as the tidings reached Wynnstay, Lady Williams Wynn hastened to the scene of the disaster, and was unremitting in her endeavours to soothe and comfort the relatives of the dead and survivors, visiting every residence where injury had been sustained.'[42]

On Wednesday 21 January 1874, a fire broke out in the workings of the Green Pit and caused a stoppage, making the work force of 550 idle. On the following Sunday there was a loud explosion and a raging fire underground, which caused the Wynnstay pits to be sealed up from February to the end of May. A commemorative medal was struck and awarded to certain staff and employees of the colliery who rendered assistance. One recipient was Edward Davies 'for courage shewn in connection with the fire at the Wynnstay Colliery.[43]

In January, 1888, 500 striking miners and boys besieged the home of Isaac Jones, manager of the Green (Wynnstay) Colliery, Ruabon.

A number of men had been dismissed for repeatedly sending up from the pit more than the percentage of slack allowed with the coal. In protest their mates marched to the manager's house to demand an interview, but on learning that he was

Workers at the Green Colliery, early 1920s.

away an attempt was made to kick open the door, whilst others threw bricks through the windows. This greatly distressed Mrs Jones and her family who were 'almost driven to hysterics', and Dr Lawton Roberts of Ruabon was sent for.

A telegram was sent to Chief Constable Leadbetter, asking him to hold the force in readiness in Wrexham, but after a few skirmishes the police sergeant at Ruabon dispersed the crowd. Later in the day Mr Jones arrived to meet a deputation of the men. They claimed that the men had been dismissed unfairly, but the manager maintained that the men had repeatedly defrauded the owners by sending up dirty coal, and in many cases their tubs contained only twenty-five per cent coal. The owners would not pay the price of coal for slack, and the men would be wise to return to work. But the deputation maintained that the incidents arose from geological and working conditions. Dismissal for these reasons was unfair, and the men would have to be re-instated before there was a return to work. But the manager was adamant. He would not negotiate under duress and referring to the attack on his home, neither would lawlessness be countenanced. If the men resumed work he would be glad to consider any extenuating circumstances.

A pit bank meeting of the men decided to continue the strike, but later in the day it was announced that an agreement had been reached and work was resumed.[44]

In August 1889, Queen Victoria made a visit to north Wales accompanied by Princess Beatrice and Prince Henry of Battenburg and Princess Alice of Hesse. The royal party stayed at Palé Hall, near Corwen, placed at their disposal by Mr Robertson. His father Sir Henry, the distinguished engineer, had died the year before.

On Friday the royal party visited Bala, on Saturday their train from Llandderfel brought them to Ruabon station, and from thence they travelled by carriage to Wrexham and Acton Park. As they drove from Ruabon station under especially decorated arches, the villagers gave them an enthusiastic greeting. On Monday the Queen visited Llangollen and Corwen, and the Princesses Beatrice and Alice with Prince Henry, returned to Ruabon in the royal train to descend the Green Pit.

On Monday morning, the Princess Beatrice, with Prince Henry of Battenburg and the Princess Alice of Hesse, with their suite, descended a coalpit at Ruabon, staying there for an hour. Of this visit the *Standard* relates:

In the lamp-room the officials explained to their guests the nature of the work carried on under the earth's surface, and the Princesses evinced much interest in all that was told them. After about ten minutes' rest they came out into the track again, and here four ordinary tubs, with the fronts knocked out, were in waiting for them. The train line was on an extremely narrow gauge, as the passage was only a few feet wide. Princess Beatrice, in the first trolley, was pushed by Major Morris, Princess Alice had Mr Boyd in attendance, and Prince Henry and the suite followed. The roof was, on the average, not more than five feet high. After proceeding in this way for about 500 yards, the company came to a party of colliers who were hewing the coal. They were lying down and 'holeing' beneath the coal. Having observed their method of working, Princess Beatrice took a pickaxe that had been specially prepared for her and attacked the coal, soon bringing down a large lump, which she claimed as her own. Princess Alice and Prince Henry tried in turn, and in due course secured their trophies, which were carefully collected and taken charge of by one of the officials. A move was then made up a side roadway, which was only 4ft high, so that all heads had to be bent low. Here the Princess Beatrice, who had previously duly

'Bottoms Up!'
Princess Beatrice firing a shot in the Wynnstay Colliery, August 1889.
A drawing from The Illustrated London News, *7 September 1889.*

Left: Aerial view of the remains of the Wynnstay Colliery.
[Clwyd-Powys Archaeological Trust 88-18-33]

Below: Derelict buildings at the Wynnstay Colliery.

Below: North Wales Rescue Brigade:
Wynnstay Colliery 'C' Team, 22 April 1924.
Back row: A. Edwards; Sergt. Major Herbert (Instructor);
J.E. Morris.
Front row: H. Gabriel; W. Matthews (Captain); T. Darlington;
E.O. Williams. Note the canary gas tester on the ground.
[Wrexham County Borough Museum]

qualified herself for the work by signing the formal document entitling her to become a shot-firer in the mines of the district, fired a shot by pushing an electric button. The site of the discharge was some fourteen yards away, in a neighbouring roadway, so that the noise of the explosion was not very formidable, and the ladies were not alarmed. As the charge was not a heavy one, the quantity of coal detached by the explosion was not great. Having thus practically tested the principles of the art of coal mining, the party returned to the trollies, and were wheeled back to the cage.[45]

Wynnstay Colliery closed in 1927, Hafod (Ruabon New Colliery) on 9 March 1968. The Denbighshire coalfield no longer exists. Ruabon is virtually a dormitory village with the majority of its people finding employment outside the Ruabon community area.

Clay Works, Brick and Terracotta Manufacture

When Queen Victoria made her visit in August 1889, she could not fail to be impressed by the prosperity of the area and, as she travelled by carriage from Ruabon Station to Wrexham, she was greeted by loyal subjects who were proud of their industry. It was reported that for this occasion of welcome and rejoicing:

> The Ruabon Brick and Terra Cotta Works are beautifully festooned, and an arch of a very pretty design, constructed of terra cotta, worked with panels of a highly artistic nature, and a great deal of other artistic work, and covered with bunting is erected near the road-way.[46]

Nature could not hide itself and the presence of the distinctive Ruabon red marl was there to be seen. The river Afon Goch betrayed the presence of clay as it carved its way across the countryside, likewise the valley of the Afon Eitha exhibited almost continuous exposures of the Ruabon marl not far south of the Gardden Lodge colliery on its course to the Dee.[47]

Further south towards Newbridge, clay was being dug in the 18th century. The Court Leet records[48] report that in 1762, John and Edward Parry were presented and fined 10s. each:

> For raising and carrying clay off a certain common called Cefn Bychan being part of the King's Waste in the township of Christionydd Kenrick in order to make earthen potts to the great annoyance of the King's subjects and the inhabitants of the sd township.

If the enterprising Parrys were fined for their opportunism, others refused to take advantage of the golden prospects of exploiting the red marl. Edward Lloyd Rowland in 1823 failed to exploit the clay 'before his house known as Gardden Lodge' to meet his debts. He was adamant that these quarries of marl should not be opened before his house to disfigure the landscape.[49] Circumstances were different forty years later when the railway had arrived to open up the market for clay products and an increasing demand for coal. Such enterprise demanded engineering skills and entreprenurial imagination, and Henry Dennis had a strong measure of these. The boring of the shafts for Vauxhall and Hafod Collieries in the late 1850s and early 1860s revealed, for example, that the N° 1 shaft of the Vauxhall Colliery passed through 431' 7" of Ruabon marl.[50]

The shafts of the old Gardden Lodge Colliery showed the lower beds of the Ruabon marl, and it was in this

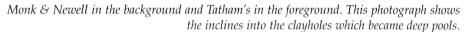

Monk & Newell in the background and Tatham's in the foreground. This photograph shows the inclines into the clayholes which became deep pools.

area that the first large scale undertaking for the exploitation of clay took place in 1883 by three companies in close proximity on either side of the Ruabon to Wrexham road.

Tatham Brick and Tile Works[51]

Henry Richard Bowers & Company, fireclay manufacturers of Chester, began their fireclay works at Penbedw, Acrefair, sometime before 1859. They came to Tatham soon after 1860, the first large-scale commercial firm to exploit the Ruabon marl — purple, green, white, yellow and red layers. A house demolished in Bank Street, Ponciau had in its debris, terracotta bricks stamped 1864 H. R. Bowers, Ruabon. *Slater's Directory* of 1869 refers to 'Tatham Brick & Tile Works, Afongoch: John Davies, manager.' In *Worrall's Directory*, 1874, Bowers is named as the owner of 'Afongoch & Tatham Tileries.' Bowers secured a thirty-one year lease from the West estate on 1 January, 1868, production then consisted of bricks, pipes and chimney-pots. In March 1877 a new lease was negotiated with the Wynnstay estate. The Tatham Works closed *c.*1910. The clay-hole was used later by their competitors, Jenks' Terracotta Works, after the closure by Bowers. It is now a land-fill site. Directly opposite over the A483 was the Monk & Newell Works, near the housing estate Gardden View, both clay-holes faced each other with the road between.

Monk & Newell

Situated on the east side of the Wrexham road, north of Ruabon village. Monk was a Liverpool man and Newell his clerk and son-in-law. There was originally a third partner, Edward Bryan of Cefn. The marl beds were 40' to 60' deep, the upper marls purple and mottled and the lower greyish purple. At the turn of the century, the brick works had thirteen round kilns and was linked by a siding to the GWR Ponkey Branch. The works closed in the 1920s. A street name 'Newell Drive' refers to their forty-year tenure, and the flooded

Ruabon Brick & Terracotta Company's works. West view (above) and general view (below).

Ruabon Brick & Terracotta Company's works.

claypit is used by an angling club.

Ruabon Brick & Terracotta Ltd. — Gwaith Jinks, 1883

This works was established in 1883 by John William Haigh, father of Reuben Haigh (1879–1951), Pen-y-Gardden. Henry Jenks, Gardden Lodge, was managing director. Later, under Reuben Haigh, W. Llewelyn Grey was managing director (from 1921), preceded by Charles S. Meadway. The works utilised the lower, more pyritous purple clays of the Ruabon marl. The original clay-hole was across the Ruabon–Wrexham road immediately adjacent to that of Monk & Newell, separated only by the aptly named Afon Goch. In 1895 the clay-hole was 50' deep, but borings had proved its depth to over 200ft. The works covered twenty acres. And twenty-five kilns produced 500,000 bricks a week, along with chimney pots, finials, encaustic-tiles, cornices, *etc*. An endless chain brought clay to the works via a tunnel under the road. In 1951 there were 105 men employed. In 1960 the works was taken over by Dennis, producing red and buff quarries and fittings. It closed *c.* 1976 and the site cleared for use as an industrial estate.[52]

The Cefn Chronicle reports that in August 1937 Frank Packard, manager gained the third award in the President's Premium Trophy competition on the subject of hot-face insulation as applied to down-draught kilns. Packard had built such a kiln and as a result new kilns of his design were built proving a remarkable reduction in fuel consumption.[53]

Wynnstay Brickworks

This was situated near Cinder's Farm east of Ruabon village on the right-hand side of the Ruabon-Overton road. It is marked in the 1873 Ordnance Survey map. We have seen earlier, that the estate made its own bricks in successive operations in the eighteenth and nineteenth centuries.

A correspondent in 1970 gave the following information:

Some of the work force in the claypit at Gwaith Jinks, c.1900.

Henry Dennis.
[Wrexham County Borough Museum]

A feature of this brickworks was that it was entirely run by three men and a boy. In 1912, I was that boy and the men were two brothers, John and Edwin Edwards, and Mark Williams. Bricks, tiles and land-drainage pipes, were produced here to provide the requirements of the Wynnstay and other estates. John Edwards was in charge, Edwin was the engineer, Mark was the clay- hole man and I was in the feeding room.

We worked from 6 in the morning until 5.30 in the afternoon, five days a week. On Saturdays we finished at one o'clock. Our programme never varied. On Mondays and Tuesdays we made floor-tiles, bricks and drainage pipes; on Wednesdays we emptied one of the two kilns. On Thursdays we filled it up again, this generally lasting the week out. Whilst this kiln was burning, the other was cooling off to enable us to start all over again on Monday morning. When the 1914 War broke out production ceased, and the men were employed on other work on the estate.

During the 1914–18 War, Mr Williams, the correspondent, enlisted in the Royal Flying Corps and on demobilisation joined the Liverpool City Police, retiring in 1946.[54]

Henry Dennis (1825–1906)

Born at Bodmin in Cornwall in 1825, he trained as an engineer, came to north Wales *c.*1850, and constructed a tramway from the Llangollen Slate Quarries to the Shropshire Union Canal. Later he was manager of Bryn yr Owen colliery near Pentre Bychan and founded the Hafod clayworks and the Ruabon Water Cº. In 1880, Henry Dennis was appointed managing director of the Ruabon Coal and Coke Cº. He was one of the first aldermen of Denbighshire County Council. Dennis is remembered as a dynamic industrialist in this area, and at the end of his life controlled the destiny of 10,000 working men. George Lerry has drawn attention to his attachment to Napoleon Bonaparte:

> On the walls of the rooms on the top landing of his home where his sons slept, huge paintings of Napoleon crossing the Alps and of other outstanding events in the career of the French emperor were hung.[55]

Dennis had the same energy and created an empire which lasted 120 years. There is a stained glass memorial to his wife, Susan Hicks Stephens, in Ruabon parish church. He was succeeded by his son, Henry Dyke Dennis. The Hafod brickworks became a private limited company, the firm was bought out by a consortium in the 1990s.

Hafod Clayworks

Hafod Clayworks is not in the community area of Ruabon, but, New Hall, the residence of Henry Dennis is, and his clayworks were situated less than half a mile away, with his offices in Ruabon High Street.

Henry Dennis realised the potential of the site whilst sinking the Hafod Colliery, adjacent to the clayworks, in 1863. He had found very rich deposits of red marl and in 1878 began to exploit these deposits. The works occupied 10–11 acres and the clayholes several more. In 1892, 360 men were employed, in 1952 there were 220 employees. George Lerry stated:

> The products of the firm were used for buildings in Oxford Street, Manchester, for the subways at Paddington and King's Cross stations in London, for flats on the Albert Hall estate, for 90 and 97 Piccadilly, London, for the Theatre Royal, Stratford-on-Avon; for the Russian Chapel in Welbeck Street, London; the Pelican Club, Soho, for mansions in Berkeley Square, for residences in Dublin and York, for buildings on the Duke of Westminster's estate, for the market buildings at Southport, and for residences overseas, including customers in Las Palmas, Grand Canaries.[56]

The export of products went on during the First World War, and in 1915 it was reported:

> The ship *Arabic*, which was torpedoed and sunk last week by a German submarine, carried some thousands

Dennis Office, High Street, Ruabon.

The decorative terracotta 'balcony' on the Dennis Office, High Street, Ruabon.

of best flooring tiles from one of the local terracotta works and which were being exported to America.[57]

The catalogue of Dennis, Ruabon proudly announced in 1900:

Since our last issue extensive additions have been made to the works to meet the growing demand upon us … with the main line of the Great Western Railway, greatly facilitating the transit of goods … the Shipping Ports are Liverpool, Birkenhead, Saltney, and Connah's Quay. The Ruabon Offices are within three minutes walk of the Railway Station, and are connected with the trunk line of the National Telephone Company, as well as by private lines with both Brick Work (Hafod and Pant), and the Company's Collieries.

The telephone number was Ruabon 1. Unfortunately the building has been demolished. This account of the building was written for the author in May 1981, by Mrs Esther M. Jones, who prefaced her account with some remarks:

I have no idea when it was built, as a guess I would say 1878. It was quite a busy place up to the time Wales Gas Board took over, and throughout the building about twenty staff were employed. The Dennis family had many interests. Coal mining, two hotels at Barmouth. Farms at Tern Hill, Tenby, and Glyn Ceiriog, in addition to those in Ruabon. They have all gone now. They made their fortune here. They were hard task-masters!

This is her account:

One feels sad to see our old buildings and landmarks disappear. One, which is of particular interest to me is Dennis' Office in High Street. It was an outstanding block of offices, built of the local red brick from Hafod brickworks, world famous for the colour and quality of their tiles and bricks. You will find bricks in all corners of the world with the stamp Dennis Ruabon underneath. I went to work in the Gas and Water Office in September 1916, during the First World War, straight from the National School, at the early age of thirteen and a half years, my wages were 7s a week. In those days the Gas and Water Companies were privately owned, and consisted of:

Rhos Gas Cº Ltd. With Gas Manufacturing Works at Johnstown.
Barmouth Gas Cº Ltd, Merioneth
Dolgelly Gas & Coal Cº Ltd, Merioneth

Henry Dyke Dennis.

Dysynni Gas C° Ltd, Towyn, Merioneth
Ruabon Water Company
Ruabon Reservoir C° Ltd

Ruabon was the Head Office, and all the accounts were sent out from there, and in those days they were all hand-written. I remember, too, that all letters were hand-written in copying ink, which had to be copied by placing them between sheets of damp tissue in a book and pressed by a hand-press. Some time later we had a Yost typewriter with a double keyboard. The directors were: H. Dyke Dennis. New Hall, Ruabon; W. Pen Dennis, Pendine, Wrexham; J. Arthur Harrop, Gwersyllt; Wm. Edwards, Ty Newydd, Ruabon; Secretary, Robert Woodford; Accountant and Cashier, Mr Albert Wynn. Later Mr Victor Dennis, Major Patrick Dennis, Mr Manton Dennis and Mr Albert Wynn were made directors.

The office had an imposing entrance hall, with mosaic flooring, and fine solid mahogany doors and staircase. The hall and corridors were panelled with decorated glazed tiles.

The water companies were taken over by the Wrexham and East Denbighshire Water Company about 1946. I left the office in 1945 and went as secretary to Major Patrick Dennis at Stansty Park, and remained there until 1947.

The office block consisted of: *Downstairs* — Gas and Water Office; Store Rooms; Caretaker's Cottage; *Upstairs* — Rev James Roberts' Office (Mr Dyke Dennis' Private Secretary); the Board Room, which had a beautiful Spanish mahogany 'D' end-table. *The Brickworks Office*: Drawing Office, several smaller offices for Dennis & Son, mining engineers; Snailbeach Gravel Company, Minsterley and the Glyn Valley Tramway.

It seems such a pity that this good building, centrally situated, should have been allowed to deteriorate, when it could have served the needs of the community in so many ways.

The Railway

The Ruabon–Wrexham coalfield was the first in north Wales to be provided with railway communications which linked it with passenger and goods services to the north-west of England via Chester in 1846, and the midlands and the south through Shrewsbury two years later. In the centre of these two railway systems Ruabon became an important junction, with later links to Llangollen and Barmouth. For a hundred years the railways provided the livelihood for a large section of the Ruabon workforce: at the station, in the signal boxes, marshalling yard, and maintenance gangs.

Before the coming of the railway system, water and waterways, and the canal navigation system, provided the major transport arteries for the industrialists. Nothing was more spectacular or innovative than the Pontcysyllte aqueduct completed by Telford in 1805 for the Ellesmere Canal Company.

Included in the opening ceremony on 21 November was the loading of five horse-drawn

Ruabon Gas, Light & Coke C° Ltd. share certificate, 1864.

A gang of workers at the Hafod brick works, 1927 (G. Griffiths, the Secretary of Bethania Chapel is second from the left).

Outside the gasworks cottage (near the Great Western Inn), where Harry Prince had a blacksmith's shop. This was formerly the retort house for the Ruabon Gas Company. Photograph taken c.1900.

wagon loads of local coal into two of the boats in the ceremonial procession from the Trevor Basin.[58] In March 1802 a tender of £3,643 was accepted for the construction of a tram-road from Trevor Basin, through Acrefair, Plas Madoc and Plas Bennion collieries, to reach Ruabon brook at Wynn Hall by 1808.[59] William Hazeldine supplied the iron rails and contracted to maintain the plate way for twelve months. Goods traffic from the many collieries and particularly from the British Iron Company after 1825, made the tramway a necessary means of transport.

In 1846 the Ellesmere and Chester Canal Company became the Shropshire Union Railway and Canal Company. Sometime afterwards, within a decade or so, the Pontcysyllte tramroad was converted into a standard guage mineral line, which was eventually linked with the Vale of Llangollen railway at Trevor station. The Pontcysyllte railway was extended in 1867 from Afon Eitha to Rhosllanerchugog. Freight traffic conveyed along this line included coal, pipes, bricks, earthenware products, zinc metal *etc.*[60]

In 1896 the GWR bought the Pontcysyllte branch and its railway stock for £51,000. In 1905 a passenger service was introduced between Wrexham and Rhos and Wynn Hall. Gradually in the 20th century the line was closed. With the closure of Wynnstay Colliery in 1927, the Plas Madoc branch went. The Pant–Pontcysyllte section finished in 1953, Rhos–Pant section 1963, and the track was lifted in 1969–70.

Ruabon station opened in November 1846. It had taken seven years of struggle to bring this about, and coincided with the height of what was called 'railway mania'. Coal owners and iron producers greeted with relief and joy the opportunity to revive their ailing industries with full production and employment providing iron and steel for the construction of lines and fuel for feeding the steam locomotives. If it was true the belching engines frightened the cows in the fields, the farmers were eager to put new acres under cultivation and to find new markets. Everyone benefited not least the workmen whose wages increased from the time of the arrival of the railway; indeed, it may be said that this marked the substantial growth of the village of Ruabon in the 19th century.

Parliamentary evidence showed that in 1844 there were almost 20,000 passengers carried by stage on coaches, *L'Hirondelle*, *Royal Oak* and *Nettle*, running on the route Ruabon–Shrewsbury–Oswestry– Llangollen. Over 117,000 travelled by other means. Building-stone, slate, timber, iron and limestone, were transported by road or canal out of the area, and wheat, flour, barley, malt, butter, and other foodstuffs were brought in.[61] The new railway would revolutionise passenger and goods traffic, increase business, and reduce prices. In 1844, Robert Roy, in promoting the line from Wrexham to Ruabon, alleged that in Ruabon only five blast furnaces

Railway staff, Ruabon station, c.1890.

were at work, and that taking 5 persons per family, 15,000 people were deprived of a means of subsistence by stopping the various works in the neighbourhood.[62]

George Stephenson projected the line from Wrexham to Ruabon in 1839, but this was dropped because of recession. A significant step forward was made in 1842 when a line was surveyed from Wrexham to Chester. No doubt it was the arrival of the Scotsmen, Robert Roy and Henry Robertson, who gave energy and direction to the scheme. They both had interests in the coalfield particularly at Brymbo, and realised the value of the mineral district between Wrexham and Ruabon as part of any scheme to link the area with Chester, Shrewsbury, and further afield. By a series of Parliamentary acts this was achieved, and amongst these the following railway systems were brought into being: the North Wales Mineral Line and the Shrewsbury, Oswestry and Chester Railways. An attempt to extend a line to Llangollen failed. Local landowners were involved: the Myddelton-Biddulphs of Chirk Castle were against railways, Sir Watkin in favour. His successors were given the right of appointing

Railway staff, Ruabon station, c.1910.

a director of the railway.[63] The Wynnstay accounts give some indication of their concern.

> 1844 1 Nov. — Expences to Oswestry to arrange with Mr West's agent as to a branch rail to the Rhos — 8s.
>
> 1844 7 Nov. — Expences to Chester to make arrangements with Mr G. Parry's desire for continuing the line to Shrewsbury — 15s.
>
> 1846 8 April — Expences to Chester to make an arrangement with the railway engineer for the alteration of the road into the tan yard at Ruabon, and the same to be allowed for the alteration of the house and part of buildings — 15s.
>
> 1849 25 July — Shrewsbury and Chester Rlwy to special train to Chester races — £26-6s.[64]

A GWR steam traction engine at Ruabon.

The North Wales mineral section opened on 4 November 1846 with the timetable advertised in the *Chester Chronicle:*

> Trains leave Ruabon for Chester at 7.30*am*, 9.35*am*, 12.30*pm*, 4.05*pm* and 6*pm*.
> Trains leave Chester for Ruabon at 9.30*am*, 11.30*am*, 2.35*pm*, and 8.15*pm*.
> Fares: First Class 3s-0d, Second Class 2s-6d, Third Class 1s-5d.
> Day tickets from Chester and Ruabon Stations First Class 4s-6d., Second Class 3s-9d. Time Tables may be had at the principal stations. Robert Roy, secretary.

An account of the opening of the first section of the Shrewsbury and Chester Railway was given:

> At 10 o'clock in the morning, a splendid train of twenty-three carriages left Brook Street Station, conveying the directors, proprieters and Co. and the Chester Blue Coat boys and their excellent juvenile band. The train on its return brought a large party of Welsh friends to this city. A second train left Chester, at 4 o'clock for Ruabon, and returned in the evening. The day was a free day and the directors were exceedingly liberal with tickets, and provided sumptuous refreshments at Ruabon. All the visitors enjoyed themselves exceedingly, and Wynnstay Park has many admirers. The line opened on Wednesday for regular traffic. The timetable will be found advertised. The trains proceed with great regularity and dispatch, and have been well loaded. This, the first north Wales line that has been opened, bids fair to become a great favourite, as it leads into the most romantic part of north Wales.[65]

Six months later, on 24 May 1847, there was an accident at Chester when the returning train to Ruabon was precipitated into the Dee by the collapse of the bridge just outside Chester. The bridge was the responsibility of Robert Stephenson, engineer, of the Chester & Holyhead Railway. The engine got across safely with its tender off the rails, but the carriages all fell into the river 36 feet below, resulting in the death of 5 of the 35 passengers.[66]

The building of the section from Ruabon to Shrewsbury demanded exceptional engineering skills. Henry Robertson was the equal of Thomas Telford in designing two great viaducts over the valley of the Dee at Cefn and the Ceiriog at Chirk. The great railway contractor, Thomas Brassey, executed the work. The Cefn viaduct is 510 yards long and 148 feet high, consisting of 19 stone arches with a span of 60 feet each. The ceremony of keying the last arch took place on 25 August 1847, and was performed by W. Ormsby Gore, MP, the first Chairman of the Shrewsbury and Chester Company '… after which the company, to the number of 300, repaired to lunch in the Goods shed at Ruabon, where no less than twenty-three separate toasts 'were enthusiastically responded to in eloquent and glowing terms'.[67] The 25½ miles of the Shrewsbury, Oswestry and Chester Junction section was opened to a temporary terminus on 12 October 1848:

> The interesting event of the opening of this line throughout, being the first line opened in Shrewsbury, took place yesterday under the auspices which we hope will auger well for the interests of the spirited proprietors.

The Directors put on a succession of free trains, and were exceedingly liberal with the tickets. The Salopians not having hitherto enjoyed direct railway communications to their magnificent county town … celebrated the event with a series of festivities … The bells of various churches were rung at intervals to mark the departure and arrival of the trains. The Mayor and Corporation processed from the Guildhall to the railway station accompanied by 'a full band of music with flags', and were taken by train to Chester and returned accompanied by the railway directors, arriving back in Shrewsbury at 2pm, they sat down to a public dinner at the Music Hall followed in the evening by a public ball and fireworks at the Lion Hotel.[68]

The next landmark in the development of the railway at Ruabon came in 1854 when the Great Western Railway Company (GWR) further consolidated its position by amalgamation with its associates, including the Shrewsbury and Chester Railway which extended its operations to Birkenhead, Birmingham, and Paddington. It has been said that when the GWR came to Ruabon it was decided to establish the company's wagon works here on account of the coalfields and iron works, but the scheme could not be realised as no land could be bought for the erection of workmen's houses.[69]

The GWR, acting through their Locomotive Superintendent, Daniel Gooch, took part in an agreement with the Ruabon Coal Company which, if sufficient coal was sent by rail for more than a 100 miles, would produce a gross revenue of at least £40,000 a year, to be doubled after two years in certain events.[70] This is just one example of the advantage of railway traffic.

It is not surprising therefore that the Vale of Llangollen Railway Co. was formed in 1858 to link up with Ruabon junction. The company hoped to secure a revenue at the rate of £20 per mile per week. This was the beginning of the GWR Ruabon to Barmouth line, a distance of $54^1/_2$ miles, which was completed over the next decade by sections: Ruabon to Llangollen to Corwen to Bala to Dolgellau to Barmouth. It was to last for about a hundred years. The closure for passengers took place on 18 January 1965 with the Trevor goods to the Monsanto Chemical Works at Pontcysyllte closing from 1 January 1968, and the Ruabon — Llangollen Goods Junction freight service ceasing three months later. The closure was a great loss to the agricultural hinterland of an isolated part of north Wales, depriving regular visitors and tourists of a picturesque railway journey through wild Wales. Perhaps the most devastating effect of the closure on Ruabon was the rapid deterioration of its once impressive railway station.

Ruabon Station

The original station was designed by the architect, Thomas M. Penson, for the Shrewsbury and Chester Railway and opened on 4 November 1846. This Italianate-style building was replaced by the present neo-Tudor type station designed by Henry Robertson, 1860.[71] On the establishment of the Ruabon link with Llangollen, the *Wrexham Advertiser* announced in October 1863:

> Ruabon Station has been much improved by the addition of a siding for the accommodation of the Llangollen trains, which, together with the down platform is covered in with a galvanized roof, which adds much to its appearance and the comfort of the travellers. We are sorry to see no indication of the adoption of gas here, as a good light is nowhere more necessary than at a railway station, and the lamps used at Ruabon are the most disagreeable kind imaginable.

In the 1930s the station accommodation made provision for a goods station, passenger and parcel station, furniture vans, carriages, motor cars, portable engines and machines on wheels, live stock, horse boxes, and a crane with a lifting power of six tons.[72]

A recent Women's Institute booklet recounted:

> 50 years ago (*c*.1930) there were 1st and 3rd class Ladies and Gentlemen's rooms, a refreshment room, a telegraph office, and a bookstand. There were 4 signal boxes, 30 sidings with accommodation for over 700 wagons, and stables for 6 horses. Sir Watkin Williams Wynn had his own private telephone line from the Hall to the booking office, and a combined saloon and hounds van located at the station throughout the hunting season. The staff complement was 62, and revenue from passengers and freight traffic was in the region of £64,000. The sidings were in constant use to and from the various industrial sites. During the war the 56 Home Ambulance train was stationed in the Gardden Lodge siding, fully equipped with men and materials, on alert at all times.

Ruabon Station, c.1900.

Wynnville Halt, Ruabon.

A steam locomotive at Ruabon, 1996, to celebrate the 150th anniversary of the opening of the station.

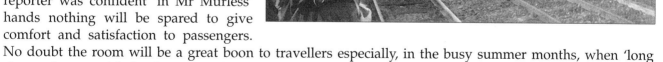

In Station Road was a well-designed residence for the station master. Still open (and listed in 1938) were Wynnville Halt by the railway bridge on the A483 Wrexham road, and Wynn Hall Halt from Rhos. Ruabon became an unstaffed halt in 1974. The refreshment rooms were opened in 1870 and consisted of 'first and second-class rooms neatly fitted with highly polished chairs and tables. ' The reporter was confident 'in Mr Murless' hands nothing will be spared to give comfort and satisfaction to passengers. No doubt the room will be a great boon to travellers especially, in the busy summer months, when 'long changes' occur with the Corwen and Dolgellau Line. '

An annual dinner was given to the railway employees at the Wynnstay Arms or other hostelries in the village before the Railway Club was opened. Until quite recently there were regular classes in first-aid and the prevention of accidents in the dangerous industrial environment. In 1896 it was reported:

> Ambulance — The examination of the Great Western Railway Ambulance class has been held at the Railway Station by Dr Drinkwater of Wrexham. Nine candidates were examined for the third certificate, seven for second, and thirteen for the first certificate.[73]

Ruabon is now a dormitory village with the majority of the population finding employment in the industrial estates outside the community area.

7. Health

At the beginning of the third millennium, the great debate in modern society concerns the funding of health and education by central government. The purpose of this chapter is to describe the provisions for community care, health and medicine in Ruabon up to the present time, and to show how these provisions evolved from the end of the 16th century under local supervision, until they became state financed through the funding of a National Insurance Scheme and the introduction of the welfare state in the middle of the 20th century.

The major source of evidence for this description are the minutes of the Ruabon parish vestry meeting and their related documents.[1] Unfortunately these are not in existence until the year 1796, but together with the records of charitable endowments which date from 1619, we are able to give a broad overall picture of the way in which the community of Ruabon cared for its sick, poor and infirm, and provided education for the young.

A feature of British society after the Reformation and the dissolution of the monasteries in the 16th century, was the way in which a great proportion of the wealth of the gentry, pious merchants and other citizens, was generously given, either in their life time or at their death, for charitable purposes. As you climb the steps to the vicar's vestry in Ruabon Parish Church, there is displayed over a large area of the wall, mounted and varnished, embalmed as it were for posterity, a 'View of Rhuabon Parish Charities from their origin to the present time. Containing a tabular statement, giving the history of the bequests from their origin to December 30th 1887; a schedule of the existing property and a summary of the application of the several charities'. This was printed by the *North Wales Guardian* in 1888 for general distribution. It was important for the general public to be reassured that there was no abuse of these sixty-seven charities conveyed into the hands of parish offices between 1619 and 1859. The first of these, the sum of £60 left by Griffith Matthews of London in 1619, was later consolidated with £20 left by David ap Richard in 1629, and the income from a piece of land, the Bronydd, left by John Eyton, gentleman, in 1624. This money was invested in land near the vicarage which amounted to 9a 1r 16p and yielded in 1857 an income of £18, which was distributed yearly on St Thomas's Day, in flannel, *etc*. The last of these charitable endowments was the sum of £400 left by Miss Rowland of the Bryn, Ruabon, the interest of which was given in weekly payments for the four almshouses in Nantygwalia.

In the 17th century there were 34 bequests, 28 in money (amounting to £577.52p), 2 rent charges, and 4 providing income from land. The majority of these gifts were to provide the poor with white bread, flannel, white gowns, and money payments. St Thomas's Day, December 21, was the most popular day for distribution.

The 18th century yielded 31 bequests, 27 in money (amounting to £1,721), and 4 providing a rent charge. Chief amongst these were the generous donations of vicar John Robinson (d.1706), through the gift of land for the endowment of the Grammar School, the Alms Houses, and educational provision for six blue-coat boys. In 1712, Ellis Lloyd of Penylan, left £200 for the Grammar School. Six years later, Sir John Wynn gave £300, the income of which purchased annually 20 coats and 32 gowns for the poor. By 1887, mainly due to vicar Richard Davies (d. 1746), a number of these charities were consolidated to buy land and farms to guarantee a realistic income to the main charitable purposes devised by the original donors. These were listed in 1887. The income for each given as:

Rhuabon Grammar School	£147-0s-0d.
National School	£20-0s-0d.
Rhuabon Almshouses Charity	£156-12s-4d.
Apprenticing Charity	£10-0s-0d

St Thomas' Day Charity	£128-13s-4d.
Bread Charities	£23-13s-4d
Bryn Almshouses Charities	£12-15s-6d

These charities were gratefully received by a large number of people. In December 1896, the *Wrexham Advertiser* reported that 'the annual gifts of beef and flannel by Sir Watkin and Lady Williams Wynn were distributed on Wednesday, the recipients who numbered about three thousand, hailing from Ruabon, Penycae, Rhos, Cefn, &c'.

It must be made clear that these charities relate to the ancient parish of Ruabon, and include in the 'area of benefit' the communities of Cefn, Pen y Cae, Rhosllanerchrgog and Ruabon, and as such were regulated by a new scheme introduced by the Charity Commission and sealed on the 18 March 1975. These twenty-one charities were consolidated to be used for the benefit of the Almshouse Charities, the Robinson Educational Foundation, and the Ruabon and District Relief in Need Charity. The vicar and churchwardens of the ecclesiastical parish of Ruabon are *ex-officio* trustees, with one representative from each of the four community councils. The trustee body is a management committee, and the resources of the charities have been enriched and enhanced over the last twenty-five years through prudent management under the oversight of the Charity Commission. This has generated more income, which enables worthwhile help to be given to needy members of the respective communities.

We have thus described the way in which people from the ancient parish of Ruabon, over the centuries, voluntarily made specific gifts towards meeting the requirements of the needy: housing, education, apprenticeship, clothing, and gifts of money. The provision of almshouses or hospitals as they were often called, was the way in which the impotent poor and the sick could be given shelter and succour. In a relatively small population, as was the old parish of Ruabon up to the end of the seventeenth century, these voluntary contributions could make a substantial difference, but nevertheless they were not sufficient, and to make up this deficiency the central government in the 16th century, through major legislation in Parliament created the first welfare state in miniature.

The intention of the Acts of Parliament of the reign of Elizabeth I (1558–1603) and their subsequent amendments, was to ensure a stable and well-ordered society under the voluntary control of the ratepayers, the officers elected by them, and the justices of the peace. Parochial welfare was administered by the vestry composed generally of the representatives of the leading rate-payers. Their scope was immense, for upon this small body of parishioners fell the burden of financing and organising the relief of the poor, the removal of strangers, the provision of medical services. According to its limited resources, always strained, the parish officers allocated benefits and made weekly grants, sometimes of a permanent duration, often to meet unexpected and temporary distress. From the cradle to the grave, parishioners, if in need, were at the mercy and discretion of its elected voluntary officers. The unmarried mother, the orphan child, the aged, were all provided for. Elementary education was organised, and apprenticeships arranged to offset the sin of idleness, the enemy of stability. The able-bodied were set to work, and public works arranged in times of unemployment. Rents were paid and housing provided. Punishment was administered to fit the crime. The absconding father was sought after, the putative father forced to maintain his illegitimate offspring, and the unmarried mother publicly censured. Although the widow and the fatherless in need were not turned empty away, the unproductive family would be moved post-haste.

Ever-increasing population in the 18th and 19th centuries, made it difficult to raise money locally to pay for these various benefits. In 1681, the population of the old parish of Ruabon was estimated as 1,082 souls. It increased four-fold to 4,483 at the first census in 1801, and almost doubled by 1821 to 7,270. The exploitation of coal, iron and clay, and the opening of the Ellesmere Canal, brought problems as well as prosperity to the parish.

The chief working official of the vestry was the overseer, who was entrusted with the distribution of thousands of pounds. Ruabon parish was troubled from time to time by incompetence and dishonesty. Mr Lovatt was 'investigated' in 1814, accused of making false entries supposing that Owen Jones's widow had received relief. He was proceeded against at the Quarter Sessions. In 1832, the vestry 'order'd that Robert Jones be appointed overseer … instead of Edward Bennion who is insolvent and confined in Ruthin Gaol', and in future, testimonials as to character and security to the amount of £500 were required. Money to be expended was raised by the setting of the Poor Rate levied quarterly by the vestry, according to the value of the land and other property. Defaulters had their goods and chattels sold. Rate assessments charter the progress of industry. In 1803 the Cefn colliery was taxed at £10 in 1805, and in 1818 professional advice was sought 'to gain every correct information relative to assessing coal works, iron works and quarries, to the Poors' Rates'.

In 1820, Ruabon vestry faced a financial crisis, and the clerk was empowered to 'negotiate with any person who may dispose to lend the parish the sum of £800 for six or twelve months'. Twelve years later, in 1832, industrial depression made the situation impossible. The overseers found it impossible to collect the rates. 'In consequence of the stopping part of the Ponkey works, and some other works, upwards of 60 men having betwixt 2–300 persons wife and children dependent on them, were thrown idle and totally destitute'. The vestry resolved 'that the Overseers should employ such of the men as have the largest families for a week in the mountain in digging lime stone to be sold for the parish behoof'. To receive further authority and assistance, the church wardens and overseers were requested to transmit these resolutions to Sir Watkin and, after hearing from him, to take such further measures as may seem best. ' It was necessary under all circumstances for the overseers to find employment, as in 1816 when it was resolved 'that persons now out of work be employed at 1s a day upon the different by-roads in the parish at the expense of the vestry. 'Another solution to the problem was emigration; 'ord'd that John Wright enquire at Liverpool what will be the freightage of passengers from there to North America' 1830. '

From the 17th century onwards, workhouses were provided for the able-bodied where they could be put to work, and parishes were given permission to join together to build a common workhouse or union. There is no record of a workhouse in Ruabon. In all probability they joined forces with either of the neighbouring parishes, Wrexham or Llangollen. The Articles of Wrexham Poor House 'for keeping of order and discipline' were extremely forbidding:

Articles of Wrexham Poor House

Whereas the said Parish Agreed the 14th day of November 1743 with Elias Price, weaver, to govern and maintain the poor admitted into the sd. workhouse with wholesome and sufficient food, washing & at fourteen pence per week each, & to employ them in manufacturing the sd. materials of wool and flax &c. for the support and benefit of this establishment.

And for the keeping of order and discipline the following articles are to be observed [below is a selection from the 12 articles].

1st. That all upon their admission into the workhouse deliver up what household goods and cloaths they have to the master.

2nd. That prayers be read morning and evening before breakfast and supper and grace said at meals & those that do not attend the prayers to lose a dinner. They are also to go to church on Sundays and holy days.

6th. That no person go out of the workhouse without leave or suffered to beg or loiter about the street or be otherwise absent than by permission the offender to be corrected by the master.

9th. That if grown persons refuse to work they are to be kept on bread & water, and if the children refuse, to be corrected by the master.

10th. That if any through negligence perform not the task given by supper time the master must oblige such to finish that night or be confined one day.

12th. That if any shd be noisy, obstinate, troublesome or any otherwise disturb the house to be confined sometime or deprived of two or three meals as the master should think fit.

The parish officers made the decision about who should receive relief. There was instruction to be found in the various manuals published for the guidance of justices of the peace and regular meetings took place to raise the rate, to scrutinise the list of the needy, and to decide on the nature of relief. The Ruabon vestry is recorded as meeting in various places: the church, the Eagles Inn (now the Wynnstay Arms), the Cross Foxes and the Talbot.

When the Ruabon records begin in 1796, the criterion for cash payments was usually labourers wages, which was generally 1s-6d a week. Money was also given as a kind of industrial benefit to those injured at work. But even money payments would hardly provide necessary relief when below the labourers' wage. Simon Jones's widow & six children were given 4s-0d a week (20p) to survive.

Poor harvests, rapidly growing demands from an ever increasing population, and the inflationary conditions created by the Napoleonic Wars all affected the stomachs of the poor during the great food crisis which occurred between 1780–1830. Food had to be bought in by the vestry with money raised by public subscription to stave off starvation in an exceptional crisis, as in the winter of 1800–01. With the price of food high, clothes were often a luxury, and large parishes contracted for the supply of clothes to the poor, whereas smaller parishes had to make do and mend. The following entry is not uncommon. 'Ordered that shirt and shift be given to John Roberts's children' (1801). The effects and clothes of deceased paupers became the property of the vestry.

There were stringent regulations concerning relief. An Act of 1697 required recipients to 'openly wear upon the shoulder of the right sleeve a badge or mark with a large Roman 'P', and the first letter of the name of the parish. This Act was repealed in 1810, but the practice was continued in Ruabon when it was decreed in 1821: 'That every pauper of this parish receiving weekly pay shall wear a badge 'PR' on some conspicuous part of their dress — and in default of doing so — shall forfeit their customary pay'. Care was taken in Ruabon: 'that every pauper and every other person do swear to their debts before payments . . . that in future the poor be paid in money and no order be given in the shops as the parish will not be accountable for their payments'. (1820) Property owners were not entitled to relief, and in 1832:

> Thomas Evans the church warden stated to the vestry that Ann Clark having become a pauper and having a house he had taken possession of the same and sold it to Jonathan Clark who paid him nineteen pounds, fifteen shillings for the same … The vestry approve of his conduct. The poor had no choice in accepting the mode of relief offered: 'Ordered that the weekly allowance to Robert Leach be discontinued he having refused to accept the vacancy in the almshouse which was offered to him by the vicar. [1798]

The Parochial Health Service

Medical aid under the old Poor Law was left in the hands of the parish officers. There were few 'doctors' available and herbal recipes were handed down from generation to generation, and the almanacs which flourished in the 18th century added to this knowledge.

Ruabon parish benefited from the large establishment at Wynnstay, and in 1780, through the arrangement of Sir Watkin Williams Wynn, received the services of Mr Lloyd, an apothecary:

> Sir Watkin to find all medicines, the chief direction of which to be Mr Lloyd: he recommends the medicines to come from the Apothecary's Hall because the druggists are not to be depended upon. Mr Lloyd to attend at Wynnstay as often as required, when not sent for, will when the family is in the country, attend once a week or oftener — when in town once a fortnight: will not go out of the neighbourhood of Wrexham without leaving word at Wynnstay, and no engagement elsewhere is to prevent his attendance there if the least necessity calls. — If any servant should meet with an external hurt that may require daily dressing: to have the liberty of sending occasionally any person qualified to observe his directions.
> Will take care of any pauper in the neighbourhood, Sir Watkin or his agent may desire …
> If a room is set apart to receive and to dispense the medicines, it will be very elegible. A fireplace in it will make it still more complete: … the still-room is a very unfit place for preparing & distributing medicines, for many reasons.[2]

Other medical practitioners included midwives and bonesetters. Relief was often given at the time of childbirth for lying-in and the Dorcas Society was instituted in Ruabon early in the 19th century to assist mothers with baby linen and other clothing. It was reported in 1850 that:

> 18 cases have been relieved, and the comfort and assistance afforded at that time have been most thankfully received, and in all cases without exception the bags of linen have been correctly returned, and in clean and proper condition.[3]

In Ruabon it was usually left to the doctor or apothecary to set the broken limb: 'Ordered that 15s be paid Elizabeth Wood of Trevor to the doctor for setting her son's leg after being broken'. (1807)

By the beginning of the 19th century we see the vestry at Ruabon tentatively beginning to cope with the problems arising from the great changes brought about by agrarian and industrial revolutions. The population explosion multiplied their difficulties. Poverty, overcrowding, dirt, disease, epidemics, dietic deficiencies, child labour, industrial disease, and injury, meant an increasing burden on the rates and a breakdown in services.

The first attempt to deal realistically with a growing number of sick was for larger parishes to employ regular medical assistance. Entries in the vestry minutes for Ruabon show that this was their solution too. In 1816, Mr Lewis, a surgeon, was engaged 'to do the parish business for £12 for the ensuing year'. Later an agreement was reached to farm it out amongst the local practitioners:

> 1821 Jan 5. It was agreed by Mr Lewis surgeon at this vestry that he would undertake to attend the paupers and other extra poor of the township of Morton Above and Below for the sum of twelve pounds for the present year and to charge one guinea for each midwifery case. Mr Roberts agreed to undertake the remaining townships of the parish for the sum of eighteen pounds for the present year upon the terms as above stated for extras. And that no other person will be employed in the parish to attend extras.

Two years later it was found necessary to employ an extra assistant, Mr Davies, and they were each paid £14.

Another medical innovation was the establishment of general hospitals and special institutions in the larger border towns of England and Wales, and the setting up of dispensaries in the smaller ones of Wales. Chester, Shrewsbury and Liverpool, provided hospital services for north Wales. Chester Infirmary, founded in 1755, was the nearest large hospital to Ruabon. In 1795, subscriptions from Ruabon included those from Parry and Jones (proprietors of Ponkey Colliery), Sir Watkin Williams Wynn, and Dr Puleston, the vicar. This enabled them to send a patient. Ruabon parish utilised the Lunatic Asylum in Liverpool opened in 1792, and Ann Bickley was conveyed there in 1813 when the parish entered into a bond of £50, and made a weekly allowance, together with a change of clothes and necessary linen. The establishment of the Wrexham Dispensary in 1833, by Sir Watkin and Griffith Taylor of Cae Cyriog, made it possible to administer to the needs of the local population on the spot, and within the first two years no fewer then 1,732 persons received attention.[4]

Preventative measures were taken against smallpox. A pioneer in the campaign for inoculation was Dr Haygarth of Chester, who founded a smallpox society there in 1778. Sir Watkin was Mayor of Chester in 1774, and an alderman of the city and a follower of Haygarth, and he made sure that Ruabon was made as safe as possible against the disease. In 1775, he paid Mr Hawkins 15 guineas 'for inoculating Mas'r Williams Wynn and provided the same for the poor of Ruabon four years later:

> One hundred and forty one paupers in the parish of Ruabon inoculated July 1779, by order of Sir Watkin Williams Wynn baronet — by me — Jno. Lancaster — 141 at 10/6 — £74-0-6.

A surviving notebook shows that the majority were under ten years of age.[5] Sir Watkin wrote in 1784:

> I am sorry to hear of the small pox being so near Wynnstay, send me by return of the post as accurate a list as you possibly can of your inoculated children & grown up people that I may determine what I will do about it.[6]

In the next generation, the Ruabon vestry took over Sir Watkin's zeal for inoculation. On Christmas Day 1806, they gave notice: 'That any poor and labouring person wishing to have their children inoculated with the cow pox may have them inoculated by applying to the General Overseer', and when regular medical practitioners were engaged by the vestry, it became one of their duties.[7]

There was a growing awareness of the need for personal hygiene. The Ruabon vestry ordered in 1826 'that a steam bath be provided for the use of the paupers, and others on payment of one shilling each time' and in 1849 a committee was appointed:

> to remove as far as is in their power the causes of sickness by promoting cleanliness and by conciliatory means endeavouring to get the various nuisances which repeated visits in different parts of the parish brought to light removed.

A fourth way in which self-improvement was promoted in the community was through the encouragement of self-help. *Self Help* was the book written by Samuel Smiles in 1859 followed by *Thrift* in 1875.[8]

Many parishes organised clothing clubs. In Ruabon in 1851 it was reported:

> This valuable institution has been established some years. While it affords great assistance to the labourer's family to obtain decent clothing, it raises his character by encouraging habits of frugality and independence. In 1850 nearly £40 was contributed in small weekly payments by 147 depositors.

Friendly societies grew up during the 19th century as a means by which the working man could protect and improve himself. The protection was against poverty and destitution, and to act as a benefit club in times of sickness and death. Improvements came through the development of social skills in the management of the affairs of the society with its regular meetings, officers, ritual and feast-day processions. The government at the end of the eighteenth century required these societies to be registered and supervised by the magistrates, to prevent sedition and unlawful strikes, and later encouraged them as a means of relieving demands on the poor rate. By 1870 there were over 32,000 registered societies in Britain with funds of about £11m. Amongst them were the Loyal Ancient Independent Order of Oddfellows, said to have had its origin in AD33. The original lodge was formed in Manchester about 1810. By 1870, there were almost half a million members drawn from the craftsmen and artisan workmen. Another society was the Ancient Order of Foresters who regarded Adam as the first forester. From about 1813 onwards the order, with its centre at Leeds, had grown to over 360,000 by 1870, with its strongest membership in rural areas.

Friendly societies were established in Ruabon at the beginning of the 19th century. Their concern for obtaining medical assistance was reported in 1870:

> Friendly Societies' and the Doctors — On Monday evening a number of delegates representing the various Friendly Benefit Societies in the neighbourhood of Ruabon, met at the Duke of Wellington Inn, and passed a resolution that they amalgamate together to advertise for and appoint a first class medical man, it being necessary to take such steps since the doctors now in Ruabon have refused to attend the societies. It has for sometime been a great grievance with many members of these societies, principally those who do not belong to a colliery or other works that have a doctor, and many of those who do subscribe to the works doctor are very dissatisfied with the attendance they get, that they have asked some of the managers to allow it to be optional with them whether they subscribe to the doctor of the works or to one belonging to their society.[9]

The Oddfellow's Anniversary for the same year was reported in full:

> The thirty-eighth anniversary of the Loyal Wynnstay Lodge of the Independent Order of Oddfellows was held with the usual ceremonies on Saturday last, at the Wynnstay Arms Hotel. Until about five years ago it was held at the Duke of Wellington Inn, when it was transferred for short time to the Court House, and finally took up its abode at the Wynnstay. It is two years since the members had their last annual gathering, the executive having voted its non-observance last year. The members mustered strongly last Saturday, there being above 300 present. At eleven o'clock they began to muster and to form the procession, the boys taking the lead, with a flag bearing the motto 'The Queen and Constitution', and accompanied by the Cefn Fife and Drum Band, conducted by Mr Brian. The Oddfellow's flag following, the executive and Dr Thomas rode in front of the New British Iron Company's Brass Band (under the leadership of Mr Johnston), also engaged by the club for the day. The procession, which was orderly and of great length, proceeded towards the Acrefair works making halts at one or two places in the Cefn and Rhosymedre, which was the tour of the day. On their arrival in Ruabon, Mr Allen (Wynnstay Arms) had prepared the dinner in his yard, admirably adapted to seat such a number of men, during the intense heat of the present season. Mr Allen's catering is so well known that it is almost superfluous to note it here, but it may not be out of place to remark that it was acknowledged by all to be exceptionally good on Saturday. After dinner the members strolled about on the bowling green, and in the evening the public were admitted there at a small charge which went towards covering the expenses of the day. Dancing was kept up with much spirit until nine o'clock, the bands playing alternately the strains required. We are given to understand that the club, in

Friendly Society procession, Park Street, c.1905, led by the vicar, Canon Sculthorpe Lewis.

Ruabon Oddfellows, c.1910.

point of numbers — nearly 450 — excels that of any other neighbouring one, whilst about 40 are juvenile members; and although during the last six months there have been ten deaths, the surplus fund amounts to above £700. The secretary is Mr Robert Edwards, Acrefair, who has held the post with credit, for 30 years, and the treasurer, Mr Edward Jones, Ruabon.[10]

In the 17th and 18th centuries in particular, the availability of the opportunity to enter into a bound apprenticeship to a master who could teach a craft, was an important avenue for a young man to obtain a stable livelihood. The great Poor Law Act of 1601 gave authority to church wardens and overseers to bind out poor children of the parish as apprentices to such persons as they thought proper. Elizabethan and Stuart Welshmen emigrated to England, many to London, and through successful careers with the guild companies accumulated wealth. Griffith Matthewes of Ruabon, the son of Edward ap Madog, was made a Freeman of the Vintner's Company in 1607, and numbered among his apprentices some of the yeomen from Ruabon and Wrexham. He left a charitable bequest to the poor, and a silver chalice to the church in Ruabon. In 1632, Thomas Nevitt remembered his education with a small endowment to the newly opened Grammar School. Apprenticeship was important in Denbighshire in the 18th century, and the magistrates in Quarter Sessions supported the efforts of the various companies to prevent persons who had not served an apprenticeship from opening a shop or following a trade. Apprenticeships were of two classes: those apprenticed by voluntary consent with the intervention of the parish officers, and parish apprentices bound by the vestry. With the development of an industrial society, the system began to break down as far as parish officers were concerned because there were too many pauper children to be found employment, and the problem was resolved by balloting. In 1823, it was ordered in Ruabon: 'that a vestry be proclaimed for the purpose of putting out poor children, who are troublesome to the parish, as apprentices'. In 1712, Ellis Lloyd of Penylan bequeathed £100 for the 'binding out' of poor children, and Edward Lloyd of Plas Madoc left a smaller sum in 1757.

Later in the 19th century, Ruabon parish vestry began to act in a responsible manner in the placing of poor apprentices and the administration of the apprenticing fund 'and in consequence of certain parties having broken their engagements as respect of boys apprenticed to them viz. John Price, tailor, widow Lloyd of Wrexham. It was determined that summonses be applied for & that they be brought up before the magistrates'.[11]

Successive vicars of Ruabon, John Robinson (1675–1706) and Richard Davies (1706–46), both endowed almshouses to provide shelter for poor men and women. John Robinson left £50 towards the purchase of lands and building an almshouse of brick or stone, for ten poor people, as near as might be to Ruabon church, with a garden at the back of the said house in common for all the poor people. The accommodation provided by vicar Robinson's bequest was for ten almshouses consisting of one room each on the ground floor, with a yard common to them all. In 1836 these houses were described as occupying 'one line of an oblong' and being occupied by five men and five women chosen by the vicar. Vicar Davies left lands for the building and endowment of four almshouses, and the sum of one shilling a week and one warm comfortable gown, coat or upper garment, every Christmas. These four additional houses were placed two at each end of the oblong, but were of somewhat larger dimensions to those of vicar Robinson and were occupied by two men and two women.

Alms Houses, Church Street after restoration in 1977.

In 1836, the Charity Commissioners reported the existence of an additional four almshouses which were unendowed. It was presumed that two may have been built in 1786 with money from surplus rents, and the other two at the expense of Richard Jones of Belan Place. These four almshouses were sited with their backs to the road and placed on the side of the oblong, parallel with Robinsons, about the centre. These eighteen houses were described as being in Almshouse Yard in Church Street, Ruabon, not far from the parish church.

It was further reported at the Charities Enquiry in 1888 that a weekly allowance of 3s. is paid to each of the 14 inmates of the endowed houses by the receiver of the charities; that there is a matron appointed to look after the old people and attend them in illness, who lives in one of the houses and receives an additional allowance of 2s. 6d a week; that coals are distributed amongst the inmates in equal proportions twice a year to the value of eight guineas; and that clothing to the value of 13s-6d is given to each inmate at Christmas and, in answer to questions by Mr Wynne Evans, the vicar, stated:

> A great many of the inmates of the almshouses do not attend church now and did not when elected. There are many of them who are members of nonconformist chapels. Mrs Davies is a great Methodist. Then there are Sarah Jones, Edward Wynne, and Mary Crowney. The last applicant attends the Primitive Methodist Chapel. William Edwards is a nonconformist. In fact five out of the 13 inmates of the houses are pronounced nonconformists, three or four are 'nonthingarians', and the rest are Church people.

In the year 2000, the Trustees meet regularly to administer the Relief in Need Charities, and the five church houses in Church Street, two in Nant y Gwalia, and three recently acquired semi-detached houses in Cil-y-Coed, Ruabon.

The community of Ruabon enjoyed its own hospital facilities from 1870 until closure on 4 June 1947. The first site of the hospital was in Church Street, in the premises occupied until 1858 by the endowed Grammar School, in the north corner of the churchyard. It was established mainly for the admission of accident cases from the adjoining collieries. As a voluntary hospital, it was supported by local goodwill, gifts, and subscriptions. It was staffed by a matron and a trained nurse.

In February 1870, Mrs Agnes Tatham, a widow from King's College Hospital, London, was appointed matron. A couple of letters from her to the hospital secretary survive: in one, by her own admission she says that her manner was 'often brusque and always plain' and in the other she requested a testimonial: 'please will you say a lot about management, something about principle and power of teaching others being well skilled in the art of nursing … ' The next matron we hear of is Miss Elizabeth Arthur who served the hospital from 1873–97. The census return for 1881 shows that she had the assistance of Miss Rachel Humphrey, a general nurse from Manchester.

The *Wrexham Advertiser* contains items of news about the hospital during its first year in Church Street. The admission of patients is faithfully reported:

> March 1870 — The temporary hospital has not been many days unoccupied. Already three patients are under treatment for severe fractures of bones and crushes. Lady Williams Wynn is unremitting in her attendance and anxiety in watching the unfortunate sufferers.

> April 1870 — Two accidents have occurred during the past week to bring into use the Accident Hospital. A workman named Daniels, at Wynnstay had his finger cut off and was attended by Dr Roberts. On Tuesday a

boy about 12 years of age, whilst working at the Green Pit, came into contact with a truck, which dislocated his hip. Dr Burton was the medical attendant in this case.

August 1870 — Dr Perkins and Dr Roberts effected an amputation upon the man Jarvis of Street Issa, who has been lying at the hospital for several weeks with an ulcerated leg.

From the beginning, the hospital received donations and annual subscriptions for salaries and maintenance. In June 1870, Lady Williams Wynn presented 'an excellent library of above forty volumes of well-selected books, to while away the monotonous hours of the suffering inmates'. In June 1885, the *Wrexham Advertiser* reported 'we learn that it is the intention of the present Sir Watkin to build an Accident Hospital at Ruabon to the memory of his uncle, the late Sir Watkin … who always took a warm interest in the present institution which has long since been considered inadequate to the requirements of this large industrial district, and during his last illness Sir Watkin revised the plans of a beautiful new structure which it was proposed to erect upon a new site'.

On the 15 May 1886 an agreement was entered into with William Edge Samuel of Wrexham, builder, for the erection of an Accident Hospital in the High St Ruabon for the sum of £1,980. The plans were prepared by W. H. Spaull, architect, of Oswestry.[12]

The general running of the hospital is described in the reports of what came to be known as the Ruabon Accident and Cottage Hospital.[13] The reports occur in 1891, 1911, and 1920. The matron nurse in 1891 was Miss Arthur, in 1911 Miss Hadfield, and in 1920 Miss Jones.

The cost of running the hospital in 1891 was £281-8s-11d, in 1911 £285-18s-10d and in 1920 £436-3s-8d, out of which £98-15-1, was for the matron's and servants' wages. Income came from annual subscriptions, donations from workmen, and collections at places of worship.

In 1891, 44 patients were in hospital for a total of 1,957 days, 38 were discharged cured, and 1 died. They consisted of colliers, brick makers, quarrymen, and a labourer. In 1911 there were 35 patients for 778 days, 21 were discharged cured, and 3 died, and amongst the injured were colliers, brick makers, labourers, a schoolboy, a clerk of works, a footman, and a mechanic. In 1920, 36 patients in hospital for a total of 1911 days, 26 of whom were discharged, and 2 died. Those injured were colliers and labourers, a fitter, 2 boys, a gardener, and a postman. In addition a considerable number of minor casualties and out-patients were treated at the hospital.

The places of employment of the workmen who donated to the hospital in 1891 were Hafod Colliery, Wynnstay Collieries, Vauxhall Colliery, J. C. Edwards, Penybont, Trefynant, Rhos Glazed brick works, Encaustic Tile Works, Potteries, Plas Kynaston Works, Rhuabon Glazed Brick, Mr Jenks Rhuabon Terra Cotta Works, Mr Bowers' Penbedw Works, Tatham Works, Messrs Monk & Newell, Ruabon, Delph Brick Works, Cefn Freestone Quarries, Messrs Corbett & Cᵒ's Works, Rhos Gas & Rhuabon Water Works.

The Medical Officers in 1911 were: Dr R. C. Roberts, Dr William Jones, Dr Lawton Roberts and Dr John C. Davies, and in 1920 Dr R. Lawton Roberts, Dr John C. Davies, Dr G. F. Jones, Dr J. C. Lawton Roberts, Dr George MacDonald and Dr A. L. Davies.

The 1891 report published a list of Christmas and New Year's Gifts — a turkey and mince pies from Mr & Mrs O. S. Wynne; a goose from Dr Jones; a piece of pork, plum pudding and mince pies from Mrs Murless, Wynnstay Arms Hotel; a currant loaf and Christmas cake from Miss Branker; Christmas letters and woollen cuffs for patients, from Miss Maude, Overton; fruit from Mrs Walter

Ruabon Accident Hospital, High Street, 1886–1947. Now demolished.

Griffith; a large pork pie and cake from Mr William Morris; tobacco from Mrs Morris; mince pies from Mrs Bushby; three bottles of wine from Mrs Franke; orange cake and wine from the Misses Edwards, Ruabon vicarage; plum pudding from Mrs Taylor, the Grammar School; contributions to the Christmas tree from Lady Williams Wynn and twenty-five others.

On the closure of the collieries during the industrial depression, it was found that there was no further use for the hospital as such, inasmuch as ordinary surgical and medical cases could more readily be treated at the Wrexham War Memorial Hospital. In these circumstances another use was found, and Sir Watkin lent it to the Denbighshire County Council as a temporary maternity hospital. It was decided, after certain internal alterations and decorations were carried out, including the conversion of a committee room into a ward of two beds, that it could be used as purely temporary accommodation of twelve beds. New equipment, including special midwifery beds and cots, a special delivery bed, and instruments were obtained, and a room previously used as an operating theatre was suitably altered to serve both as an operating theatre and a labour ward. A staff consisting of a matron, two sisters, three probationers, a cook, and two maids, was appointed.

The hospital was re-ordered to provide accommodation for as many as possible of the abnormal cases seen at the newly established ante-natal clinics, by the County Obstetric Officer, who would be in charge of the hospital. It was opened for the admission of patients on 23 August 1935. 'In the 4 months and a week from then until the end of the year, 67 cases were admitted; 39 babies were born; 40 operations were performed. There was one maternal death … The average stay in hospital was 20 days'.[14]

There were seven sets of twins and one set of triplets born in 1944. The hospital closed on the 4 June 1947. The Wynnstay family offered the building to the parish council for use as a memorial building to the seventh baronet who died in May 1944. The offer was declined, and for a while the building became the Wynnstay Estate Office, until it was demolished in the 1960s.

General Practice
We have seen how the Ruabon vestry began to employ qualified medical practitioners at the beginning of the 19th century. From this group of apothecaries, surgeons, and doctors, emerged general practitioners or family doctors. In Ruabon, the history and development of this profession is to be seen in one family which had five generations of doctors over a period of nearly 170 years.

The first of these was *Richard Roberts* (1795–1862). Born in Oswestry, he was living at Tir y Fron by 1814, and was a member of the Royal College of Surgeons in 1815. His talents were quickly recognised, and he was used by the vestry to provide medical attention to the poor. Being Welsh speaking, he was close to his patients as is illustrated by two pieces of surviving evidence. The first is a bill of 1826 for 'saddling the horse at 2*am*, travelling four miles and compending twelve pills'. The other memory of him was that he frequently carried chickens in the pockets of his long riding coat for consumption by patients he thought more in need of nourishment than medicine. His practice was extensive and varied, and in 1853 he was a surgeon with the British Iron Company.

Richard Chambers Roberts (1815–91), the second doctor in the family, qualified at University College Hospital, London, in 1837, later becoming an FRCS. In 1845, he married Catherine Roper Lawton, one of the many descendants of the martyr, Sir Thomas More. Ruabon was growing in population and prosperity, and in his early years the doctor travelled on horseback to see his patients, and later went around in a phaeton, dressed in a frock-coat and top-hat. He was fond of gardening, and in old age would often go round his patients' gardens before seeing them. Once he collected some strawberries and on his next visit found the ripe fruit sprinkled with cayenne pepper. He kept a parrot in his kitchen, which would warn the maids of the approach of the old man, by coughing furiously. Industrial conditions were dangerous and operations were carried out in primitive circumstances, an example of which was an amputation of a collier's hand, performed in an isolated cottage on the moors at midnight where the collier held in his other hand the only available light, a small dip candle. Richard was gazetted as Lieutenant of the 2nd Denbighshire Rifle Volunteer Company. He was interested in ornithology, and there was a collection of stuffed birds and mammals at 11 High Street.

Richard Lawton Roberts (1846–1922), was medically the most distinguished member of the family. He studied medicine at University College Hospital, London, and between 1865 and 1869 won several gold and one

Ruabon Doctors.
Top L–R: Dr Richard Roberts (1820–58); Dr Richard Lawton Roberts (1873–1920); Dr Glyn Cadwalader Roberts (1951–83).

Middle L–R: Dr William Stephen Davies (1935–47); Dr John Chambers Lawton Roberts (1906–58); Dr John Lawton Roberts (1946–81).

Bottom: Dr Arthur H. Turner (1883–1963).

Dr Richard Lawton Roberts on his rounds accompanied by his chauffeur.

silver medal. In 1873, after receiving his MD, he returned to Ruabon to help his father in the practice. In 1878, he married Christiana of Fennant Farm, Johnstown. In the course of his career he wrote several books: one on ambulance works (published in 1885 and running to five editions) — he was an honorary life member of the Ambulance Association; *Nursing and Hygiene* (published in 1890); a volume on British poisonous plants and *A Dietary for Invalids* (a hand-written book). He converted one room of 11 High Street into a laboratory, and decided to study for the Diploma of Public Health. Because the medical practice was a busy one, he would get up at 5 am to pursue his studies and took the degree in 1889.

He became Public Medical Officer of Health for Wrexham Rural District, and his professional duties included the post of Medical Officer to Wynnstay Colliery and to the Ruabon Brick and Terracotta Works. In 1887, he was presented with a silver salver by the British Iron Company 'in recognition of his kindness and valuable medical services'. In the same year he received a presentation from the underground workmen at Plas Kynaston Colliery. He was a justice of the peace and for many years served as vicar's warden in Ruabon Parish Church. With his wife he promoted district nursing, striving to raise money to provide Queen's Nurses from the Queen Victoria Jubilee Institute. The cost of a nurse in 1900 was £80–90 a year:

> …commendable effort made at Ruabon to raise funds for the maintenance of a trained nurse. Dr Lawton Roberts, JP has taken a lively interest in the movement in Ruabon.

> Mrs. Roberts would be always at hand to give help, under the directions of the medical men, to workmen and their families and the poor, in cases of accident, sickness, and (if need be) of child birth. She would visit the sick, tend and wash them *etc.*[15]

In 1919, Christiana Roberts received a silver jug from the Ruabon and District Nursing Association as a mark of appreciation of her services as Honorary Secretary since its formation in 1904.

For much of his career Dr Roberts' transport was a horse and dogcart but, in about 1905, he bought a car on the suggestion of Henry Dennis of New Hall. This was not a great success. It had no windscreen and the seats were perched rather high, with no protection against the weather. Richard Roberts died in 1922, and his obituary in a Wrexham newspaper described how 'his kindly manner, strict and conscientious attention to his duties and his generosity had won for him the greatest esteem and warmest affection'. For a considerable portion of his career, his partner was Dr G. MacDonald of Cefn.

John Chambers Roberts (1879–1965) succeeded his father, becoming known to everyone as 'Dr Jack'. At the age of four he attended Miss Booth's school at Bryn Hall. He later went to Charterhouse, Clare College, Cambridge, and St Thomas' Hospital, London. In his first year at medical school, he developed tuberculosis. His doctors prescribed fresh air, and from June to August of that year he lived in a tent on the edge of Ruabon Mountain, taking his meals at one of the farms. For the winter he was sent to Brighton. He was a fine sportsman and captained both his college and the hospital football team, and there are pictures of him representing Ruabon at football and cricket. In 1910, he married Ethel Timms, and the following year went down with pneumonia which prevented him enlisting for military service on the outbreak of the First World War. Later in life, he was diagnosed as having Parkinson's disease. Though given no more than ten years to live, he continued practising medicine to the age of 79, and died in his 87th year. His obituary described him as 'self-effacing, quiet, kindly and easy to approach, and with a keen sense of humour'. Further, 'he was deeply loved by his patients, and had a real interest in them and their families'. He was more than once described as 'the best loved man in Ruabon' and 'because of his kind and understanding nature, he was sometimes approached by girls in trouble' and he would have to go and help the families come to terms with the problem once he had told them the news'.

Jack's surviving brother, Richard Chambers Lawton, intended to follow in the family medical tradition, but was called up in 1914 after obtaining his first medical degree. He joined the King's Shropshire Light Infantry and was awarded the Military Cross. He had been a keen sportsman playing cricket for Denbighshire and Rhos. He played hockey and later, as his health deteriorated, bowls. Following damage to his lungs, a result of inhaling of poison gas in the war, he went down with tuberculosis in the 1930s and the 1950s. In the Second World War, along with Major Ormrod of Penylan, he organised the local Home Guard. All the guns, ammunition and other equipment, were stored in the attic and cellars of his home in Ruabon, and on training evenings there would be a string of men coming to the house to collect equipment.

Dr John Lawton Roberts (1917–82) was the fifth in succession to follow in the family tradition. He trained at St Thomas' Hospital, London. Whilst there he did some work with Sir Bernard Spilsbury, who is known as the father of forensic science, and developed a strong interest in this subject. He joined the Indian Medical Service in 1942 as captain, later major, with General Slim's VI Army. He served in Burma and north-east India and was mentioned in despatches for distinguished service. Dr Roberts married Rosemary Cynthia Edwards from Leicester in 1946, and returned to the family practice in the same year. During his thirty-five years of medical service to the area, he saw major changes in the running of the practice — from an essentially family concern, with his mother as receptionist, accountant and manageress — to a team of five doctors and full time secretarial staff. Like his father and grandfather, he took a keen interest in ambulance work, acting as an examiner for the St John's Ambulance Brigade. He formed, and for twenty-five years played host to, an amateur chamber music ensemble; and shortly before his retirement he resumed his interest in photography.

Dr John lived only a few months into retirement. He is remembered, with affection, for his unassuming manner and quiet sense of humour, and his sound judgement of people, strong sense of duty and total integrity, gained him the respect of his professional colleagues, as, indeed of everyone who knew him.

Neither his son John, nor his daughter Ann, took up medicine, both becoming teachers. His widow Rosemary, moved to Marford in 1984, and so ended the family's 170 year connection with Ruabon.[16]

Ty Newydd, General Practitioners
Across the High Street at Ty Newydd was another medical practitioner, Dr William Jones, described in the census of 1891 as a surgeon and physician. I have no knowledge of his successor, but in 1920 Dr Henry Turner (1883–1963) came to Ty Newydd having served as a medical officer in the Middle East during the First World War, and as a general practitioner in Liverpool. Dr Turner held surgeries at his home, Ty Newydd, and at Rhos, and was associated with the miner's penny-a-week scheme. His wife, Annie Lyon, whom he married in 1908, was a qualified nurse, and with her help they nursed some patients at Ty Newydd. A qualified surgeon, he carried out many operations at the Ruabon Accident Hospital, and helped to bring many babies into the world. He retired in April 1960 and died in July 1963. Dr Turner was a Freeman of the City of York where he had been educated at St Peter's School, and was buried in the city.

Ruabon Medical Centre
In 1984, the Surgery became the Medical Centre. The practice, founded in 1820, was keeping up with the times.

Doctor John Lawton Roberts retired in 1981, and died suddenly in February 1982. Dr Glyn Roberts retired in 1983, and was succeeded as senior partner in the practice by Dr Khan. From three doctors in 1977, the practice had grown to four in

Dr Turner's residence, surgery and nursing home at Ty Newydd, High Street.

Ruabon Medical Centre.

1991, and increased to five in 2000.

The confident relationship of trust between doctors, nurses and patients, is seen for example in the support for the Equipment Fund established in 1984. This is a charity fund which receives its income from the proceeds of donations made to the practice. The fund has purchased nebulisers, an ECG machine, sterilizer and physiotherapy equipment (used in Ruabon Clinic).

The facilities provided by the Medical Centre, besides regular consultations and referrals, are: nurses clinics (twice daily); asthma clinic (twice a month); diabetic clinic (once/twice a month); minor surgery (once a month); ante-natal clinic (once a week);well-woman clinic (once a week). Regular assessments are made on hypertensives, cholesterol and thyroid. Influenza clinics, annually. Family planning service by request.

The Partners
Dr M. Iqbal Khan, MB, BS
Dr Colin C. Jones, MB, ChB
Dr David Cluett, MB, BCh, MRCGP
Dr Philip I. Davies, MB, BCh.
Dr Mary Prendergast, MB, BCh

Ruabon Medical Centre Staff, 2000. Back row: Julia Bailey; Cecilia Roberts; Sharon Jones; Debbie Rogers; Julie Cooper; Eirawen Roden; Sue Kassab; Valerie Jones; Lorna Burge. Seated: Dr D. Cluett; Dr C.C. Jones; Dr M.C. Prendergast; Dr M.I. Khan; Dr P. Davies.

8. The Community in the 19th and 20th Centuries

This section looks at the idea of community in Ruabon in the 19th and 20th centuries. Ruabon has become identified with the groups created within the area. Some have been described earlier and are continuing into the third millennium: religion, education, industry, agriculture, and medicine. The dominance of the Williams Wynn family at Wynnstay created a community within a community, an estate which owned a large portion of the community area, and influenced village life at many points.

Housing Developments

The village began to expand considerably after 1888. Major housing development took place along the road from Ruabon to Wrexham. First of all on the right hand side with the building of Tai Clawdd houses, by the Yorke family of Erddig in 1888. These are situated outwards from the old toll house. Other new buildings on this side of the road included the North and South Wales bank (now the HSBC Bank), and Ty Newydd (now demolished). On the other side of the road, the Accident Hospital was built in 1886, the first development since Dr Roberts' house was built by Edward Lloyd Rowland of Gardden sometime in the 1820s. From here to the railway bridge was land belonging to the Bryn Hall estate, which had been recently purchased by Henry Dennis from Captain Conran. Dennis decided to sell off the estate in seventy lots as 'building plots being part of the parklands adjoining the said mansion and having excellent frontages to the main road

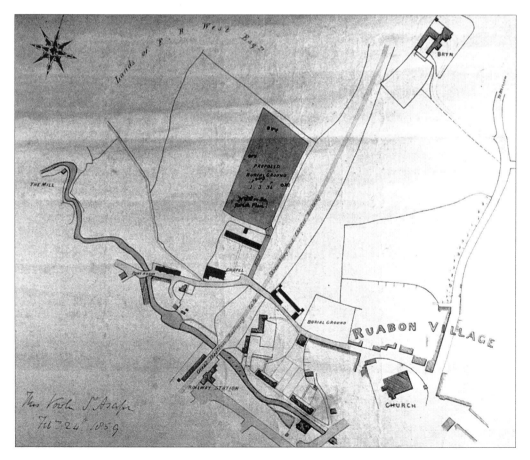

Bryn Fields before development.

Bryn Fields after development.

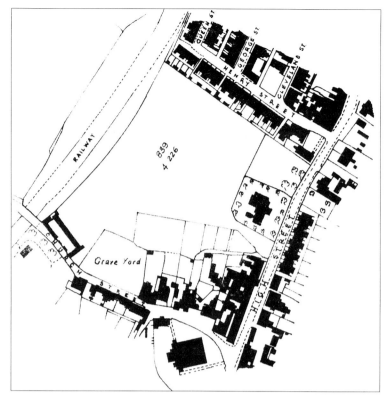

leading from Wrexham to Ruabon'. The sale was at the Wynnstay Arms, Ruabon, in April 1891:

Mr S. T. Baugh, the auctioneer, congratulated the inhabitants of Ruabon upon what was probably the first sale of land ever held in the village, and said he was glad there was so good an attendance. Lot 2 was first put up, which consisted of 360 yards, with a frontage to the main road leading from Wrexham to Ruabon. The bidding was started at 2s and rose to 4s-3d per yard, Mr Lloyd, Oswestry, being the purchaser on behalf of the Primitive Methodist church, Ruabon, as a site for their new chapel. The same body bought no. 3 at the same price, consisting of 294 square yards. Lot 4 was put up, but was with-drawn, and afterwards privately bought on behalf of the Welsh Calvinistic Methodists. Lot 5 (420 yards), after some spirited bidding, was knocked down to Mr W. H. Thomas, Cefn, at 4s per yard. Lots 7 to 12 were not sold. Lots 14 and 15 (296 and 400 yards respectively) were purchased by Mr Bradley, Wrexham, at 4s-6d per yard. Lot 6, having frontage to the proposed new road, and consisting of 333 square yards, was bought at 2s-9d per yard by Mr R. A. Jones, Bridge Street. Lots 58, 59, 60 and 61, comprising 1,028 square yards, was knocked down at 2s-9d per yard to Mr John Davies, Park Street, Ruabon. Lots 66, 67, and 68, were purchased by Mr H. W. Laycock, Ruabon, at 1s-9d per yard. Lot one consisted of the mansion, outoffices, &c. The bidding commenced at £500 and gradually rose to £750, when the lot was knocked down to Mr Benjamin Owen, builder, Wrexham. Lot 23 (216 square yards) was sold to Mr Lloyd at 2s-3d per yard. Lots 28 and 29 (466 square yards) were bought by Mr Simpson at 2s-3d per yard. Mr Langford, Ruabon, was the purchaser of Lots 49 and 50 (400 square yards) at 2s-3d per yard. This concluded the public sale, but several purchases were afterwards privately effected.[1]

As a result of the sale there was the creation of improved housing development, and the establishment of an area which rivalled the old village in size. On this land was built Henry Street Methodist Church, Cleveland Street Welsh Baptist School Room, Bryn Street English Presbyterian Church, shop premises, and a new Police Station. Streets of houses were built, known collectively as either Bryn Fields or Dennis Town. In the 1910 valuation return to the Inland Revenue, the Domesday Book ownership of the property is given.[2] Some of the owners were: Cleveland Street, four houses owned by Robert Griffiths, Park Street, four by Sarah Davies, Chirk, and six by the trustees of the Baptist chapel. Henry Street

County Buildings (Police Station) and the Villas, c.1910.

Wynnville, 1927.

houses had a variety of owners including shops and houses by R. A. Jones. The United Order of Odd Fellows owned five houses in Bryn View, and two in Queen Street. The Ancient Order of Foresters owned all the fourteen houses in the terrace named after them. The same number of houses in John Street were in the ownership of Robert Jesse Wright, Henry Street. The largest property owner in this new development was Mrs. Sarah Gethin, Glansevern, Shrewsbury, who owned the six villa residences, twelve in Beech Terrace, and the fifty-two properties near the Railway Bridge called New Hall View but known as 'long row', now demolished.

The next major housing development took place in April 1926 when Council Houses were built by the Wrexham Rural District Council on the land opposite the 1891 Bryn Fields site, and again up to the railway line where a railway stop was opened bearing the same name as the new estate, Wynnville. Initially the scheme was for one hundred houses, and by the beginning of the Second World War the estate included, Wynnville, Wynn Avenue, North Avenue, East Avenue, and New Hall Road. Mr R. A. Jones, JP, performed the ceremony of cutting the first sod, attended by Sir Watkin, members of the Denbighshire County Council, Wrexham Rural District Council, and Ruabon Parish Council. Afterwards they were entertained to tea at the Parish Hall where musical items were rendered by Councillor Gethin Davies and Inspector Owen Jones. It was reported, 'Mr W. F. Humphreys, whose firm had been referred to as a 'hustler', said that when engaged on the Rhos scheme he endeavoured to beat the record set up by the Liverpool Corporation by building one house per week'.

Another phase of council house development took place after the Second World War with the development of the triangle from the top of New Hall Road via Albert Grove, which stretched to Maes y Llan, running to Stanley Grove, Hampson's Grove and William's Close. Twenty-five years later there were further developments in the creation of Daniel's Drive, Turner House, and Wat's Dyke View. In the 1980s sheltered accommodation was provided on the site of the demolished Bryn Hall at St Michael's Close, and in nearby warden-controlled accommodation.

A number of private houses and shops were built before and after the First World War in New High Street, Maesyllan Lane, and on the Penycae Road above the Grammar School. The major private housing estate developments took place in the 1950s in Vicarage Fields for Monsanto employees, and after the 1960s in the Pont Adam Crescent scheme. In the 1990s new houses have been built in High Street on the site of Ty Newydd in Church Street opposite the Old Grammar School, in Park Road opposite Grenville Terrace. In 2000 the field opposite New Hall and the out-buildings at Wynnstay Hall are the sites of private property development.

Law and Order

An office of importance from the 16th century onwards was that of the parish constable. His duties unpaid, multifarious and demanding, the constable was a servant of the parish and of the justices. As such he was responsible for the observance of the many local statutes regulating the life of the local community — the maintenance of law and order, the suppression of disorderly houses, the apprehension of felons, their conveyance to gaol, and for the maintenance of the stocks. Every parish had its stocks. Those in Ruabon stood outside the church gates, and the roundhouse against the church yard wall.

Until the year of 1841 Ruabon parish had burial police, appointed to control large groups of mourners, but the vestry were of the opinion that they were, 'a heavy, useless, unnecessary expense, and they authorised the church wardens and high constable to petition the magistrates to discontinue it'. The constables were fully engaged on fair days:

The Round House, Bridge Street.

whereas complaints and quarrels are continually made at the Fairs held in Ruabon respecting the placing of standing carts, stalls *etc.* to the detriment, danger, and inconvenience of public business on the said fair days — we…authorize the Constables and Police Officer to remove all standing carts etc. which obstruct and incommode the public business on the said fair days…[3]

In 1851 it was decided that three paid constables should be appointed for Ruabon parish, 'one to live at Ruabon and have the charge of the lock up', the others were stationed at Cefn and Rhos. In the same year, 'fifty efficient persons' were nominated to serve as constables for the ensuing year. The constable in his supervision of the local fairs and trading in the parish acted on behalf of the community in seeing that correct weights and measures were used. This was necessary in the colliery districts when there were innumerable complaints and riots directed at the 'Tommy Shops'. Ruabon parish produced a new set of weights in 1815 but by Easter Monday 1825, 'it appears that the Scales and Weights belonging to the parish are not to be found. Ordered that the Cryer be requested to cry the same on Sunday next to be delivered into the custody of the Vestry Clerk'.

The Round House, Bridge Street

The Round House, Bridge Street, is a late-18th century stone structure and was probably the parish lockup. J. Watkin Ellis recounted, '…it contained two iron-framed bedsteads, one on each side. I have no knowledge of prisoners being actually detained there, but some of the old inhabitants assured me that it was built for that purpose. Possibly another place of detention was provided'.[4] This was the Old Court House built as a school for Thomas Madeley's scholars in 1824, it probably became the centre of justice in Ruabon. On the mid-nineteenth century map it is shown as the Court House with a robing room and prison. It was here that the Petty Sessions were held, and in the hot summer days with the door open the National School children on there way home would strain to hear the proceedings. It probably lasted as the Court House for forty or fifty years. The census returns show that the Ruabon police sergeant lived in Park Street.

The New Police Station 1897

The architect was Richard Lloyd Williams, County Surveyor at Denbigh. The land was part of the Bryn Hall estate, and Henry Dennis sold the county the site of 860 square yards at 5s-3d per square yard or £225-15s. The tender of Messrs Jenkins and Jones of Johnstown for £1,795 for erecting the Court House was accepted. The work was started in 1896, and completed by 1897, although work on drainage, sewerage, painting and boundary walls, continued until about 1899. The following is the report from the *Wrexham Advertiser*, 8 May 1897:

Opening Of The New Court — On Monday the new county buildings were opened. The building is on the main road, and although possibly not in the most central position, it is very conveniently situated. It consists of a capital dwelling house, magistrate's private room, police office, weights

The 1897 Police Station after closure and conversion to retail premises.

and measures inspectors' office, and a spacious court house, possibly the finest of its size in the principality. There are two ordinary cells with a good exercise yard. Mr Hooson presided, when a noted character named Thomas, a returned convict, who has served several terms of imprisonment, was charged with stealing a ladies satchel, containing 3s. and a silver thimble, the property of Miss Ann Davies, of New Broughton, who was on a visit to her brother at the Moreton Inn on the 27 *ulto*. He was committed to the Assizes.

Public Services

Gas Works

There was a gas works opened in October 1863 on the approach to Pont Adam. It was reported that the parish church was to be lighted up for the first time the following Sunday evening.[5]

Water

A water company was formed in the late 1870s with Sir Watkin as chairman. He observed 'that the formation of the company had been of great blessing to that populous locality, as without it many must even up to the present time been without a proper supply of water'. It was stated by a shareholder that there was still a very large number of cottages in Ruabon parish still without a proper supply of water.[6]

Sewerage and Sanitation

In 1891, Henry Dyke Dennis campaigned for the provision of mains sewerage for the village. When writing to the Rural Sanitary Authority he expressed the inadequacy of services and their effect on dwelling houses. Nearly all the sewerage was carried into Ruabon brook, which he alleged was the cause of an increase in the number of scarlet fever cases. The situation was made worse by the keeping of pigs near the back door. Dennis pointed to the parts of the village where conditions were appalling. Complaint was made regarding a cess pool which served the newly-erected houses at Tai Clawdd from which a most unpleasant smell wafted over the Church school yard. He reminded the authorities that a new hospital had been opened, new houses built (fifty or sixty of them) in Bryn Fields, without provision for the disposal of waste.[7]

Fire Engine

In April 1928 the parish council discussed the provision of fire-fighting equipment. Sir Watkin drew the council's attention to his fire engine at Wynnstay which members decided to inspect and report back on at the next meeting in July. It was reported that the fire engine was in excellent condition, but it was resolved to enter into agreement with the Borough of Wrexham for the services of their fire engine for twelve months.

Library Services

A lending library was formed in 1850 in connection with the National Schools, 'containing about 180 volumes suited to both old and young. A ticket may be obtained for a month, a quarter, or a year, by application to Mr Humphries the school master, who attends at the school after service on Sunday afternoon to exchange the books.[8] In connection with the library a reading room was established, 'an important institution, as connected with education, and the mental and moral improvement of the neighbourhood' and held in a class room open every evening from six till ten, and on Saturdays from four to nine.[9] In March 1933 the Parish Council discussed the scheme offered by the County Library for the provision of books, reporting that it would cost 7s-6d for a paid

The new Library.

Allotment holders and some of the Parish Councillors, c.1920.
Back row: Dave Jarvis; Ernest James Wilcock; John Ridge; John Williams; R. Everitt; Charlie Edwards; Ed. Evans.
Middle row: John Gibbons; John Jones; Walter Nicholas; Parker Richards; George Saint;
George Hughes; Alf Pemberton; Robert Leighton; Ed. Price.
Front row: David Owens; John Jones (Snr.); George Richards; John Jones (Jnr.); William Morris; Tom Edwards.

librarian to be appointed for one night a week. By October arrangements had been made with the Parish Hall committee who had agreed, 'the use of one room for the storing of books in cupboards under the proposed county library scheme, and for the issuing of books on one night per week for two hours each evening for the sum of thirty shillings per annum'. This service was enthusiastically taken up by the villages. In February 1934 it was reported, 'that 347 members were enrolled, and an average of 341 books were issued weekly'.[10] The library left the Parish Hall, and eventually arrived at the purpose-built library in the late 1970s.

Allotments

The gardens on the new housing estates were insufficient to produce enough vegetables to supplement the diet and income of large families. There was a nation-wide campaign at the beginning of the twentieth century to improve the health of the population. This was taken up in Ruabon in 1911 when all members of the Parish Council formed themselves into an allotment committee which supervised allotment gardens near the cemetery, at Tatham beyond Maes y Llan Farm, and Fron Goch gardens. During the First World War John Gibbons, a member of the Parish Council and the honorary inspector, distributed leaflets from the board of agriculture on gardening, pigkeeping, and autumn gardening. A public meeting was held in April 1918 about the allotments and, as a result, twenty-two new gardens were applied for and granted. There were sixty-four allotment gardens at Tatham, twenty-nine or thirty in older lots, altogether about 150 gardens in Ruabon district.[11]

Roads and Bridges

The Highway Act of 1555 made parishes responsible for the repair of roads, and surveyors were appointed by them to report on repairs needed which were paid for by the raising of a local rate. Bridges became the responsibility of the Justices of the Peace and their repair was dealt with at the County Quarter Sessions, and it is principally from this source that we learn about the major bridges in Ruabon. Here bridges are necessary for crossing the river Dee at Newbridge, and the Afon Eitha at Rhuddallt and Pont Adam. Quarter Session records for the county of Denbigh contain many items relating to bridges.[12] In 1708 there is an order for the inspection of all bridges rebuilt or repaired since the great flood of 1706, and there are accounts of repairs to Pont Adam, Ruabon, Hen Bridge, Lower Bridge, Green Bridge,and New Bridge, throughout the eighteenth century. Bridges are mentioned in the Court Leet records:

> 1733, We present the bridge leading from Ruabon to Rhuddallt to be out of repair…about £3 will repair.
> 1763, The inhabitants of the parish of Ruabon for not getting rails along the King's Highway … from Ruabon

churchyard wall towards the bridge on the road leading to Oswestry, about £1 will do the same.

1766   …for not railing between the King's Highway and the river near the almshouses…£10 will do the same.

1768   …for not making a footbridge to go over the water opposite Plas Madoc and Richard Lee's fields. £1 will do the same.[13]

The Wynnstay rentals provide some information on the making of new roads in the eighteenth and nineteenth centuries. A feature of these years was the establishment of turnpike roads. By these means roads were repaired and improved. The roads were administered by trusts authorised by private acts of parliament on which tolls were charged. To administer these, toll houses or toll bars were erected to stop and levy a charge on travellers' vehicles and cattle. There was a toll house on the High Street where René's hairdressers is, another toll bar at Plas Madoc, and at the top of the Wynnstay Hill on the Overton road. In 1785 the Justice of the Peace ordered Mr John Rowland of Plas Bennion to appear to answer a complaint of assaulting Margaret Pool, collector of tolls at Ruabon Turnpike. Also his conviction and order to pay £10 compensation to Samuel Horath, surveyor, 4 January 1785.[14]

1767, 3 September. Paid Meredith Hughes for surveying and planning the intended new road to Wynnstay £3-3s-0d.

1822, 28 January. Received of Mr Thomas Evans, money which had been previously lent by Sir Watkin to the Commissioners of Ruabon District for the new Bangor Road

1826, 14 January. By cash to Mr Thomas Evans, treasurer to the Ruabon Turnpike Road Commissioners, on account of the new line of road from New Bridge to Ruabon £160, another £520 had been paid previously.

J. Watkin Ellis revealed:

when the new road from Ruabon to Newbridge was engineered, the contour was changed; previously the Bridge End Inn then known as the Bricklayers' Arms Inn, was practically at the same level as Duke Street, as an examination of the river bridge will confirm. The old road to Newbridge and on to Chirk left the village at a spot near the former Wesleyan Chapel, opposite Station Road, passed through what is now the enclosed parkland, running through the Cross Keys, well within the present park along Offa's Dyke and terminating close to the present bridge over the Dee at Newbridge. The new road was laid about the same time as the new bridge was erected.

The Wynnstay rentals confirm that this was *c.*1826.

Motor traffic ensured a higher standard of maintenance of the roads. From 1910 onwards some of the main roads in Ruabon were tarred. The council was given the option of having the main roads tar sprayed in future, instead of watered. In 1911 the parish council asked the county, 'to fix a speed limit not to exceed twelve miles per hour for motor cars going through the village of Ruabon'. The newspaper reported on 28 June 1913:

In view of the heavy motor traffic, with its attendant dust nuisance, the County Council have begun tar painting in the village. This week the road leading to the entrance to Wynnstay park has been tarred, and it is understood that the main street is to receive similar treatment. Several large motor buses have passed through this week, most of them being bound for Llangollen, and on Monday last the members of the Liverpool City Fire Brigade motored through to Llangollen where they spent their annual outing.[15]

The 1980s and 1990s in the Ruabon area witnessed a road building programme to be favourably compared with the works of Thomas Telford and Henry Robertson in the 19th century. In August 1987 the £14 million Ruabon by-pass was opened by the Minister of State for Wales, Mr Wynn Roberts, MP. It is a three-mile long dual carriageway which runs southwards from Wrexham. Three years later in June 1990 the five-span viaduct which crosses the river Dee was opened to traffic. To celebrate this engineering feat the Rotary Club of Llangollen, with help from the Oswestry Club and the Canal Boat Trust of Llangollen, organised a walk which attracted between 20 and 25,000 walkers, with many others crossing over after officials had finished counting.

Meeting Places for the Community

One of the favourite meeting places was the Village Room in Park Street now called the Constitutional Club. Next door was the Goat Public House and the area was called the 'Goat Bank'.

The opening of the A483 Ruabon by-pass, 1987.

This was the centre of the huge fairs held in the village periodically, when the streets were well nigh impassable and stalls displaying all kinds of articles were set up — sometimes beyond the confines of the village…Crowds came from far and near to buy workmen's tools, household utensils, wearing apparel, eatables of all kinds including butchers' meat in great quantities and sometimes livestock was marketed. The purchasers naturally followed the crowd to patronise the 'hobby horses', swings, and innumerable shows provided for their entertainment.

There is in the centre of the space a circle with a surround of shaped stones. This in the old days was the Market Hall, divided into stalls, which were opened for trade once a week…It seems a pity that this open space, 'the Goat Bank' was used for building purposes. It was quite a pleasant feature of the old village…[16]

There was an annual fair in February held on the last Friday. The next was 22 May:

1880 The May Fair — the annual May Fair was held on Friday week and was as usual a small one, this being the smallest fair of the year. There was a fair representation of livestock. Barren cows and heifers were sold at low figures while milking and calving cows demanded a good price. There was also a large quantity of pigs which fetched high prices.[17]

And the Onion Fair on the 20 November:

1863 The Onion Fair…there was but a small show of cattle which fetched average prices; pigs were plentiful and sold better than at Wrexham; butter sold at 11^{1}/2d to 1s.-2d.; cheese from 4d to 7d; onions were as usual very plentiful and sold from 1d. to 1^{1}/2d per pound; mutton 5d to 7^{1}/2d per pound; beef 5d to 7d per pound.[18]

The Goat Public House was converted into a 'Cocoa House, as part of the 19th century movement to resist the evils of intemperance by providing congenial surroundings with the opportunity for education and moral improvement:

1865 Opening of the Goat Cocoa House. On Friday evening the long looked for Cocoa House was opened. It is situated in the best possible position, the Ruabon Public House company having converted the Old Goat buildings into a very attractive cocoa room. They are well furnished. In the shop are an ample supply of eatables of every kind, with the usual non-intoxicating beverages, and tea, cocoa and coffee. On the left of the shop there is a smoke room where the splendid bagatelle board of the Ruabon Working Men's Association has been erected. The games of chess, draughts and dominoes are also afforded. To the right of the shop there are also two other rooms used as dining and reading rooms. Here there is a capital supply of daily and weekly newspapers. There are also good rooms upstairs. The marble top and wooden tables are used. The walls are hung with the 'British Workman' wallpaper and the entire house is very neat, clean and attractive. The rooms supply a long required want and will be appreciated by the inhabitants as a boon. Already a very good business has been done and they are in a fair way for success.

The Working Men's Association, 1864

Next door to the Cocoa Rooms was the Village Room. How this building was used when Madeley's school was closed has not been discovered. The purpose envisaged when the Working Man's Association was opened in October 1864 was explained at length by the vicar of Ruabon, E. W. Edwards. Its major function was to give young men an opportunity of spending their week day evenings in reading and self improvement, without being engrossed in the temptation of the public house. The vicar was supported by the schoolmaster, Mr Allott, who acted as secretary and read out the rules. The association was to elect a committee to consist of the working men themselves, who would meet once a month. Subscribers and members would meet once a year. The charge to members was 6d a month, with expenses calculated about

Constitutional Club, Park Street.

10s. per week. For the benefit of the Association there would be a library, and a number of newspapers would be available. It was made clear that intoxicating drinks would be forbidden on the premises. Fifty-four members had joined at the first meeting. The first annual report in 1865 was not very optimistic. Membership had increased to sixty-four members, but the average numbers in attendance during the winter months was twenty-nine, and it was thought necessary to close the room from April to October. The chief subscriber of £5 was Sir Watkin who 'with his usual liberality and readiness to further any good cause' gave the room to the association, and promised to light it with gas and make it comfortable. Named amongst the subscribers were the New British Iron Company, G. H Whalley, MP, J. Kenrick, W. Kenrick, and the Gardden Lodge Coal Company. The annual report for 1870 shows that the Association is stable, with the average readers of newspapers forty per month, and increased attendance and funds. After the hard political battles in the 1880s and the loss of this parliamentary seat in 1885 to the Liberals, the name of the association was changed to the Working Men's Conservative Club, and later to the Constitutional Club.

Public Houses

There were many public houses in Ruabon: the Bridge Inn, the Vaults, the Duke of Wellington, the Wynnstay Arms and the Great Western. Others were the Phoenix at Pont Adam, the Feathers, and Cross Foxes in Church Street, and in Tan Lan the Talbot, the Goat, and the Royal Oak.

George Hammond Whalley (1813–78).

George Hammond Whalley, 1813–78

A colourful character who lived at Plas Madoc in the 19th century was George Hammond Whalley who claimed descent from Edward Whalley, first cousin to Oliver Cromwell and John Hampden. Just as Henry Dennis had a high regard for Napoleon Bonaparte, Whalley had an equal preoccupation with Oliver Cromwell, particularly in his hatred of the Jesuits and Puseyites. He obtained the property of Plas Madoc, which had been heavily mortgaged by Thomas Youde, and took a part in local affairs entering into some local industrial partnerships, including the Cambrian railway. He was an able barrister and an expert on the law of tithes and was for some years liberal member of parliament for Peterborough. Ironically he died on 8 October 1878 at King William's Tower, near Llangollen, and was buried in the Lloyd vault at Ruabon. There is an intriguing account of a demonstration in Plas Madoc park in August 1865 to mark the anniversary of the Temperance Society and the Band of Hope:

On Monday last, Plas Madoc Park, the residence of G. H. Whalley Esq, MP, was the scene of a Temperance demonstration of a very pleasing character. The first part of the ceremonial consisted of a tea party, which took place in a large tent belonging to Mr T. Rowlands of the Nag's Head brewery of this town...After tea a variety of innocent games were improvised for the indulgence of which Plas

Madoc park affords such ample scope. The more robust of the male sex betook themselves to football, while the more gallant of the same sex joined the fair ones in a game of 'Kiss in the Ring', always one of the favourite pastimes at Temperance Fêtes. The Penycae band gave an additional touch of merriment to the proceedings, varied occasionally by the singing of the children. The weather was delightfully fine and nothing occurred in any way calculated to mar the enjoyment of the happy company.

In the evening a public meeting was held, over which G. H. Whalley Esq. was called to preside, and on taking the chair the honourable gentleman was received with loud acclamation. In the course of the remarks he made, he said that he had expected to have amongst them that evening the son of that noble patriot Garibaldi, but although they had been disappointed that evening, he hoped that on some future occasion they would have the pleasure of seeing him 'amongst' them. The chairman then proceeded to picture the benefits accruing from the practice of temperance principles and was frequently interrupted by the plaudits of the assembly.[19]

The Hospitality at Wynnstay

In a previous chapter the great events associated with the rites of passage of the Williams Wynn family were described. Here are a few extracts to illustrate their power to charm and welcome people to the hall from the neighbouring communities and to allow the park to be the playground of the village:

> To the Editor of the *Wrexham Advertiser* Christmas Eve 1863 — Sir Watkin and Lady Wynn's Liberality.
> Sir — 'I think it would be wrong of us if we didn't say a word about the kindness we received at Wynnstay this Christmas. You know it is the custom in this neighbourhood to go about singing on Christmas Eve, and among several others that went out the Band and Glee Society, connected with the New British Iron Company's Works, went to Wynnstay and after playing several Welsh airs before the mansion, were all invited to supper, where there was plenty of beef and venison provided for us, together with plenty of Sir Watkin's old ale. After supper was over we were invited to sing several Welsh airs before Sir Watkin, Lady Williams Wynn, and a number of visitors. We were then taken to see the new rooms, the grandeur of which I am not able to describe to you Mr Editor, but I can tell you this we never saw such a sight before, nor did I ever dream of such grandeur. Afterwards, the Glee Society, accompanied by the band, sang, *God Bless the Prince of Wales*. We were then taken to the cellar to taste the Prince of Wales's ale, which was brewed on his marriage day, and the young lady singers with us were taken to have some refreshments that were provided for them. We afterwards made the best of our way home, all speaking of Sir Watkin and Lady Williams Wynn's kindness, wishing them a long life and happiness in this world. This terminated one of the merriest Christmas Eve's that we ever witnessed.' — Yours truly, A Singer.[20]

Sir Watkin was president of the Ruabon and Rhos Cottages Horticultural Society, which later was known as the Ruabon and District Horticultural, Industrial and Poultry Society. In 1875 their exhibition as usual was in Wynnstay Park under the supervision of a working committee of thirty members, including the Post Master, Schoolmaster, the Police Sergeant, and his Inspector. As usual the exhibition was competitive with prizes for fruit, flowers, and vegetables open to those, 'who are in receipt of weekly wages'. Extra prizes were offered to school children for marking, tucking, holing and plain sewing. Another class, Local Industry and Cottage Produce, invited models of flower gardens, the best-made labourer's shirt etc.

Another show held on Bank Holiday 7 August 1895 was lively with sports as well as produce, fireworks, the Ruabon Silver Band and the Boy's Refuge Band. The printed programme included interesting adverts:

> R. D. Pierce — Practical watch and clock maker — Jeweller and Optician, the Old Bank, Church Street, Ruabon. Birmingham House, Ruabon is noted for the best goods at remarkable prices — Hardware, earthenware, ironmongery, small ware, fancy goods, stationery, wall papers 2d. per roll and upwards. W. E. Richards, Birmingham House, Ruabon.

The Foresters enjoyed their fête in Wynnstay Park in May 1913:

> Ruabon Courts of the Ancient Order of Foresters held athletic sports and choral competitions at the Wynnstay park on Whit Monday. Notwithstanding the unpleasant state of the weather there was a strong muster of members at the morning procession and it was witnessed by a large number of people at different places on the route which included the principal streets of Ruabon and Johnstown and Pont Adam. The Ruabon Silver Band conducted by Mr J. Griffiths, headed the procession, being followed immediately by the Chief Ranger H. Manning and other officials of the Court.

The Mayre Fayre, 1954.
Mrs Albert Roberts crowning Rosaline
Brentnall.
Back row: Rosemary Davenport;
Sylvia Pierce; Dorothy Jones;
Ann Saunders; Edith Johnson;
Joyce Williams; Christine Price.
Middle row: Angela Smith; Eileen
Wright; Barbara Jones; Renée Morgan;
-?-; Kathleen Hughes.
Front row: Valerie Joseph; Elizabeth
Wood; Kathleen Leighton;
Pauline Northall.

Another event to take place in the Park was, 'the Mayre Fayre'. Mrs Audrey Bowen has provided me with her memories:

> I believe the first carnival to be held in Ruabon was soon after the First World War. I had heard stories of Wild West shows taking place in the field bordering station road, crockery sales by the Wynnstay Hotel, and events on the Goat Bank. It was when these travellers stopped visiting, that Ruabon decided to have its own annual carnival, and eventually it moved from the station field to the large field inside the Wynnstay Park Gates near Park Street. Over the years it became a bigger and better known event, and people from around the area flocked into the Park every August Bank Holiday Monday, having previously lined the streets to watch the procession of jazz bands, Morris dancers, street collectors waving their tins under the noses of hundreds of bystanders, and at the rear the splendid retinue of the Queen and her attendants beautifully attired in gowns made by lady members of the committee and riding in a carriage provided by Sir Watkin Williams Wynn.
>
> It was a great afternoon starting with the crowning of the Queen followed by competitive events held in the large arena and, in most years, concluding with a thrilling high-wire acrobatic turn. The ladies of the church were kept busy at their stalls or helping in the large tea tent. The gentlemen had their own tent where they had drinks with friends and visiting acquaintances! The afternoon came to and end about 4.30*pm* when the Queen and her retinue left the field awhile to prepare for the Ball held in the Parish Hall. A lovely night to conclude a great day. The Ruabon Silver Band made their splendid contribution. How hard the men of the village worked preparing for the event, and the ladies who made the lovely dresses year after year, sewing for hours and hours, and my father, Victor Bowen, the secretary, who started preparing for the next carnival as soon as he had rolled down his sleeves at the end of the one previous.

An account of the 1937, 'Ye Olde Mayre Fayre' gives the flavour of the event:

> The procession included the Langley Mills, Prize Carnival Band, Boys and Band of the Heswall Nautical Training School, Boy Scouts and Girl Guides, and the various dancing troupes and jazz bands. In Wynnstay Park the Festival Queen, Miss Peggy Garmston, was crowned by Lady Bushby. The Queen's retinue consisted of attendants: Rosemary Griffiths, Eileen Griffiths, Alice Jones, Bettine Edwards, Myfanwy Williams, Audrey Bowen, Doreen Davies, Gwen Jones. Train-bearers: Margaret Page, Sybil Reid, Ann Raisewell, Doreen Jones, Eileen Parry, Sybil Bailiff. Crown-bearer: Linda Jones. Heralds: Ifor Owen and Sidney Diggory. A bouquet was presented by Margaret Sedgbeer to Lady Bushby. [Also present was] Ex-Queen: Molly Evans; Attendants: Minnie Stal, Hilda Davies, Connie Allmand, Edna Edwards, Sheila Lloyd, Eva Lightwood, Connie Valentine, Hilda Edwards. Train-bearers: Jean Evans, Alberta Edwards, Jean Crewe, Barbara Teague.

The main events of the afternoon were the jazz band and dancing-troupe contests but the crowd also enjoyed excellent displays of the boys of the Heswall Nautical School and Miss Woodford's Ruabon School of Dancing. The Ruabon Silver Band played throughout the day. There were large entries for the competitions, and the displays of the troupes reached a high standard…The day was concluded with a grand carnival ball in the parish hall, when music for dancing was provided by Fred Roberts and his band.

Venison Day

Wynnstay Park was always a fascinating place to explore, with perambulation created by Capability Brown in the 18th century alongside the lake, past the column, the ice-house, the boat-house, and the bath grounds. No doubt there were encounters with the red fallow deer in the park. Special memories of the duties of the keepers have been related by Mr A. C. C. Brown:

My grandfather, Mr Allan Brown, came to the Ruabon Hills as Head Keeper in the late 1800s. I believe a Mr Wynne Corrie had a lot to do with the appointment. He leased the Moor, I think he also occupied Park Hall near Oswestry. In the 1901 season, 3,301 brace of grouse were shot. Prior to 1906 the best day's bag was 638$^{1}/_{2}$ brace (that was in 1905). Sometime after the 1914–18 War my grandfather moved into Cae Clapiog.

My grandfather George Campbell was recruited as the Glanllyn keeper in the late 1880s. He was interviewed for the job by Sir Watkin on Perth railway station. One of the requirements was that he should be able to make nets! He could and got the job. As Bala Lake was part of the Glanllyn estate I suppose net-making was relevant. He moved down to Ruabon about 1910 and set up home in the Kennel Cottages. With four sons and two daughters he needed both cottages.

My father married Ethel Kate Campbell at Pen-y-Lan Church in 1924. I think my mother was a servant of the Hall for her wedding cake was baked by Mrs. Hancock, the cook at the Hall.

Before the war the younger Campbell children attended the church school in Ruabon. The two older sons served with the Gordon Highlanders during the war, Colin was killed on the Somme in 1916, and his name is on the tablet in the Lychgate. George was wounded a couple of times and ended the war in Italy.

About fifteen red and twenty fallow deer were kept in the park. The herds roamed freely within the confines of the deer fence and the park wall. The park was divided into four, but the animals would easily jump the internal fencing to change their feeding area.

Captain Waters and before that a Mr Addison was the Park Keeper. George Campbell combined the duties of Park Keeper, Game Keeper (he reared pheasants), and Deer Keeper. I doubt if he was paid for the three jobs! He also kennelled the Glanllyn gun dogs.

In July, August and early September, the cull of the stags in the park used to take place. Barren hinds were taken earlier or later depending on numbers, condition, and the requirements of the hall. The number to be taken was decided upon by the agent acting on the information provided by the park keeper. This information would cover such details as the numbers, condition, and maturity of the stags in the herd of red deer, with a similar assessment being made on the bucks in the herd of fallow deer.

The day of the killing was arrived at in consultation with Mr Burgess the butler, and Mrs. Hancock the cook, for should Sir Watkin wish to have venison on the menu, the quantity and timing was of the essence. Usually if a stag was to be killed then a haunch would be sufficient for the cook's requirements, and if a buck was killed then she may require both haunches. It would all depend on the numbers dining with Sir Watkin at Wynnstay. The venison had to be consumed shortly after being delivered to the Hall; there were no freezers in those days.

Once Sir Watkin's requirements were known, Mr Campbell, the Park Keeper, would set a date to stalk and kill the selected stag. In the summer months before the rut, the stags, after feeding/grazing would leave the herd for a sheltered spot under the trees or in the bracken — a favourite place being in the dingle below Ty Gwyn (this was used by the army as a 'live' training ground during the 1939–45 World War). For a stag Mr Campbell used a .450 double-barrelled Sharples Express rifle firing from a range of 100–150 yards. A single shot to the head was all that was required to ensure a kill, at a shilling a round the Scot was 'awfie' canny.

Once the shot was fired and the stag fell, the firer had to get to the carcass quickly and stick it with his hunting knife. This was very important as the quality of the venison depended upon the carcass

Wynnstay and the deer in Wynnstay Park. T. Barber after J.P. Neale, 1829.

being properly and quickly bled. It was also quite a dangerous task, for when the point of the knife entered the neck behind the jawbone there was some kind of reflex action which caused the head to twitch and an unpleasant bruising from the points of the antlers could befall the unwary. It was said that a ghillie in the Scottish Highlands had lost an eye performing a similar task.

The next part of the exercise, almost as difficult as locating the stag, was to track down Sam Bishop, the knackerman. He lived below the stables behind the Wynnstay office. He was a surly resentful fellow who was, or so it appeared, always a couple of days overdue for a wash and a shave. He wore a twill jacket with whipchord breeches, brown leggings and boots, topped off by a brown bowler hat. The outfit would have been handed down from further up the social scale.

The knacker cart was a specialist vehicle, and it's main purpose was the recovery of dead cattle, horses, and other animals, from the surrounding farms to be transported to the kennels. The diameter of the wheels was between 3' 6" and 4' with a cranked axle which placed the floor about 18" above ground level, making the task of loading and unloading a heavy carcass less difficult. The cart was pulled by a mule every bit as stubborn as Sam! It took a lot of 'verbal' encouragement from Sam to get the show on the road! This combination could often be seen in Park Street outside the Wynnstay Arms, that is the knacker cart and mule — Sam would be inside!

Having got the knacker cart loaded up, it was driven to Cae Clapiog where it was unloaded and the carcass placed on a flat barrow-like device which had handles at each end and without wheels, the loaded barrow was carried into the slaughter house where the head and feet were removed and the skinning started. With the skin off the belly and legs, a gimbal was inserted in the shanks and the carcass was hoisted up by a block and tackle for the skinning to be completed, and the innards removed. Mr Campbell was usually assisted by his son or son-in-law for this part of the operation. He was most meticulous, the skin had to be removed correctly, the entrails removed completely, and the carcass thoroughly cleaned with water and cloths. Once this was done to his satisfaction, it was taken across a small yard and hung in the larder, a round building with zinc gauze windows, which made it fly-proof, and there it would hang for at least a week.

The cutting-up usually took place on a Thursday or Friday with the needs of the Hall being satisfied first, the order being collected by Mr Jim Rolfe, the chauffeur. On the Saturday morning estate workers families and others, who having heard on the grapevine that venison was available, would turn up at Cae Clapiog hoping to buy some. Of the many customers there are a couple of regulars who come to mind, there was Mr Griffiths who used to walk from Broth Lodge Cottages (a round trip of some three miles) and who would ask for, 'some neck please Mr Campbell' with a hearty chortle, and she would get a good-sized piece duly cut up, for nine old pence. The other was Mrs. Hewitt, who lived in Burton Terrace, whose husband cycled to Cae Clapiog to collect a joint of venison (a return journey of about ten miles).

The perks of the job? The offal on the day of the kill, the hide after it had dried out on the wall of the out-building — it made a floor covering of sorts, and the horn from the antlers which was used to re-handle knives and forks.

The Parish Hall

We have seen that there was an active social life connected with the nonconformist chapels and the church: literary societies, Sunday schools, choirs and football teams, which met in the schoolrooms at the National and County, at the Congregational, Baptist and Wesleyan and Calvinistic Methodist churches. What was needed in the village was a 'neutral zone' unconnected with a particular denomination. Perhaps symbolically the idea of a parish hall was chosen as the memorial to those valiant men who fought and died in the Great War. It was formally opened by Sir Watkin in February 1922, followed on the same day with a whist drive and a dance. Soon it became 'the centre of all village activities. The main room held snooker exhibitions, wrestling matches, dances, and receptions; the St Mary's players staged many productions there. The ante-rooms provided facilities for committee meetings and coffee mornings, and also housed the library. When not used for other purposes, the hall became the local cinema. The building was demolished in 1974 to make way for a parking ground when plans to make a new centre went ahead'.[21]

The Parish Hall was not an architectural wonder, but it had its own air of mystery and excitement for the initiated whether stage-struck, romantically inclined, or snooker kings. It obviously influenced the intellectual development of one young man, Eddie Bowen Jones, who grew up in wartime Ruabon, and has written an account of the local cinema mogul:

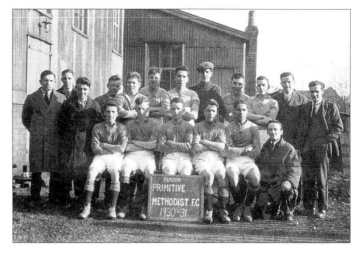

Primitive Methodist Football Club,
1930–31 outside the Parish Hall.
Back row: Redvers Parry; Douglas Hughes;
Fred Reynolds; Leslie Jones; Bert Bithell; Phil Williams;
George Clarke; Lawton Hughes; Ken Haynes;
Willie Jones; Walter Jones; Edgar Edwards.
Front row: Amos Blything; Ivor Jones; Gwilym Jones;
-?-; Arnold/Graham Hughes; Cyril Richards.

The Boss — For many of us brought up during the war the 'pictures' or 'movies' are indelibly stamped on our memories. The Odeons, the Rialtos, the Majestics and the like were places of excitement and escapism. The 'Picture Place' at Ruabon was no exception. Even with its tin roof and variable acoustics many happy hours were spent in the thrilling or chilling company of a Walter Pidgeon or a Boris Karloff and also in the reassuring care of Albert, Jimmy Edgar, Beryl, and Joe.

I could write a paragraph about each of these kindly but formidable characters who worked at the 'Picture Place' who were remarkable not only for their hard work (two houses Monday, Wednesday, Friday and Saturday — one house Tuesday and Thursday, together with a Saturday matinée) but also for their concern. Those were troublesome times.

Here, however, I want to give prominence to a figure we children knew as the 'Boss'. Mr Jervis — I never knew his Christian name — was a middle-aged or old man — everyone was old! — of slight stature with a moustache and formal clothes which were neither shabby nor smart. He was a man of few words who, it was reputed, had great wealth invested in cinemas as far afield as Oswestry and Ellesmere. That he was a man of considerable wealth and influence was never in doubt, because it was well-known that those who were involved in the 'Pictures' business had to hobnob with Hollywood stars occasionally. Confirmation of this was easily at hand, to refute the incredulous, in the shape of his large Chrysler car.

The car, which he parked on what is now the National Westminster car park, next to our house Bryn View, was of a golden hue (or seemed so), and if my memory serves me, it had masses of chrome embellishments both inside and out. It had thick chunky doors and a shape which spoke of unlimited horsepower. Some of the windows were partly curtained, and the two door pillars had attached to them two cornet-like receptacles or vases for flowers. Cars in Ruabon at this time were as scarce as hen's teeth, especially since my late father's Austin car had been requisitioned by the government to tow the NFS tender. This Chrysler car made the other cars look ordinary and ancient. We, of course, were in the know about cars, because of our connection with Ling's Garage, but in any event, seeing was believing, for had we not seen such a limousine in the numerous shots of 'Down Town' New York or 'Skid Row' Chicago, in the company of Cagney, Greenstreet or Toler?

That the Boss was a gangster and crook was well known. Did he not appear in Ruabon without warning, and nearly always when it was time to go to bed, and did he not leave suddenly and silently, sometimes with and sometimes without a brief case or round metal containers? I never saw him carry a violin case, but there was no doubt in my mind that he had one. Furthermore, no one knew where he lived or whether he put flowers in the cornet-shaped receptacles when he had made a 'hit' for the mob.

The other possibility was that the Boss was a spy. Ruabon, with its new Bryn bridge, its marshalling yards — a phrase we learned from the wireless — and its army camp obviously made spying a lucrative pastime. So secret were the Boss's

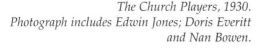

The Church Players, 1930.
Photograph includes Edwin Jones; Doris Everitt
and Nan Bowen.

antecedents, and his comings and goings, little confirmation was needed. Confirmation there was, however, when as sure as eggs, the Germans bombed the Gorse, just missing the bridge and the Wynnstay camp.

After this thundering event, without my knowing, or perhaps noticing, the Boss disappeared, never to be seen again. Soon the war was over, and I suppose spies became redundant. Sometimes, even now, on murky Autumn evenings when passing the bottom of Henry Street, I fancy I hear the crack of tops and whips and conkers and, even about those youthful noises, I hear the Boss's car purring away on 'our back'. It may be the Boss sits low inside behind the curtained window waiting for the decline of television, though, hopefully, not for another world war.

The Recreation Ground

This formed part of the Maes y Llan field. The ground was purchased in September 1931 for £297-10s. In 1932 the Miners Welfare Fund donated £500 to equip a playground for children of fifteen years or under. Tennis courts were opened on 1 July 1933. The privilege of performing the ceremony, in the regrettable absence of Sir Watkin, was given to Dr and Mrs Lawton Roberts. There was an amusing correspondence between Dr Turner who objected to the effect of noise from the recreation ground on the patients in his nursing home at Ty Newydd, and the parish council who threatened to sue him for the trespass of his poultry!

The Community Centre

In 1947 the Wynnstay estate offered the accident hospital, recently closed as a maternity hospital, as a centre for social purposes generally, and to be known as the Watkin Williams Wynn Memorial Hall. After carefully examining the conditions for use, the suitability of the building and maintenance costs, the offer was reluctantly declined.

The opportunity for a community centre came in the 1970s when St Mary's Aided School was demolished and replaced by a modern building. It was decide that the developed site was to be shared with the community. Incorporated in the plans were a community hall, a large meeting room with a kitchen, an office and chambers for use by the Community Council, the usual offices, parking facilities and a public playing field, with a football pitch suitable for league matches.

The community centre was officially opened on 8 June 1976 by Councillor Noel Isfryn Wright. Officers of the centre were Councillor F. H. Williams, JP (Chairman of the Management Committee); Mrs A M Warburton, (Secretary); Clwyd Councillors D. Hughes and J. Williams (Treasurer); Councillor H. L. Brown; Councillor J. R. Fenner and Mr T. R. Evans (headteacher of St Mary's Aided School).

Queen Victoria's Visit to Ruabon

Ronnie Knox-Mawer, a former High Court Judge in Arabia and the South Seas, described the visit of Queen Victoria to Ruabon through the eyes of his great aunt, Mrs R. A. Jones (d.1946), who related her memories to him in the early 1930s:

> It was my great aunt, Mrs Jennie Jones, JP, of Bryn View, Ruabon, who first told me about the visit of the Queen to Wales. She was talking about Queen Victoria of course, and showing me the photographs.
>
> To me as a small boy the two ladies seemed frighteningly alike. Both were small and stout, dressed in black, with expressions of stern disapproval. Also, their two deceased husbands were both called Albert. The late Albert Jones, JP, (proprietor of a hideous edifice in bright orange-red Ruabon brick, known as The Stores) lay in a tomb of royal proportions surmounted by an enormous stone 'so that the little bugger never got up again', as was said in the village. I sometimes visited the cemetery with my aunt, walking up a bleak hill overlooking the derelict colliery. At the top another monument was always pointed out, that of great Uncle Isaac Jones. 'He was the one who met with the Royals', Aunt Jennie told me. 'He always thought a lot of himself', she went on, clattering the tea cups back on to the tray, 'but after all that fuss there wasn't a hat in Wales big enough to fit him'.
>
> Apparently the highlight of the royal visit was a descent of our village coal-mine, the Green Pit, where Isaac Jones (I.J.) was Underground Manager. In preparation for the great event it seemed the royal party had actually changed their clothing at I.J.'s house, Tir-y-Fron, which overlooks the colliery. Great aunt Jennie's account always ran the same, word for word, like some Arthurian legend.[22]

Queen Victoria came to Ruabon in 1889 whilst staying at Palé Hall, Henry Robertson's house, near Corwen.

On Saturday, 24 August the Queen, with Princess Beatrice, Prince Henry of Battenburg, and Princess Alice of Hesse, arrived by train from Llandderfel at 4.15*pm*. The *Illustrated London News* devoted three issues to the royal visit to Wales and the *Oswestry Advertiser* published a special edition. Describing the arrival at Ruabon, Knox Mawer continued:

Queen Victoria's carriage leaving Ruabon Station escorted by the Denbighshire Hussars Yeomanry.

Next day it was the turn of Ruabon, Sir Watkin's home village, through which the royal cavalcade passed en route for Wrexham. This was when another member of Aunt Jennie's family had his moment of glory. 'Your grandfather, Jack', she explained, 'he was Clerk to Sir Watkin, you see, and made responsible for decorating the High Street'. This was her cue to produce the picture cut from the *Illustrated London news*. 'That's his Triumphal Arch' she said.

My concentration would then be required on a dog-eared page of the *Wrexham Advertiser* describing Grandfather's plywood masterpiece as 'a very good resemblance of masonry.' The dour mining village of Ruabon was particularly lacking in historical remains. Nothing daunted, Grandfather had remedied the deficiency by designing his Triumphal Archway in the style of a medieval battlement. In addition he erected a row of Venetian masts with coloured bunting to hide chimney stacks, and disguised the coke-ovens with Union Jacks and Welsh Dragons. As a result of Grandfather's enthusiasm, Ruabon High Street looked, according to Aunt Jennie, 'smarter than the promenade at Llandudno!'

This quaint fantasy was evidently accepted by Sir Watkin's decorations committee which presented Grandfather with an elaborate mahogany writing set, 'as a memento of his honorary services.[23]

The *Oswestry Advertiser* gave a lengthy account of the wonderful decorations prepared for the Queen:[24]

At the Ruabon Station there are profuse decorations of heraldic shields surmounted by flags, and festoons of bunting, erected by a staff of men from Paddington and some of the station men. On the road leading from the station to the main road, venetian poles are erected on both sides of road with heraldic shields and flags, and at the bottom of the road opposite Mr Griffith's shop the Ruabon Horticultural Society have erected a splendid triumphal arch, of which the groundwork is heather. On the turrets a good deal of bunting is displayed, and over a floral crown in the centre floats the Royal Standard. The arch is profusely decorated with choice flowers and over it is the motto, 'Our beloved Queen' in floral design. From there to the Wynnstay Arms Hotel, venetian masts have been erected at equal distances along the road, all bearing heraldic shields, and devices of flags, and festoons from mast to mast with bunting.

In the churchyard a stand for 1,000 of the National School children is erected, this also decorated with bunting, and from the top of the church, festoons and flags float to venetian masts erected near the gate. The gate is decorated with heraldic shields and flag, and bears the motto, 'God save the Queen' and 'Duw a gadwo y Frenhines'. The Wynnstay Arms Hotel is ablaze with large shields surmounted with flags, with festoons of bunting from window to window. In the middle of the road, opposite the entrance to Wynnstay park, there is a group of venetian masts decorated with flags and trophies of flags, connected with the houses on both sides of the road, with festoons, and surmounted by the crown. Just after passing the hotel there is a triumphal arch, in imitation of a castle (a very good resemblance of masonry). This is decorated with flags and royal shields, and over the centre the royal standard floats, supported by the ensigns. On the side which would be seen first by Her Majesty, there is the motto, 'God protect our Queen', and on the other side, 'God save the Queen'. Opposite the Gardden Lodge an arch of venetian masts spans the road with the words, 'Welcome' on both sides in floral devices. It is also profusely decorated with flags and flowers, and has a very graceful appearance. This is surmounted by the royal crown. At the Accident Hospital flags and trophies are displayed, with festoons from there to the roadway. The decorations are carried out by Messrs J. Defries and Son, of London, and the town has a most airy and graceful appearance. Lining the wall of the hospital were the scholars from Lady Williams Wynn's School wearing Red Riding Hood cloaks.

From Ruabon, the whole length of the road to Wrexham is festooned with venetian flags, from venetian masts, on which are fixed shields and trophies of flags, and it presents a very lively appearance. The Ruabon Brick and Terra Cotta Works are beautifully festooned, and an arch of a very pretty design, constructed of terracotta, worked with panels of a highly artistic nature, and a great deal of other artistic work, and covered with bunting, is erected near the road-way. At Afongoch an arch of venetian poles, with flag and festoons, and the motto, 'Welcome', in yellow letters on a red ground is erected. Opposite the Vauxhall colliery, Mr George Saint had the superintendence of a stand, which was tastefully decorated with evergreens, heather and festooned gracefully. A large flag was flying on the pithead and the works generally displayed clouds of bunting. All Johnstown is decorated. In the middle of the village the royal standard floats. At Moreton Inn, flags and bannerets were displayed, and a stage is erected. Opposite, near the Old Gardden Hall colliery, a spacious stage is erected by the Rhos Primitive Methodists for the use of the members and friends. The large waste heaps of the Brandy Coke Ovens are disguised with bunting. At Fir Tree Cottage (Mr Forshaw), and Tanyclawdd (Mr G. E. Woodford), there was a display of bannerets, &c. At this a stage was also erected and each stand has an appropriate motto. From Johnstown to Wrexham the festooning continues and at the smithy an arch of venetian poles, festooned is erected, bearing the motto 'May Agriculture flourish', and a little lower down at Croes Foel, one of the most artistic efforts is seen. It is an arch constructed by Messrs Womersley of Leeds. It is constructed of poles, round which bark has been placed, and in the crevices of the bark flowers and ferns have been placed. The arch is 30ft. span, and the bases are each 6ft. by 5ft. On the bases are large medallions bearing the letters V. R. and A. E. (Albert Edward). A large shield with banners rises from the centre, and from the four masts at the sides streamers flutter and festoons cross. The whole has a most graceful experience, and was erected at the entire expense of Mr T. Ll. FitzHugh, Plas Power. The Bersham colliery, as well as numerous houses in the neighbourhood of Rhostyllen, are decked with bannerets and streamers. A handsome flag and other decorations gives proof of the loyalty of Mr Cooper, the Black Lion Inn. At Esclusham Church a large stand is erected for the reception of all the schoolchildren of the village.

The general decorations from the end of the Station road, Ruabon to the Moreton Inn, a distance of nearly a mile and a half, were in the hands of the Ruabon sub-committee, which consists of Sir Watkin Williams Wynn, Bart, Messrs. Simon Yorke, Philip Yorke, O. S. Wynne, Captain Ormrod, Messrs H. Dennis, E. Lloyd Jones, G. Thomson, J. S. Laycock, H. C. Murless, the Rev E. W. Edwards, the Rev W. Taliesin Davies, the Rev J. W. Thomas, Rhosymedre, the Rev E. M. Edmunds, the Rev John Jones, Messrs F. Morris, G. Saint, T. Jackson, Dr R. C. Roberts, Dr Lawton Roberts, Dr William Jones, Messrs W. Morris, John Davies, Walter Griffiths, R. A. Jones, Albert Jones, Thomas Hughes, Dyke Dennis, John Dawson, George Garside, W. Pemberton, A. C. Gibson, George Beckett, H. Jenks, Robert Lloyd, and Joseph Owen, honorary secretary and treasurer.

R. A. Jones with his prize winning pony 'Princess Ena' outside the Accident Hospital, 1908.

The First World War[25]

In many ways people were prepared for the First World War. Patriotism was a familiar theme of school assemblies. Love of Wales was imbued by the singing of *Hen Wlad fy Nhadau* and stories of St David. Pupils were mustered and drilled in the playground where the Union Jack flag was saluted, *God Save the King* sung, and the greatness of the Empire, where the sun never set, exulted. When Empire day was celebrated at the council school on Friday afternoon 23 May 1913, the assembly took place out of doors with the presence of about

Officers and men of the 4th Bn Royal Welsh Fusiliers (Territorial Force) in Park Street, Ruabon, 5 August 1914. These men had just been rushed back from thier annual camp at Aberystwyth and were about to entrain for Northampton from where, in December, they were sent to France. They served with 1st Division until September 1915 when they became a pioneer battalion of the 47th (London) Division. The spelling of the regiment's name was changed from 'Welsh' to 'Welch' in 1920

three hundred parents and friends. Unconsciously war was becoming part of the mentality of the people in the jingoistic atmosphere which possessed the British on the eve of war. Sir Watkin speaking to the National Service League in April 1913 said that when he raised two companies to go out to the South African War twelve years before, he was surprised to see so many men who were unfit for service at the village room. The Church Lad's Brigade wore khaki for their summer camp in 1913. Drilling, training, and time under canvas, were a dress rehearsal for what was to come. The first Ruabon Boy Scout troop, under the command of their scoutmaster R. G. Richards, camped at Rhagatt near Corwen in August 1913 where, 'practice in signalling, ambulance, scouting and tracking were the most important items of routine'.

It is not surprising that when war came in August 1914 there was a patriotic fervour of hysterical proportions. By the end of hostilities in November 1918, out of a population of 3,500 the parish of Ruabon supplied over 650 men to the various forces of His Majesty the King, and of these eighty-one names appear on the War Memorial as having made the supreme sacrifice. With Wynnstay Park the parade ground for drilling and training the local volunteers, with the marching of men from the Royal Welsh Fusiliers barracks at Wrexham, and with the railway platform a regular mass of khaki it was not surprising that so many got the message that their country needed them.

Troops marched through Ruabon bound for France on the declaration of war in August 1914. In October the headmaster of the Council School recorded, 'Mr C. H. Jones called here to wish us goodbye, he having

enlisted for active service', the log book entry for the next day said 'gave an attendance half-holiday to scholars as one of the Royal Welsh Fusilier battalions of Lord Kitchener's army marched to Wynnstay Park'. The battle of the Marne stayed the advance of the Germans in September. Ypres saw the offensive drift towards Christmas. In April 1915 the parish council under the chairmanship of Sir Watkin launched a vigorous recruiting campaign when the noble baronet accompanied by the recruiting committee marched through the streets of Ruabon headed by the Royal Welsh

'Your Country Needs You!'
Recruitment at Ruabon, 1915.

Church Lad's Brigade members in khaki uniform at their annual camp during the First World War. Left 1915, below 1917 (World's End).

Fusiliers and their band. In August two of the staff of the council school, Miss N. Daniels and Miss J. Hughes, left to become Red Cross nurses. A situation of stalemate and stagnation made the war static. A line of trenches in southern Belgium and northern France from the English channel to the Swiss border became the Western Front.

If the women of Ruabon couldn't join their men folk in France or Gallipoli, they made every effort to help them. Money was collected to purchase wool for knitting socks and mittens. In July 1915 the Ruabon sewing party organised a 'cake and apron' sale in the village room to purchase materials for making garments and socks. In the same month some of the produce of the Congregational Churches anniversary service was sent to sick friends and hospital patients, and the eggs to wounded soldiers. On 10 July there was a memorial service in the parish church to Private Eddie Jones of Park Street who was shot when doing stretcher work, and Joseph Haycock of Gyfelia, who was seriously wounded and died not long after. A roll of honour was unveiled to the scholars of the Primitive Methodist church who had joined the army. A meeting was held on the Goat Bank in August 1915 to mark the anniversary of the declaration of war. It turned out to be a demonstration of solidarity with a large attendance. Sir Watkin presided, and amongst the speakers was the Reverend W. B. Jones of Penycae, the first non-conformist minister to enter the recruiting campaign:

> He dwelt upon the righteousness of the war, and said it was the duty of every citizen of the empire, to do his or her best in the present crisis. There was no room for shirkers, and he had two sons now serving with the Colours. He had great pleasure in moving the following resolution, 'For this anniversary of the declaration of righteous war, this meeting of the residents of the Ruabon district records its inflexible determination to continue to a virtuous end the struggle in the maintenance of those ideals of liberty and justice which are the common sacred cause of the Allies.[26]

The sinking of the ship *Arabic* the same month, carrying best flooring tiles to America, brought home the German U-boat menace and the extent of the conflict, as did the Russian flag day to support our allies on the eastern front. When Lance Corporal A. E. Owen of Foundry House, Wynn Hall, came on leave in December

The Tiger Stores, used as a rest centre for travelling soldiers.

after fifteen months in the trenches, a musical evening and smoking concert was held in his honour at the Great Western Railway inn. The years of 1916 and 1917 have been called the great slaughter. In February 1916 the French lost 720,000 men at Verdun, in June the naval battle at Jutland was a stalemate, and from July to November the unsuccessful allies attack on German lines in the Somme valley, France, resulted in total casualties of 107,000 men, and in consequence Lloyd George became Prime Minister. Pupils from both elementary schools were taken to see pictures of the Battle of the Somme at Cefn parish hall. The nation prepared itself for more sacrifice and effort with the introduction of daylight saving 'British Summertime', to give more assistance to an increase in food production, and an appeal for war savings. The headmaster of the council school spent the whole of his summer vacation working voluntarily in a YMCA hut at Park Hall Camp, Oswestry, whilst the troops at Passchendaele in a very wet summer were up to their waists in mud. The Tsar abdicated in March 1917, the Americans came into the war in April, and the last year of the Great War was marked by weariness and shortage of food.

Private Davenport, ready to leave for the Front.

A soldier's rest was established in the summer of 1917 when Sir Watkin placed the old Tiger Stores, at the bottom of Station Road, at the service of the soldiers who were unable to continue their journeys when they arrived on the last train from Shrewsbury or Chester, and desired to go up the branch line. Mr Fred Davies, headmaster of the council school, was the honorary manager. It was reported to be a great boon and 180 men had received accommodation from September 1917 to February 1918.

Sugar was rationed in January 1918. In February, 'a public meeting was held in the village room convened by the Parish Council and presided over by Sir Watkin … who in his opening remarks called upon every man, woman and child, to set forth to produce as much food for the use of the nation as soon as possible. Mr Walsh, Government Agricultural Inspector, gave an excellent address upon the relative value of potato seed, and the need for all to do their utmost in the production of food generally'. The schools closed in March for food registration, and their managers were requested to provide a plot of ground for raising food production. From 4 March meat, butter, and margarine, were rationed. More applications were made to the parish council for allotments. A year earlier the grass plot on the 'girls' side of the council school was cut up into eleven plots for cultivation by the villagers. But in spite of food shortage, Ruabon people were determined and prepared to make further sacrifices. This was demonstrated in April when Mr Edwin Richards, secretary of the war savings campaign, 'organised a procession of the silver band, the Wynnstay fire engine, decorated and manned by members of the Church Lads Brigade in their khaki uniform, and a number of lads carrying Union Jacks. They paraded the streets, the band playing and this attracted a number of people to the government bank, where a capital meeting was held and addresses given by Sir Watkin, the Reverend D. J. Bowen, and Alderman R. A. Jones. The campaign raised £1,125 for saving certificates, and £4,225 for war bonds. This was April 1918, and in the same week the soldiers' parcel funds committee dispatched to 258 Ruabon soldiers serving overseas, a postal order for 14s-6d each, and to sixteen officers, a box of cigars each, value 12s-6d.

The Spanish 'flu' epidemic reached Ruabon in July. The Girls' Department of the National School was closed and several work places were hit. It continued into 1919

Sergeant. J. Evison, DCM, MM, of The Green. Ruabon's most decorated serviceman of the First World War.

when the clerk of the Wrexham Rural District Council instructed, '…during the prevalence of the influenza epidemic the local district council are empowered to sanction the payment for additional nursing assistance and the services of a medical practitioner in those cases where the cost cannot be met by the patients themselves'. The epidemic had a heavy impact on children and young people: 228,900 died in Britain as a result.

Determined to keep up the morale at home, a Flag and Fête Day was held on 31 August 1918:

> The Flag and Fête day was organised through the friendly societies. In the morning there was flag selling by young ladies and scouts, a sale of garden and farm produce was held on the Goat Bank, and a war souvenir and fancy work exhibition was held in the village room …At four o'clock a fine procession was formed composed of the Foresters, Shepherds, Oddfellows, Boy Scouts and Church Lad's Brigade, headed by the Rhosddu and Acton Brass Band. They paraded the principal streets and proceeded on to the vicarage lawn where dancing was kept up until 9 o'clock. There were displays in ambulance, bridge building, and physical drill, by the 1st Ruabon Scout Troop. A good number of people gave produce and the net result of £60 was given to the soldiers' parcel fund.

As autumn approached the Germans began to retreat and hit by food shortages, mutiny, and civil demonstration, the Kaiser abdicated on 9 November. At 11*am* on 11 November the Armistice was declared. The *Wrexham Advertiser* recorded the reception of the announcement in Ruabon:

> When the news was made known that our terms were signed, much excitement prevailed. Flags were hoisted, the church bells were rung, the miners at Wynnstay colliery came up from the pits and a general holiday spirit prevailed. Many of the soldiers who were home on leave or returned home on Monday were warmly greeted. In the evening the 1st Ruabon Scout Company and the Church Lads Brigade paraded.

There is no mention of the Armistice in the National School log book because it was closed, owing to influenza and fever.

The war came to an end on a weary note. Everyone in Ruabon had done their best. There was a pride in the service men, some of whom had the distinction of being decorated for gallantry. On the home front, Wynnstay was a munitions factory. Support for the war effort came from the whole community. Naturally the peace celebrations involved the whole of Ruabon. The Council School log book recorded the Treaty of Versailles between the Allies and Germany, '1919 Peace was signed at 3.12*pm* on Saturday 28 June at Paris. I assembled the School today (30th), and spoke on the importance of this historical event. We sang patriotic songs.'

To mark the occasion local celebrations were organised in the village on 18 July 1919. The Community Council minutes record:

> The men assembled at Lodge 8 under the leadership of Sir Watkin Williams Wynn, CB and marched through the principal streets of the village headed by the band of the Royal Welsh Fusiliers,

✝
Our Absent Friends.

Charles G. Taylor, M.V.O., R.N.	William Evans
Edward Jones	Thomas McLaren
Clifford Robinson	Robert Ridge
Thomas Reed	David Jones
Joseph Haycocks	Arthur Trevor Lewis
William Henry Rogers	Albert Williams
John Wyatt	Enoch Griffiths
William Griffiths	John Thomas Morgan
Dyke Davies	Charles Jones
Thomas Jones	Thomas Lloyd
William Lawton Roberts	William Roberts
Arthur Morris	Alfred Samuels
James McLaren	David Edwards
William Stanley Jones	Thomas Vaughan
Colin Campbell	George Sedwick
Harry Hughes	Arthur Jones
Edwin Hampson	Humphrey Jones
John Allen Sangers	Levi Arthur Humphreys
James Williams	Richard Charles Benyon
Joseph Samuels	Robert Lloyd
Thomas James Matthews	Charles Nicholas
John Henry Williams	Thomas Hughes
Walter Lockey	Charles Jones
John Kempster	John Mortimer Jones
Frederick Johnson	Joseph Edwards
Morris Roberts	Sydney Gordon Hughes
Charles Edwards	John William Jones
Thomas Smith	Albert William Fowles
William Carter	Ellis Hopley
Frank Pumford	William Jones
Robert Davies, D.C.M.	William Lowe Percival
Percy Hughes	William Lawton Wooley
George Webster	Thomas Colley
George Jones	William Hughes
Alec. Meredith	R Emlyn Evans
Harry Harding Davies	Thomas Albert Dobbins

The men from Ruabon who lost their lives in the First World War.

Wrexham, to the Council School yard. This was followed by a supper in the council schools, after which the usual toasts were drunk … dancing in the yard until 10*pm*. At 11*pm* the sailors and soldiers and wives and friends attended a dance in the schools. On the morning of 19 July 1919 a Public United Peace Thanksgiving service was held in the parish church.

The village memorial to those who fought and died in the conflict was the parish hall. The memorial of the parish was the lychgate entrance to St. Mary's Church on the south east. The memorial lychgate was designed by the architect T. H. Hogg of Wrexham and erected by G. F. Roberts & Sons, Trevor. Built of Cefn stone, the upper part is carved in Wynnstay oak. The cost was £425, exclusive of oak. Inscribed on marble slabs are the names of the fallen and, 'their names liveth for evermore'. Carved over the oak gates on the cross beam is the inscription, 'erected in honour and gratitude 1914–18'. The lychgate was dedicated on 31 October 1920 by the Venerable W. Fletcher, Archdeacon of Wrexham, at a service conducted by the vicar, Canon J. Sculthorpe Lewis. Amongst the congregation were territorials, ex-servicemen, the Church Lads Brigade and their bugle band, and the Ruabon Silver Band. At the unveiling of the memorial tablets by Sir Watkin the band of the Royal Welsh Fusiliers played.

Between the Wars

To make 'a country fit for heroes to live in' was the slogan at the end of the war. The parish hall was erected to be the social centre of the village. Ex-servicemen were given the Institute in Tan Lan. The building was the former site of the Welsh Independent chapel which returned to the Wynnstay estate when the Congregational church was opened in 1858. The ex-servicemen became part of the national organisation, the British Legion. J Watkin Ellis remembered the Institute:[27]

> Immediately after the First World War the Institute as it stood and all that it contained was handed over to the British Legion … the Institute was a democratic institution, the officials appointed by vote of the members in which were included all sections, from the professional class to the labourer. They were good mixers, a social and friendly spirit prevailed, and all worked and played harmoniously. I was privileged to act as secretary for many years and can vouch for this 'happy family' feeling. On the first floor there was a first-class library, and in this reading room were the usual daily papers, weekly periodicals, and monthly magazines in considerable variety. On the ground floor there was a good full-sized billiard table and chairs to accommodate those playing chess, draughts and dominoes.

Although they had their own meeting place many of them had but little money to spend, with starving families to support. In 1920 the headmaster of the council school recorded, '24 May, owing to the prevailing distress in the district owing to the lock-out of the miners, it has become necessary to feed many necessitous cases amongst the school children.' Twenty-eight from this school attended. The Great Strike of 1926 created more hardship. Ironically on Armistice Day a school concert was arranged at the parish hall in aid of the local Distress Committee. The total proceeds were £18-8s-9d with admission at 6d only.

Wynnstay Colliery closed in 1927, causing further unemployment. The school was the heartbreak house of the depression. The headmaster wrote in 1929, [I] 'received a request from the organiser as to the number of children who require boots. This is in connection with the Lord Mayor's Mansion House fund.'

A fortnight later he commented:

> Have now got all scholars who were granted boots fitted up. A feature of this investigation has been to reveal

the small wage earned by so many of the parents and the wonder as to how they manage to live and keep their children so nicely dressed.

On 14 February 1923 the teachers of the infants department of the council school, 'unanimously agreed to an abatement of five per cent of their salaries in accord with the Geddes axe which smashed peoples' hopes. The means test, a rigorous investigation conducted when an application was made for 'dole' or benefit, was the task of the local Relief Committee. Some parents were supposed to find money for their children. Mrs. Marjory Williams of Avondale, a pupil at the Girls' County Secondary School, Ruabon, remembers how lucky she was to go to London:

> In 1924 a party of about 36 girls with the headmistress and two mistresses went to London by train. From Paddington we went in a double decker bus around London: to St Paul's cathedral and the Tower of London and saw the crown jewels. We stayed at a large hotel for three nights. On the second day we visited the British Empire Exhibition at Wembley; Hughes and Lancaster of Acrefair had a stand in charge of which was the brother of one of our party. We spent two days at the exhibition. We saw Queen Mary but she didn't take any notice of us! One evening the older girls went to the theatre with the headmistress, whilst the two mistresses took the rest of us for a walk around the area of the hotel.
>
> On another school expedition we went to Cricieth to see the total eclipse of the sun. We travelled by train overnight to be there by 5am but unfortunately it was teeming with rain, and we were not allowed to leave the train.

Things began to improve in the 1930s. Council houses provided better accommodation. Milk for school children was introduced:

> 1934, 1 October, commenced milk scheme today. The milk is pasteurised and supplied by Cefn Co-operative Society in third pint bottles at a half-penny each. Ninety children took the milk the first day, and by the end of the week the number increased to one hundred and twenty.

The economy was improving by the time war came in 1939. National morale was good and the events of the silver jubilee of King George V and Queen Mary in 1935, the abdication of Edward VIII in 1936, and the coronation of George VI and Queen Elizabeth in 1937, gave the nation a sense of a new beginning. For the coronation day celebrations the council school flew their new flag for the first time, the red dragon of Wales, alongside the Union Jack. Many men in Wales joined the territorial army for extra money and a free summer holiday. After Munich, war became inevitable. It was declared on 3 September 1939.

There were differences between the two great wars of the 20th century for the people of Britain. For civilians the war was more immediate and realistic. The sound of the siren was heard more often in Ruabon, bombs were dropped, and the radio brought the war into the living room as families listened attentively to the nine o'clock news, the rousing speeches of Winston Churchill, and the light entertainment programmes that mocked Hitler, Mussolini, Tojo and the likes, reducing them to the level of cartoon characters. Laughter dispelled fear.

Wearing uniform gave an opportunity to identify with conflict as a contestant. You were not a spectator if you were in the Home Guard, Red Cross, St John's Ambulance, an Air Raid Precautions (ARP) warden, a railwayman or a member of the voluntary services. Women served in the armed forces, the Land Army, or did the work of men in the forces. The presence of the Royal Engineers at Wynnstay brought the troops into the heart of the village to experience the warmth and hospitality they hoped their own boys would receive. The NAAFI operated in the Wesleyan Chapel school room at the bottom of Station Road with an efficient committee: Mrs Bryn Roberts, Mrs Diggory, Mrs Ingham, Mrs Haigh, Mrs Bunty Leighton, and Mrs Dilys Everett. Corned beef, sausages, tomatoes, beans and eggs, when available, were served up on toast or in sandwiches. And from time to time a free ration of chocolate. Gas masks, identity cards, and ration books, broke down class divisions to some extent, and was a movement towards social equality. Perhaps the most important factor, in this area, was that for victory to be achieved the mining communities were needed after the dreadful neglect of the Depression.

Extracts from the council school log book provide a war diary from 1939 onwards:

1939

9 August — Re-opened this morning. Gas masks for the whole parish were distributed from the school on Friday, Saturday and yesterday and as the distribution was not completed, we used classroom one and the open air classroom.

31 August — Learned from the wireless this afternoon that owing to the international situation, the government has decided to carry out its plans for the evacuation of school children and all schools are to close. I understand that the school is to be the reception centre for the village but have no official intimation, or any information whatever. At about 5*pm* the emergency rations for the evacuees arrived. These consisted of 61 tins of biscuits, 1,200 tins of nestles milk (sweetened and unsweetened), 743 tins of Libby's corn beef, 2 large cases and 8 dozen packets of Cadbury's chocolate and 584 carrier bags. These were put up by a band of willing helpers who completed their task by 11.30*pm*.

1 September — The school assembled at 9*am*. The scholars sent home until September 11th. The first batch of evacuees arrived just before noon and consisted of scholars from Chatsworth Street school, Liverpool. Later in the day came infants from Chatsworth Street and Rathbone schools, Liverpool.

3 September — (War was declared with Germany at 11*am* and the Prime Minister, Neville Chamberlain addressed the nation)

Sunday. Scholars, teachers and parents of St. Francis Xavier, Roman Catholic Junior Boys' School arrived this afternoon. The total number of evacuees received in Ruabon is 447, including parents and infants.

6 September — Convened meeting to consider situation at 6*pm* this evening. It was felt the accommodation in the local school was sufficient to enable work to be carried out without resorting to the 'double shift' system. The following suggestions were agreed to:

    I   The Francis Xavier School, juniors and infants should attend Ruabon C of E School.

    II Chatsworth Street scholars should attend Ruabon Council school.

    III Ruabon Council infants should use the school and the two afternoons at the parish hall, if available, alternating with Chatsworth street infants and Rathbone infants.

14 September — Dr Mary Share Jones medically examined all evacuees this afternoon.

15 September — School re-opened for our scholars this morning.

20 November — As the school is not fitted with dark blinds for 'blacking out', the times of morning and afternoon sessions have been varied for winter months …closing at 3.15*pm* …to enable the caretaker to clean before the 'blackout' time.

1940

29 January to 16 February — Weather continues to be extremely severe. It is generally considered that this is the severest winter for over fifty years.

24 May — Empire Day — made a collection for providing tobacco for troops which realised £1-0s-9d.

30 May — Visited by Dr Clarice Hughes who treated children whose parents had consented to their immunization against diptheria.

3 June — Second inoculation of children against diptheria.

6 July — Visited by County Architect who explained plans for air raid precaution. In the event of an air raid scholars are to be assembled in corridors and the back half of each classroom. Corridors are to be buttressed up, windows treated with anti-splinter preparation, and half-inch mask wire netting. School will be provided with stirrup pump.

16 July — Lecture on wartime cookery given to a good attendance of housewives at 3.15*pm* in the central hall.

30 August — This district had its first experience of air raids during the night 29/30 when from about midnight to 3*am* German planes dropped bombs over a wide area, setting the mountain on fire.

31 August — From 10*pm* last night waves of German bombers dropped high explosive and incendiary bombs on the surrounding district. Fortunately only one fell in Ruabon, in Pentre Clawdd fields. This caused breakage of many windows in the village but only dislodged gas mantles from school.

2 September — 48 children present this morning. The majority of people have been seeking shelter in cellars during the weekend and have lost much sleep. Planes pass over the village each night.

5 September — Siren sounded at 2.30 this afternoon. Children were in the corridor in less than one minute and cheerfully sang while German planes passed about twenty feet over the school at the time when the siren was going.

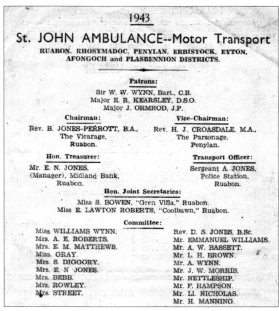

St. John Ambulance, Ruabon area, 1943.

9 September — Planes continue to pass over nightly and as many bombs have been dropped, people seek shelter in cellars. In accordance with instructions we commence school at 10*am* from today.

19 December — We held the usual Christmas treat in the central hall this afternoon. As the children were taking their places the siren sounded an air raid warning, and children were marched into the corridor where they cheerfully sang songs for half an hour. In spite of the difficulty of obtaining food, the tables were as generously filled as in former years, the chief items missing being chocolates and oranges.

1941

8 May — For the last eight nights the siren has sounded while German planes have passed on their way to heavily bomb Merseyside, the all-clear sounding about 4*am*.

1942

20 January — The school has been scheduled as a rest centre in case of a blitz. During the past week the black-out curtains have been fixed, a quantity of stores and equipment delivered.

1943

17 May — 'Wings for Victory' week commenced today. The target set for the school was £100. Amount collected this morning was £152-11s-6d.

People were healthier under war-time rationing and the introduction of school meals was one of the great advances in child care. When the scheme was mooted for Ruabon in 1942, it was estimated there would be about seventy-five children whose parents wished them to have school meals. When they were served for the first time in February 1943 it was recorded, '129 were served. Great difficulty in accommodation. Not possible to fit any more in.'.

Ruabon Burial Joint Committee, 'senior citizens responsible for the well-being of Ruabon, post 1945'.
Back row: W. Davies; H. Hough; E. N. Jones (Treasurer); T. R. R. Griffiths; G. R. Everitt; F. Hampson;
A. W. Bassett; W. D. Blanchard; J. Valentine.
Front row: T. Aston; A. E. Pemberton; P. Lloyd; Emmanuel Williams (Vice-Chairman); A. Wynn (Chairman);
A. H. Squire (Clerk); W. E. Richards; G. Davies; H. M. Green.

The death of Sir Watkin Williams Wynn in May 1944 marked the end of an era, although he lost his seat as Member of Parliament in 1885, he was a member of Denbighshire County Council, Wrexham Rural District Council, and Ruabon Parish Council. The tight grip Wynnstay held on village affairs was loosened forever.

Peace came in 1945, the Germans surrendered in May, and the Japanese in August. The parish council arranged for the peace celebrations to take place on 29 September with tea parties in the schools for children of three years of age and over and elderly persons, a programme of sports in Wynnstay park followed by a bonfire and fireworks on the recreation ground. The parish council asked Mrs. Bryn Roberts and the WVS to prepare the teas.

After long years of war and economic depression, the parish council made plans for housing development and improved community facilities. On New Years Eve 1946 a dance was held to raise funds for the recreation ground reconstruction plan. Three hundred tickets, admission two shillings and sixpence, were sold and the 'Bohemian' Dance Band Wrexham engaged. Arrangements were made for a variety concert at the parish hall by Madame Blackshaw Jones with Mr F. Hinchcliffe, stationmaster, chairman; a Sunday evening concert by the Broughton male voice choir at the council school; and an offer of the loan of a boxing ring for a boxing show from the Physical Training Corps at Wrexham Barracks accepted.

Wynnstay Hall was sold to Lindisfarne College in 1949, but the army huts used by the Royal Engineers during the war had been turned into an international settlement camp for forty mid-European families, mainly Polish and Latvian, fleeing from Russian terror, with a sprinkling of Italians and British wives. After becoming naturalised, they were eventually dispersed, some of them being re-housed and settling down in the Ruabon district.

Another group absorbed into the Ruabon village community fifteen years later were the people of Plas Bennion. The story of the last years of this small community on the border of Penycae is told by Mrs Betty Humphries (née Ellis).

Plas Bennion

Plas Bennion was a close knit and caring community. It had sixty houses, thirty-seven in Ruabon parish, and another twenty-three over the railway crossing in the parish of Penycae. There were three shops, all of them stocked to provide the needs of a community which had little or no transport. They sold everything. Joe's operated from the front room of 15 Plas Bennion Terrace, until it closed on the outbreak of war in 1939. Bob Hughes traded from his kitchen of 3 Sweeny Mount, and Dinah Daniel's general store was in the kitchen of 6 Wynn Hall Terrace. There were four small farms: Plas Bennion, Davenport's, Bryn Issa sometimes referred to as the Engine House, Ty'n Pistyll, and Tai Bithel which ceased farming just before the Second World War.

Plas Bennion flourished as an industrial community from the time of the Lloyds in the 18th century and the old mine workings were

Above and right: Plas Bennion (now demolished).

still in evidence in the 20th century. During the Second World War the men dug out a tunnel leading to the 'B' pit to make an air raid shelter. An old brickyard, the kilns, was demolished in 1933. The remains of Plas Bennion Hall, together with four cottages, were swept away in the 1960s. The Church of the Good Shepherd was always well attended, until the thirty-one houses were demolished and the residents moved to Ruabon and Plas Madoc. Many continued to return to worship until the church was closed in 1982. The chapel, Capel Carmel, was supported on special occasions by the church people as was the Church of the Good Shepherd.

During the Second World War many of the young men joined the armed forces. Two of them were killed and one was taken prisoner by the Japanese. Others, colliers, worked in the mines at Hafod, Bersham, Gresford, Llay Main, Black Park, and Ifton. Some found employment at Monsanto. A searchlight battalion of the Royal Artillery arrived in 1941 and established a camp here. They were made welcome and soon became part of the community until they left around 1944. The local men joined the Home Guard, A.F.S., A.R.P., and the Special Constabulary. The women worked at the Royal Ordnance Factory at Marchwiel or the engineering firm of Hughes and Lancaster, Acrefair, now Air Products. I joined the ATS [Auxilliary Territorial Service].

Evacuees from Liverpool were billeted at Plas Bennion. They enjoyed their stay and returned at the end of the war except for one boy who remained and who died in Ruabon in 1999 aged seventy years.

Social activities in the community took place in the building known as the 'room'. Mrs Annie Roberts was the 'local impressario' and arranged the 'Penny Hop' on a Friday night where the young people learned to dance and here in the 'room' concerts and plays were staged with the young people taking part. Plas Bennion had a football team which broke up when the lads went into the army. The team played on a ground belonging to Ty'n Pistyll farm. This was the highlight for all. It was a good team. Girls and boys played cricket and rounders in summer but in winter the marsh would freeze, and there was great fun sliding and slithering since none had skates.

Plas Bennion was a wonderful place to live and all who lived there will never forget it.

Gyfelia

There is a story of an 18th century highwayman, Dick the Devil, who had a favourite spot on the old road in Gyfelia, Devil's Ditch, where he used to hold up the coaches as they neared the Old Swan coaching inn. Otherwise, life in Gyfelia in the north-east of the community area was fairly ordinary. Gyfelia is approached from Johnstown, the Bangor road linked it in its time of prosperity, a hundred years ago, to the Dennis brickworks and Hafod colliery. Education and religion were found close by at Eyton. The Dennis family established nearby at New Hall and Astridge took an interest in the village, and presided at times of national celebration such as the return of the servicemen at the end of the Second World War when Mrs. Dennis presented wallets at a barn dance arranged to greet them.

The census of 1891 reveals the major occupation of the inhabitants as coal-mining. Here the names of heads of households are given:

Gyfelia: Wm Roberts, woodman; Thomas Pritchard, stoker; John Massey, retired grocer; Abel Roberts, road labourer; Edward Roberts, general labourer; Robert Williams, farmer; Letitia Kay, charwoman.

Gyfelia Terrace: John Hughes, engine driver; Lloyd Pritchard, coal-miner; Charles Hughes, general labourer; Wm Lee, agricultural labourer; John Lloyd, colliery labourer; John Pemberton, general labourer.

Gyfelia Cottages: John Jones, coal-miner; William Hales Taylor, coal-miner.

Gyfelia Farm: Thomas Massey, farmer, wife and nine children.

Moreton Manor: Uriah Morgan, wife and six children, farmer and shopkeeper.

The Waggoners: Joseph Haycock, wife and ten others in the household.

Coal-mining continued to provide work until the mines closed in the late 1960s. In 1934 Herbert Hughes of Gyfelia Terrace was the youngest member of the rescue team which faced the horror of the Gresford Colliery disaster. He was gone for days and when he returned his daughter Brenda asked him where he had been? He replied, 'in the cornfield', and he would never talk about his experiences.

The landlord of the Waggoners in 1891 was Joseph Haycock, and one of his sons, John, succeeded him as landlord and must have been the perfect host, winning the respect of his customers by his prowess in many fields of sport, with over thirty trophies on display.

Pen y Gardden.

In 1914 John Haycock received an international cap as a member of the Welsh Quoiting XI which defeated England. He played in a final trial at Wrexham for the international soccer team when Billy Meredith was in the match. He won a prize for hurdling, and in 1898 won a magnificent clock for success in the 120 yards race at Stansty Park, Wrexham. As a horticulturalist he was an example to the locals who must have envied his green fingers. In 1907 he won a gold medal for dahlias and in 1928 three trophies at the *Daily News* show in Southport presented by the National Sweet Pea Society. During the 1914–1918 war out of 3,000 entries he was awarded first prize, value £100 for the best collection of three vegetables at the *Daily Mail* Home Grown War Food Exhibition. He submitted three potatoes, three onions and three carrots. Another hobby was racing pigeons. These were the activities pursued by miners in their spare time with the opportunity of showing at a multitude of venues from mid-summer to late autumn.

The Waggoner's Inn is now closed, but the community survives.

Gardden

Gardden is situated in the north-west corner of the parish. Extracts from the census returns of 1891 reveal what a busy place it was. A description of occupations is given and in some instances names of the heads of households.

Gardden Hall: William Pritchard, farmer and builder.

Gardden Cottages: John Evans, engine man; living in other cottages — shoemaker, coal-miner, colliery worker, coal-miner.

Gardden Lodge: Henry Jenks, retired African merchant.

Gardden Lodge Cottages: ostler, farm labourer.

Pen-y-Gardden: John W. Haigh, colliery proprietor, in the household Reuben aged 12 years.

Pen-y-Gardden Cottages: John Pemberton, butcher — and a brick turner, general labourer, blacksmith, coach man.

Tatham Cottages: William Haywood, terracotta burner.

Offa Cottages: carter, labourer.

Offa Terrace: James Roberts, baker; David Rogers, gardener; John Rowland, coal-miner.

Mill Farm: Ann Lloyd, laundress.

The Tithe Apportionment 1844 gives the ownership and acreage of the farms:

Gardden — The Reverend Henry William Marker, Trustee for Miss Kenyon, an infant, 81a-0r-4p.

Pen-y-Gardden — Landowner Miss Parry, occupier, Robert Johnson, 59a-31r-9p.

Tatham's landowner — The Honourable Frederick West, occupier — Elizabeth Jones.

The atmosphere of Gardden in the 1880s is captured by J. Watkin Ellis:[28]

I should say that this portion of Ruabon from what is known as the Bryn Bridge, so called from the mansion on the adjoining estate, to Afongoch is the most altered of any part of Ruabon. Seventy years ago the main road was narrow and on the left-hand side leading from the village, GWR branch line to Aberderfyn ran about forty yards from the road, crossing the by-road to Tatham by way of a level crossing and entering what was then Gardden Lodge Colliery, well inside their works.

At the level crossing gates was a well-known attendant known to all and sundry as 'Sam the Coedloedd', quite a character of importance seldom found in these days. Just beyond the crossing were several cottages, afterwards engulfed in the clay pit. Close to the spot where the bridge now stands were several other cottages, one of which was straw thatched … From the opposite side of the bridge there used to be a public path running east, over the GWR line and on to the old Wrexham Road (Dennis's Lane), another path lost to the public. On the right hand side there were two cottages on the road side, afterwards the site of Monk and Newell's brickworks — the only buildings on that side from the old village to Afongoch proper.
'Sam the Coedloedd' directed the firm of Monk and Newell to the clay-bed. When they persisted in erecting their sheds on the Ruabon end in what was then a field, he pointed out to them that it was on that spot where the best clay would be found…
What a change in a few years! Two brickworks and a colliery gone; the whole countryside altered and now developing into a miniature Lake District. On the Gardden estate there were at least three good quarries, now derelict, which supplied a first-class quality of freestone to all parts of North Wales, Lancashire and Cheshire…

Mr Eddie Bowen Jones writes with the same nostalgia. Remembering Gardden, he writes:

Standing on the bridge at Ty'n-y-Rhagau looking towards the Rocky Woods one would have seen on the left Mill Cottage, though why it was called Mill Cottage I do not know as there seemed no running water readily available at this point. It was an old property, and has now been modernised almost beyond recognition. At the back of Mill Cottage ran an open gully which was used to run the extracted water from the Afoneitha for the purposes of the railway at Ruabon station and I think the sluice gate is still in position near the wooden bridge which crosses the Afoneitha near the Ty'n-y-Rhagau waterfall which may have been used as a mill race.

The wooden bridge leads to Rocky Woods. Above the Afoneitha at Ty'n-y-Rhagau one can see the red brick houses, built I believe by Reuben Haigh, brickmaster. The houses in the 1930s were occupied by the Misses Parker, Mr Llewelyn Grey…Before crossing the road bridge at Ty'n-y-Rhagau on the left-hand side was a gipsy caravan or wagonette which was occupied by a German lady who was obviously very religious as she had a harmonium in her little caravan and sang hymns. The outside of the caravan was emblazoned with religious emblems and legends such as 'Sin is Death', 'God is Love'. We children thought this lady to be a witch, and we would run past her shouting and screaming. Before the war certainly I knew this lady to be a very gentle person, as one day my nain R. A. Jones, who had by this time suffered a stroke, had stopped in her bath chair outside, and we were served tea in the middle of the highway.

Looking towards Tatham Farm where the Allens were farming at this time one could see a long row of houses at right angles to the highway. They were stone, and I remember Miss Carrie Rogers lived at one of the properties and Eddie Griffiths' family lived in another of them. On the Afoneitha side of these cottages was an exposed coal seam and I think Mr Eddie Griffiths' father extracted coal from there as others must have done from time to time. Crossing the Ty'n-y-Rhagau bridge moving up the hill was another mill cottage, and I seem to remember here through the cottage in the cellar ran a stream.

At the top of the hill leading towards Tredville Bridge the Pen-y-Gardden Lane and the entrance to Tatham Farm, one comes across an entrance to Pen-y-Gardden although I never remember it being used until it was re-opened recently. The house is now called Pen-y-Gardden Hall but it was not so called until say 1980. The house in the 1920s was occupied by Mr Reuben Haigh and his wife and family. The house was refurbished in or around 1912 as can be seen from the timbers imported from the United States supporting the rather grand oak staircase. Of the three cellars they included two wells and all the cellars are of different ages which suggest that the present building was not the only one to have been constructed on this site. The odd thing about this house is that the front door seems to be facing the 'wrong way', *i.e.* towards the Rocky Woods rather than towards the highway below. It has been said that one of the owners of the house had fallen out with the Wynnstay family and would not have his house facing Wynnstay Hall. In the 1920s Reuben Haigh used to breed shire horses on the farm abutting the house, and one would see them being led away from time to time, or at least the stallions, to service mares on local farms. The formal gardens at Pen-y-Gardden contain a pistyll which discharged it's water into a carved stone leaf of quite considerable size, and this was near a conservatory or gazebo which fell into disrepair and was demolished after the war.

The lane to Pen-y-Gardden runs upwards in a loop passing an entrance to Pen-y-Gardden and its farm. The loop then borders the hill-fort and then runs downhill past the site of Gardden Lodge (now demolished), then borders the site of the old brickyard which closed in the 1960s. The loop I refer to is ingeniously contrived to afford drainage, or otherwise parts of it would have become a watercourse long since.

The brickyard which comprised about a dozen kilns was served by the clayhole now in the process of being used as a landfill. It was famous among the children of the village for its 'lizards' and some flooded parts of the clayhole contained small fish. Above the clayhole towards Tatham Farm was the bakelite factory managed by Mr Hulse. During the Second World War this factory ran apace, but closed I think shortly thereafter. Looking from that factory one could see the Bryn Bridge at Ruabon where the ambulance train was first stationed just over the Bryn Bridge on an unusual industrial railway line. The ambulance train was manned by soldiers, one of whom was known in the village as 'Blondie'.

From the bakelite factory looking across the main Ruabon/Wrexham highway, one could see the Monk & Newell brickyard, but there was a white cottage and a chimney there before the war, and I think I can remember the chimney being demolished as indeed I remember the adjoining Bryn Bridge being reconstructed. Rumour was rife in the village when the war broke out that the first target for Hitler's bombers would in fact be the Bryn Bridge in whose reconstruction a mechanical digger called 'The American Devil' was used. I believe it was then that the railway halt at Wynnville may have been constructed.

The Monk & Newell brickyard ran from the Bryn Bridge right to Afongoch and terminated there with two large pools, formerly clay holes, one of which is now used for fishing, the other having been filled in some years ago. These pools were dangerous and therefore, were an attraction to children and they were the site of two suicides at least which upset the village very much. Mr Haigh also kept his greyhounds near the pools.

Haigh participated in Ruabon affairs from time to time, but his best remembered contribution, I suppose are his cricketing exploits. He played in his earlier days with Dr 'Jack' Lawton Roberts, R. A. Jones (grocer), Rev D. J. Bowen, Mr J. C. Murless, and others. He was survived by Mrs. Haigh, who continued to live at Pen-y-Gardden for some time, and his nephews Mr Jimmy Thomas, of Rhos Cricket Club fame, and Mr Roddy Thomas.

Shops and Trade

At the beginning of the 20th century Ruabon had a variety of shops. The radical increase in the population in the nineteenth century brought its stresses and strains, but these were more than compensated for by an improvement in the quality of life. There was more fresh food as the means of transport improved and provided Ruabon with an important railway junction, bringing in fresh food and sending away manufactured goods. In the village were self-contained communities in Tan Lan, Brynfields and Church Street, where shops were patronised by large households, and fellow-adherents of the church or chapels. The village supplied a great variety of goods to business and professional men and the local farmers. To walk down High Street as a child with money in your pocket must have given great pleasure.

The Post Office

The most important public building used by the majority of the inhabitants of Ruabon was the Post Office. J. Watkin Ellis observed:

The first Post Office I remember occupied the site of the present Haven Café (on the corner of Church Street, opposite the Wynnstay Hotel), kept by Edward Morris … The next Post Office was in Church Street, quite a small provision for the public, accommodating three or four persons at the most, with glass shutters separating the office from the public, on which you knocked to

Ruabon Post Office Staff outing to Rhyl. 1921/2. Mrs W. B. Jones holding Iris.

Ruabon Post Office Staff, c.1910.
Included are:Mr Taylor (postman); Mr W. B. Jones
(Postmaster); Miss Lizzie Owen (telephonist);
Mr Llewellyn Nicholas (postman).

gain attention and the stamps you required. The Post Office was afterwards established at the top of Ysgoldy Hill, on the west side. This was a great improvement and provided more accommodation for the public. A new Post Office was built, which provided all the necessary requirements for the public.

This 'new Post Office' was a fairly large red-brick building on the left hand-side between the Wynnstay Hotel at the entrance to Tan Lan. Ruabon was an important sorting office supplying a large rural area.

The Post Office used the railways as soon as they were established, and an important link was therefore made in 1846 when the railway station opened.

Bryan Martin Davies.

Mr Bryan Martin Davies
Mr Bryan Martin Davies has brought distinction to Ruabon through his service to the Welsh language. A native of Brynaman, Carmarthenshire, Mr Davies came to Ruabon Boys' Grammar School in 1959 to teach Welsh. It was whilst he was head of the Welsh department in Ysgol Ruabon that he won the Crown for poetry at the National Eisteddfod in two successive years: Ammanford 1970 and Bangor 1971. In 1978, Mr Davies moved from Ruabon to teach Welsh at Yale Sixth Form College, Wrexham, where he remained until retirement in 1985. Mr Davies has published books of verse:

Darluniau ar Grynfas, 1970; *Y Golau Caeth*, 1972; *Deuoliaethau*, 1976; *Lleoedd* (Winner of Welsh Arts Council Prize), 1984; *Pan Oedd y Nos yn Wenfflam*, 1988.

Translations: *Nadolig Plentyn yng Nghymru* (*A Child's Christmas in Wales*, Dylan Thomas), 1978; *Prolog Chwedlau Caergaint* (A metrical translation of Chaucer's *Prologue to the Canterbury Tales*), 1983.

Novel: *Gardag*, 1988.

Voluntary Organisations

The strength of a community may be measured by its ability to meet together for a diversity of purposes which are for the mutual benefit of the group. Over the last 150 years, organisations have died out, and after a short while been revived. Amongst these are sports and youth groups. Some organisations have left but little trace behind, with no records to mark their strength and contribution.

Sport
The second half of the nineteenth century saw the development of team games. Chapels, churches and small hamlets raised their own teams. In Ruabon organised sport was influenced by the reform of the Grammar School. A. L. Taylor, the headmaster, was a competent cricketer and played regularly with the school team. Sir Watkin had his own chaplain at Wynnstay and young clerical gentlemen played in the Wynnstay cricket team. In 1888 the football league was set up and attracted young men from the coal-mines. Other team games played in Ruabon were tennis, hockey, and bowls.

[continued on page 208]

Slater's Directory 1895, Ruabon.

Private Residents

Booth, Misses Charlotte & Frances, Plas Madoc Hall

Brancker, Mrs. Helena, Tynllan

Davies, David Llewelyn, Park Side

Davies, Thomas, Plas-yn-wern cottage

Dennis, H. Dyke, Hafod House

Dennis, Henry C.E., J.P., New Hall

Douglas, J. Campbell, Bank House, Church Street

Doxey, Thomas, Plas-yn-Wern

Edmunds, Rev. E.M., Tai Clawdd, High Street

Edwards, Rev. Canon Ebenezer W., M.A., Vicarage

Edwards, William, Bryn End

Griffiths, Nathaniel Robert, Plas-newydd

Haigh, John, Penygardden

Hope, Cecil A., Penynant

Hughes, Lieut-Col. H.R., Wynnstay

Jenks, Henry, Gardden

Jones, Rev. John, Duke Street

Jones, Edward, Woodlands

Jones, Isaac, Tiryfron

Jones, William, Tynewydd

Kenrick, Llewelyn, Wynn Hall

Laycock, J.S., Hafod Cottage, Parkside

Maguire, James, Tai Clawdd, 4 High St.

Malyn,B.A., Rev. R.H. Bryn Hyfryd Villas

Morris, Charles, Tai Clawdd, 6 High Street

Morrish, Frederick, High Street

Peters, Wm., Tai Clawdd, 7 High Street

Roberts, Jas., Tai Clawdd, 10 High Street

Roberts, R. Lawton, M.D., High Street

Taylor, Rev. Alfred Lee, M.A.

Turner, Miss E.H., Brooklyn House

Woodford, George Edward, The Bryn

Wynn, Sir Herbert Lloyd Watkin Williams- bart., D.L. J.P,. Wynnstay

Yardley, Edward, Bryn Hyfryd villas

Commercial

Bailiff, William, hair dresser, Duke Street

Barmouth Gas Co. Limited (registered offices), George E. Woodford, secretary

Beckett, George, tailor, High Street

Booth, Charlotte & Frances (Misses), ladies' boarding school, Plas Madoc Hall

Bowers, H.R., brick & tile manufacturer, Penbedw & Taltham Fire-clay works

Chambers, W. & J., watch makers, High Street

Coombs, T.A., engineer, Linslade

Davies, George & Son C.E. Feis. Inst. P.A.London, M.S.I.C. Paris &c. (established 1835; British, foreign and colonial patents obtained, designs and trademarks registered; 'self help to Patent Law', new edition, price 6d.), Leinster chambers, 4 St. Ann's square, Manchester. T.A. 'Inventor, Manchester'

Davies, John, joiner & builder, Epworth House, Bryn

Dennis -, manufacturers of red, blue and buff bricks, terracotta, encaustic & tesselated tiles, glazed bricks, ridging, roofing tiles, flooring quarries, sanitary pipes &c. T.N. 1 Nat.; T.A. 'Dennis Ruabon'

Dennis, Hy., civil & mining engineer

Dolgelly Gas & Co. Limited (registered offices), George E. Woodford secy

Douglas, J. Campbell, accountant, North & South Wales Bank Ltd. (branch) Church Street

Doxey, Thomas, agent to the Wynnstay Collieries Ltd. Ruabon

Dutton, E.K. & Co., Fels. Inst. P.A. London (civil & consulting engineers & scientific experts; solicitors of patents for inventions in Great Britain & abroad & agents for the registration of trademarks & designs; established thirty years), 5 John Dalton Street, Manchester. T.N. 752; T.A. 'Dotus Manchester'. New & revised pamphlet containing latest information, gratis & post free

Dysynni Gas Co. Limited (registered offices), George E. Woodford, secy

Edwards & Co., grocers, High Street

Edwards, J.C., terracotta, glazed brick, encaustic tile & brick & tile manufacturer, Terra Cotta Works. T.A. 'Edwards, Ruabon'. See advertisement.

Edwards, Richard, hosiery manufr. St. Martins (Salop), near Ruabon.

Edwards, William C.E., civil & mining engineer, Bryn end. T.A. 'Central'

Evans, David, boot maker High Street

Ferguson, Walter, shopkeeper, Afoncitha

Franks, O.A.H., Vaults P.H. Bridge Street

Graesser, Rob., manufacturing chemist. T.N. 3 Nat.; T.A. 'Graesser, Ruabon'

Griffith, Walter, grocer & draper, Bridge Street

Griffiths, Nathaniel R., mining engineer, Plas Newydd

Griffiths, Robert, butcher

Hughes, Lieut.-Col. H.R., head agent for Sir Herbert Lloyd Watkin Williams-Wynn bart.'s estates, Wynnstay

Hughes, Harriet (Mrs.), milliner & dress maker, Church Street

Hughes, Thomas, superintendent to the Refuge Assurance Co. Limited Bryn House, Henry Street

Hughes, William H., iron founder, Plaskynaston foundary

Jenks, Henry, managing director of the Ruabon Brick & Terra Cotta Co. Limited.

Jones & Jones, grocers, Henry street

Jones, Ann (Mrs.), shopkeeper, Bridge street

Jones, Evan, builder & contractor, Glenoffa

Jones, Hugh, coach proprietor, Bryn Hyfryd Villas

Jones, John, bootmaker, Duke street

Jones, John, Bridge End Inn

Jones, Robert A. grocer, Bridge Street

Jones, Sarah (Mrs.), Duke of Wellington P.H., Duke Street

Jones, William, L.R.C.P. Lond. M.R.C.S. Eng. surgeon, Tynewydd

Jones, William, tailor, Park Street

Kenrick, Llewelyn, solicitor & commissioner for oaths, Church street

Langford, Joseph, bootmaker, Henry Street

Laycock, J.S., local agent to the Wynnstay home estate, Wynnstay.

Leighton, William G., grocer, Brynfield

Littlehales, Alfred P., agent, Tai Clawdd, 1 High Street

Lloyd, Robert, vestry clerk & clerk to burial & lighting board, Cambrian House, Church Street

Monk & Newell, brick & tile mfrs

Morgan, William, sculptor, Tai Clawdd, 5 High Street

Morris, William, grocer & draper, Church Street

Murless, Philip, Wynnstay Arms

North & South Wales Bank Lts. (branch) (J. Campbell Douglas accountant), Church Street

Owen, Joseph, Moreton Inn

Pemberton, Robert, beer retailer & maltster

Prince, Charles, blacksmith, High Street

Prince, Mary (Mrs.), dress & mantlemaker, Tai Clawdd, 8 High Street

Prince, John, blacksmith, Tanyclawdd

Reynolds, Ernest, painter, Church Street

Rhos Gas Co. Limited, George E. Woodford secretary

Roberts & Son, saddlers & harness makers, High street

Roberts, David, butcher, Park Street

Roberts, Evan, saddler, High Street

Roberts, R. Lawton M.D. surgeon, High Street

Rogers & Jackson, ironmongers & china &c. dealers, Church street & at Wrexham

Rowlands, L. & Co. chemists & oil & colourmen, High Street

Ruabon Brick & Terra Cotta Co. Limited, brick manufacturers, Henry Jenks, managing director. T.A. 'Bricks, Ruabon.'

Ruabon Coal & Coke Lim. (The)

Saint, George jun. manager to the

Bridge Street.

Bridge Street.

High Street.

Midland Bank.

Henry Street

Above left: Poster advertising R. Albert Jones, The Stores, Ruabon.

Above right: High Street, 2000.
Right: High Street, 2000.

Vauxhall Colliery Co. Limited, Vauxhall House

Saint Thomas E.W. mining engineer, Tai Clawdd, 3 High Street

Smith, W.H. & Sons, booksellers, Railway station

Smith, Mary Jane (Miss), milliner & dressmaker, High Street

Taylor, William, sculptor, Henry St.

Teirw Hill Road Stone Co. Limited (William Edwards Secretary) quarry proprieters; quarries, Glyn Ceiriog, Chirk

Vauxhall Colliery Co. Limited, coal proprieters, George Saint, jun. Manager

Williams, David R. shopkeeper, Oakleigh

Williams, Francis, butcher, Bryn

Williams, John, builder & contractor, Oakleigh

Woodford, George E. secretary to the Barmouth Gas Co. Limited, Dolgelly Gas Co. Limited, Dysynni Gas Co. Limited & Rhos Gas Co. Limited

Wyndham, Henry, manufacturer of glazed stoneware, sewerage pipes & fire-clay goods 'The Delph' Brick & fire-clay works. T.A. 'Wyndham, Ruabon'

Wynnstay Collieries Limited, colliery proprieters, Thomas Doxey, agent. T.A. 'Wynnstay Collieries, Ruabon'

Farmers

Cooper, Mrs. Hannah, Clwt
Davies, Edward, Ty Carrol
Davies, James, Plasynclawdd
Davies, John E. Plas Issa
Davies, Thomas, Pant-y-Garn
Davies, William, Coedleodd
Davies, William, Tai Nant
Dennis, Henry & Co. top of Cefn Farm
Dennis, Walter Pen, Hafod House
Dicken, John, Christwnydd
Dodd, Joseph, Crab Mill
Edwards, Edward, Pen-y-Bryn
Edwards, James C.
Edwards, Joseph, Pen-y-Bryn
Edwards, Robert
Edwards, Walter, Pentre
Edwards, William, Rhos-y-Madoc
Ellis, Edward, Penymais
Evans, John, Graig, Penlan
Evans, Samuel, Plasdrain
Evans, Thomas, Penbedw
Gabriel, Samuel, Stryt Issa
Green, Mrs. Jane, Crabtree Green
Griffiths, Mrs. Sarah & Son, Moreton Issa
Griffiths, Mrs. Catherine, The Mill
Griffiths, Nathaniel R. Ty Newydd

Griffiths, Robert
Haigh, John W. Pen-y-Gardden
Hope, Cecil A. Pen-y-Nant
Hughes, Hugh, Pen-y-Bryn
Hughes, Thomas, Sycamore Farm
Hughes, Thomas, Ysgubor ucha
Hughes W.C.
Hutchinson, Nathaniel, Tyddyn Ucha
Huxley, Edward, Caia
Jackson, Edward, Upper Nant
Jones, David, Caillyd
Jones, Enoch, Brynteg
Jones, Lewis, Morton Issa
Jones, Parry, New Buildings
Jones, Robert, Pen-y-Cae
Jones, Robert, Ty-Brith
Jones, Thomas, Cinders
Jones, Thomas, Yewtree-Issa
Jones, William, Plasmadoc
Kenrick, Kenrick, Dynhynlle Issa
Lloyd, John
Massey, Thomas, Gyfelia
Morgan, Uriah, Gyfelia
Moore, Benjamin, Tanyclawdd
Morris, John, Onew Fawr
Morris, John, Plas Ucha
Murless, Phillip R. Llwynhowel
Owen, Joseph, Moreton
Parker, Noah, Bryn Farm

Parry, Thomas, Park Farm
Parry, Thomas, Tymawr
Philips, Alfred, Caesoil
Phillips, Andrew, Tyddyn Ucha
Phillips, Charles Herbert William, Penybryn Hall
Phillips, Ellis, Pant Hill
Price, John, Wern
Price, Richard, Pentre Issa
Price, Robert, Drefechan
Price, Thomas, Dryll Farm
Pritchard, Benjamin, Prefechan
Pruett, J.A., Plasyclawdd
Pugh, John, Park Eyton
Randalls, S.T., Newbridge
Roberts, Edward, Middle Sontley
Roberts, Edward, Pant Glas
Roberts, Mrs. Mary J. Cinders
Roberts, Robert William, Yellow Oak

Farm
Roberts, Thomas, Coedloedd
Roberts, William, Coedloedd
Roberts, William, Rhos Farm
Sands, Samuel, Lower Farm
Sharpe, Richard, Pentre Issa
Stevens, John, Dunenfechan
Taylor, John, Rhosymadoc
Taylor, William C. Tan y Clawdd
Thomas, Edward, Ty Gwyn
Thomas, Elias, Rhos-y-Madoc
Thomas, James Lloyd, Drill Drefechan
Thomas, John, Drefechan
Thomas, Joseph, Hafod-y-Ucha
Thomas, William, Drefechan
William, Mrs. Margaret & Son, Pentreclawdd
Williams, John M. Tainant
Williams, Robert, Gyfelia

Williams, Robert, Tyn-y-Pistill
Williams, William, Bryn by Powell & Hafod
Williams, William, Ty Mawr

Bryn-Pen-y-Lan
Private residents
Buncombe, Rev. Thomas, B.A., The Parsonage
Ormrod, Peter J.P., Penylan Hall

Commercial
Foulkes, John, shopkeeper
Taylor, Frank, blacksmith

Bennett's Business Directory, 1922

Ruabon, a village, civil and ecclesiastic parish is in the Wrexham county court area and rural district of Denbighshire, 5 miles S.W. of Wrexham. The acreage of the civil parish is 5,906 with a population of 3,387. It has a head post, money order and telegraph office and a telephone call office in the Wrexham area. The station is on the G.W.R. between Shrewsbury and Chester. The industries are mining and the manufacture of bricks and tiles. Early closing day, Wednesday.

Bailiff, G, hairdresser, Duke St.
Barmouth Gas Co. Ltd, High St.
Beckett, G., mcht tailor, High St
Bridge End Hotel (close to Station) — R.E. Davies, proprietor. Teas and refreshments provided. Good stabling.
Cefn & District Co-Operative Society Ltd., New High St.
Chapman, Miss, confectioner & tobacconist, High St.
Davies, D.C., grocer, baker and provision merchant, Bryn Shop
Davies & Ling, motor garage proprietors
Duke of Wellington, close to station- Dave W. Jacubs, proprietor. Accommodation for cyclists and tourists. Teas and refreshments provided.
Dysynni Gas Co., Ltd., High Street
Edwards, E. nurse, Grenville terrace
Eggington, E. T. & G., milliners & costumiers, Bryn House
Ellis, John, corn merchant; and at 15 Queen St. Wrexham
Evans, G. fishmonger, 3 Central Buildings, Henry St.

Fletcher, W. & R., Ltd., butchers
Great Western Hotel, near Station
Griffiths, R. butcher, Park St.
Hough, S, refreshment room, Church St.
Hughes, F, cycle and motor repairer, Duke St. All kinds of motor and cycle accessories in stock
Hughes, G., joiner
Jones, J.W. hairdresser, New High St.
Jones, R., bootmaker. High St.
Jones, R. A., grocer, Brynfield
Kenrick, Ll., solicitor
Latham, E., coal merchant, Oakland
Lee & Sons, Posting & Livery Stables, Bryn. Tel. No. 28. Motor car on hire by time or distance, with experienced chauffeur
Squire, Mrs, registrar of births & deaths
Lee Bros., fruiterers, Brynfield
Leighton, R., assistant overseer, Parkside
Lewis, H. confectioner, New High St.
Liberal Association Rooms, Bryn Estate
Lloyd, E., grocer, draper, high-class confectioner, tobacco and cigar merchant, Bridge st
London Joint City and Midland Bank Ltd. High Street
Parry, Miss M., first-class milliner, 4 New High St. Latest styles and fashions.
Pearl Insurance Company Ltd., Branch Office: High Street
Prince, Mrs., costumier, High St.
Price, tobacco, cigar & cigarette stores, High St.
Refuge Assurance Company, New High Street
Rhos Gas Co., Ltd., High Street
Richards, W E, ironmonger, etc., Birmingham House
Roberts & Maginnis, Welsh Silica Brick & Ganister Works, Trevor, Specialite: Dinica Silica Bricks. Ground Ganister for all kinds of furnaces. Silica cement,

etc. Tel. Add. 'Silica, Ruabon'. Tel. No. 17 Ruabon. Established 1873
Roberts, A. E., cycle dealer, Henry St.
Roberts, Miss F., A.R.C.M., A.T.C.L., music teacher, Brynhyfryd
Roberts, R. J. boot stores, High St.
Roberts, R. L. & J. C., surgeons
Rowland & Co., chemists, High Street
Ruabon Brick & Terra Cotta Co., Ltd.
Ruabon Coal & Coke Co Ltd, mnfrs of glazed sanitary stoneware
Ruabon Constitutional Club
Ruabon Council School — Headmaster (mixed) F. Davies
Ruabon County School — Headmaster D. J. Bowen
Ruabon Garage (The), motor engineers, 3 New High St. - see advt.
Ruabon National School - Headmaster (boys) J. Owen: Headmistress (girls) Miss Morris
Ruabon Working Men's Association and Literary Institute
Ruabon Water Co., Ltd., High St.
Smith, W. H. & Son, booksellers
Smith, Mrs., Confectioner, High St.
Taylor, D., monumental mason, Station Rd.
Thomas, J.E., tailor
Treadwell, Miss M., highclass confectioner, tobacconist and grocer, Oakleigh
Vauxhall Collieries Ltd.
Waggoners Inn, Gyfelia
Working Men's Conservative Association
Wyman & Sons, Ltd., newsagents, Railway Station
Wyndham & Phillips, brick makers
Wynnstay Arms Hotel
Wynnstay Collieries, Ltd.

Bennett's Business Directory, 1936

Ruabon, a village, civil and ecclesiastic parish is in the Wrexham county court area and rural district of Wrexham, 5 mile S.W. of Wrexham. The acreage of the civil parish is 5,906 with a population of 3,263. It has a head post, money order and telegraph office and a telephone call office in the Wrexham area. The station is on the G.W.R. between Shrewsbury and Chester. The industries are mining and the manufacture of bricks and tiles. Early closing day, Wednesday.

Bailiff, G., hairdresser, Duke Street

Barmouth Gas Co. Ltd., High Street

Beckett, G. & Son, merchant tailors, High Street

Bentley, G., monumental mason, Station Road

Bowen, wireless depôt, Henry St.

Bridge End Hotel (close to station)

Carless, A.W., coal merchant, Tan-y-La

Cefn & District Co-operative society Ltd, New High Street

Chapman, Jas, butcher, Vincent Street

Clay, Miss, confectioner, Henry Street

Corfield, A., grocer, Church Street

Davies & Horspool, confectioners, High Street

Dennis Ruabon Ltd, brick works. Offices, High Street.

Dolgelley Gas & Coal Co., Ltd, High Street

Duke of Wellington, R Howard

Dysynni Gas Co. Ltd, High Street

Edwards, G.O., grocer, New High Street

Edwards, R., butcher, High Street

Eggington, E.T. & G., milliners & costumiers, Pontadam

Evans, G., fishmonger, 3 Central Bldgs, Henry St

Evans, M.V., clerk to justices

Fletcher, W. & R., Ltd., butchers

Grand United Order of Oddfellows, State Insurance Office, Railway terr (L. Nicholas)

Great Western Hotel, near station, A E Pemberton

Griffiths, R. & Son, butchers, Park Street and Henry street

Hayward, Mrs., Hardware dealer, Church Street

Ruabon Nursing Home, Ty Newydd, Mrs Turner

Hughes, C., fruiterer, New High Street

Hughes, G., joiner, Duke Street

Hughes, H., haulage contractor

Hughes, J., fruiterer, Duke Street

Hughes, M., confectioner, High Street

Hughes, R.W., relieving officer, Church Street

Jones, D., Coal merchant, Park Street.

Jones, J.W., hairdresser, New High Street

Jones, R., bootmaker, High Street

Jones, Mrs R.A., grocer, Brynfield

Jones, T., Penylan nurseries

Kenrick, Ll. & Co (M V Evans), solicitors, High Street

Leighton, J.L., newsagent, Henry Street

Lewis, H., confectioner, New High Street

Lewis, H., general stores, High Street

Ling & Co., motor garage

Lloyd, E., general stores, Bridge Street

Matthews, fried fish shop, High Street

Midland Bank Ltd., High Street

National Provincial Bank Ltd.

North Wales Brick & Tile Works, Ltd.

Pearl Insurance Co. Ltd., Branch Office: High Street

Phillips,Walter, grocer, Oakleigh Shop

Piper, J.H., bootmaker, Henry Street

Post Office. J.E. Davies, postmaster

Price, P., boarding house, Spring Lodge, Church Street

Prince, Mrs. costumier, High Street

Pritchard, Mrs, grocer, Brynfield

Refuge Assurance Co., High Street

Reilly, E., confectioner, High Street

Rhos Gas Co., Ltd., High Street

Richards, W.E., painter, Pontadam

Roberts, A.E., cycle agent, High Street

Roberts, J.C.L., surgeon

Roberts, S.E., grocer, High Street

Rowland & Co., chemists, High Street

Ruabon Brick & Terra Cotta Co., Ltd.

Ruabon Coal & Coke Co., Ltd., manufrs of glazed sanitary stoneware

Ruabon Constitutional Club

Ruabon Council School, Headmaster (mixed) A.W. Bassett

Ruabon County School — Headmaster, Rev. D.J. Bowen

Ruabon County School for Girls. Headmistress: Miss Mary Jones

Ruabon National School — Headmaster (boys and girls), T.H. Simpson

Ruabon Nursing Home, Ty Newydd, Mrs Turner

Ruabon Water Co., Ltd, High Street

Smith, W.H. & Son, booksellers

Squire, A.H., clerk to Ruabon Parish Council

Squire, Mrs, registrar of births & deaths

Thomas, J.E., tailor, Brynfield

Turner, A.H., (M.B., B.S., London, etc.), surgeon, Ty Newydd

United Service Club, Tan-y-Lan

Vaults (The) — P Rowlands

Waggoners Inn, Gyfelia

Williams, Mrs P., fried fish shop, Duke St.

Working Men's Conservative Association

Wyman & Sons, Ltd, newsagents, Railway Station

Wyndham & Phillips, brick makers

Wynnstay Arms Hotel — Mrs M.E. Murless

High Street, c.1910.

Llewelyn Kenrick.
[Wrexham Magistrates Court]

Soccer[29]

Ruabon made a significant contribution to Welsh soccer through the influence of Samuel Llewelyn Kenrick (1847–1933). Kenrick was a member of the Wynn Hall family and practised as a solicitor in Ruabon becoming clerk to the magistrates and later coroner for East Denbighshire. He first played soccer as a pupil of Ruabon Grammar School,then as a young man in Shropshire and later for the Plas Madoc club between 1874-78, helping in its transition to the famous Druids. Kenrick won five international caps for Wales between 1876–1881. In January 1876 he founded the Football Association of Wales at a meeting in the Wynnstay Arms, Ruabon.

Other Welsh soccer internationals connected with Ruabon were:

William Ellis Bailiff, b. Ruabon 1882. Goalkeeper, four caps for Wales. Played for Ruabon 1906–1907.
Edward Bowen, b. Ruabon 1858. Played in most positions, 2 caps, teams included Druids, Wynnstay.

Thomas Blundell Burnett, b. Liverpool 1852. Goalkeeper, one cap, Ruabon 1876–1880.

Knyvett Crosse, b. Pontesbury. Halfback/forward, three caps. Played for Druids 1877–1878, 1879–1883. Ruabon 1878–1879. He was employed as a bookstall manager for W. H. Smiths at Ruabon station. Crosse was the licensee of the Cross Foxes, Ruabon, for several years until the public house was closed by Sir Watkin, patron of the Druids, *c*.1889.

Emrys Ellis, b. Plas Bennion 1904. Three caps, wing-half, son of a miner, an outstanding cricketer and footballer at Ruabon Grammar School. At Bangor University, and later headmaster of Weston Rhyn school.

Dr Daniel Grey, b. New Mill, Lanarkshire, Scotland 1848, died Ruabon 1900. Practiced medicine in Ruabon, half-back, forward, two caps. Played for Druids 1874–1880. A founder member of the F. A. of Wales.

Edward Hughes, b. Ruabon 1876. Centre-half, fourteen caps. Played for Everton and Tottenham.

Ralph Stanley Jones, b. Ruabon 1876. Outside left, one cap. Played for Druids 1895–1902.

Robert Albert Jones, b. Ruabon 1876. Outside left, one cap. Played for Druids 1882–1885; Ruabon; Wynnstay 1889–1890. Albert Jones was a good all-round athlete and began playing for the Druids after leaving Ruabon Grammar School. He got into the first team in 1882, and his 'complete ball control' and 'fine dribbling qualities' made him the ideal wing partner for Jack Vaughan. In 1886 he was promoted from Ruabon goods station to booking clerk at Market Drayton, and from then on his football appearances became rarer. Work commitments forced him to turn down an invitation to face Ireland in 1886. By 1890, he had his own grocery and provisions business in Ruabon, and had virtually retired from soccer. Jones became a councillor in Ruabon, was later made an alderman, and served on the Druids F.C.G. committee.[30]

James William Lloyd, b. Ruabon 1881. Wing half, two caps. Played for Ruabon 1877–1878.

Robert William Matthews, b. Plas Bennion 1897. Centre-half, three caps. Fought in the battle of the Somme. Played for a number of clubs until 1934, later manager of Llangollen F.C. … 'He was a fitness fanatic throughout his life and a keen cyclist until almost eighty years of age. Matthews was known as 'Billy white Hat' for his distinctive headgear, which could be seen above the hedgerows as he rode by.[31]

The most famous Ruabon soccer player is Mark Leslie Hughes, born Wrexham 1963, educated at Ysgol Maes y Llan and Ysgol Rhiwabon, and a member of their teams. In a long playing career spent at Manchester United, Barcelona, Bayern Munich (on loan), Chelsea, Southampton, and Everton he has won seventy-two Welsh international caps, an FA cup winner's medal, and played in a European Cup Winners Cup Final. In 2000 he is manager of the Wales team.

There have been many soccer teams in Ruabon, notably those which represented the various places of worship in the village and were part of their Sunday schools and youth groups; amongst them the Primitive

Ysgol Maes y Llan, 1973-74.
Back row: Timmy Williams; Kevin Millington;
Alan Roscoe; Arfon Hughes; David Morris; Geoffrey
Pate; Mr Delwyn Jones (Headteacher).
Front row: Daryl Hughes; John Dodd; Stephen Williams;
Mark Hughes (Captain, later Welsh International);
Malcolm Jones; Joseph Mark Williams; Ian Williams.

St Mary's Youth Team, 1963.
Back row: Desmond Edwards; Ron Breeze; -?-;
Julian Roberts; Arnold Edwards; Chris Jones;
Peter Richards; Cliff Samuels; Alan Owens;
Bill Edwards.
Front row: John Morris; James Edwards; John
Venn; Billy Bride; Phil Davies.

St Mary's Senior Team, 1963-64.
League Champions, League Cup Runners-Up;
Rhosymedre Cup Winners.
Back row: Tudor Jones; Tony Jones;
Malcolm Bryant; Alan Davies;
Bryan Wynn; Barry Wynn.
Front row: Arthur Moreton; Tony Hughes;
Graham Collins; Glynne Evans; Bobby Jones.

Ruabon Cricket Club, 1907.
Back row: A. Adams; J. W. Thorpe;
W. Payne; H. C. Sturgeon; W. Bowler;
T. Longdin; G. Clay.
Seated: Rev P.R. Bartley; R. A. Jones;
R. Haigh (Captain); Rev D. J. Bowen.
Front: Lloyd Rogers.

Methodist Chapel team and St Mary's started in 1963. Plas Bennion had a strong football team until 1939.

Cricket

Ruabon Grammar School was basically the home for cricket in Ruabon from the days when the Rev A. L. Taylor became headmaster in 1856. Here the talent of youngsters was spotted and nurtured. The Rev D. J. Bowen who came to the school in the 1890s was an excellent cricketer, captaining the Ruabon village side for a number of seasons. At the annual meeting of the club held in March 1913 it was said 'Mr Reuben Haigh had the best batting average last season and the honours with the bowling went to the Rev Bowen for the thirteenth time'. Efforts to form a 'youths cricket club' were made by Charles Henry Lloyd in 1871 and in January 1884 an amateur concert to raise funds was organised by the vicar, E. W. Edwards, Dr Lawton Roberts and the Rev J. B. Armstrong, private chaplain to Sir Watkin. Teams from Wynnstay and Ruabon competed in the various Wrexham leagues for a number of years at the beginning of the 20th century. Lindisfarne College had a good cricket team which had fixtures with independent school elevens throughout north Wales with pupils winning representative honours.

Reference to other sports is found in the *Wrexham Advertiser*. Hockey and tennis were played at the Girls' Secondary School as well as in village teams. A cyclist club was formed in the village in 1897. A ladies hockey team was in existence in 1913. Tennis was played in the village especially at the beginning of the 20th century, and courts were provided on the recreation ground in 1933. Before this, there was the vicarage tennis club which possessed two courts in 1922. The club was open to the senior members of the Sunday School and the girls' Friendly Society. Bowls has been a popular pastime in Ruabon for over a hundred years with greens at Wynnstay, Maes y Llan, and elsewhere.

Ruabon Sports Association

The Ruabon Sports Association is an unincorporated trust set up in 1994 to oversee the construction of a new sports pavilion and the provision of sports facilities for the village. The trust has six trustees: Councillor John Henry Davies, Chairman; Mrs Dorothy Blake, Mr G. Bithel, Mr C Wright, Mr Alan Roberts and Mr Steve Owen. Funds were raised for the pavilion by a grant of £70,025 from Sportlot, the lottery sport fund for Wales, towards the £100,000 needed for the construction of a new pavilion in Maes y Llan lane adjoining the bowling green. The pavilion was opened by Mr Mark Hughes.

Cllr John Henry Davies with international soccer player Mark Hughes at the opening of the new Sports Pavillion.

The sports association was formed to provide changing and other facilities for bowls, football, tennis, and netball; coaching sessions are provided. It is used by other groups and is becoming a general social base for the wider community. The pavilion has proved to be extremely useful and popular, and a building of which the Association and community are grateful and proud.

Young People's Groups

Every place of worship provided facilities for the large numbers of young people who were members of their Sunday schools. At the end of the nineteenth century the Temperance movement, the Blue Ribbon Army, was strong in the non-conformist chapels as was the Band of Hope. After the Second World War the church ran a strong youth club, Cymru y Groes. A purpose-built youth club in Stanley Grove has been in existence for many years.

Other youth groups are: Scouts, Cubs, Guides and Brownies. The Boy Scouts were formed by Robert Baden Powell, 1907–1909. Baden Powell was a household name for his command of Mafeking during its long siege during the Boer War. The first mention of Boy Scouts in Ruabon is in 1913 when in January F. Matthison received a life-saving certificate signed by the Chief Scout Baden Powell for his gallantry in stopping a runaway horse. In August of the same year the 1st Ruabon Troop under their scoutmaster, R. G. Richards, camped near Corwen. After the Second World War from 1946–67, the Ruabon Scout Troop was loyally served by Mr Harold Parry.

> Ruabon Scout Group as part of Llangollen District reformed in 1977/8, with a cub pack and leaders, Eve Evans and Pat Brown. There being no Scout headquarters, they met in the local school. Once established they decided to start up the Scouts with Jim Davies as leader. By 1979 the Cubs had become so popular they started a second pack with leader Rosaline Jones. They were known as 1st. Offa and the original pack was named 1st. Wynnstay. The group had now moved to the Youth Club Building. All parts of the group thrived and continued to meet in district events, camping and learning new skills. In 1983 Ian Jones from the Scouts was chosen to represent Llangollen district at the world jamboree in Canada. This was a great honour. By now the Scout Association had decided to involve boys of a lower age, six to eight, the idea being to give them the chance of meeting together with other boys after school to have fun and games. They were to be known as Beavers. The first one in Llangollen district was at Ruabon, the leader being Rosaline Jones. When HMS *Beaver* visited Liverpool they joined with hundreds of other Beavers to meet the captain and his crew and roam all over the ship. This was a great excitement for boys so young.
>
> The Ruabon Scout group is still going strong in all aspects, although leaders and assistants have changed through the years. Rowland Jones retired from the association in 1998 having served as Chairman, Cub Leader and finally Scouter in charge, leaving the group in the hands of Mrs. Mem Love, Mrs Bottomley, and their assistants. We always need people to volunteer to help these children.[32]

A Jamboree was held at Wynnstay park in the 1960s. Mr Roy Jones was in charge of a flourishing Lindisfarne troop for many years.

The first mention of Girl Guides I have found is August 1913 when, 'the local troop of Girl Guides, fifteen in number, left Ruabon for a week under canvas at Barmouth. Mrs. Birkett Roberts of Tai Clawdd was in charge of the troop'. Guiding has continued since then, together with the Brownies. In the 1920s Miss Sally Bowen was the captain.

The meeting place in the late 1950s and early 1960s was the Scout Hut located in Wynnstay Park. This was unfortunately vandalised and burnt down. Guides and Brownies continued to meet in various places — St. Michael's Roman Catholic Church, Bryn Hall, the Community Centre, and the Youth Club in Stanley Grove.

The Girls' Friendly Society (GFS)

This was a youth group for girls attached to St Mary's parish church in Ruabon. The GFS in Ruabon flourished between the two world wars 1919–1939 under the able leadership of Miss Sally Bowen. They specialised in exercises to music. The Ruabon branch of the GFS represented the diocese of St Asaph in the 1920s in national competitions held at the Albert Hall.

The Church Lads Brigade

A uniformed group for boys which emerged from the Boys Brigade in 1891 and was founded by Walter Mallock Gee, and by 1893 had spread through England and Wales. Mention is made of the Church Lads Brigade in Ruabon in 1913; by this time they wore khaki uniforms and were under the command of the Rev D. J. Bowen. Mr Ronald Breeze was in charge from 1946–1963, and Mr J. Owen was the bandmaster.

An early Scout group with their band.

1st Ruabon Ranger Guides, c.1943, outside the Police Station, Vincent Street (Headquarters: The Village Room, Park Street).
Back row: Cerys Wright; Audrey Bowen; Hazel Owen; Blodwyn Jones; Jean Evison; Margaret Pumford; Sheila Owens;
Gwyneth Morris; Thelma Chapman; Phyllis Jones; Joan Smith; Betty Hughes; John E. Griffiths (First Aid Instructor).
Front row: Hazel Williams; Miriam Owen; Patricia Morgan; Barbara Teague; Sally Bowen (Captain);
Llewelyn Gray (President); Margaret Sedgebeer; Joan Thrift; Kathleen Pumford; Megan Evans.

1st Ruabon Guides, c.1943.
Back row: Jean Prince; Margaret Page;
Dorothy Evison; Betty Sutcliffe; Eluned
Griffiths; Dinah Wilson; Lilian Jones;
Eira Matthews; May Milnthorpe.
Front row: Sybil Bailiff; Margaret Jones;
Mary Evison; Eileen Parry; Sally
Bowen (Captain); Sybil Reed; Marie
Crewe; Margaret Hughes.

Cubs.
Back row: Aaron Jones; Steffan Williams; Philip Walker;
Edward Bottomley; Michael Jones; Jonathan Montgomery.
Front row: Dafydd John -?-; Joseph Holman;
Jamie Edwards; Alex Jones; Joseph Price.

Brownies, 1976.
Fiona Wilkinson; Susan Everett; Carolyn Hughes;
Jennie Jones; Julie Lane.

Beavers, 1999.
Included are: Rhys Powell; Matthew Edwards;
Simon Holland; Owen Luke;
Jack Price; David Bailiff; Andrew -?-; Geoffery Pettit.

Church Lads Brigade Parade, 1959.
John Page (Standard Bearer); Major Jones (Inspecting
Officer); Captain R. Breeze; Brian Hughes; -?-; -?-;
Tony Wilkinson; Bryan Owens; Graham Roberts;
Peter Jones; Bruce Leighton.

Ruabon Silver Band, c.1914.

Entertainment

It is hard to imagine a world without electricity, radio, television and computers, but this is what Ruabon lacked during the first decades of the twentieth century. Churches and chapels encouraged social activities with literary/debating societies and lectures, illustrated by lantern and glass slides. Schools were the venue for entertainments until the Parish Hall was built.

The extracts below are reports of events recorded in the *Wrexham Advertiser*:

15 February1884 — Amateur entertainment at Wynnstay…in the large dining room, in aid of Ruabon Working Men's Library Institute … performers were the Wynnstay Choir, Wrexham Hand Bell Ringers, the Rev J. B. Armstrong readings from *Pickwick* created roars of laughter.

4 February 1913 — Operetta. A performance of the pretty operetta *Dick Whittington* at the National Schools, Ruabon, by a company mainly composed of juveniles. As Dick Whittington, Miss Blanche Bowen quite captivated the audience. There was a cast of about forty members.

12 April 1913, — Cantata the *Passion of the Cross* performed at the English Presbyterian Church by a choir of fifty voices, conducted by Mr Dan Davies.

18 February 1922, — Concert. The Ruabon United Prize Choir gave a concert in aid of the Primitive Methodist Church in the parish hall.

29 April 1922 — Operetta, *Zurika, the Gypsy Girl* in the parish hall. The Misses Blanche and Sally Bowen were responsible for the training of the performers who numbered over fifty. They also took two of the leading parts themselves.

The Ruabon Silver Band

I do not know the date of the beginning or the end of the Ruabon Silver Band, but they were formed before the beginning of the First World War until the 1950s. They had a band room at the end of Paddock Row and were always, 'on parade' in Ruabon for fêtes, recitals, flower shows or parades:

1913, 21 June — The Silver Band. During the summer evenings, the Silver Band are giving selections of music on Saturday and Sunday evenings in different parts of the parish with a view of clearing off the debt of £27 still remaining on the instruments which originally cost £320. The band secretary is Mr W. E. Richards, and the treasurer, Mr T. Longdin.

Ruabon Silver Band, 1925.
Back row: A. Wynn; R. Bailiff; E. Bithell; D. Hughes; J. Bithell; A. E. Owen; H. Edge; E. Jones; D. Hinsley; G. Jones; T. Jones.
Middle row: P. Owen; R. Roberts; I. Jones; F. Evans; J. H. Owen; T. Daniels; T. Davies; W. Davies; W. Jones; W. Jones; J.T. Jones;
G. Evans; G. Bailiff; T. Wright. Front row: E. Valentine; F. Owen; B. Jones; F. Duckett; Mr Nettelship; Mr Richardson; J. Owen
(Bandmaster); W. W. Wynn (President); W. Evans; J. Jones; W. Hughes; W. Edge (Treasurer).

WVS, 1950s.
Included in the photograph are: Mrs Amy Owens; Mrs Ethel Parry; Mrs Marie Morgan;
Mrs Olive Williams; Mrs Jones Perrott; Mrs Collins; Mrs Linda Samuels; Mrs Vi Owens; Mrs Jones;
Mrs Lizzie Edwards; Mrs Vi Robinson; Mrs Page; Mrs M. Kilfoyle; Mrs Hughes; Mrs Bessie Brown.

26th. August 1922 — Instrumental Recital — under the conductorship of bandmaster J. Owen the Ruabon Silver Band gave an excellent recital on the Station Field, Ruabon, on Sunday evening.

St. Mary's Church Players
Amateur dramatics flourished between the wars and up until the 1970s. St Mary's Church players lasted as long as the parish hall. Edwin Jones was a noted comic character amongst a number of experienced performers.

Women's Royal Voluntary Service (WRVS)
A group of the Women's Royal Voluntary Services then the Women's Voluntary Service (WVS) was formed in Ruabon during the Second World War under the leadership of Mrs Bryn Roberts. The Ruabon W.V.S. was reformed by Mrs Bessie Brown in 1953 with the assistance of the area organiser, Mr Kelly of Ruthin. In those days of the Cold War, with the perceived threat of Russian invasion they prepared themselves for war. One year they spent all day on a site by the entrance to the Vicarage fields with orders to build an emergency kitchen. They prepared vegetables and over a huge fire made stew which later in the day was taken to Bodhyfryd Hall in Wrexham where it was served to underprivileged children.

Ruabon Women's Institute[33]
The first president was Mrs Dyke Dennis of New Hall, Ruabon, but her untimely death in 1947 saw Lady Williams Wynn of Wynnstay Hall installed as president, an office she held for the next nineteen years. Her home at Belan was the venue for the June meetings during these years, when it took the form of a garden party.

   During the first year of its life Ruabon WI increased its membership to 115, and although by then the subscription charge had increased to 3s. membership continued to rise, and Ruabon became the second largest institute in Denbighshire.

   Along with other institutes, Ruabon responded to the government's request to produce and preserve food immediately after the second world war to eke out food rationing. A canning machine was purchased, members took instruction and on a rota basis went along to a house in Paddock Row to can their produce. At this time the WI jam image was born, as what was not canned was made into jam. A Produce Guild was formed in the county, subscription 1s-0d, and bulletins were issued containing recipes and useful tips and hints.

   This was the beginning of many 'firsts' such as a Guild of Learners which arranged schools and lecturers on various crafts and 'make-do-and-mend', and 'Can I help you' schools, very useful in those post-war years.

Women's Institute 50th Anniversary, 1996
Back row: M. Baxter; Y. Evans;
L. Whitworth; B. Ellis; S. Thompson;
K. Ackerley; J. Griffiths; E. Butler;
P. Jones; M. Pealing; G. Fowles;
A. Potter; D. Williams; P. Roberts;
B. Morgan.
Front row: S. Hill; M. Thelwell; J. Williams;
G. Forgrave; O. Thomas (President);
M. Jones; C. Matthias; M. Williams;
D. Evans; P. Asquith (obscured);
Jean Morris.

The National Savings club was very successful and continued for many years and the interest generated, supplied a very useful contribution to Institute funds. The honorary secretary, one year, was honoured with an invitation to a Buckingham Palace garden party.

The institute choir, consisting of 30 members, was formed in 1948. They built up a large repertoire of two-part songs and were called upon to entertain other institutes as well as hospitals and chapels and each Christmas they went carol singing to the old people's home. The choir took part in all-group eisteddfods and in the jubilee celebrations in Denbigh. We had an equally successful drama group, one-act plays being their speciality, and in 1951 the two groups combined to give an excellent concert in the parish hall in aid of 'The Dame Agnes Memorial Fund'.

Ruabon's membership may have waned somewhat over the years and many members grown considerably older, but it has always taken as full a part as possible in all aspects of W.I. activities, ranging from sports teams to the 'Going For Gold' fun run, an exhibition of arts and crafts in the local library during 'promotion fortnight', obtaining merit stars in County exhibitions, and staging a tableau for 'Scene 80', to entering two quilts, one knitted and one embroidered, for the national competition, and having the embroidered one selected for the big Olympia event.

Institute members have always played a full part in the activities and well-being of their village and county with many members actively engaged in the many projects, committees, and servicing units on offer; the tree planted in a pleasant spot outside the new library building to commemorate the Queen's Jubilee in 1977 signifies the depths of its roots in the community.

During our fifty-four years many changes have taken place, but we hope to continue to promote with enthusiasm the highest principles of the Women's Institute.

Churches Ladies Guild, May 2000.
Back row: Rosemary Davies (President); Audrey
Powell (Vice President).
Standing: Ann Jones; Margaret Hughes;
Elizabeth Owens; Emma Davies; Marjorie Roberts;
Beryl Edwards; Nans Hughes; Iola Evans; Mary
Jones; Roseline Jones; Pauline Davies; Sarah Hill;
Marian Jones; Beti Evans; Dorothy Taylor;
Wendy Hughes (Treasurer).
Sitting: Kathleen Robinson; Evelyn Robinson;
Mair Jones; Sheila Brookfield; Gwyneth Owen;
Evelyn Robinson; Bronwen Jones; Carolyn Hughes.
Front: May Thelwell; Anne Oliver; Doris Weaver;
Audrey Roberts (Secretary).

Ruabon Churches Ladies Guild

This women's group first met in October 1984. The sharing agreement between Anglicans and Roman Catholics in 1980 led to the building of the Church Hall. The Ladies Guild was perceived as an ecumenical women's group and the officers of the guild are drawn from Anglicans, Roman Catholics, Congregationalists, Wesleyan Methodists, Welsh Presbyterians and Welsh Baptists. The average attendance is thirty members for the meetings held every month, apart from August. The first president was an Anglican. The present in 2000 is a Methodist. In March there is a Welsh evening to celebrate St David's Day, and in December a Christmas carol service.

The Wednesday Club[34]

In the late sixties, following the closure of the coal mines, new industry moved into the area bringing key-workers, some of whom settled in Ruabon with their wives and families, many with young children. The weekly visit to the clinic for the welfare of their children gave the wives an opportunity to meet with other newcomers in similar circumstances and to make new friends. The health visitor, Miss E. Griffiths, suggested the formation of a club which would benefit the mothers by providing a social activity away from their daily routine. A committee was formed, chaired by Mrs Barbara Hadwin, and 'The Ruabon Mothers Club' came into being. The clinic was made available for the evening meetings, the first of which was held on 5 February 1969, when a slide show of local views was given by Mr and Mrs Street.

The name was changed to 'The Wednesday Club' at an early stage when it was decided to open membership to all ladies over sixteen, whatever their status. Meetings were held on the first and third Wednesdays of each month at the clinic up to the time when the new community centre was opened in 1976, where the meetings have been held since.

Club activities have included, talks on a wide variety of topics of interest, demonstrations, celebratory dinners, and theatre outings. The club has also made numerous donations to various charities.

Ruabon Royal British Legion: Men's and Women's Sections

These branches met separately for general meetings but came together on special occasions and annually for a service of remembrance on the Sunday nearest 11 November to mark the Armistice of 1918 and the end of the Second World War in 1945. Wreaths were laid on this occasion at the parish church lychgate by the Legion

Wednesday Club, September 2000.
Back row: Nancy Thomas; Marjorie Phillips; Anneke Bibby; Dorothy Jones; Dorothy Barnwell;
Gwyneth Baines; Mary Thomas; Annette Brixton-Lee; Edna Griffiths; Ann Edwards.
Front row: Audrey Roberts; Doreen Williams; Hilda Richards; Audrey Crosbie; Clare McCabe; Doreen Price; Ennis Davies.

Ruabon Royal British Legion Women's Section, 1976.
Mrs Marie Morgan, Mrs Royal British Legion, local district.

and other organisations who attend the parade.

The purpose of the Royal British Legion is to support comrades and their families, to provide financial support and retirement homes for those who need them. The extent of death and injury in the First World War, particularly the loss of limbs, blindness and shell shock, led to Earl Haig making a special appeal for annual funding to help relieve such suffering, of which the red poppy of Flanders was chosen as the symbol of sacrifice. Both the Ruabon sections of the Royal British Legion have been active in the sale of poppies.

After the First World War, the Institute in Tan Lan became the men's headquarters. This building was later modernised, but unfortunately was destroyed by fire. After the Second World War the women's section met in the council school with the support of Mrs Haigh, Mrs Albert Roberts, Mrs Diggory, Mrs. Ingham, and the Dowager Lady Williams Wynn, their president. The women's section ceased to be active in 1995 and their standard was laid up in the parish church in November of that year. The men's section is still active and meets on the first Wednesday in the month at the Constitutional Club. The branch officers are Alf Thelwell, President; Ernie Pugh, Chairman; Idwal Meredith, Vice-Chairman; Ron Ankers, Welfare Officer and Secretary. The branch were successful in being awarded the cup for the highest amount of money collected for the sale of poppies in 1997.

Friendly Societies
Friendly societies came into existence at the end of the eighteenth century. Their main purpose was to offer some security to working men who relied on day wages to receive support in times of sickness, and their widow's death benefit. These two insurances were supplemented at the beginning of the twentieth century by the introduction of statutory national insurance schemes. Nevertheless some societies continue to flourish.

The main societies in Ruabon in the nineteenth century were the Independent Order of Oddfellows and the Ancient Order of Foresters. Government regulations required that their rules be approved by parliament. Both of these societies have rules which stipulate elaborate

Ruabon Royal British Legion, 1970s.
Standard Bearer Mr Bill Edwards.

Ruabon Royal British Legion Men's Section, 1997.
Cup winners for poppy selling. Ron Ankers; Ernie Pugh;
Idwal Meredith.

Royal Antediluvian Order of Buffaloes.
Presentation of shield to Brother J. T. Rogers by
Brother R. L. Brown, January 2000.
L–R: Iorwerth Lloyd; Keith Eaton; Jack Rogers;
Charlie Thomas; Peter Thomas; Derek Trantor;
Ron Morgan; Pat Williams;.
Front: John Parry; Ray Brown.

ritual and regalia at branch meetings. On their anniversaries joint processions were held in the local villages, culminating in a dinner at a local public house. Weekly contributions were made to enable each of the 'clubs' to engage the services of a medical practitioner for the treatment of their members. A practice which is compulsory is the attendance at brother members' funerals and the following of the coffin. When the Bryn Fields were developed after 1891 both Oddfellows and Foresters purchased houses. These branches continue to meet.

Another friendly society is the Royal Antediluvian Order of Buffaloes. The Ruabon lodge is affiliated to the Wrexham and District Provincial Grand Lodge, and meets on Friday evenings at the Constitutional Club. It has elaborate rules, ritual and regalia. The Order supports local charities of which the Special Care Baby Unit at the Maelor Hospital in Wrexham was chosen for 2000.

The Ruabon Pre-School Play Group and Play Group Plus

Ruabon Pre-School Play group was started early in 1970 by a group of mothers under the leadership of Mrs. Joan Landon. The Supervisor was Mrs. Brunhilde Farrow and her assistant, Mrs. Dorothy Owen. The first meeting place was in the Youth Club building in Stanley Grove. A term later the playgroup moved to the clinic where it settled for a few years until accommodation problems meant a search for new premises. By this time Mrs Dorothy Barnwell became the supervisor and Mrs Yvonne Laine the leader.

New premises were found in the basement of Rhagluniaeth, Tan Lan. There was a lot of scrubbing, cleaning, painting and decorating to do, and husbands and fathers and any handyman available were roped in to help. Rhagluniaeth was a quaint building with lots of little rooms, and the children loved it.

Fund-raising was constant and a number of successful events were held. One of the first was a Christmas Fayre in the old parish hall when the queue for Father Christmas stretched down the High Street. Other events were well supported such as coffee mornings, and cheese and wine evenings. As the building was old it was eventually considered unsafe for children; so once again they packed their bags and moved to the small room in the community centre.[35]

Ruabon Pre-School Play Group.
Left: a visit to the Fire Station.
Above: Busy with activities.

In 2000, the Ruabon Pre-School Play Group and Play Group Plus meets in the community centre on Monday, Wednesday, Thursday and Friday mornings, from 9.15*am* until 11.15*am*, under the leadership of Mrs. Chris Madsen and Mrs. Shirley Massingham. They describe their purpose:

> The aim of our play group is to provide pre-school children with a wide range of enjoyable and stimulating opportunities of learning through play. We have a safe and happy environment where children can gradually get used to being away from Mum for a little while. This helps them greatly when the time for 'big school' arrives. Our facilities include a wide range of toys and equipment which are both fun and educational.

Children also learn good social skills at play group especially when it comes to snack time. A nutritious snack and drink are provided at every session. The children are taken on several outings during their time at play group, these have included visits to the library, dentist, fire station, and to Ty Mawr country park. We also encourage visitors to the group such as the community dentist and, on a more fun theme, shows such as puppets and even a disco! Parents/carers are encouraged to take an active role in the running of the play group, such as forming a management committee and helping out at the group.

In addition you may be interested in our Playgroup Plus sessions. These are held on the same days as the play group, in the same hall from 11.30*am* until 2.45*pm*. These sessions are designed for the pupils attending St Mary's nursery class as an extension to their school day. The pupils are brought to the session by school staff and must be provided with a packed lunch. These sessions have proved very useful as they let the children gradually adapt to the lengthier school day they will face once in the reception class. Again, an introductory booklet is available, and Chris and Shirley will be happy to provide any further information.[36]

Ruabon and District Club for the Physically Handicapped

This club draws its members from Ruabon, Rhostyllen, Acrefair, Rhos, Penycae, Johnstown and Llangollen, and is well served by a large number of voluntary helpers who assist in the activities and generally join in the fun. Fund-raising activities give the opportunity for the sale of work produced by members, and help to finance the enjoyable annual outings.

The Senior Citizens Centre, Maesyllan Lane

In 1951 the parish council obtained a corrugated iron building to use as a baby clinic and senior citizens rest centre. This was an ex-army nissen hut used by a searchlight detachment situated at the end of the lane leading to Pentre Clawdd. Such was the popularity of the venue and the continuing supply of babies that the building served this dual function until a new clinic was opened in the new civic centre off High Street.

Not to be outdone, the parish council arranged for the tin hut to be replaced by a new prefabricated building for the purpose of a senior citizens centre. Councillor Harold Jones, chairman of the community council opened the centre in

Ruabon & District Club for the Physically Handicapped.
Presentation to retiring President, Mrs Eira Ellis.
Back row (standing): Lily Griffiths; Fanny Blaze; Marion Lane; Doreen Williams; Nancy Hughes; Noel Hughes; Pam Gawler; Alan Roscoe; Gwyneth Fowles; Bronwen Jones; George McGill; Sheila Brookfield; Gwenda Davies; Les Hamer; Mabel Jones; Rosa Williams; Tom Williams; Jean Griffith; Anna Lena Bradbury; Barbara Paton.
Middle row (seated): Mrs Edwards; Violet Jones; Maureen Blaze; Jane Lloyd; Leonora Crewe; Kate McGill; Elsie Davies; Doreen Grifiths; Gwen Richards.
Front row (standing): Marjorie Pealing; Heulwen Edwards; Eira Ellis.
Present, but obscured: Meirwen Williams. Absent: Mr & Mrs Harry Hill.

Old People's Federation, founder members Ruabon Branch.
Back row: Rosie Caulfield; Lucy Griffiths; Mrs Edge; Mrs Owen; Mrs Jordon; Teddy Jones; Doris Jones Owens; Bob Davies; Mrs Williams; Mrs Amy Jones; Mrs Edwards; Mrs Williams; Mrs Dot Williams; Mrs Whiddon; Mrs Saunders; Mr Harold Jones; Mrs Harold Jones; Mrs Lil Jones; Miss Pardoe; -?-; Mr Lewis Williams. 2nd row: Mr George Jones; Mrs Vi Jones; Mrs Teddy Jones; Mr Ted Samuels; Miss Williams; Mrs Hewitt; -?-; Mrs Lizzie Jones; Alice Rogers; Alice Davies; Mrs Woodfine; Mrs Moreton; George Winters; Mrs Dido Williams; Mr Teddy Jones; Mrs Gertie Roberts; Mrs Thomas; Mrs Delia Williams; -?-; -?-; Mrs Brook. Front row: Mr Wynn; Mrs Elsie Wynn; Stan Moreton; Sid Rogers.

1982, when it was dedicated by the vicar, the Rev Bill Pritchard, and the Roman Catholic priest, Father Antony Jones.

In 2000 there are two senior citizens organisations meeting in the centre. One of them is run by Mrs. Audrey Jones and Mrs. Mary Owens. They arrange occasional meetings and bingo on Monday evenings. The other is the National Federation of Old Age Pensioners founded in 1976 which held its meetings in the Community Centre until January 2000, when the group moved to Maes y Llan Lane to be in a central position. The chairman is Mr Les Owens, the secretary Mrs Rosa Hughes, and the treasurer Mrs Marie Morgan, all founder

The first Ruabon Baby Clinic, held at the Old People's rest and Recreation Centre, Maesyllan Lane, 1952.
Nurse Griffiths; Mrs Bassett; Mr & Mrs Lloyd; Mr & Mrs Griffiths; -?-; Dr Islwyn Jones; Nurse -?-; Mr Hughes; -?-; Mr E. Williams; Rev. Jones Perrott; -?-; Mrs Jones Perrott, -?-.
Seated: Pat Jones (and Ann); Iola Evans (and Mervyn); Lady Williams Wynn; Eirlys Ducket (and Stephen); Mrs Smith (and Carol); Kath Jones (and Lesley); Mr Pumford (and David).

members. A social afternoon is held on Wednesdays with an annual trip in June and a Christmas meal together.

Ruabon, Cefn and District Credit Union

This was the first credit union to be operative in north Wales and it has been in existence since 1992. A credit union is a non-profit making financial co-operative (or community banking service) which offers a convenient saving and low interest loans service to its members. Savings must be regular, and after an initial savings period of approximately three months, members may apply for a loan at a very competitive rate of APR 12.68% (July 2000).

Credit unions are run by volunteers so that costs are minimal, and in the case of the Ruabon, Cefn and district credit union, they are only restricted by an area boundary. The credit union offices are the George Edwards Hall, Cefn; The Tenant's Association, Plas Madoc and the Community Centre, Ruabon.

Ruabon Heritage Trust

This body is enrolled with 'Entrust' as an environmental body under the landfill tax regulations. The Trustees are the Reverend Godfrey Caine Jones, chairman; Mr Roland Fenner, clerk and treasurer; and Mr Alun Richards. Entrust had contributed towards the refurbishment and re-hanging in a new frame of the six bells of St Mary's Shared Church, Ruabon. This work was undertaken in 1998 by John Taylor Bell Founders Ltd, Loughborough, at a cost in the region of £50,000. In the same year Entrust supported the publication of a new edition of the guide book, 'Ruabon Parish Church' by the Venerable T. W. Pritchard.

Another promotion of the Ruabon Heritage Trust, with the support of Entrust, is the establishment of the Ruabon Heritage Trail, which was successfully launched by the Mayor and Mayoress of Wrexham, Councillor and Mrs Neil Rogers, on Tuesday, 18 July 2000. Wrexham County Borough Archaeological Department provided information and advice regarding the trail route to the Trust. The text of the trail guide was written by pupils of Ysgol Rhiwabon with illustrations by Timothy Morgan.

Greys Club — Established April 1996

The club held its first lunch as an informal gathering for men. There were ten foundation members. Its name was approved, after a light-hearted competition, and the word 'Greys' is derived from a painting of the charge of the Royal Scotts Greys, hung in the lounge of the Duke of Wellington, the club's first venue. Permission was sought from the Regimental Museum curator, who also approved the club tie insignia of a white horse against the Prince of Wales' feathers and standing on a plaque with the word 'Greys' upon it. The badge was designed by a member, and a club tie is now displayed in the museum in Edinburgh.

At present there are twenty members, and a waiting list to join. Members meet for lunch each month in the

Launching of the Ruabon Heritage Trail, July 2000.
Back row: Alun Richards (trustee); Richard Clarke; Peter Hollershead (Shanks Waste Solutions); Stephen Grenter (WCB Archaeologist); Ingrid Emerson (Groundwork); Rev G. C. Jones (trustee); Alice Thomas (Groundwork); Gwyneth Owen; Brian Robinson; Roland Fenner (trustee); Mrs Bradbury; Raymond Hesketh; Angela Culloten; Malcolm Crosbie; Audrey Crosbie; Beti Evans; Dorothy Taylor.
Front row: Hayley Dodd (Pupil Ysgol Rhiwabon); Cllr & Mrs Neil Rogers (Mayor & Mayoress); Richard Perry (Pupil Ysgol Rhiwabon).

Bridge Inn, Ruabon. There are no rules, titles, or subscriptions. The club exists solely to create a forum for men in which a mixture of all sorts and conditions can meet together for fellowship and conversation.

The foundation lunch is held in April and there is a special lunch to celebrate Christmas. The club does not adhere to any social, political or religious dogma, although from time to time conversation may stray in to all these areas. Admission is by invitation only.[37]

Age Concern Cymru (Ruabon Branch)

This charity finds its outlet in Ruabon through the manning of a voluntary shop where articles are sold in aid of Age Concern. A substantial income is derived from this activity and is distributed to members of the local community over sixty-five in various ways, for example, smoke alarms. Members of the committee in 2000 included Dr Khan, Cllr Cyril Williams and Mr Ronald Breeze. Volunteer helpers are May Owens, Kath Clarke, Mair Roberts, and Colin Edge.

The Greys Club, 2000.
Back row: Jack Words; Rev Tegid Jones; Peter Maitland;
Rev. Colin Gibbs; Brian Robinson; Roland Fenner; Roy Jones;
Rev. Arthur Moseley; Richard Griffith.
Front row: Des Gough; Don Biggs; Len Evans; Malcolm Crosbie;
Rev. Godfrey Jones; Newton Matthias.
Missing: Merton Purslow; Bill Davies; Hubert Humphreys;
Bill Roberts; Derek Owens.

The Ruabon and District Field Club

The Field Club was founded on 8 February 1918. The main driving force behind the foundation was Mr W Bezant Lowe, MA, FCS. About sixty-five members were present at the first meeting on 25 February 1918 when the Rev D. J. Bowen, MSc, headmaster of Ruabon Grammar School, was chosen as the first president of the Field Club and its purpose defined:

> The object of the club is to encourage the study and practical knowledge of animal and plant life in the field, geology, archaeology and photography, particularly in the neighbourhood of Ruabon.' The club has a winter programme of monthly meetings with speakers and a summer programme of excursions to places of interest.

In 1992 Miss Bronwen Jones the president for that year published a brief history of the Ruabon Field Club. In 1993 a dinner was held to celebrate the seventy-fifth anniversary of the club when its membership was nearly a hundred. In February 2000 the Field Club invited the Venerable T. W. Pritchard to celebrate the millennium by writing a history of Ruabon. The President for the millennium year 2000 is Mrs Ann Owen.

Ruabon & District Field Club
Committee, 2000.
Back row: Val Dyer (Treasurer);
Bronwen Jones; Derek Owens;
Roland Fenner (Vice President);
Wendy Hughes (Asst. Treasurer);
Malcolm Crosbie; Sylwyn Jones;
Jean Broadmeadow; Eddie Griffiths.
Front row: Gwyneth Williams
(Excursion Secretary); Dorothy Taylor
(Minute Secretary); Beti Evans
(Secretary); Ann Owens (President);
Myra E. Smith; Jean Horne (Transport
Officer).

Notes

Chapter 1: Beginnings and Settlement

1. *Prehistoric and Roman Remains of Denbighshire*, Ellis Davies & William Lewis, Cardiff, 1929, p.392.
2. ibid., p,392.
3. ibid.
4. ibid., p.394.
5. ibid., p.397.
6. *Prehistoric and Roman Remains of Flintshire*, Ellis Davies & William Lewis, Cardiff, 1949, p.454.
7. *Archaeologia Cambrensis*, vol. 92, 1937, 'Y Gardden Hill-fort', Willoughby Gardner, p.156.
8. ibid., p.158.
9. *A Tour in Wales*, Thomas Pennant, London, 1784, vol. 1, p.373.
10. Gardner op. cit. p.157.
11. *Offa's Dyke*, Sir Cyril Fox, British Academy, 1955.
12. *West Midlands Archaeology*, 40, 1997, p.57, report by Hugh Hannaford.
13. I am graetful to Clwyd-Powys Archaeological Trust and to Ian Basty, Offa's Dyke Archaeological Management Officer for their advice.
14. This is part of the Ruabon Heritage Trail.
15. *Antiquaries Journal*,vol. 65, part 1, 'The Construction of Offa's Dyke', D. H. Hill, pp. 140–2.
16. Fox, op. cit.
17. *Wrexham Leader*, 'Looking Back', 20 August, 1999.
18. *History of Ruabon*, A.N. Palmer, p.55.
19. *The Age of Conquest: Wales 1063–1415*, R. R. Davies, Oxford, pp.129–30.
20. *The First Extent of Bromfield and Yale, 1315*, T.P. Ellis, Cymmrodorion Records, Series No. XI, 1924.
21. op. cit., p.399.
22. op. cit. p.127.
23. *Lordship and Society in the March of Wales, 1282–1400*, R. R. Davies, Oxford, 1978, p.289.
24. The gazeteer and survey is based on the study of A. N. Palmer's *History of the Parish of Ruabon*, made about one hundred years ago but not published until 1992 (Bridge Books, Wrexham). It is used in conjunction with other sources.
25. In 1950, J. Watkin Ellis wrote a number of articles in the *Cefn Chronicle*, 'Points of Local Interest', from which some of this information is derived.
26. ibid.
27. ibid.
28. DRO DD/WY/874.
29. Details of Plas Newydd are found in *Houses of the Welsh Countryside*, Peter Smith, 2nd Edition, Royal Commission on Ancient and Historic Monuments in Wales, HMSO, 1988.
30. J. Watkin Ellis, op. cit.
31. ibid.
32. ibid.
33. Palmer, op. cit. p.54.
34. DRO DD/WY/960.
35. The demesne is land reserved for the lord's own use.
36. These are common names for medieval fields.
37. I saw this map at the Wynnstay Estate Office some twenty years ago.
38. DRO DD/WY/8342.
39. DD/VR/9/118 Ruabon 1910.

Chapter 2: Wynnstay

1. This chapter depends on *Country Life* 'Wynnstay, Denbighshire', 23 March 1930, 6 April 1972, P. Howell & T. W. Pritchard, *Transactions of the Denbighshire Historical Society*, vols. 27, 28, 29, 30, 'Sir Watkin Williams Wynn 4th Bart., 1749–89', 'An archectectural history of the mansion of Wynnstay, Ruabon: political influence, rise and decline', T. W. Pritchard, published as *Wynns at Wynnstay*, Old Court Press, Caerwys, 1982.
2. *History of the Parish of Ruabon*, A. N. Palmer, Wrexham, Bridge Books, 1992.
3. *The Wynn Family of Gwydir*, J. Gwynfor Jones, Aberystwyth, 1995, p.53.
4. *History of Caernarvonshire, 1284–1900*, A. H. Dodd, Denbigh, 1968.
5. *Archealogia Cambrensis*, vol.95, 1940, 'Wynnstay 1683–6', F. Jones, pp.54–5.
6. NLW, Agreement dated 10 November 1719.
7. *Politics in Eighteenth Century Wales*, Peter D. G. Thomas, UWP, Cardiff, 1998, p.160.
8. *Life in the English Country House*, Mark Girouard, p.256.
9. *Country Life*, 23 March 1972.
10. Thomas, op. cit. p.156, quoting *Wynnstay and the Wynns: a volume of varieties*, Askew Roberts, Oswestry, 1885, p.12.
11. *Gentleman's Magazine*, XIX, 1749, p.473.
12. ibid., quoting from a Chester newspaper.
13. This follows design number 6 in the Victoria and Albert Museum. The account for £485 is in the NLW.
14. Finished 1775/7 *Wynns at Wynnstay*, T. W. Pritchard, p.27f.
15. Roberts, op. cit. p.15.
16. *Gentleman's Magazine*, May 1770.
17. NLW Wynnstay 115/2, pp.65–79.
18. *Historical Manuscripts Commission, 14th Report Appendix, Pt.IV,*p.502, R. Kenyon to Mill Kenyon at Peel.
19. NLW Wynnstay 122, p.497.
20. *Cambrian Directory*, 1808, pp.543-6.
21. *Byegones*, 1882, p.133.
22. A Jacobite club founded in 1710 to promote the restoration of the Stuarts. Members names were on a rosta (hence the name Cycle) with a white rose in the centre.
23. *My Life and Times*, C. J. Apperley (Nimrod), 1927, p.55.
24. *Byegones*, May 1880, p.61.
25. *The Beauties of England and Wales: North Wales*, J. Evans, 1812, vol. 17, p.580.
26. *Gentleman's Magazine*, 1811, p.486.
27. ibid., 1820, pt. 2, p.461.
28. *Royal Visits and Progresses in Wales*, Edward Parry, 1850, p.440.
29. Askew Roberts, op. cit. p.24.
30. Three verses from a series of three line *englynion* entitled *Chwedlau'r Doethion,* published in Iolo Manuscripts, 1848. The English translation by Bryan Martin Davies.
31. For a full account of these activities see *A History of Fox-hunting in the Wynnstay Country and part of Shropshire from the beginning of this century to the end of the season 1884–5*, T. H. G. Puleston, 1893 and *A Short History of Sir Watkin Williams Wynn's Hounds*, Ralph Greaves.
32. op. cit. p.131.
33. *Chester Chronicle*, 5 December 1885.

Chapter 3: Churches and Chapels

1. *The Dissolution of Valle Crucis Abbey*, D. Pratt, 1982, pp.108-9.
2. *Records of the Court of Augmentations Relating to Wales and Monmouthshire*, Board of Celtic Studies, UWP, 1954. ed. E. A. Lewis & J. Conway Davies, p.87, *History of Ruabon*, A. N. Palmer, p.80.
3. Palmer, ibid., p.90 and fn.
4. *The Welsh Elizabethans*, F. J. Harries, 1924.
5. *History of the Diocese of St Asaph*, D. R. Thomas, 1908, edt. vol. 1, pp.96–7.
6. *A History of the Older Nonconformity of Wrexham*, A. N. Palmer, Bridge Books, re-print 1988.
7. NLW SA/FB/1, p.6.
8. Palmer, *Older Nonconformity of Wrexham*, p.124–5.
9. NLW Wynnstay 115/6.
10. NLW SA/RD/28.
11. NLW SA/FB/182.

12. NLW SA/QA/1.
13. NLW SA/QA/4.
14. NLW SA/QA/10.
15. FRO Leeswood MS.
16. NLW SA/QA/14.
17. NLW SA/QA/15.
18. This account depends upon *Hanes yr Achos Eglwys y Methodistiad Calfinaidd, Rhiwabon*, E. P. Jones, Cymric Press, Wrexham, 1934.
19. *Wrexham Advertiser*, 4 January 1862.
20. ibid., 7 December 1895.
21. ibid 26 September 1896.
22. ibid 12 April 1913.
23. ibid 21 August 1913.
24. ibid 1930.
25. This account relies on the *Centenary Booklet*, published 1958.
26. DRO DD/WY/1316, 25 February 1822, Conveyance of Cottage and Garden at Tan y llan upon trust to build a meeting house for Protestant Dissenters, Thos. Rogers, Mary Anne Rogers, Sarah Rogers, Edward Rogers. Trustees W. Williams, John Pearce, William Davies, *etc.*
27. DRO DD/WY/1445, 4 February 1857, Conveyance (1) Rev. John Pearce Guernsey, Minister of Gospel; Rev. Wm. David, Rhydyceisiaid, Minister of Gospel; John Jones, Ruabon, Farmer; William Jones, Ruabon, butcher; *etc.* (2) Sir WWW Chapel or Meeting House as in 1316 consideration £151-3s-6d.
28. *Welsh Wesleyan Methodism, 1800-1858*, A. H. Williams, Bangor, 1935, p.117.
29. NLW SA/FB/2, p.297.
30. DRO DD/WY/1377, 13/14 March 1839.
31. DRO DD/WY/1509, 13 August 1901.
32. DRO ND/40/54–5.
33. *Wrexham Advertiser,* 7 & 14 March 1896.
34. DRO ND/40/54–5.
35. DRO ND/1/53.
36. This account relies on a booklet published for the centenary of Ruabon Methodist Church, Henry Street, 1892–1992, by Sheila Brookfield, see p.7.
37. ibid., p.7. See the *Religious Census of 1851, vol.II, North Wales*, edt. Ieuan Gwynedd Jones, UWP.
38. 1981, pp.151–4.
39. Ruabon Vestry Minutes, 31 July 1868.
40. *Archaeologia Cambrensis*, vol. 40, 1885, pp.128–30.
41. 1877.
42. *Parochial Duties, Practically Illustrated*, H. C. Ridley, Henley on Thames, 1829, pp.18 & 19, quoted in *A Different Kind of Gentleman*, B. Heaney, Archon Books, 1976, pp.38–9.
43. NLW SA/DR/50.
44. DRO DD/DM/1140 the land and buildings conveyed to the Representative Body of the Church in Wales, December 1928.
45. *Wrexham Advertiser*, 9 September 1922.
46. *Winds of Change, the Roman Catholic Church and Society in Wales, 1916–1962*, Tristan Owain Hughes, UWP, Cardiff, 1999, p.21.
47. *Wrexham Advertiser & Star*, 6 August 1955.
48. *The Universe*, 4 June 1959.

Chapter 4: Schools

1. This account relies on 'A History of Ruabon Endowed Grammar School', T. W. Pritchard, *Transactions of the Denbighshire Historical Society*, vol. 20, 1971.
2. NLW Carreg Lwyd MS II, 93. See also NLW *Journal*, vol. 9, p.264.
3. DRO DO/WY/6719.
4. *Chirk Castle Accounts*, vol. II, W. M. Myddelton, p.147, fn 825.
5. *The History of Wem* — taken from a manuscript of the late Rev'd. Sam Garbet, A.M., Wem, 1818.
6. NLW SA/QA/4, 1749.
7. NLW Leeswood MS 816.

8. Ruabon vestry minutes 30, 31/12/1815.

9. *Report of the Charity Commissioners, Denbighshire, 1837*, 1893.

10. ibid.

11. *Report of the Commissioners of Inquiry into the State of Education in Wales, pt. III, North Wales, 1847*, pp. 72–3.

12. Ruabon vestry minutes 4/10/1852.

13. Public Record Office E/27/6419, 29/12/1853.

14. ibid. 10/1/1854.

15. DRO DD/WY/8659, 1855.

16. Parliamentary Papers, British Museum Return, relating to Endowed Grammar Schools 467 p.276.

17. PRO E/27/6423, Report of J. L. Hammond.

18. *Aberdare Commissioners Report*, vol. II, evidence of A. L. Taylor, p.253f.

19. *Byegones*, 1895/6, p.355, 17 June 1896.

20. DRO CD/E/1/54.

21. DRO CD/E/1/58.

22. Further information on the school is to be found in *Ruabon Boys Grammar School — a collection of pictures*, Dennis W. Gilpin, Bridge Books, Wrexham, 1999, particularly the period from 1894 to 1978.

23. DRO CD/E/1/17. Refers to the minutes of the Denbighshire education Committee, 1919, pp.11–3, 95–7. These were published annually and provide much of the information.

24. *Wrexham Advertiser*, 30 September 1922.

25. DRO CD/E/1, 12 March 1934.

26. NLW SA/QA/15 Visitation Returns under Ruabon.

27. Charity Report, 1893, Ruabon, Denbs.

28. DRO DD/WY/66288.

29. op. cit.

30. They did not realise that the land belonged to Sir Watkin. He bought the building and gave the purchase price towards the erection of the National Schools in 1848.

31. FRO D/E/588.

32. Charity Commission 1837.

33. Parliamentary Papers 1842, vol. 17, Evidence No.:35 Thomas Madeley schoolmaster Ruabon.

34. op. cit.

35. NLW SA/Misc/52 under Ruabon.

36. DRO E/LB/89 National School log book.

37. The story of the building of the council school in Ruabon is to be found in the minutes of Denbighshire Education Committee, vol. 211f.

38. ibid., vol. 215.

39. ibid., vol. 218.

40. ibid., vol. 234.

41. ibid., vol. 256.

42. *Wrexham Advertiser*, 27 July 1912.

43. I am grateful to Mrs C. M. Giller for the extracts from the log book she made for me in the 1980s.

44. He died tragically in 1946.

45. *The Story of Education in a Welsh Border Parish or the Schools of Cefn Mawr, 1786–1933*, E. K. Jones, Wrexham, 1933.

46. This acount relies heavily upon *Lindisfarne College: a Brief History, 1891–1991*, L. Roy Jones, Wrexham, 1991.

47. ibid., p.13.

48. ibid., p.15.

Chapter 5: Penylan

1. His memorial is in the north aisle of Ruabon Church.

2. DRO DD/PL/166.

3. Observations by Mr Graham Phillips.

Chapter 6: Industry

1. This account relies on articles written by the late Ifor Edwards and published in the *Transactions of the Denbighshire Historical Society*, vol.9 'The Charcoal Iron Industry of East Denbighshire, 1630–90', pp.23–53, and vol. 10 *c*.1690–1770, pp. 49–97, ibid. vol.31, 'The British Iron Company', pp.109-148 and vol.32, 'The New British

Iron Company', pp.98–124.

2. *Transactions of the Denbighshire Historical Society*, vol.9, pp.28–29.

3. ibid., vol.10, p.58, Plas Madoc Hall was demolished in the 1960s. A housing estate now occupies the site.

4. *Beauties of Wales*, J. Evans, vol.2, London, 1812, p.585.

5. *Topographical Dictionary of Wales*, Samuel Lewis.

6. *Transactions of the Denbighshire Historical Society*, vol.32, 'G.W.R. Pontcysyllte Branch', D. Pratt.

7. *Transactions of the Denbighshire Historical Society*, vol.31, p.110.

8. *A History of the Parish of Ruabon*, A, N, Palmer, Bridge Books, Wrexham, 1992, pp.38–41 and *Transactions of the Denbighshire Historical Society*, vol.31, pp.113–8.

9. This account relies on *The Collieries of Denbighshire*, G. G. Lerry, Wrexham, 2nd edition, revised and enlarged by Ifor Edwards, p.13.

10. ibid.

11. NLW Bodrhyddan MS dated 1565.

12. NLW Chirk Castle MS 10164.

13. CD (*Collieries of Denbighshire*), p.11

14. *Transactions of the Denbighshire Historical Society*, vol.6, 'Notes at Random on Eighteenth Century Denbighshire', Emlyn Rogers.

15. *Transactions of the Denbighshire Historical Society*, vol.12, p.114.

16. NLW L1303, 1719–1733; L1305, 1762–1780.

17. *The Torrington Diaries*, J. Byng, (ed.) C. B. Andrews, London, 1934, vol.1, p.177.

18. NLW Wynnstay 123, p.35.

19. ibid., p.477.

20. op. cit.

21. For the troubles of 1830 see CD and *Transactions of the Denbighshire Historical Society*, vol.13.

22. *Transactions of the Denbighshire Historical Society*, vol.15, Rogers, p.144.

23. ibid., p.155f.

24. *Commission Children's Employment in Mines, 1842.*

25. ibid., p.367.

26. ibid., p.368.

27. ibid.

28. ibid., p.370.

29. ibid., p.371.

30. ibid., p.381.

31. *Geological Survey, Wrexham, 1928*, p.78; CD, p.63.

32. CD, p.144.

33. ibid., p.63.

34. ibid., p.26–7.

35. ibid., p.84.

36. ibid., p.124.

37. ibid.

38. ibid., 132.

39. ibid., 159–60.

40. ibid., 153f.

41. see photographs in text.

42. *Wrexham Advertiser*, 1863.

43. DRO NTD/965.

44. DRO NCD/38; *Wrexham Leader*, 23 January 1976, 'Looking Back', Silin (ed.).

45. *The Guardian*, 28 August 1889, p.1286.

46. *Oswestry & Border Counties Advertiser*, 28 August 1889.

47. *The Geology of Wrexham*, 1928, p.105.

48. op. cit.

49. 'Permian Marls of the Wrexham and Ruabon Districts', I. Edwards, *Transactions of the Denbighshire Historical Society*, vol.20, 1971, p.243.

50. *Geology of Wrexham, 1928*, p.104.

51. The account of the individual clayworks depends on *Transactions of the Denbighshire Historical Society*, vol. 20, I. Edwards, 'Permian Marls'; ibid., vol.35, I. Edwards, 'Claymakers and Clay Workers in the Old Parish of Ruabon'; ibid., vol.36, I. Edwards, 'Gazeteer of Clayworks in the Wrexham and Ruabon District'.

52. *Transactions of the Denbighshire Historical Society,* vol.36, p.78.
53. *Cefn Chronicle,* 6 August 1937.
54. *Wrexham Leader,* 5 June 1970, 'Looking Back', Silin (ed.).
55. *Transactions of the Denbighshire Historical Society,* vol.1, 'Henry Dennis', George Lerry.
56. *Transactions of the Denbighshire Historical Society,* vol.8, 'Industries of Denbighshire', George Lerry, p.109.
57. *Wrexham Advertiser,* 28 August 1915.
58. *Railways of the Dee Valley,* pp.11–13.
59. *Transactions of the Denbighshire Historical Society,* vol.32, 'G.W.R. Pontcysyllte Branch'.
60. ibid., p.44.
61. *A Regional History of the Railways of Great Britain, Vol. XI, North and Mid Wales,* Peter E. Baugh, David & Charles, 1980, p.38.
62. *Henry Robertson, Pioneer of Railways,* George Lerry, p.24.
63. *History of the G.W.R.,* E. T. MacDermott, 1927, p.341.
64. NLW Wynnstay Rentals.
65. *Chester Chronicle,* 6 November 1846.
66. MacDermott, op. cit., p.343.
67. ibid., p.344.
68. *Chester Chronicle,* 13 October 1848.
69. J. Watkin Ellis, 'Points of Interest', *Cefn Chronicle,* 11 February 1950.
70. MacDermott, op. cit., p.406.
71. *Buildings of Wales: Clwyd,* Edward Hubbard, Penguin, 1983 (under Ruabon).
72. *Official Handbook of Stations,* 1938, Railway Clearing House, London.
73. *Wrexham Advertiser,* 15 February 1896.

Chapter 7: Health

1. The Ruabon parish records are to be found in the DRO, Ruthin.
2. NLW Wynnstay MS 124, p.49.
3. NLW SA/MISC/3.
4. *The History of Wrexham,* A. H. Dodd, 2nd edition, Bridge Books, Wrexham, p.257.
5. NLW Wynnstay 115/38.
6. NLW Wynnstay 115/14/10.
7. DRO Ruabon vestry minutes, 11 February 1816.
8. W. E. Gladstone, 1890, recorded message on Edison's new phonograph for a meeting of the Mutual Building Association of New York in which he said: 'thrift is the symbol and instrument of independence and of liberty, indispensable condition of all permanent human good'.
9. Wrexham Advertiser, 1870.
10. ibid., 6 August 1870.
11. DRO Vestry minutes, 16 June 1851.
12. DRO DD/WY/6846.
13. FRO D/E/3163.
14. DRO Annual Reports for the Denbighshire Medical Officer, 1935, pp.32, 33.
15. *Ruabon Free Press,* 6 September 1901, DRO NTO/773.
16. I am grateful to Mr John Lawton Roberts for providing this information about his family.

Chapter 8: Community in the 19th and 20th Centuries

1. *The Llangollen Advertiser,* 10 April 1891.
2. DRO VR 9/118.
3. Ruabon vestry minutes, 20 June 1845.
4. J. Watkin Ellis, 18 February 1950.
5. *Wrexham Advertiser,* 31 October 1863.
6. ibid., 28 February 1880.
7. *Wrexham Leader,* 'Looking Back', 15 April 1977, Silin (ed.).
8. NLW SA/MISC/52 Ruabon.
9. ibid.
10. Ruabon parish council minutes.

11.　ibid.

12.　DRO QSD.

13.　NLW Wynnstay 1305.

14.　DRO QSD/SR/300/31–3.

15.　*Wrexham Advertiser*, 28 June 1913.

16.　J. Watkin Ellis, 18 February 1950

17.　*Wrexham Advertiser*, 29 May 1880.

18.　ibid., 21 November 1863.

19.　ibid., 26 August 1865.

20.　ibid., 2 January 1864.

21.　A booklet prepared by the Ruabon Women's Institute, *c.*1980s.

22.　*The Weekend Telegraph*, 26 August 1989.

23.　ibid.

24.　A complete record of the royal visit to Wales in 1889 reprinted from the *Oswestry & Border Counties Advertiser*, 28 August 1889.

25.　This account is based on the school log books of the council and church schools and the *Wrexham Advertiser*, 1913, 1915, 1918 and the community council minutes.

26.　*Wrexham Advertiser*, 14 August 1915.

27.　J. Watkin Ellis, op. cit., 18 December 1950.

28.　ibid., 25 February 1950.

29.　This section relies on *Whos Who of Welsh International Soccer Players*, Gareth M. Davies and Ian Garland, Bridge Books, Wrexham, 1991.

30.　ibid., p.114.

31.　ibid., p.135.

32.　Information provided by Mr Rowland Jones.

33.　Information from a booklet published by the Ruabon Women's Institute in the 1980s.

34.　Information provided by Mrs Audrey Crosbie.

35.　Contributed by Mrs Dorothy Owen.

36.　Information provided by Mrs Chris Madsen and Mrs Shirley Massingham.

37.　Information provided by Mr Rowland Fenner.

Sources

1. Manuscript collections

Denbighshire Record Office
   Census returns
   Education records
   Nonconformist records
   Ruabon parish records
   Estate MSS/collections
   Penylan
   Wynnstay
   Ordnance Survey records

National Library of Wales
   Wynnstay MSS
   St Asaph diocesan records

2. Principal journals
Archaeologia Cambrensis (indexed)
Transactions of the Denbighshire Historical Society (indexed)
 In these transactions the major articles relating to Ruabon have been contributed by Ifor Edwards, George Lerry, Derek Pratt, Bill Pritchard and Emlyn Rogers.

3. Official publications
Children's Employment Mines Parliamentary Papers, 1842
Report of the Commissioners concerning Charities County of Denbigh
Report of the Commissioners of Enquiry into the State of Education in Wales, 1847
Nonconformist statistics, 1905
Royal Commission on Welsh Church, Diocese of St Asaph statistical returns, 1907
CADW listed buildings

4. Books
These are given in the text notes

5. Newspapers
Cefn Chronicle
Chester Chronicle
Illustrated London News
Llangollen Advertiser
Oswestry and District Border Advertiser
Wrexham Advertiser
Wrexham Leader